Robert South

Animadversions upon Dr. Sherlock's book,

entituled A vindication of the holy and ever-blessed Trinity

Robert South

Animadversions upon Dr. Sherlock's book,
entituled A vindication of the holy and ever-blessed Trinity

ISBN/EAN: 9783337895655

Printed in Europe, USA, Canada, Australia, Japan

Cover: Foto ©ninafisch / pixelio.de

More available books at **www.hansebooks.com**

Animadversions

UPON

Dr. *SHERLOCK*'s Book,

ENTITULED

A Vindication of the Holy and Ever-Blessed Trinity, &c.

TOGETHER

With a more Necessary Vindication of that Sacred, and Prime Article of the *Christian Faith* from his New Notions, and False Explications of it.

Humbly offered to His Admirers, and to Himself the *Chief* of them.

By a Divine of the Church of England.

LONDON,
Printed for *Randal Taylor*, near *Stationers-Hall*,
MDCXCIII.

A PREFACE, OR, INTRODUCTION To the following Animadversions.

TO *be Impugned from without, and Betrayed from within, is certainly the worst Condition that either* Church *or* State *can fall into; and the best of* Churches, *the* Church *of* England, *has had experience of Both. It had been to be wished, and (one would think) might very reasonably have been expected, That, when* Providence *had took the Work of destroying the* Church of England *out of the* Papists *Hands, some would have been contented with her* Preferments, *without either attempting to give up her* Rites *and* Liturgy, *or deserting her* Doctrine. *But it has proved much otherwise. And amongst those, who are justly chargeable with the latter, I know none, who has faced the* World, *and defied the* Church *with so bold a Front, as the* Author *of Two very* Heterodox Books; *the first*

Entituled, A Discourse concerning the Knowledge of Jesus Christ, *&c. Published in the Year*, 1674. *And the other*, A Vindication of the Doctrine of the Holy and ever-Blessed Trinity, *&c. Published in the Year* 1690. *And (as one would think) Wrote purposely, to let the World see that the Truth cannot be so much shaken by a direct Opposition, as by a* Treacherous, *and* False Defence. *I shall in this* Preliminary Address *to the* Reader, *pass some brief Remarks upon both these* Books. *But first upon this, which I have here undertook to Animadvert upon. It is now of about Three Years standing in the World, and I have wondered, even to Astonishment, that a Book so full of* Paradoxes,*and those so positively,as well as absurdly delivered, could pass* Unanswered *for so long a time. For the* Author, *having therein advanced a Notion immediately and unavoidably inferring* Three Gods, *has yet had the Confidence not only to Assert it, but to Declare it* Heresie and Nonsence *to think, or hold otherwise; that is, in other Words, to call the whole* Christian Church, *in all Ages and Places*, Fools and Hereticks. *For I do here averr, and will undertake to prove it, (as far as a Negative may be proved)* That no Church *(known to us by History, or otherwise)* ever held this Notion of the Trinity before. *And must we then be all* Fools and Hereticks, *who will not acknowledge the* Three Persons of the Blessed Trinity to be Three distinct Infinite Minds, or Spirits, *that is, in other Terms, to be* Three Gods? *And can so Learned, and every way Excellent a Clergy bear this? For if they could not, whence is it that some Writers amongst them, while they are declaring their dislike of his* Opinions, *yet do it with so soft an Air, and so gentle a Touch, as if they were afraid either to* Condemn *the* Opinion, *or to* Attack *the* Author? *Nay, and some I find creeping under his Feet with the Title of* Very Reverend, *while they are charging him with such* Qualities *and* Humours, *as none can be, justly, chargeable with,*

and

and deserve Reverence *too. For my own part, I franckly own, That I neither* Reverence, *nor* Fear *him*; *that is, I Reverence none, who gives whole* Communities *and* Churches *such Words, nor Fear any One, who Writes such Things, and in such a manner. For even those* Mean Spirits, *who can both* Court, *and* Censure *him in the same Breath, complain,* That he gives no Quarter, *where he supposes he has his Adversary upon the least Advantage. And if this be his Way and Temper* never to give Quarter, *I am sure he has no cause to expect any, whatsoever he may find. But still, methinks, I can hardly believe my Eyes, while I read such a* Pettit Novellist, *Charging the* Whole Church *as* Fools and Hereticks, *for not Subscribing to a* Silly, Heretical Notion *solely of his own* Invention. *For does he, or can he think to Live and Converse in the World upon these Terms? and to throw his* Scurrility *at* High, *and* Low, *at all* About *him,* Above *him, and* Below *him (if there be any such) at this insufferable rate? Does he, (I would fain know) in this speak his* Judgment, *or his* Breeding? *Was it the* School, *the* University, *or* Gravel-Lane, *that taught him this Language? Or does he never reflect upon himself, nor consider, That though* he *does not, others assuredly will? One would think by his Words and Carriage that he had ingrossed all Reason and Learning to Himself: But on the contrary, that this his scornful looking down upon all the World besides, is not from his standing upon any higher ground of Learning, and Sufficiency, than the rest of the World; and that he* Huffs *and* Dictates *at a much more commanding rate than he* Reasons, *the perusal of my Ninth, Tenth, and Eleventh Chapters will, or (I am sure) may sufficiently inform the* Impartial Reader; *and shew him how many things there are in this our Author's* Vindication, *which too much need Another, but admit none. In the mean time, I do, and must declare both to himself, and to all others, That the forementioned Charge of* Heresie *and* Nonsence *(as he has laid it) is so*

very

very Rude, Scandalous, *and* Provoking, *that it is impossible for the* Tongue, *or* Pen *of* Man *to reply any Thing so severely upon him, which the foulness of the said Expression will not abundantly warrant both the Speaking and the Writing of.*

The Church of England *is certainly very Merciful;* Merciful *(as a Great* Judge *once said of K.* Charles II.) even to a Fault. *For who, by her silence upon what this Bold Man has Wrote, and the Encouragement he has since received, would not be shrewdly induced after some considerable number of Years (if his stuff should live so long) to believe, that his Notions were the* Current Doctrine *of our* Church, *or, at least, of our* Church-men *at that time? None then opposing them, most over-looking them, and some countenancing and advancing the Author of them; and, perhaps,* for them *too. This is truly the Case; and I hope to do the* Church of England *so much Service at least, as to break the Universality both of the* Silence, *and the presumed* Acceptance, *by one plain, resolute and full* Negative *put in against it. For upon a due Consideration of the Things vented by this* Author, *and comparing them with the Proceedings and Zeal of the* Primitive Church *in its* Councils, *I do from my Heart believe, That had he lived and publish'd this Book in those Days, and Asserted,* That the Three Divine Persons in the Trinity were Three distinct Infinite Minds, or Spirits. *And that* Their Personal distinction consisted only in Self-Consciousness, and their Unity only in Mutual-Consciousness. *And withall, That the Terms* Essence, Nature, Substance, Person, *and* Hypostasis, *or* Subsistence, *&c. applyed to the* Godhead *and the* Divine Persons, *served only to perplex, obscure, and confound Men's* Apprehensions *of them; and for that cause ought to be laid aside; I say, I do not in the least question, but that all and every one of these* Propositions, *would have been*

Ch. Justice Scroggs.

been publickly and solemnly Condemned *in* Council, *and the* Author *of them (as high as he now carries his Head, like another* Abbot Joachim) *severely dealt with for Asserting them; and that upon great Reason. Forasmuch, as the Two chief of those Terms,* viz. οὐσία *and* ὑπόστασις, Substance *and* Subsistence, *were equally with the* ὁμοούσιον *it self opposed by those Two grand* Arian Hereticks *and Furious Disturbers of the* Church, Ursacius *and* Valens, *who with their Accomplices vehemently contended to have them all wholly suppressed and disused. So that as for the* οὐσία *of the* Father *and the* Son, *they would have* παντελῶς οὐδεμίαν μνήμην, *no mention at all to be made of any such Thing; and as for the* ὑπόστασις *it ought* οὐδαμῶς ὀνομάζεσθαι *not so much as to be named concerning any of the* Three Persons. *And, as one Reason for this, they alledged the satisfaction of* Tender Consciences. *Which shews, That* Tender Consciences *are such Things, as may, some time or other, put the* Church, *not only to part with its* Liturgy, Rites, *and* Ceremonies, *but its very* Faith *also for their sake. But right, or wrong, those Two* Arian Incendiaries *pressed hard for the Abolition of these* Two Words; *as this* Author *also does in this his* Vindication;

Having first rejected the ὁμοούσιον in those Words. Τὸ μὲν ὁμοούσιον καὶ τὸ ὁμοιούσιον ἐκβαλλόμενοι ὡς ἀλλότριον τῶν γραφῶν. *Athanas. de Synodis Arimini & Seleuciæ, Tom.* 1. *P.* 904. *Edit. Colon.* 1686. In the next place, *p.* 906. they proceed to cashier the Terms οὐσία and ὑπόστασις, in the following Words. Τὸ δὲ ὄνομα τῆς οὐσίας, ὅπερ ἁπλούστερον ἀπὸ τῶν πατέρων ἐτέθη, ἀγνοούμενον δὲ τοῖς λαοῖς σκάνδαλον ἔφερε, διότι μηδὲ αἱ γραφαὶ τοῦτο περιέχουσιν, ἤρεσε περιαιρεθῆναι, καὶ παντελῶς μηδεμίαν μνήμην τοῦ λοιποῦ γίνεσθαι. Ἐπειδήπερ καὶ αἱ θεῖαι γραφαὶ οὐδαμῶς ἐμνημόνευσαν περὶ οὐσίας Πατρὸς καὶ υἱοῦ, καὶ γὰρ οὐδὲ ὀφείλει ὑπόστασις περὶ πατρὸς καὶ υἱοῦ καὶ ἁγίου πνεύματος ὀνομάζεσθαι. For this see also *Socrat. Hist. lib.* 2. *cap.* 29. and *Theodoret Histor. lib.* 2. *cap.* 18. *&* 21. *& Sozomen's Histor. lib.* 4. *cap.* 18.

Vindication; *treading hereby exactly in the ſteps of thoſe* Bleſſed Leaders; *who, no doubt, underſtood the Intereſt of their baſe Cauſe well enough, and were both* Self-Conſcious, *and* Mutually-Conſcious, *how much they ſerved the deſign, they drove at, by what they did. And, ſince Things were ſo in former days, what hinders, but that in theſe latter Days likewiſe, the ſame, if not prevented, may happen again? And, that* One, *who, (though he carries himſelf, as if he were able to teach the whole World, yet, for ſome certain Reaſons, profeſſes himſelf a* * Learner ſtill) *having already exploded the Terms* Subſtance *and* Subſiſtence, *as not to be uſed about the* Trinity, *may, upon the winning proſpect of ſome* Approaching Advantage, *(as, where Advantage is the* Teacher, *ſome care not how long they* continue Learners) *be very eaſily prevailed upon to ſend the* ὁμοούσιον *packing after its Fellows, and to abandon and caſt off that too? For, though ſuch an One ſhould give the* Church his Oath *to the contrary, there is no ſecurity from thence, but that a* Perpetual Learner *(by a due waiting upon* Providence) *may, all in convenient time,* Learn *to forget it too: And a* Self-Contradictor *having freely allowed a Thing at one time, as freely and fully diſown it at another.*

* See his Preface to his Caſe of Allegiance, *p.* 5. *line* 15.

Wherefore it was, no doubt, upon a moſt ſerious conſideration of the force of Words *in Conjunction with the* Tempers of Men, *That the* Sixth General Council *(and* Third *of* Conſtantinople) *was ſo jealouſly concerned, and ſo remarkably ſtrict to fence againſt all* Hereticall Miſchief *from that Quarter; as appears from the* Concluding Article *of the* Synodical Sentence *pronounced by the ſaid* Council *againſt the* Monothelites, *as we find it thus ſet down in the* Acts *thereof.* Theſe Things therefore, being thus with the utmoſt care and exactneſs, on all ſides, formed and drawn up by

Τέτων τοίνυν μετὰ πάσης πανταχόθεν ἀκριβείας τε καὶ ἐμμελείας παρ' ἡμῶν διατυπωθέντων, ὁρί-

by us, We Decree and Enact, That it ſhall not be lawful for any one to Produce, Write, Compoſe, Conceive, or Teach another Faith, or this in any other way, or manner. But as for thoſe who ſhall preſume to Compoſe, or Contrive another Faith, or Publiſh, Teach, or deliver forth another Creed, to ſuch as ſhall be ready to come over to the Acknowledgment of the Truth from Heatheniſm, or Judaiſme, or any other Sect whatſoever, or ſhall introduce any *unuſual* way of ſpeaking, or *new Invented Terms*, as tending to Subvert all that has been defined by us, if they be Biſhops, or in Clerical Orders, we decree, That they ſhall be deprived of their Biſhopricks, or ſaid Orders; or if they be Monks, or Lay-men, that they ſhall be Anathematized.

ζομεν ἑτέραν πίστιν μηδενὶ ἐξεῖναι προφέρειν, ἤγουν συγγράφειν ἢ συντιθέναι ἢ φρονεῖν ἢ διδάσκειν ἑτέρως. Τοὺς δὲ τολμῶντας ἢ συντιθέναι πίστιν ἑτέραν ἢ προκομίζειν ἢ διδάσκειν ἢ παραδιδόναι ἕτερον σύμβολον τοῖς ἐθέλουσιν ἐπιστρέφειν εἰς ἐπίγνωσιν τῆς ἀληθείας ἐξ Ἑλληνισμοῦ ἢ ἐξ Ἰουδαϊσμοῦ ἤγουν ἐξ αἱρέσεως οἱασοῦν, ἢ καινοφωνίαν ἤτοι λέξεως ἐφεύρεσιν πρὸς διατροπὴν εἰσάγειν τῶν νυνὶ παρ' ἡμῶν διορισθέντων· τούτους εἰ μὲν ἐπίσκοποι εἶεν, ἢ κληρικοὶ, ἀλλοτρίους εἶναι τοὺς Ἐπισκόπους τῆς ἐπισκοπῆς, καὶ τοὺς Κληρικοὺς τοῦ κλήρου, εἰ δὲ μονάζοντες εἶεν ἢ λαϊκοὶ ἀναθεματίζεσθαι αὐτούς. *Concil.* 6. *in Actione* 17. *ſeu ultimâ, circa finem.*

So that we have here a clear and full Declaration of a General Council, *againſt all teaching, not only* ἕτερόν τι, *but alſo* ἑτέρως; *that is, not only againſt delivering another Faith, but againſt delivering the ſame in another way, or manner, than the* Council *had ſettled, and againſt the uſe of all new-Invented Terms, all* καινοφωνία, *or* ἐφεύρεσις τῆς λέξεως, (Self-Conſciouſneſs, *and* Mutual-Conſciouſneſs *themſelves not excepted) as in the Judgment of the* Council, *deſtructive in their conſequence to the* Faith *declared; and all this upon pain of* Deprivation, *or* Anathematization, *as the Quality of the Persons concerned should happen to be. According to the rigour of which Sentence, and the Proceeding of the* Church *in those* Ages *sutable to it*, Deprivation, *or* Suspension, *would, no doubt, have attended this Author, had he then lived and produced his new Terms, in defiance and reproach of the former received ones. And if such a punishment had actually befallen him, he would have found, that in those Days, Men were not wont either to be* Suspended, *or* Deprived *in order to their* Promotion.

I know indeed, that in the Apology *lately put out by him for Writing against the* Socinians, *he utters some Things contrary to what he had Asserted in this his* Vindication of the Trinity. *But this the Reader ought not at all to be surprized at; it being as Natural to some Men to* Write *as to* Breath, *and to* Contradict *themselves as to* Write: *And no Man of Sence, who knows this* Author, *will reckon that he knows his Judgment, or Opinion from any Book Wrote by Him, any longer, than till he Writes another; nor from that neither, till he has Wrote his last.*

Having given the Reader *this short* Prelibation, *or* Taste *of the Book, which I shall more particularly and fully examine presently, I think fit to remark something also upon that other Piece mentioned by me, and Entituled,* A Discourse concerning the Knowledge of Jesus Christ, *&c. A Book fraught with such Vile and* Scandalous Reflexions *upon* God's Justice, *with reference to* Christ's Satisfaction, *that it may deservedly pass for a* Blasphemous Libel *upon both. And I do seriously think, that never was any Book* Licensed, Published, *and suffered to pass* Uncontrolled, *more to the* Disgrace *of the* Church of England *than this, which the* Reader *will quickly see upon his Reading some Passages of it; which, I am sure, if he be but* Christianly disposed, *he cannot do, but with extreme Horrour. But before I direct the* Reader *to his* Blasphemies, *I shall lay before him*

him one Grand leading Absurdity, which utterly Evacuates and Overthrows the whole Doctrine *of* Free Grace, *and the* Redemption of Mankind thereby; *and indeed, by Consequence, the whole* Oeconomy *of the* Christian Religion.

And it is that Wonderful Assertion concerning the Goodness of God, *in Page* 44. of his Knowledge of Christ, *viz.* That it is not possible to understand what Goodness is, without Pardoning Grace. *Now certain it is, that* Natural Reason, *by its own light, is able from the* Common Works *of* God's Providence, *to collect* the Knowledge of God's Goodness; *as St.* Paul *expresly told those* Heathens *of* Lycaonia, Acts 14. 17. *and therefore, if the* Knowledge *of* God's Goodness, *necessarily implies in it, the* Knowledge *of* Pardoning Grace, *it will follow, That the* Heathens *by understanding* one *from the* Works *of* Providence, *must needs understand and know the* other *also; and consequently, that the* Knowledge *of* Pardoning Grace *is not owing to* Revelation, *nor the* Gospel *necessary to make a Discovery of it to Mankind. A Bless'd Principle, and Foundation, no doubt, to establish the New-designed Scheme of a* Natural Religion *upon! For it is not unknown, what Projects were on foot amongst some, when this Book was Wrote, though the* Author *had the ill luck to be left in the Lurch, and not seconded in the Attempt.*

But in opposition to this Paganish *Assertion, I do here affirm,* That if *God* may *be Good,* and that, both as to the *Essential Attribute* of his *Goodness*, and as to the actual Exercise of the same, without the *Pardon of Sin*, then it is not *impossible to understand the Goodness of God without Pardoning Grace. The Consequence is evident. For whatsoever any Thing* is, *it is capable of being* understood to be. *And as for the Antecedent, that is manifest from these Considerations.*

First, *That* God *was* Good, *and exerted Acts of* Goodness, *before there was any* Sin *in the World, and therefore might be, and undoubtedly was,* understood *both as* good, *and as exercising his* Goodness, *by the Angels before the Fall of any of them, and for that reason before* Pardon of Sin *could come into Consideration.*

In the next Place, God *had been* Good, *and had exercised his* Goodness, *had Men and Angels been Created* Impeccable; *and, I am sure, it is no Contradiction to hold, That they might* have been *Originally made such, as all Glorified Spirits now actually* are.

And Lastly, God *is and may be understood to be* Good, *even in respect of those, whose Sins shall never be pardoned. And therefore that Assertion of this Author,* That it is not possible to understand what Goodness is without Pardoning Grace, *is apparently false and absurd; as drawing after it One of these Two Consequences.*

First, *That either we cannot understand the Creation and Support of* Angels, *and of this visible World, and particularly of* Mankind, *to have been Acts and Instances of the* Divine Goodness (*which yet, no doubt, were very great ones.*) *Or,*

Secondly, *That we cannot understand them as such, but by understanding them also to imply in them* Pardoning Grace. *And if so, then, supposing the* Creation *of* Man, *and his Sin after his* Creation, *and the* Goodness *of* God *remaining still entire, notwithstanding Man's Sin, (as it certainly did) it will follow, that* Pardoning Grace, *having (according to the forementioned Principle) a necessary Connexion with, or result from the said* Goodness, *must have fallen in of course, and by necessary consequence from thence. And then, Where could be the* Freedom *of this* Grace? *Nay, Where could be this* Grace *it self? For the very Nature of* Grace *consists in this, that it be an Act perfectly* Free; *so free,*

free, that God *might have chosen, after* Man *had sinned, whether he would ever have offered him any Conditions of* Pardon, *or no; And if he had not, Men might, notwithstanding that, have abundantly known and understood the* Goodness *of* God, *by several other Acts and Instances, in which it had sufficiently declared it self. So that the foregoing Assertion is nothing but a gross Paradox, and a Scurvy Blow at all* Revealed Religion *besides, if the* Knowledge of Pardoning Grace *could, or may be had without it.*

And now after this Absurdity *presented to the* Reader's *Examination; I shall point out to him some of the* Blasphemies *also that occurr in the same Book. Such as are these that follow.* The Justice of God *(says he)* having glutted it self with Revenge on Sin in the Death of Christ, henceforward we may be sure he will be very kind, as a Revengeful Man is, when his Passion is over. *Knowledge of Christ*, P. 46. *Again*, The Sum of the Matter is, That God is all Love and Patience, when he has taken his fill of Revenge; as others use to say, That the Devil himself is very good when he is pleased, *P*. 47. *Again*, The Death of Christ (*says he*) discovers the Naturalness of Justice to God; that is, That he is so Just, that he has not one Dram of Goodness in him, till his Rage and Vengeance be satisfied; which, I confess, is a glorious kind of Justice. *And presently after.* Now the Justice and Vengeance of God having their Actings assigned them to the full, being glutted and satiated with the Blood of Christ, God may pardon as many and great Sins as he pleases, *P*. 59. *And sutable to this, he likewise calls the Method of* God's *saving Sinners upon a Previous Satisfaction made to his Justice, as necessary for the Remission of Sin*, God's Trucking and Bartering with Sin, and the Devil for his Glory, *P*. 52. *Concerning which and the like Expressions uttered by this* Great-Good

Good Man *(as a certain poor Wretch calls him) I cannot but out of a due Zeal, and concern for that* Eternal Truth, *by which, I hope to be Saved, declare,* That the Tongue that ſhould Speak ſuch things, deſerves to Speak no more; and the Hand that ſhould Write them, to Write no more. *And great pity it is, that at this time, and in this caſe alſo, his Aſcendant* had not tyed up his Hands from Writing. *For ſee, how one of the* Leading Diſſenters *Inſults over our* Church, *upon occaſion of theſe Horrid Paſſages.* Is this *(ſays he)* Language becoming a Son of the *Church of England?* Ought it not more juſtly to have been expected from a *Jew*, or a *Mahometan?* From *Servetus*, or *Socinus*, (from whom alſo it was borrowed) than from a Son of the Church, in a Book publiſhed by Licence and Authority? *And thus he goes on, equally Chaſtiſeing his Arrogance, and Expoſing his Ignorance; the poor* Church's *Reputation all the while paying the Scores of both. As to the Licenſing of which Book, here ſo ſeverely reflected upon, it did indeed meet with a Perſon (as it were) framed for the very purpoſe. For none certainly could be ſo fit to ſtamp an* Imprimatur *upon a Book Wrote againſt* Chriſt's *Satisfaction, as One, who while he was* Eating the Bread, *and* Wearing the Honours *of the* Church, *could ſtab the* Doctrine *of it to the Heart, by Writing for* Tranſubſtantiation. *And then in the next place, for its paſſing Uncontrolled, it had really been to be wiſhed, That the* Clergy *in* Convocation, *in the laſt eſpecially (in which ſo many of them acquitted themſelves ſo exceeding worthily upon other Accounts) would have vouchſafed to wipe off this groſs Blot from the* Church *by a due Cenſure paſſed upon the forementioned Poſitions; ſo reproachful to that, and ſo Contumelious to our Common Chriſtianity. For what vaſt advantage the* Diſſenters *have taken from hence to Scandalize and Beſpatter the Government and Governours of our* Church, *is but*

Owen's Vindication againſt Sh. p. 47, 48, &c.

too

too well known, and cannot be too much Lamented; and I heartily wish, That it had been a Scandal *only* Taken, *and not* Given. *And the rather do I represent this as a Work fit for the* Convocation; *since this* Author *has given the World such a Notable Proof, That nothing but a* Convocation *can Convince, or work upon him.* [illegible] of [illegible] P. 5.

And thus I have given the Reader *a Specimen of the* Doctrines *of this* Author *in these Two Books of his. In the former of which, he affects to be the* Socinian's *humble Servant, by Ridiculing and Exploding* Christ's *Satisfaction of* God's *Justice; and so in effect, the whole Mystery of the* Gospel: *And in the latter he pretends to oppose them by such a* Vindication of the Trinity, *and of* Christ's Incarnation, *as one would think, were Wrote by themselves. But whatsoever it is, that he either pretends, or intends (as it is hard to know the latter by the former) this Character I shall give of him as a Writer, That there is hardly any one Subject which he has Wrote upon (that of* Popery *only excepted) but he has Wrote both* for it *and* against it *too: Not that I say, that he has Printed all which he has so Wrote; for Printing is not the only way of Publication; and this I will say besides, That where he has not* Printed, *he has* Acted *it with a Witness. And yet even for Printing; could any thing be Wrote and Printed more sharp and bitter against the* Dissenters, *than what this Man Wrote in his Answer to the* Protestant Reconciler? *And yet how frankly (or rather fulsomely) does he open both his Arms to embrace them in his Sermon Preached before the* Lord Mayor, *on* Nov. . 1688? *Though I dare say, That the* Dissenters *themselves are of that Constancy as to own, That they were of the same Principles in* 88, *that they were of in* 85. *But the Truth is, Old Friendships cannot be so easily forgot. And it has been an Observation made by some, that hardly can any one be found, who was first tainted with a* Conventicle, *whom a* Cathedral *could ever*

after

after cure; but that still upon every cross Turn of Affairs against the Church, *the irresistible Magnetism of the* Good Old Cause, *(as some still think it) would quickly draw him out of the* Good Old Way. *The Fable tells us of a* Cat *once turned into a* Woman, *but the next sight of a* Mouse *quickly dissolved the Metamorphosis, cashiered the Woman, and restored the Brute. And some* Virtuosi *(skilled in the* Useful Philosophy *of* Alterations) *have thought her much a gainer by the latter change; there being so many unlucky turns in the World, in which it is not half so safe and advantagious to* Walk Upright, *as to* be able to fall always upon one's Legs.

But not to hold the Reader *too long in the Entrance of the Work, which I am about to present him with, I do here assure him, That, in the following* Animadversions, *I have strictly pursued this* Author *in every part of his new* Hypothesis, *I have answered all his Arguments, not omitting so much as one, or any Thing that looks like one. And if I have thought fit sometimes in a short Remark or two, here and there to refresh the* Reader *and my self, by exposing his* Bold *and* Blind *side together; yet this has still been my method, throughly to dispatch the Argument, before I offer to divert upon the Author.*

As for that part of his Book, which peculiarly concerns the Socinians, *I leave him and them to fight it out. My business is to shew, That the* Doctrine *of our* Church *is absolutely a stranger to his Novel and Beloved Notions: It knows them not: It owns them not; nor ought we to look upon him, so far as he Asserts and Maintains them, to be any True and Genuine Son of it: And consequently, whether he worries the* Socinians, *or (which is much the more likely) the* Socinians *worry him, the* Church of England *is not at all concerned.*

Well, but since this Author has concluded the whole World in Ignorance (himself, I suppose, still excepted from so general a Doom) What must we do in so sad a Condition? Must we all take up in Scepticism, and acknowledge, that nothing is to be known? What then will that old Principle of Nature, πάντες ὀρέγονται τοῦ εἰδέναι, serve for, but to tantalize and torment us? For must we thus think, and thirst, and desire to know, and, after all, find nothing to be known with any thing of plainness, evidence, and demonstration? Why, Yes; to comfort us under this Cimmerian darkness, and to shew, that God has not given us our Intellectual Faculties wholly in vain: There is one certain thing in the World, *viz. The Doctrine of the Trinity*; That is, to say, *of three distinct Persons, all united in one and the same numerical Divine Nature,* which is *wonderfully plain, easie, and obvious to be known:* Though still, thanks to our Author for it, who by a New-found Exposition, and Explication of it, has bestowed this piece of Charity upon the World as to render it so. For thus, in *Page* 58. *line* 2. of his Book, Explaining the Union of the three Persons in the Godhead, by *Self-Consciousness, and Mutual-Consciousness,* (which words shall be throughly considered in their due place) he says, *That this is very plain, and intelligible, and makes the three Persons to be as much one, as every Man is one with himself.* And certainly it is hardly possible for any thing to be more plain and clear, more evident and intelligible, than *that every Man is one with himself.* (Except it be only when he *contradicts* himself.) Again in *Page* 65. *line* 31. he tells us, That his Notion of *Self-Consciousness, and Mutual-Consciousness, seems to him to make a Trinity in Unity as intelligible, as the Notion of one God is.* And in *Page* 66. *line* 2, 3. *That it gives a plain, and intelligible Solution to all the Difficulties, and seeming Contra-*

dictions in the Doctrine of the Trinity. And ſurely that thing, from which *all difficulties are removed*, and about which, *all Contradictions are ſolved*, cannot be imagined to have any difficulty remaining in it at all. And again, in *Page* 68. *line* 26. he roundly tells us, That the Explication given by him *of a Trinity in Unity, is a very plain and intelligible Account of this great and venerable Myſtery; as plain and intelligible as the Notion of one God, or of one Perſon in the Godhead.*

And in good earneſt, the Notion of one firſt Cauſe of all things, and of one Supreme Being, and conſequently of one God, is ſo eaſily demonſtrated, or rather, with ſuch a broad light, ſtares all Mankind in the Face, even without any demonſtration, that if the *Trinity in Unity* be as plain as this is, it is hardly poſſible for any thing to the Reaſon of Man to be plainer: and the *Arrians*, and *Socinians* are ten times more inexcuſable, than ever I thought them before. Again, in *Page* 73. *line* 11. having affirmed, *The Trinity to be a moſt Sacred and Venerable Myſtery*; within 6 or 7 Lines after, he ſays, *If Men would but conſider it according to his Hypotheſis* (which he there ſets down) *then a Trinity in Unity is a very plain, intelligible Notion.* Again, in *Page* 74. *line* 9. *There will appear* (ſays he) *no difficulty, or abſurdity in the eſſential Union of Three Minds by a mutual Conſciouſneſs to each other.* But will this Man conclude, That where there is no *Abſurdity*, there is therefore no *Difficulty* neither? So that, that which removes one, muſt needs remove the other too? It is ſtrange to me, That any one who pretends to argue cloſely, ſhould place two words ſo vaſtly different upon the ſame level. But again, in *Page* 82. *line* 30. he tells us, *That this gives an intelligible account of one of the moſt difficult Problems in all School-Divinity*, viz. *That the whole Trinity is not greater than*

any

any one Perſon in the Trinity. And again, in *Page* 85. *line* 14. *This Notion* (ſays he) *gives a plain account too of that Maxime* of the Schools, *That all the Operations of the Trinity,* ad extra, *are common to all the Three Perſons.* So that by this time we ſee here all things relating to the Trinity, made *plain, eaſie*, and *intelligible*; and that, ſince this Man has ſhewed his skill upon it, all knots and difficulties are wholly cleared off; ſo that now none are to be found, though a Man ſhould beat his Brains as much to find them, as Divines did heretofore to ſolve them. And therefore well may he magnifie the Exploits of ſuch a Triumphant Hypotheſis,as he does, firſt in his Preface, *Page* 1. *line* 13. (which though it be always placed firſt in Books, yet is generally written laſt) Having told us, *That his Original Deſign was to vindicate the Doctrines of the Trinity, and Incarnation, from thoſe pretended Abſurdities, and Contradictions which were ſo confidently charged on them:* He adds theſe words, *This* (ſays he) *I am ſure I have done; for I have given a very eaſie and intelligible Notion of a Trinity in Unity.* If he has, 'tis well. But (how great ſoever the aſſurance is, which he utters this with, as he had always a very great ſtock of it) I dare aver, That he has here ſaid more of himſelf, than any Divine of Note, ſince Chriſtianity came into the World, ever durſt ſay, *He was ſure of*, before. But as high as this ſounds, in *Page* 85. *line* 27. he raiſes his Voice ſomething higher, or at leaſt is more particular in the Encomiums he beſtows upon this his Performance in theſe words: *Thus* (ſays he) *I have endeavoured to explain this great and venerable Myſtery of a Trinity in Unity. And this I may ſay, That I have given not only a very poſſible, and a very intelligible Notion of it, but ſuch alſo, as is very agreeable to the Phraſe, and Expreſſions of Scripture, ſuch as preſerves the Majeſty of the Article, and ſolves all the diffi-*

culties of it. By which account, as we ſee that our Author is not wanting to the Commendation of his own Hypotheſis (as it is pitty but *Self-Conſciouſneſs*, and *Self-Commendation* ſhould go together) ſo we ſee alſo, that he does it upon three diſtinct Heads, or Topicks, which, therefore, by his good leave, we will as diſtinctly conſider.

And Firſt, for it's being ſo agreeable to the *Phraſe and Expreſſions of Scripture*, I hope amongſt theſe, ſome conſideration ought to be had of ſuch Texts of Scripture, As that forementioned one in the 1 *Corinth.* 13. 12. Where (no doubt, with reference to the Myſteries of the Goſpel, of which this is one of the chief) *we are ſaid to ſee but as through a glaſs darkly, and to know but in part*, &c. neither of which, can I perſwade my ſelf to think, is only another Expreſſion for *knowing a thing plainly, eaſily, and intelligibly, and without any difficulty.* The like may be ſaid of that place in 1 *Pet.* 1. 12. where the Apoſtle ſpeaking to the Saints, he wrote to, of the things reported to them by ſuch as had preached the Goſpel (amongſt which, this Doctrine, doubtleſs, had it's place, or an equal difficulty at leaſt) he adds, That they *were ſuch things as the Angels deſire to look into.* The *Greek* word is παρακύψαι, which all Interpreters lay a peculiar weight and Emphaſis upon; as importing both the earneſt intention of the Inſpector, and the difficulty of the object inſpected, from the Poſture of ſuch as uſe to ſtoop down for the better diſcerning of ſuch things as cannot otherwiſe be well perceived, or look'd into. And now, is not this (think we) a moſt proper and fit poſture for ſuch as view and look into things very *plain, obvious, and intelligible?* And yet, I doubt not, but the *Angels*, who are ſaid to uſe it, could very eaſily give us the Philoſophy of *Rain, Snow*, and *Ice*, of *the Fires burning*, and *the deſcent of*

Stones,

Stones, and *other heavy Bodies*, which yet this Author will allow *no Man of sense and reason* (without forfeiting the reputation of both) to presume *to give a Philosophical Account of*: Whereas, in the mean time, the *Trinity* is declared to be a very *plain, easie, and intelligible Notion*, even to such Persons as can give no such Account of the other. And thus much for the *Agreement of his Hypothesis with the Phrase and Expressions of Scripture.*

The next head of its commendation is, That it preserves the *Majesty* of this great Article (as he words it:) But in much the same sense, I suppose, as his *Refusing the Oath*, preserved the *Majesty* of King *William*, and *his taking it*, the *Majesty* of K. *James*: But, that it *preserves it so, as to have a singular virtue to encrease Men's Veneration of it*, this I very much question, and demur to: forasmuch as that old Observation that *Familiarity breeds Contempt*, holds too frequently, as well as undeservedly, no less in Things than in Persons; which we are more apt to venerate at a distance, than upon a clear, plain, and full knowledge of them. I do not say, That Men ought to do thus; but such is the present state of Nature, that thus they use to do. And it is worth our marking; That where a Man is said to know a thing perfectly, he is said *To be Master of it*; and *Mastership* (one would think) is not naturally apt to create in the mind, any great awe for the thing, it is thus Master of. But be it, as it may; this I am sure of, That as the Scripture tells us, *That things revealed belong to us*, so the same Scripture tells us also, *That there are secret things, which* (by a kind of sacred enclosure) *belong only to God*, *Deut*. 29. 29. And till God shall think fit to reveal to us the Nature of the *Trinity*, I, for my part, shall reckon it amongst those *Secret things*: And, accordingly, with all the Pious submission of an humble

Reason

Reason falling down before it, adore and admire it at a distance; not doubting, but that for this very cause, That Men should do so, God in his Infinite Wisdom thought fit to spread such a Cloud and Veil over it. And therefore I cannot but think, that that Man expressed the due measures of our behaviour to this, and the like Mysteries, extremely well; who being pressed in the Schools with an Argument from the Trinity, in opposition to the Question held by him, gave it no other Answer but this: *Magister, hoc Mysterium Trinitatis ex quo argumentaris, est potiùs flexis genibus adorandum, quàm curiosâ nimis indagine ventilandum.* The Respondent who made this Reply, had the Repute of a Learned and Eloquent Man; and I think this Reply represents him a very Pious, and Discreet one too.

And therefore, as for the third and last Topick, upon which our Author would recommend his Hypothesis about the Trinity, *viz. That it solves all the difficulties of it.* I fear, from what hath been last said, that it will prove as far from being a *Commendation*, as it is from being a *Truth*; especially when the Author himself, after his saying so, in *page* 85. immediately adds, and that in the very next words, *Page* 86. *line* 1. *That there may be a great deal more in this Mystery than we can fathom,* &c. But now, if our Author will in this manner utter one Assertion, and immediately after it subjoyn another which quite overthrows it, who can help this? *For that a great deal more should remain in this Mystery than we can fathom*, or that there can be any thing unfathomable in that, *in which there is nothing difficult*; or that any thing can *be difficult*, after such an Explication given of it, as *solves all the difficulties of it* (for that is his very word in *Page* 85. the last *Line*) I must freely confess, surpasses my Understanding, to conceive; and God bless his Understanding, if it can.

It

It must be confessed indeed (as I hinted before in my Preface) that in a short Treatise lately Published by him, and entituled, *An Apology for Writing against the* Socinians, he seems to deny *the Notion of a Trinity to be comprehensible and easie*, Page 15. telling us, "*That there* " *must be infinite degrees of knowledge, where the Object is* " *Infinite; and that every new degree is more perfect than* " *that below it: and yet no Creature can attain the highest* " *degree of all, which is a perfect Comprehension; so that the* " *knowledge of God may encrease every day, and Men may* " *write plainer and plainer about these matters every day,* " *without pretending to make all that is in God, even a Tri-* " *nity in Unity, comprehensible and easie*, which he calls, *a* " *Spightful and Scandalous Imputation.* By which angry words it is manifest, that he would fain rid himself from those Inconveniences which his former unwary, and absurd Assertions had involved him in. But by his favour, the *Truth* of the Charge shall take off the *Scandal* from such as make it, wheresoever else it may fix it. For I have fully shewn, That in this his *Vindication*, &c. he has frequently (and as clearly as words can express a thing) affirmed, *a Trinity in Unity to be a plain, easie, intelligible Notion*: Where, by *Plain* must be understood either 1*st*. such a *Plainness*, as excludes all Doubts and Difficulties whatsoever: In which sense alone a thing can be said to be simply and absolutely *plain*: And in this sence also it can admit of none, and much less of *Infinite degrees* of *plainer* and *plainer*; since that, which excludes *all* doubts, certainly can exclude no more. Or 2*dly*, The word may be taken in a Lax, Popular, and Improper sense; for that which is so *Plain*, as to have no considerable doubt, or difficulty remaining about it. But, now, the Notion which Men have of *God*, or *of the Trinity*, can never be truly said to be *Plain*, in either of these

Some Remarks upon his Apology.

these Senses, and therefore not at all. For in the first, to be sure, it cannot: No, nor yet in the second. For let Men know never so much of any Object, yet if there remains more of that Object actually unknown, than either is, or can be known of it, such a knowledge can never render, or denominate the Notion of that Object (even in the common sense of the word) *Plain.* And so, I hope, our Author will allow it to be in the *knowledge*, Men have of *God*, and *the Blessed Trinity.* And, whereas he lays no small stress upon this, *That Men may write plainer and plainer of these matters every day*: I must here remind him, That the word *Plainer* in the *Comparative* Degree does not couch under it the *positive* signification of *Plain*, but denotes only a less degree of difficulty, and signifies no more than, That a Thing, or Notion, is not quite so difficult, or obscure, as it was before; which it may very well not be, and yet be far from being *Plain*, in either of the two foregoing senses, laid down by us. And therefore, though we should admit, *That Men might write plainer and plainer of the Trinity every day*; yet I affirm notwithstanding, that *the Notion of a Trinity in Unity*, can in no sense be truly said to *be plain and easie*, and much less, *very plain and easie*, as this Author has expresly affirmed it. So that if this be a *Scandalous Imputation*, it is easie to judge, to whom the Scandal of it must belong.

But besides all this, I see no cause to grant this Author that, which he so freely takes for granted, (for I think it very questionable) viz. *That Men may write plainer and plainer of the Trinity every day.* For, so far as the Writers of the Church have informed us about this great Mystery, the Catholick Church for above these 1200. Years past, has not only had, and held the same Notion of a Trinity, but has also expressed it in the same

way

way and words, with the Church at this very day. And for so much of this Mystery, as Divines could give no Account of then, neither have they given any clearer Account of it ever since; nor has the Church hitherto advanced one step further in this Subject: which is an evident demonstration, that it has already proceeded as far in it, as the Reason of Man could, or can go. And as for any further Discoveries of it, which this Author pretends to from two Phantastick words, found out by himself, it will not be long, before they shall be throughly *weighed in the Balance*, and *found as inconsiderable* as *the Dust of it*.

But there is one thing more, which I must not pass over; and it is this: That in the Passage, I transcribed from him, he lays down that for a certain Principle, which is indeed an Intolerable Absurdity, viz. *That where the Object is infinite, there must be infinite degrees of knowledge*. Now it is most true, That nothing but *Infinite knowledge can adequately comprehend an infinite Object*. For which reason, God alone can comprehend himself, and he does it by one simple, indivisible act, uncapable of Parts, or *Degrees*. But as for *Degrees* of any sort, whether of *knowledge*, or any thing else, nothing but a Finite Being is capable of them; and therefore for this Man to *assert infinite degrees of knowledge*, when Uncreated knowledge is uncapable of *Degrees*, and Created knowledge uncapable of *Infinite Degrees*, is a gross thick piece of Ignorance, in the first, and commonest Rudiments of Philosophy.

But to return to his Absurdities about the *plainess, and easiness of the Notion of a Trinity in Unity*, and therein to be as short with him as I can, I shall only demand of him, Whether he does in this *Apology* retract and renounce all that in his *Vindication* he has Asserted quite contrary to what he has since delivered in his *Apology*.

If he does, let him declare so much, and I have done; but till then, no regard at all ought to be had to his *Apology*; as serving for nothing else, but to shew, That according to his accustomed way, and known Character, he has denyed some things in one of his Books, which he had positively, and expresly affirmed in another; and consequently proving, *That the Apology, which denies a Trinity in Unity to be comprehensible and easie, and the Vindication, which forty times over affirms it to be plain and easie*; nay, *very plain and easie*, ought to pass for the genuine, undoubted Works of this Author, though they had never born his Name.

Wherefore upon the Result of all, what shall we, or what can we say to the fore-cited Particulars, which with so much positiveness over and over assert the *plainess, and intelligibility of the Notion of a Trinity!* Which yet has hitherto amazed and nonplus'd the whole Christian Church. For if it be really so *plain and intelligible*, as this Author tells us, it must to my Apprehension unavoidably follow, either that a Mystery *is a very plain intelligible Notion*, or that the *Trinity is no Mystery.* I shall not here presume to take this Author's beloved word out of his Mouth, and cry *Nonsence*, and *Contradiction.* But certainly if the Trinity *be a Mystery*, and a *Mystery* in the nature of it imports *something hidden, abstruse*, and by *bare reason not to be understood*; then to say, *we may have a plain, as well as an intelligible Notion* of it; nay, *plain even to a demonstration*; this, to say no more, is as like a Contradiction, as ever it can look.

But really our Author has shewn himself very kind and communicative to the World: For as in the beginning of his Book he has vouchsafed to instruct us how to judge of *Contradictions*; so in the Progress of his Work he has condescended to teach us (if we will but learn)

learn) how to *speak* and *write Contradictions* too. There remains therefore only one favour more, *viz.* That he would vouchsafe to teach us how to *reconcile* them also. For I, for my own part, think it every whit as hard a task to reconcile Contradictions, *as to reconcile* Protestants; and, I hope, much harder. And yet this latter he has endeavoured to prove in a certain Book, wrote by him in the Year 1685, a thing not to be done. But whether it can, or no, I am sure, he has hardly publish-ed any Book since, but what manifestly proves, That there is great need of some *Reconciler* to do the other.

Answer to the *Protestant* Reconciler, *Chap.* 3.

But why do I speak of reconciling Contradictions? It would be a very troublesome work, if it could be done; and a very uncomfortable one, when it could not: And therefore our Author (to give him his due) has attempted a much surer, and more compendious way of clearing himself of this imputation, than such a long and tedious way of reconciling inconsistent Propositions, could possibly have been. For having Asserted, *That we cannot justly charge a Contradiction, where we cannot comprehend the Nature of the thing said to be contradicted*; and that, in the next place, *there is nothing in the World (which he knoweth of) the Nature of which we can throughly understand, or comprehend:* I hope it follows, That, where nothing can or ought to be contradicted, none can be guilty of a Contradiction. And this, I suppose, none will deny to be an Expedient, every way answerable, and equal to our Author's Occasions: For otherwise I cannot see what can stand between him and the charge of many Scurvy, Contradictory Assertions; but that which shall effectually prove, and make out to us, *That indeed there neither is, nor can be any such thing as a Contradiction.*

CHAP. II.

Containing an Account of ſeveral Terms, commonly made uſe of in Diſcourſing of the Divine Nature and Perſons; and particularly ſhewing the Propriety of applying the Words, Eſſence, Subſtance, Nature, Infinity, *and the like, to this great Subject; and laſtly proving this Author's Exceptions againſt the uſe of them about the ſame, falſe, groundleſs, and impertinent.*

OUR Author ſeems ſo deſirous to advance nothing upon this ſublime Subject, but what ſhall be perfectly new, that in order to the making way for his particular Novelties, he Quarrels with almoſt all the old words, which Divines, in their Diſcourſes about the Divine Nature, and Perſons, were heretofore accuſtomed to make uſe of. He can by no means approve of the words *Eſſence, Subſtance, Nature, Subſiſtence,* and ſuch like; as reckoning them the *Cauſes of all the Difficulties, and ſeeming Abſurdities,* that are apt to perplex Mens minds in their Speculations of the Deity, and the Trinity, 4 *Sect. p. 68, 69, 70.* and therefore they muſt be laid aſide, and made to give way to other Terms, which he judges properer, and more accommodate to thoſe Theories. To which purpoſe, though our Author has fixed upon two purely of his own Invention, (which are to do ſuch

ſuch wonderful feats upon this Subject, as in all paſt Ages were never yet ſeen nor heard of before, and which I therefore reſerve in due place to be conſidered of particularly by themſelves) yet at preſent the Author ſeems moſt concerned to remove, and caſhier the fore-mentioned uſeleſs, cumberſome words, and to ſubſtitute ſome better, and more uſeful, in their room: Such as *Eternal Truth and Wiſdom*, *Goodneſs and Power*, *Mind and Spirit*, &c. which being once admitted, and applyed to all Diſputes about the Divine Nature (and an *Act of Excluſion* paſt upon the other) the way will become preſently ſmooth and open before us, and all things relating to the Myſtery of the Trinity (according to our Author's own excellent words) be made *very plain, eaſie, and intelligible*. Nevertheleſs, *as I may ſo ſpeak* (to borrow another of our Author's Elegancies) *let not him that putteth on his Armour boaſt as he that putteth it off*. A great *Promiſſor*, with a great *Hiatus*, being much better at raiſing an expectation, than at anſwering it. And hitherto I can ſee nothing but words, and vapour: Though after all, it is Performance, and the iſſue of things alone that muſt ſhew the ſtrength and reaſon of the biggeſt *Pretences*.

Now for the clearer, and more diſtinct diſcuſſion of the matter in hand, I ſhall endeavour to do theſe 4 things.

I. I ſhall ſhew, That the ground upon which this Author excepts againſt the uſe of the Terms, *Nature*, *Eſſence*, *Subſtance*, *Subſiſtence*, &c. in this Subject, is falſe and miſtaken.

II. I ſhall ſhew, That the ſame Difficulties ariſe from the Terms, *Truth*, *Wiſdom*, *Goodneſs*, *Power*, &c. uſed for the Explication of the Divine Being, that are objected againſt *Eſſence*, *Subſtance*, *Nature*, and the like.

III. I shall shew, That these Terms do better, and more naturally explain the Deity, or Divine Being, than those other of *Truth*, *Wisdom*, *Goodness*, &c. And,

IV. And Lastly, I shall shew, That the Difficulty of our Conceiving rightly of the Deity, and the Divine Persons, does really proceed from other Causes.

These four things, I say, I will give some brief Account of.

But because the Subject, I am about to engage in, is of that Nature, that most of the *Metaphysical*, and *School-Terms*, hitherto made use of by Divines upon this occasion, will naturally, and necessarily fall in with it, I think it will contribute not a little to our more perspicuous proceeding in this Dispute, to state the Import and Signification of these Terms, *Essence*, *Substance*, *Existence*, *Subsistence*, *Nature* and *Personality*, with such others, as will, of course, come in our way, while we are treating of, and explaining these. And here, first of all, according to the old Peripatetick Philosophy, which, for ought I see, (as to the main Body of it at least) has stood it's ground hitherto against all Assaults: I look upon the Division of *Ens*, or *Being* (a summary word for all things) into *Substance* and *Accident*, as the Primary, and most Comprehensive (as we hinted before in our first Chapter.) But that I may fix the sense and signification of these Terms, all along as I go, by giving them their respective Definitions, or at least Descriptions, where the former cannot be had, I look upon *Ens*, or *Being*, to be truly and well defined, *That which is*; tho, I must confess, it is not so much a perfect Definition, as a Notation of the word from the original Verb *est*. For to define it by the Term *Essence*, by saying, *That Ens, or Being, is that which has an Essence*, though it be a true Proposi-

Propoſition, yet I believe it not ſo exactly proper a Definition; ſince the Terms of a Definition ought to be rather more known than the thing defined: Which in the fore-mentioned Caſe is otherwiſe. As for *Subſtance*, I define that to be a *Being not inhering in another*; that is to ſay, ſo exiſting by it ſelf, as not to be ſubjected in it, or ſupported, this way, by it. *Accident*, I define, a *Being inherent* in another, as in a Subject ſupporting it, and without which it cannot exiſt, or ſupport it ſelf. Which Diviſion being made by Terms contradictory, viz. *Inhering* in *another*, and *not inhering in another*, muſt needs be adequate, and perfect, and fully comprehenſive of the whole that is divided thereby.

But now, beſides theſe two Terms of *Subſtance* and *Accident*, there is another aſſigned by Logicians, Metaphyſicians, and School-men, called, a *Mode of Being*, viz. ſuch a thing, as being added to another, does not make any addition of another Being, or degree of Being to it, but only reſtrains, and determines it; and may be defined an *Affection of a thing, or Being*, by which the Nature of it, *otherwiſe indeterminate* and *indifferent*, is *determined* to *ſome certain reſpect*, *ſtate*, *or condition*. Thus, whereas the Nature of a thing may be conſidered either as yet in it's Cauſes, or as actually produced, and exiſting out of them, either of theſe is a *Mode* of that Nature; the firſt rendring it only *Potential*, the other *Actual*: Nor is this a meer *Ens Rationis*, foraſmuch as it affects the Being of a thing antecedently to any Operation of the mind paſſing upon it. And the Reaſon aſſigned by ſome Logicians for the allowing and aſſerting theſe *Modes*, is this: That ſome things muſt neceſſarily be admitted to belong to *Being*, which are not *Beings* themſelves, to prevent an *Infinite progreſs in Beings*. For ſince every thing is capable of being defined, or deſcribed,

bed, and yet nothing can be defined merely by it ſelf, (an Identical Propoſition being no Definition) it muſt needs be defined by ſome thing or other, diſtinct from it ſelf; but now if that be alſo a *Being*, then that likewiſe muſt be defined by another *Being*, and that by another, and ſo on *in infinitum*; which would be moſt abſurd: whereas, if this definition, or deſcription of a thing be made by ſome *Modus of it*, which is not ſtrictly and properly a *Being* it ſelf, the thing preſently ſtops here, without any neceſſity of proceeding to any more *Beings*. But perhaps it will be here ſaid, if theſe *Modes* are not ſo many meer *Nothings*, or *Entia Rationis*, what order, or rank ſhall they be placed in? Since thoſe ten heads of *Being*, which we call *Prædicaments*, cannot ſeem the proper Receptacles of things, which we own not to be properly, or formally, *Beings*. I Anſwer. That though they are not *Beings*, properly ſo called, and ſo not directly, and upon their own Account, placeable under any of the Ten fore-mentioned Heads of *Being*; yet ſince they are Appendages of *Being*, as cleaving to it, and depending upon it, they are accounted under, and reduced *to* thoſe reſpective Heads, or *genera* of *Being*, to which the *Beings* modified by them, do directly belong. Now the Nature of theſe *Modi* being thus accounted for, we are, in the next place, to take notice of the *difference* reſulting from them, which we call *Modal*; and that is either between two, or more, ſuch *Modes* differing from one another; as the Perſonalities belonging to ſeveral Perſons, differ amongſt themſelves; or when a thing, or Being, differs from the Mode affecting it; or Laſtly, when ſeveral things thus modified, or affected, do by vertue of thoſe Modes differ from one another; and thus the Perſons in the Bleſſed Trinity may be ſaid to differ amongſt themſelves.

I pro-

Chapter II.

I proceed now to those other Terms of *Essence*, *Existence*, *Nature*, *Subsistence*, and *Personality*. And first for *Essence*: as I shewed, that *Ens*, or *Being*, might be truly defined, *That which is*; so *Essence* may be as truly and properly defined, *That by which a thing is what it is*; that is to say, by which it is Constituted in such a kind, or order of *Being*: And this difference I take to be founded in the different ground, upon which we conceive of the same thing. Accordingly the *Essence* of a thing, no less than the thing it self, may be considered, either as yet in the *Power of its Causes*, and only producible by them, or as *actually existing*, and produced by them. By which we see, that an *Essence*, as such, may be indifferent to exist, or not exist; and that from hence springs the difference between *Essence* and *Existence*. There is indeed a Reality ascribed to it, even without Existence: But that is not properly a reality in the thing it self, but partly in respect of the power of its Causes enabling them to produce it; and partly, because it is properly the Subject of *Science*, and capable of having true Propositions formed of it, and Demonstrations built upon it: As we may form as true Propositions of a Rose in Winter, and demonstrate all the Properties of it, as of their proper Subject, by their proper respective Principles, as well, as while it is actually flourishing upon the Tree. And this is all the reality which I think can be ascribed to *Essence*, in its separation from *Existence*. As for *Existence* it self, it may be defined, that *Mode, or Affection of Being*, by which *a thing stands actually produced out of the power of its Causes*; or, at least, not actually included in any Cause; in which sense God himself *does exist*. From whence it appears, That in Created Beings, *Essence* bears no such necessary Connexion with *Existence*, since it is not necessarily included in the Nature of any finite Being, that it must needs be produced, or actually Exist. But it must be confessed, That *Existence* being a perfection, and, in God especially, a very great one, must of necessity be included in his very *Essence*, as containing in it (formally, or eminently) all sorts, or degrees of perfection. The next Term is *Subsistence*, which is a Mode of Being, by which a thing exists by it self, without existing in another, either as a part in the whole, or an *Adjunct* in the *Subject*. I say an *Adjunct*, not an *Accident*, for a Substance may be an Adjunct. And, I think, if we would assign a way, by which the humane Nature of Christ exists in the Person of the λόγος, we shall hardly find out a fitter, than to say, That it exists in it, as an Adjunct in the Subject. For it is certain, That it does not exist in it, as a part in the whole; since by this means, the second Person in the Trinity, must, till his Incarnation, have wanted one part of his Person. But I shall not be positive in the Application of this Term here. In the mean time it must be observed, That *Essence and Subsistence really differ*, (so far as a Modal difference is reduced to a Real) not only in Created Beings, but also in Uncreate. In Created, it is evident; forasmuch as a part divided from the whole, loses the Subsistence which it had from thence, but still continues its Existence, as being still a Substance actually subsisting by it self, and not inhering in any Subject, as Accidents do. Nor is it less evident in the Deity it self, and the Divine Persons belonging to it. For one and the same undivided *Existence*, as well as one and the same *Essence* or Nature belongs to all the three Persons equally, whereas yet every Person has his own proper distinct *Subsistence* by himself; which must make as great a difference between Existence and Subsistence, as that which unites several Persons into one Nature, and that which

which perſonally diſtinguiſhes them from one another. And then alſo for Chriſt's Perſon, with reference to his humanity; though this *ſubſiſts* by the Subſiſtence of the λόγος, yet it do's not properly *ſubſiſt* by the *Exiſtence of it*, (ſince every diſtinct Nature muſt have its own diſtinct *Exiſtence*) which ſhews, That even in the Oeconomy of this Divine Perſon, *Exiſtence* and *Subſiſtence* muſt be conſidered as formally different; ſince ſomething, we ſee, may relate to, and be affirmed of one, which cannot be affirmed of, or bear the ſame relation to the other. Now, whatſoever Being, or Nature, this *Mode of Subſiſtence* does belong to, that is properly called a *Suppoſitum*; as being a thing, which by no means exiſts in any other, but as a Baſis, or foundation, ſupports ſuch things, or Beings, as exiſt in it; from which alſo it receives its Name of ὑφιστάμενον. And the Conſequence of this is, That as *Subſiſtence* makes a thing, or Being, a *Suppoſitum*; ſo ſuppoſitality makes it *incommunicable*; ſince that which makes it uncapable of exiſting in another, muſt alſo hinder it from being Communicated to another. And another Conſequence of the ſame is, That every *Suppoſitum, or Being, thus Subſiſting by it ſelf*, is a compleat Being; that is, ſuch an one as is not made for the *Completion of any other*: For whatſoever is ſo, muſt naturally exiſt in it, as a *part* does in the *whole*, or at leaſt be originally deſigned ſo to do. This Account being given of *Subſiſtence*, and of a *Suppoſitum*, which is Conſtituted ſuch by it, it, will be eaſie to give an Account alſo what a *Perſon* is; which is properly defined *Suppoſitum Rationale*, or *Intelligens*. So that as a *Suppoſitum* is *ſubſtantia ſingularis completa per ſe ſubſiſtens*; ſo the *Ratio Intellectiva*, being added to this, makes it a *Perſon*, which is a farther perfection of Suppoſitality, and the utmoſt perfection of Subſiſtence, as Subſiſtence and Suppoſitality is the utmoſt

Bound and Perfection of Existence in all Beings not Intelligent.

If it be here now asked: Whether *Subsistence*, or *Suppositality* added to bare *Nature*, does not make a Composition? I Answer, That in Created finite Persons it does, but not in Uncreated and Infinite: And the reason is, Because though all Composition implys Union; yet all Union, is not therefore a Composition, but something higher and transcendental; so that in the Divine Persons of the Trinity, the Divine Nature, and the Personal Subsistence coalesce into one, by an Incomprehensible, Ineffable kind of Union and Conjunction. And if this does not satisfie, (as I think it rationally may) I must needs profess, That my Thoughts and Words can neither rise higher, nor reach further.

Having thus stated and fixed the signification of the fore-mentioned Terms, I cannot but remark these two things of the Term, or Word, *Essence*. As,

1. That it is sometimes taken not only for the *Ratio formalis entis*, but simply and absolutely for an entire Entity, or Being it self. And.

2. That those two other Terms, *Nature* and *Form*, are for the most part used as Terms equipollent, and of the same signification with it: *Nature* being the *Essence* of a thing considered as an Active, Productive Principle; and *Form* being the *Essence*, or *Nature* of a thing, as it is the chief Principle, giving Being and Perfection to it, in the way of Composition. Nevertheless it is sometimes also applyed to simple uncompounded Natures promiscuously with the other. So that we see here, That *Essence*, *Form*, and *Nature*, generally taken, are only three formally distinct Considerations of one and the same thing; which I thought fit to take notice of, to prevent all cavil, or mistake about the use of these Terms.

I have now gone over, and severally given an Account of the Notions of *Being*, *Substance*, *Accident*, *Modes of Being*, *Essence*, *Form*, *Nature*, *Subsistence* and *Personality*; and hereby, I hope, laid some foundation for our clearer, and more intelligible discoursing of the great Article we have undertook to rescue from a false *Vindication*: There being hardly any one of all the foregoing Terms, of which a clear and distinct Notion is not highly requisite to a clear, explicite, and distinct consideration of the Subject now before us. Concerning which, I think fit to note this, That (so far as I can judge) the thing now in dispute is not, what fully and exactly expresses, or represents the Nature of God (for nothing can do that:) But what is our best and most rational way of conceiving and speaking of him, and subject to fewest Inconveniences; and for this, we shall debate it, whether this Author, or we take the best course.

These things being thus premised, and laid down, we shall now resume the four Heads first proposed to be spoken of by us, and Discourse of them severally: And,

1. I shall shew, That the Ground upon which this Author excepts against the use of the Terms *Substance*, *Essence*, *Subsistence*, &c. in treating of this Subject, is false, and mistaken. His Exceptions against them we find in *Page* 68, 69, and 70. of his Book. "*The great* "*difficulty* (says he) *of conceiving a Trinity of Persons* "*in one Infinite and undivided Essence, or Substance, arises* "*from those gross and material Ideas, we have of Essence* "and *Substance, when we speak of the Essence, or Substance* "*of God, or Created Spirits.* We can form no Idea of Sub-"stance, but what we have from matter; *that is something* "*extended in a triple dimension of length, breadth, and* "*depth, which is the Subject of those Qualities, which in-*

"*here*

" *here and ſubſiſt in it. And therefore, as matter is the* " *Subject of all ſenſible Qualities, ſo we conceive ſome ſuch* " *Subſtance of a Mind, or Spirit, which is the Subject of* " *Will and Underſtanding, Thoughts and Paſſions; and* " *then we find it impoſſible to conceive how there ſhould be* " *three Divine Perſons, which are all Infinite without three* " *diſtinct Infinite Subſtances, each diſtinct Infinite Perſon* " *having a diſtinct Infinite Subſtance of his own: And if* " *we grant this, it ſeems a plain Contradiction to ſay, That* " *theſe three diſtinct Infinite Subſtances are but one Numeri-* " *cal Infinite Subſtance*, &c. Thus far our Author: And I freely grant, That this does not only *ſeem* (as he ſays) but really is a *Contradiction.* And, before I have done with him, I will prove to him alſo, That to ſay, *That three diſtinct Infinite Minds are but one Numerical Infinite Mind*, (which ſhall be effectually laid at his Door) or, *That three diſtinct Infinite Minds, are not three diſtinct Infinite Subſtances, or Eſſences*, are as groſs, and palpable Contradictions as the other. But he goes on in the ſame Page a little lower. " *We know nothing* (ſays he) *of the* " *Divine Eſſence, but that God is an Infinite Mind; and if* " *we ſeek for any other Eſſence, or Subſtance in God, but an* " *Infinite Mind; that is, Infinite Wiſdom, Power, and* " *Goodneſs, the Eſſence of God, though conſidered but as* " *one Numerical Perſon is as perfectly unintelligible to us, as* " *the one Numerical Eſſence, or Subſtance of three Divine* " *Perſons in the ever-bleſſed Trinity.* In which words, I think this Author guilty of a double Abſurdity. One, That he ſuppoſes a *Mind* not to be an *Eſſence*, or *Subſtance*; and it is manifeſt, that he does ſo, ſince he finds fault with *Subſtance*, and puts *Mind* in the room of it: Whereas a *Mind* is really a *Subſtance*, or *Nothing*; not that there is *nothing* in the World beſides *Subſtance*, but nothing elſe which *a Mind* can be properly ſaid to be.

His

His other Abſurdity is, his ſuppoſing *Mind, Wiſdom, Power*, and *Goodneſs*, to be the ſame; whereas *Wiſdom* and *Goodneſs*, are not properly a *Mind*, but the Affections, or Attributes of a *Mind*. And here let not our Author tell me, That they are all one and the ſame thing in God: For that is no News; yet nevertheleſs, *Mind, Wiſdom, Power, Goodneſs*, &c. are *formally* diſtinct from one another, and ſo not affirmable of one another: And in ſpeaking of things, the *formal* differences of them muſt ſtill be attended to: God's *Juſtice* and his *Mercy* are one pure ſimple Act in Him; but he that ſays, His *Juſtice* is his *Mercy*, ſpeaks abſurdly for all that: And he who ſays, That a *Mind* is *Wiſdom*, or *Goodneſs*, or *Power*, &c. ſpeaks juſt at the ſame rate.

But again in *Page* 70. " *It is this groſs and material* " *imagination* (ſays he) *about the Eſſence and Subſtance of* " *the Deity, which occaſions all the difficulties about the No-* " *tion of one God, as well as of a Trinity in Unity. For* " *we cannot imagine how any Subſtance ſhould be without a* " *beginning, how it ſhould be preſent in all places without* " *parts and without extenſion, how Subſtance, Eſſence, Ex-* " *iſtence, and* all Divine Attributes and Powers (*which are* " *diſtinct things in Created Spirits*) *ſhould be all the ſame* " *and one ſimple Act in God*, &c. From all which we are (according to this Author) to conclude, That the Terms *Subſtance, Eſſence*, and *Exiſtence*, ought to be laid aſide in all Diſcourſes of the Deity; as ſerving for nothing but to cauſe in us thoſe falſe Notions of it. Nor are thoſe only excepted againſt, but alſo all *Divine Attributes and Powers*; for in his laſt words (newly quoted) he equally joyns and puts them all together. And what monſtrous work this muſt needs make in our Conceptions and Diſcourſes of God, ſhall, I hope, in the proceſs of this Diſpute, be made to appear.

In

In order to which, I do here first of all in opposition to what this Author has Asserted about *Substance* and *Matter*, lay down this Proposition, *viz.* That Substance in the proper Nature, and Notion of it, includes no Communication with, or respect to Matter at all. And this I prove to him by one plain Argument, before I proceed to any thing that is Metaphysical, viz. *That there was Substance in the World before ever there was Matter*; and therefore the Notion of the former does not essentially include in it the Notion of the latter: For, surely, if the Being of one might be without the Being of the other, the Notion of the one may be no less without the Notion of the other too. Now that there was Substance in the World before Matter, I prove from this, That there was a *Being existing by it self*, in the World, before Matter, and therefore there was *Substance*: For this is the very definition of *Substance*, That *it is a Being existing by it self*, and consequently they must reciprocally infer one another, as the definition and the thing defined by it always do. And then, that there was a *Being thus existing by it self*, before Matter, is proved from hence, That there was a Being which produced Matter, which nothing but a Being existing by it self could do. And now I would fain know of our Author, Whether we may not have a clear and distinct Conception of such a Being, without so much as thinking of Matter. And if we may, (as I see nothing to hinder us) then it is false, that the Notion of Substance does necessarily engage our thoughts in, or confound them with the Idea of Matter. Besides, all the World does, and must allow, that we may have a full and perfect Conception of a *Genus*, or Generical Nature of a thing, without considering any of its *Species*. And withall, that it is impossible, that such a Generical Nature should include in it any one of the Specifick

cifick Differences of the things, which it is Communicable to, and which are contained under it; for if ſo, then one *Species* would include in it the Specifick difference of the other oppoſite *Species*; foraſmuch as including in it the Generical Nature, it muſt include all that is included in that Nature too: Which would be infinitely abſurd. But now Subſtance is a Generical Nature, equally communicable both to Material and Immaterial Subſtances, as to two diſtinct *Species*; and conſequently in its Preciſe Conception, implys nothing of Materiality in it; and for that cauſe may be conceived and known, and diſtinctly repreſented to our minds without it. Nay, and to ſhew further the difference between *Subſtance*, and *Matter* in the proper Notions of each, This Propoſition, *Subſtance is not Matter*, is certainly true; true, I ſay, *particularly* though not *univerſally*; that is, with reference to all thoſe Subſtances, the Nature of which excludes all Matter, as the Nature of Angels, and of the Souls of Men, confeſſedly does. But now, if the general Nature of Subſtance eſſentially implyed in it Matter, it could not be truly ſaid of any one particular Subſtance in the World, *That it is not Matter*. Mr. *Hobbs* I know, makes *Subſtance* and *Matter* Commenſurate, or rather the ſame. But methinks, though ſome have lately wrote after him in his lewd Politicks,no Divine ſhould venture to fall in with him in his Natural Philoſophy too, for fear of ſome certain Conſequences, which, it is too well known, muſt follow from it. In a word, the firſt thing to be conceived in God, is, *That he is a Being*; the next, *That he is a Being exiſting by it ſelf*; that is, in other words, *He is a Subſtance*: And therefore, I hope, we may both form an Idea of Subſtance, and afterwards apply it to God, without plunging our ſelves into the groſs Imagi-

 nations

nations of Matter. And so far do all other Divines, and Philosophers differ from this Man, that they affirm the word *Substance* much more properly, and really applicable to God, than to any of the Creatures; which certainly it could never be, if it implyed any such essential cognation to Matter, either in the Nature, or Notion of it.

It is evident therefore, That there is no necessity from the thing it self to justifie this Author's Objection. And as for those gross and Material Imaginations of Substance, taken up and borrowed from Material Corporeal things, nothing can be inferred from thence to his purpose. For is it good arguing to conclude, That because a thing is actually thus or thus, it cannot possibly be otherwise? Do not some form to themselves gross and absurd Imaginations of God the Father, from that Expression of the *Ancient of Days*, Dan. 7. 9. representing Him to their thoughts, as an Old Man sitting in Heaven? But may not others therefore, who are wiser, conceive more worthily of him, without laying aside that Scripture-expression? If it be a good Argument (as it is all our Author brings) that Terms, which may occasion gross and Material Imaginations in the minds of Men, ought not to be applyed to God; then I hope it is as much an Argument in one thing as in another. And accordingly I desire to know of him, Whether the Terms *Begetting*, and *being begot*, *Father* and *Son*, are not very fitly applyed to, and used about the Divine Persons? And if so, Whether they are not altogether as hard to be abstracted from material Imaginations, as the Notions of *Essence*, or *Substance* are, or rather, indeed, much harder? I believe all thinking Men will conclude they are. Nay, and I shall venture to tell him further, That these two words, partly through their Corporeal signification, and partly through

through the weakneſs of Men's minds, have occaſioned more difficulties about the Notion of a *Deity*, and a *Trinity* too, than ever the words *Eſſence*, or *Subſtance* did, or perhaps could do: And yet, for all that, the Spirit of God has thought fit to make uſe of them to expreſs ſo ſacred a Myſtery by. But this Man ſhould have remembred, That how groſs and Material ſoever the Repreſentations of things are, which our ſenſes firſt make to us, there is a *Judicium Correctivum* in Reaſon, as the ſuperiour faculty, which is to conſider and ſeparate what is groſs and Material in them, from what is otherwiſe, till at length by rejecting ſome Notions, and retaining others, it finds out ſomething even in the moſt Material things, which may truly, properly, and becomingly be applyed to the pureſt and moſt Immaterial. But to give a fuller Account of this matter, we muſt obſerve, That the Idea of *Subſtance* may be ſaid to be taken from *Matter* two ways.

1. Remotely and *Occaſionally*; as the Obſervation of Material Things may firſt ſet Reaſon to work, which in the ſtrength of its own Diſcourſe may draw from thence the knowledge of Immaterials, as the Apoſtle tells us in *Rom.* 1. 20. That the *Inviſible things of God, from the Creation, were clearly ſeen and underſtood from the things that are made*, viz. Such viſible ſenſible Objects, as Men daily converſe with: And if ſo, then ſurely theſe do not neceſſarily diſpoſe the mind of Man to groſs and Material Imaginations of the things ſo apprehended by it. But

2. The Idea of Subſtance may be ſaid to be taken from Matter *immediately* and *exemplarily*, as when the Imagination does, (as it were) tranſcribe and copy one from the other, and take one for the repreſentation of the other; and this, I confeſs, muſt needs imprint a very

ry groſs Idea of *Subſtance* upon the Imagination : And to this way may be referred all thoſe groſs and Material Ideas of Subſtance, which this Author ſo much exclaims againſt. But then, all this is from the neglect of the Perſon, in not imploying his Reaſon to correct and refine the firſt reports of Sence, as it might and ought to have done ; and if from hence we conclude an utter Incapacity in the thing it ſelf to be improved and heightened into Immaterial Repreſentations, and thereupon to be conceived and ſpoken of agreeably to them, we muſt even expect a Teacher to be ſent down from Heaven to furniſh us with a new Language, or we muſt ſhut up our Mouths, and put up our Pens, and not ſpeak, or write of Divine matters at all.

And therefore whereas this Author further adds, in *Page* 70. *That we cannot imagine how any ſubſtance ſhould be without a Beginning, and how it ſhould be Preſent in all places.* I tell him, This is not the Point in Controverſie, Whether we can imagine it, or no ? But I tell him withal, That it is as eaſie for the mind of Man to conceive all this of *Subſtance*, as of any thing elſe whatſoever. For, Why not *a Subſtance without a Beginning*, as well as *Truth, or Wiſdom, or Goodneſs*, without a Beginning ? I ſay, Let him ſhew me ſome ſolid Reaſon why. In the mean time, I can tell him, That of the two, it ſhould ſeem leſs difficult to imagine the Eternal Exiſtence of *Subſtance*, than of *Truth* ; ſince Subſtance is in order of Nature before it ; as the Subject muſt needs be before that which affects it. Though in very deed, the main difficulty here, is not ſo much to find out which of thoſe Perfections may be the moſt eaſily conceived to have been without a Beginning, as it is to bring the mind to a full and clear Conception, How any thing at all is ſo? while it finds it ſelf wholly at a loſs in running up its thoughts

thoughts ſtill higher and higher, without any bound or ſtint to determine them. And this it is, and not the particular Nature of Eſſence, or Subſtance, that nonpluſſes and confounds our Reaſon in theſe unlimited Speculations. And whereas he goes on in the next words, and tells us, That we cannot imagine, How *Subſtance, Exiſtence, and all the* Divine Attributes *and Powers ſhould be all one and the ſame ſimple Act in God?* I Anſwer. What if we cannot? Muſt nothing be applyed to God, but what ſhall let us into the full knowledge of all that is difficult and myſterious in the Divine Nature? Or will this Man ſay, That the Application of the Terms *Eſſence* and *Subſtance* to God, is the true cauſe and reaſon, why we cannot apprehend, *How Subſtance and Exiſtence, and all the Divine* Attributes and Powers, *are one and the ſame ſimple Act in God?* For this is the thing that he has been profeſſedly driving at, and therefore ought to prove. And beſides, as what he has here alledged, is nothing to his purpoſe, without the proof of that, ſo it is all but a meer fallacy, *a fallacy of the Accident:* For albeit, we cannot apprehend how all theſe Attributes are one and the ſame ſimple Act in God, yet ſurely it will not follow hence, that we cannot apprehend them ſingly and ſeverally by themſelves, and as we ſo apprehend them, apply them properly and fitly to God. And here I cannot but take notice of a way of Arguing uſual with this Author, as, *I cannot conceive*, and *I cannot underſtand*, and *I cannot imagine*, &c. After which, as if he had laid down irrefragable Premiſes, he concludes, That the thing it ſelf is not to *be conceived, underſtood*, or *imagined*. But for my part, I muſt be excuſed, that I cannot allow this Man's ſingle Judgment (or prejudice rather) for the univerſal Standard, or meaſure of humane Reaſon; or that ſuch a way of diſcourſing proves any thing but the

aſſuming

assuming humour of him who uses it; and one strangely full of Himself, instead of better things.

In conclusion therefore, I do here assert, That the gross and Material Imaginations which Men form to themselves of *Substance*, proceed not from the thing it self, but from the grossness and fault of the Persons who take up these Imaginations. And accordingly I affirm to this Author, That that Assertion of his in *Page 69. That we can form no Idea of Substance, but what we have from Matter*, is false, and manifestly proved to be so. And moreover, That it is not only as possible, but as easie to form in the mind, a conception of a *Substance, or Being Existing by it self* (which is all one) as abstracted from, and strip'd of all conception of Matter and Corporeity, as it is to frame to our selves a conception of *Truth*, or *Wisdom*, or of a Being eternally True and Wise, separate from all those gross Qualifications: And consequently that the word *Substance*, with others of the like import, may be most fitly and significantly applyed to the Divine Nature and the Persons of the Holy Trinity, which was the thing to be proved.

But because our Author avers, in *Page* 70. *That if we consider God as Truth and Wisdom, which is his true Nature and Essence, without confounding our mind with some material conceptions of his Substance* (as he had already affirmed all conceptions of Substance must needs be) *then these things (viz.* the Difficulties before-mentioned concerning our Apprehensions of God) *are all plain and easie.* Where, by the way it is observable, That he *calls Truth and Wisdom the true* Nature and Essence *of God*; whereas in this very *Page*, as well as in 68. he had excepted against the Term *Essence*, no less than that of *Substance*, as (by reason of the gross Material Ideas raised by it in the mind) very unfit to be applyed to God. So happy

is

is this Author above other Men, that he can rectifie the most improper words and expressions barely by his own using them.

But because he is so positive in making the Terms *Truth* and *Wisdom* an effectual Remedy against all the Inconveniences alledged from the Terms *Essence* and *Substance*, as applyed to the Deity, this brings us to our second *Proposition*, *viz*. That the same Objection lies against the Terms *Truth*, *Wisdom*, *Goodness*, &c. as applicable to the Deity, that are made against *Essence, Substance*, *Existence*, and the like. In order to the proving of which, I shall observe, That *Truth* may be taken in a three-fold sense.

First, For the truth of Propositions, which is called Logical.

Secondly, For an Affection of Being, which is Truth Metaphysical. And

Thirdly and Lastly, As it is a Qualification of Men's Words and Actions, and consists properly in an Agreement of the mind with both.

Concerning all which I observe, That the Truth of Propositions is no further eternal, than as it exists in the mind of God. That the Metaphysical Truth of Things is eternal, or not eternal, as the Being, or Thing it belongs to, is, or is not so. And for the Moral Truth of Men's Words and Actions, it is no more eternal than the said Words and Actions, the proper Subject of them, can be said to be. This premised, I would here ask our Author, Whether the first Notions we actually entertain of *Truth* and *Wisdom*, are not drawn from the Observations we make of these things in Men; that is, in Beings sensible and Material, and consisting of Body as well as Soul, and accordingly cloathed with sensible Accidents and Circumstances? I cannot imagine that he

will

will deny this, ſince we do not ſpeak immediately, or converſe viſibly with God, or Angels; and I ſuppoſe alſo, that he now ſpeaks of *Truth*, *Wiſdom*, *Goodneſs*, &c. not as they are exhibited to us in Books, or Propoſitions, but as they actually exiſt and occurr in perſons, and conſequently as they are firſt apprehended by us in Concretion, or Conjunction with Men; that is, with Beings ſo Compounded, Qualified, and Circumſtantiated, as above expreſſed, and as we find, ſee and obſerve them, in Men's Words and Actions, in what they ſpeak, and what they do; and theſe are certainly very ſenſible things, and ſuch as incurr into, and affect the ſence as much as Matter it ſelf can do. And if ſo, I deſire to hear ſome ſatisfactory Reaſon, Why the Obſervation of *Subſtance* in Material Beings, and our firſt *Occaſional* collection of it from thence, ſhould ſo neceſſarily pervert, and cauſe ſuch a groſſneſs in our Conceptions of it, as to make it hardly (if at all) poſſible to conceive of *Subſtance*, without the groſs Conception of Matter; and yet that the ſame conſideration and cauſe ſhould not equally take place in *Truth* and *Wiſdom*, and equally pervert and thicken our Apprehenſions of them, when they are equally drawn from ſenſible, groſs, and Material Objects, *viz.* the Words and Actions of Men, which they both Exiſt in, and Converſe about? For I can ſee no ground why the ſame Reaſon ſhould not infer the very ſame thing, and the ſame Antecedents draw after them the ſame Conſequents, whatſoever they are applyed to. For the Argument *à Quatenus ad omne*, &c. is certain and infallible.

If it be here ſaid, That *Truth* and *Wiſdom* in the proper Notion and Conception of them, imply no Communication at all with Matter: I Anſwer, That as the Notion of them is Abſtracted, and gathered up by the Diſcourſes

Discourses of Reason it does not; but so neither does that of *Substance*, after such an Act of the Mind has passed upon it. So that hitherto the Case is much the same in both.

But to carry the matter a little further. *Truth* and *Wisdom* as observed in and amongst Men, are certainly finite Things. For whatsoever exists in a finite *Subject* (whatsoever the *Object* be which it converses about, or is terminated upon) is certainly it self finite also. And here I would have this Author tell me, Why a Notion drawn off, and borrowed from finite Things, should not be as apt to perplex and confound our Minds, when applyed to an Infinite Being; as a Notion abstracted from a *Material Being*, can be to distract and confound our Thoughts when applyed to an Immaterial? I must confess, I can see nothing alleageable for one, which may not be as strongly alledged for the other. All that can be said, is what has been mentioned already, *viz.* That Reason may, and does, extract some Notions from a finite Being, that may be properly applicable to an Infinite, due allowance made for the disproportion between both; and in like manner I affirm, That it can and does draw Notions from a thing endued with Matter, which may as well agree to Things Spiritual and Immaterial. So that I cannot perceive, that *Truth*, *Wisdom*, or *Goodness*, have upon this Account any Preheminence, or Advantage over *Essence*, *Substance*, *Existence*, and the like Terms at all, but the one may be applyed to the Divine Nature as well and properly as the other.

But this is not all; for I affirm in the 3d *Place*, That *Essence*, *Substance*, *Nature*, *Existence*, and other Terms equipollent to Being, considered precisely in and by themselves, are naturally fitter to express the Deity by, than those other Terms, *Truth*, *Wisdom* and *Goodness*, contended for by our Author. This is our Third Propofition ; and for the proof of it I firft appeal to that high and glorious Account, which *God* himfelf gave of his own Nature, when *Mofes* defired to be informed of it, viz. *I am that I am,* Exod. 3. 14. In which he defcribes himfelf only from his *Being* and *Subftance*, which indeed rendered him more eminently, and even more *fubftantially*, and truly *a Being or Subftance*, than all other Beings, or Subftances whatfoever, which, in comparifon of him, can hardly be fo much as faid to *Exift*, or *Be*. And I am perfwaded, that God knew his own Name and Nature, and withal, how to give the beft and moft proper Declaration of Both, as well as the Author of *Self-Confcioufnefs,and Mutual-Confcioufnefs* does or can pretend to do. And indeed this feems to have been the very Character by which God would be then known to all the World, *viz.* All the Rational part of the Creation ; for it was fent to his People, then living under, and with a Heathen Prince, to anfwer them and him even in thofe Notions of a God, which meer Nature fuggefted to all Mankind ; and confequently were fo known and received by them, that they could not eafily queftion, or deny them. For otherwife we know God addreffed himfelf to the fame People afterwards in a Character extreamly different, and more peculiar, viz. *A God Merciful and Gracious, Long-fuffering, abundant in Goodnefs and Truth, and pardoning Iniquity, Tranfgreffion, and Sin,* Exod. 34. 6, 7. Which, it feems, was the Opening a Particular Attribute to them, which the bare Account of his Being (as known as it was) could not fufficiently inform the World of before.

But to proceed to other Confiderations, vaftly indeed inferiour to this, but yet of fingular ufe in their degree, to direct our Speculations about thefe Matters,

I

I have ſome other Things to offer in behalf of the Propoſition laid down by us.

As Firſt, That all Divines hitherto have looked upon, and profeſſedly treated of *the Divine Nature and Attributes*, as different and diſtinct from one another; ſtill conſidering the firſt as the *Subject*, and the other as the *Adjuncts* of it; or, at leaſt, as Analogous to theſe Terms as they ſtand properly applyed to other Things. According to which Notion, as the *Subject*, or that which is Analogous to it, naturally both precedes and ſupports the *Adjuncts*; ſo all Notions importing the Divine *Nature*, *Being*, or *Subſtance*, are to be accounted as *the Subject*, in reſpect of all God's other Attributes, or Perfections, whether they be *Truth*, *Wiſdom*, *Goodneſs*, *Power*, *Eternity*, *Omniſcience*, or any other whatſoever. Which being ſo, I do here affirm, That the Terms *Eſſence*, *Subſtance*, *Exiſtence*, and others Synonymous to them, ought to have the Precedence of the other Divine Perfections, commonly called *Attributes*, in their Application to God, and that upon a three-fold Account, *viz*.

1. *Of Priority.*
2. *Of Simplicity.*
3. *Of Comprehenſiveneſs.* Of each of which ſeverally.

1. For that of *Priority*. As we have already obſerved. That the firſt thing in order of Nature Conceivable of God, is, *That he is a Being*; and the next to it, *That he is a Being exiſting by it ſelf*, or (in another word) *a Subſtance*; ſo the ſame is yet further evidenced from this, That the Notion of Being, or Subſtance, is that, which fully anſwers and determines the laſt Queſtion and Enquiry, which can be made concerning God. For if we deſcribe his Nature by any particular Attribute, or Per-

 fection,

fection, and be thereupon asked, *What that is?* And having given an Anſwer to that Queſtion, be afterwards urged with another, and perhaps another; and accordingly, after an Anſwer given to thoſe alſo, the Enquiry be ſtill continued, till at length we Anſwer, *That God is a Being; a Being exiſting by it ſelf*, that is, *a Subſtance.* Then we muſt of neceſſity ſtop, and can go no further; which makes it evident even to a Demonſtration, That this is the firſt and Original Notion which we have, or can have of God. Foraſmuch as that which anſwers the laſt Enquiry, or Queſtion, naturally made concerning any thing, is certainly the firſt Thing into which the Being, or Reaſon of that Thing is reſolved. And thus much for *Priority.*

Paſs we now to the *Second Thing*, which is the *Simplicity* of theſe Terms. For *Primum in omni genere ſimpliciſſimum.* So that when we ſay, *God is a Being exiſting by it ſelf*, viz. *A Subſtance*; this includes in it no reſpect to, and much leſs any Conjunction with any other Thing or Notion whatſoever: But on the contrary, *Truth*, *Goodneſs*, *Power*, &c. are all Affections of Being, or Subſtance, and ſo connote a Relation to, and a Conjunction with it, as their *Subject.* So that to give you the ſame thing in words at length, *Truth* and *Goodneſs* are nothing elſe but *Being, or Subſtance, with theſe Qualifications*, or Being and Subſtance under ſuch certain reſpects formally determining them to ſuch a condition, *viz.* either of *Conformity* to the *Underſtanding*, as *Truth* determines them, or of *Conformity to the Will*, as *Goodneſs* does. So that in theſe, and all other the like Attributes, *Being or Subſtance* do, as it were, paſs from their abſolute and Original Simplicity by the Acceſſion of the fore-mentioned Perfections ſuperadded to them.

And

And then in the *Third and last place*. For the *Comprehensiveness* of Being, or Substance, above any one, or more of the Divine Attributes, This also is evident; forasmuch as it runs through and contains them all, which no other particular Attribute does, or can be said to do. And certainly that which signifies *Being* in the whole compass and perfection of it, should be much more properly applicable to God; than that, which signifies *Being* only under some certain and particular determination of it, as every one of his Attributes does, and no more. For we cannot say, That *God's Justice, Mercy, Wisdom, Holiness and Power*, are properly contained under, and formally attributable to his *Truth*, but they are all contained under, deducible from, and referible to his *Being or Substance*. So that it may properly be said, That God is an *Infinitely True, Wise, Good, Holy, Omnipotent, Omnipresent Being* or *Substance*. But we cannot with any propriety of Speech pitch upon any one of the other *Divine Attributes*, and in like manner affirm all the rest of that one. As to say that God is an Infinitely Wise, Good, Eternal, Omnipotent, Omnipresent *Truth*. This (I say) cannot be equally said: For though the Thing be fundamentally true, yet the Expression is neither Proper, nor Natural: Forasmuch as *Goodness, Justice, Omnipotence, Omnipresence*, and the like, are not the proper Affections of Truth, but they are properly so of *Substance*, or *Being*. And moreover, Whereas this Author will needs have the Terms *Substance, Essence and Existence* discarded, and the Terms *Truth, Wisdom and Goodness* put in their room, when we speak of the Divine Nature; I desire him to give me some good Reason, why he pitches upon *Truth, Wisdom and Goodness*, rather than upon *Eternity, Omnipotence and Omnipresence*. For these, in their proportion, express the *Divine Nature*

ture as much as the other; but neither the one nor the other can grasp in the whole Compass of the *Divine Perfections*, so as to be properly denominable from all and every one of them, as *Substance, and Essence*, and such other Terms as barely import *Being*, are found to be. I conclude therefore, that in our Discourses of *God, Essence, Substance, Nature*, and the like, are so far from being necessary to be laid aside, as disposing our Minds to gross and unfit Apprehensions of the Deity; that they are much fitter to express and guide our thoughts about this great Subject, than *Truth, Wisdom*, or *Power*, or all of them together, as importing in them both a *Priority*, and a greater *Simplicity*, and larger *Comprehensiveness of Notion*, than belong to any of them; and these surely are Considerations most peculiarly suted to, and worthy of the Perfections of the *Divine Nature*.

I have now done with my *Third Proposition*, and so proceed to the *Fourth and last*, viz. *That the Difficulty of our Conceiving rightly of the Deity and the Divine Persons, does really proceed from other causes, than those alledged by this Author*. I shall assign three: As,

First, *The Spirituality of the Divine Nature. For God is a Spirit*, Joh. 4. 14. And it is certain that we have no clear, explicit and distinct Idea of a Spirit. And if so, must we not needs find a great difficulty in knowing it? For we know things directly by the Ideas, the *Species Intelligibiles*, or Resemblances of them, imprinted upon the Intellect, and these are refined and drawn off from the *Species Sensibiles*, and sensible Resemblances of the same imprinted upon the Imagination. And how can a Spirit incurr directly into that? Indeed not at all. For we can have no knowledge of a Spirit by any direct Apprehension, or Intuition of it; but all that we know of such Beings, is what we gather by Inference,

Di-

Diſcourſe, and Ratiocination: And that is ſufficient. But

2. The Second Reaſon of our Short and Imperfect Notions of the Deity, is, *The Infinity of it.* For this we muſt Obſerve, That we can perfectly know and comprehend nothing, but as it is repreſented to us under ſome certain Bounds and Limitations. And therefore one of the chief Inſtruments of our knowledge of a Thing, is the Definition of it. And what does that ſignifie, but the bringing, or repreſenting a Thing under certain Bounds and Limitations, as the *Greek* Word διορισμὸς manifeſtly imports. Upon which Account, what a loſs muſt we needs be at, in underſtanding or knowing the *Divine Nature*, when the very way of our knowing ſeems to carry in it ſomething oppoſite to the thing known? For the way of knowing, is by *Defineing*, limiting and determining; and the Thing known is that, of which there neither are nor can be any Bounds, Limits, Definitions, or Determinations. And this, I think, is not only a ſufficient, but ſomething more than a ſufficient Reaſon, why we ſtumble and fail, when we would either have, or give a diſtinct Account of the Deity.

3. A Third Reaſon of the ſame, eſpecially with reference to the Trinity of Perſons belonging to the *Divine Nature*, is, *The utter want of all Instances and Examples of this kind.* For when a long and conſtant courſe of Obſervation has ſtill took notice that every numerically diſtinct Perſon, and every *Suppoſitum* has a numerically diſtinct Nature appropriate to it, and Religion comes afterwards, and calls upon us to apprehend the ſame Numerical Nature, as ſubſiſting in three Numerically diſtinct Perſons; we are extreamly at a loſs how to conform our Notions to it, and to conceive how that

can

can be in three Persons, which we never saw before, or in any thing else, to be but only in One. For humane Nature, which originally proceeds by the Observations of sense, does very hardly frame to it self any Notions, or Conceptions of things, but what it has drawn from thence. Nay, I am of Opinion, That the Mind is so far governed by what it sees and observes, that I verily believe, that had we never actually seen the beginning or end of any thing, the Generality of Men would hardly so much as have imagined, That the World had ever had any beginning at all: Since with the greatest part of Mankind what *appears*, and what does *not appear*, determines *what can*, and *what cannot be*, in their Opinion.

And thus I have shewn three Causes (which I take to be the True Causes) why we are so much to seek in our Apprehensions of, and Discourses about the Divine Nature, and the three Glorious Persons belonging to it. And the Reason of them all is founded upon the Essential Disparity which the Mind of Man bears to so disproportionate, and so transcendent an Object. So that it is a vain thing to Quarrel at Words and Terms, especially such as the best Reason of Mankind has pitched upon as the fittest, and properest, and most significant to express these great things by. And I question not, but in the Issue of all, Wise Men will find, That it is not the defect of the Terms we use, but the vast incomprehensibility of the thing we apply them to, which is the True Cause of all our Failures, as to a clear and distinct Apprehension and Declaration of what relates to the Godhead.

From all which I conclude, That the Terms, *Essence*, *Substance*, *Nature*, &c. have had nothing yet objected against them, but that they may still claim the place, and

continue

continue in the uſe, which the Learned'ſt Men the *Chriſtian* Church has hitherto had, have allotted them in all their Diſcourſes and Diſputes about the Divine Nature, and the Divine Perſons; which are confeſſedly the greateſt and moſt Sacred Myſteries in the Chriſtian Religion. But as in my time, I have obſerved it a practice at Court, That when any one is turned out of a conſiderable Place there, it is always firſt reſolved (and that out of *merit foreſeen*, no doubt) who ſhall ſucceed him in it: So all this ado in diſmounting the Terms *Eſſence*, *Subſtance*, *Nature*, &c. from their ancient Poſt, I perceive, is only to make way for theſe two ſo highly uſeful and wonder-working Terms, *Self-Conſciouſneſs*, and *Mutual-Conſciouſneſs*. And therefore let us, with all due and aweful Reverence (as becomes us) expect their Auguſt appearance, and for a while ſuffer the *Mountain* to ſwell, and *heave up its Belly*, and look big upon us, and all in good time, no doubt, we ſhall have the happineſs to ſee and admire, and take our meaſures of the *Mouſe*.

But before I cloſe this Chapter, to ſhew how like a Judge upon Life and Death, this Man ſits over all the formerly received Terms, by which Men were wont to diſcourſe of *God*, Sentencing and Condemning them as he pleaſes; not content to have caſhiered the words *Eſſence*, *Subſtance* and *Nature* from being uſed about this Subject, he has as great, or greater a Quarrel at the word *Infinite*, as applyed to *God*; and I ſhall here give his Exceptions againſt it in his own words, being ſuch, as I believe few would dare to utter but himſelf, and approaching ſo near, or rather quite coming up to Blaſphemy, that it may be truly ſaid, That he has not ſpoke more blaſphemouſly of *God's Vindictive Juſtice* in his *Book of the knowledge of Chriſt*, than he has ſpoken of

See my Preface.

of *God's Infinity* in this: For in the 77, 78, 79. *Pages* he expresses his thoughts of it thus. *The truth is* (says he) *this very word* Infinite *confounds our Notions of God, and makes the most perfect and excellent Being the most perfectly unknown to us. For* Infinite *is only a Negative Term, and signifies that which has no end, no bounds, no measure, and therefore no positive and determined Nature, and therefore is Nothing* (mark that) and withal, *That an Infinite Being, had not Use and Custom reconciled us to that expression, would be thought Nonsence and Contradiction.* Which I am so far from granting him, that I affirm, if there had never been any thing in the World besides *God* alone, it had yet been most True and Rational. But he goes on. *For* (says he) *every Real Being has a certain and determined Nature, and therefore is not infinite in this sence, which is so far from being a Perfection, that it signifies Nothing Real.* Thus he discourses: And yet this word *Infinite* has been universally received and applyed to the *Divine Nature,* by Learned Men in all Places and Ages; and I desire this Man to tell me, How, if this word *Infinite* were so liable to be thought *Nonsence* and *Contradiction,* this could possibly come to pass. For what he speaks of *use and custom reconciling us to this Expression,* is Impertinent, and begs the Thing in dispute. For still I would know of him, how a word so utterly unfit to express the thing it was applyed to, could ever pass into *Use* and *Custom,* so as to be took up, approved, and made use of by all Mankind. Let him prevail with the whole World to speak *Nonsence*, and to use words that *signifie nothing*, if he can. But this Man, before he played the *Aristarchus* at this rate, should have done well to have considered, That every Term is not *Negative*, which has a *Negative* Particle in the Composition of it. Of which, innumerable Instances may be given. And if he he does not know this, for all his flirting at his *Socinian* Adversary, as if he *knew neither* Greek *nor* Latin, *P.* 95. it is a scurvy sign that he is not so over-stocked with either of them as to have any to spare.

And therefore, whereas he goes on in *Page* 78. and pretends there to explain this word *Infinite*, he might have kept his explication to himself. For no body ever used it otherwise, but so as to signifie a *Positive Perfection* by it, but yet withal connoting an *Illimitation* belonging to it. It signifies, I say, a Thing *Real, Absolute and Positive*, but still with a Connotation of something, which is to be removed from it, and denied of it; such as are all *bounds and limits* in respect of that Substantial, all-comprehending perfection of the *Divine Nature*. In a word, the thing principally signified by this Term, is *Positive*, the Thing Consignified, or Connoted (which is but Secondary and Consequential) is a *Negation*. And this sufficiently overturns all his odd Descants upon it. But if, after all, our Minds cannot fully master this Notion, Persons, as thinking as he can be, know and acknowledge, that it is not the *word Infinite*, but the *Thing Infinite*, that renders them so short and defective in this matter.

But it is pleasant to see him take his Turns backwards and forwards in speaking of this Thing. *There is (* says he) Page 78, *a measure of the most Absolute and (in this sense) Infinite Perfections*; and if such a *measure* there be, then I hope there is as much *Nonsence* and *Contradiction* in the word *Immense*, as in the word *Infinite*; and withal, if there is even in the most Absolute and *Infinite Perfections*, a *ne plus ultrà*, and an *ultimum quod sic* (as the School-men, who were never bred at St. *Mary Overies*, are apt to speak) then I confess, That an *Infinite*, with all these Qualifications about it, must needs (according to his beloved Dialect) be *Nonsence and Contradiction*; and that of the highest rank. And again, P.79. *We know not* (says he) *How far Infinite Wisdom, and Power, and Goodness reaches*, (and thus much is very true) but then (says he again) *we certainly know that they have their* Bounds, *and that the Divine Nature is the utmost* Bounds *of them*. By which words if he means, That they have their fixed determinate Notions, whereby they are formally distinguished among themselves, as well as from other Things, it is right. For the Notion of *Infinite Wisdom* is so bounded, that it cannot be said to be *Infinite Power*, or *Infinite Power* to be *Infinite Goodness*, or the like; but still the Thing couched under all these is *Infinite*, and neither has nor can have any *Bounds* set to its Being. And if he should here reply, That then the Notion of *Infinite Wisdom*, *Power*, and the like, are false Notions, as not answering the Things they are applyed to. I Answer, That they are indeed imperfect and *inadequate*, as not fully answering the Thing it self, but they cannot be said to be *false* for all that. But on the contrary, if he will needs have the thing hereby signified to have any Real Bounds or Limits of it's Being; then it will and must follow, That in the forecited words he has with Accurate and Profound Speculation presented to us *An Infinite with* Bounds, *and the Divine Nature* (which has no Bounds) *made the* Bounds *of it*. These are the very words he uses; and withal delivered by him with such a Magisterial Air and Contempt of the whole World besides, who have hitherto approved and made use of these Expressions (and that in a sense and signification not to be born down by every self Opiniator, after so long and universal a Prescription) that so much Confidence cannot be sufficiently wondred at, nor too severely rebuked.

And

And therefore to review a little the foregoing particulars, and thereby to take ſome eſtimate of the Man; Where ſhall we find ſuch another Inſtance of a *private Presbyter*, who in the Communion, or rather in the very Boſom of ſo pure and Orthodox a Church, as this our Church of *England*, ever before durſt, in ſo great an Article of the *Chriſtian Faith*, draw his Pen againſt all the Writers of the Church Ancient and Modern, Fathers and School-men, and with one daſh of it explode and ſtrike off all thoſe received Terms by which they conſtantly explained this Myſtery, as not only uſeleſs, but miſchievous in all Diſcourſes about it? Whereas (not to anticipate what I intend more particularly and fully upon this Head in my eighth Chapter) I ſhall only affirm thus much at preſent; That the *Greek* Writers in expreſſing the *God-head*, or *Divine Nature*, whenſoever they do not uſe the words, Θεότης, or τὸ Θεῖον, conſtantly expreſs it by φύσις and οὐσία, and ſometimes by ὑπόστασις, while οὐσία and ὑπόστασις were commonly uſed in the ſame ſenſe. And likewiſe the *Latines*, where they expreſs not the ſame by *Deitas*, or *Divinitas*, do as conſtantly expreſs it by *Natura* and *Subſtantia*; which words ſtand now particularly condemned by this Preſuming Man; and that, not only in defiance of all the Ancients, but alſo of the Church of *England* it ſelf, which has ſet her Authorizing ſtamp upon thoſe two words *Subſtance* and *Perſon*, by applying them to this Subject both in her *Articles* and *Liturgy*. In the firſt of them teaching us, *That in the Unity of the Godhead there are three* Perſons, *of one* Subſtance, *Power and Eternity.* Artic. 1. And in her Liturgy rendring the *Athanaſian Creed* by the ſame words, *Neither confounding the* Perſons, *nor dividing the* Subſtance. As likewiſe that Paſſage in the *Nicene Creed*, by the *Son's being of one* Subſtance *with*

with the Father. And again in the Doxology at the Communion on *Trinity Sunday*, it gives us these full and notable words, *One God, one Lord, not one only* Person, *but three Persons in one* Substance. After all which, with what face can this strange, Anomalar Son of the Church (while he is sucking her Breasts, and at the same time poysoning the *Milk*, with which she should feed her Children) I say, with what face can he aver to the World, That this word *Substance* thus embraced, owned and used by her, ought to be thrown away, as the Direct Cause of all the Errours Men are apt to fall into, about this great Mystery? and that we can have no *Notion of Substance*, but what *implys in it something gross and material*? Which, were it so, can any one imagine, that the Church of *England* would ever have made use of such a *word*, as could serve for nothing, but a Snare and a Trap to betray the Understandings and Consciences of Men, into such Errours as may cost them their Souls? This is so fouly Reflexive upon her, that I would have any Man living give me a good Reason, Why this Author should not be call'd upon by Publick Authority to give the Church satisfaction for the scandal given to all the Orthodox Members of it, by the Contumely and Reproach which he has passed upon those *Terms* and *Words* which she has thought fit so solemnly to express her *Faith* and her *Devotions* by. But some Men, (such is the Regard had to her Laws and Discipline) will venture to utter and write any Thing, that the Bookseller will pay them for, though they throw their Conscience and Religion into the Bargain.

Some further Remarks upon his Apology.

But *God* himself, *who resisteth the Proud*, seems to have took the Matter into his own Hands, and (to shew his Controlling Providence over the Minds and Hearts of Men) has at length brought this Scornful Man *to eat his own*

own words (the hardeſt Diet certainly that a proud Perſon can be put to) and after all the black Dirt thrown by Him upon the *School-men* and their *Terms*, to lick it off again with his own Tongue. So that after he had paſſed ſuch a Terrible killing Doom upon theſe words, *Eſſence*, *Subſtance*, *Subſiſtence*, *Suppoſitum*, *Perſon*, and the like, here in his *Vindication*, all on a ſuddain, in a relenting fit, he graciouſly reaches out his *Golden Scepter* of *Self-Contradiction*, and reſtores them to Life again, in his *Apology*. And that the Reader may behold both ſides of the Contradiction the more clearly, I think it the beſt and faireſt way to give him the *ſenſe* of this Author (if it may be ſo call'd) in his own words.

Vindication.	*Apology.*
" I Have not troubled " my Reader with the " different ſignification of " *Eſſence*, *Hypoſtaſis*, *Subſi-* " *ſtence*, *Perſons*, *Exiſtence*, " *Nature*, &c. which are " Terms very differently " uſed by the *Greek* and " *Latin* Fathers, *and have* " *very much obſcured this Do-* " *ctrine inſtead of explain-* " *ing it*, P. 101. l. 12.	" HE (*viz.*) the *me-* " *lancholy Stander-* " *by*, is very angry with " the School-Doctors, as " worſe Enemies to Chri- " ſtianity, than either Hea- " then Philoſophers, or " Perſecuting Emperours. " 'Pray what hurt have " they done ? I ſuppoſe he " means the corruption of " Chriſtianity, with thoſe " Barbarous Terms of *Per-* " *ſon*, *Nature*, *Eſſence*, *Sub-* " *ſiſtence*, *Conſubſtantiality*, " &c. *which will not ſuffer* " Hereticks *to lie concealed*
" The School-men have " no Authority where they " leave the Fathers ; *whoſe* " *ſenſe they ſometimes ſeem* " *to miſtake*, *or to clog it*	

" *with some peculiar Niceties* " *and Distinctions of their* " *own*, P. 138. l. 28.

" The Truth is, that " which has confounded " this *Mystery* (*viz.* of the " Trinity) has been the " vain endeavour to reduce " it to Terms of Art, such " as *Nature*, *Essence*, *Sub-* " *stance*, *Subsistence*, *Hypo-* " *stasis*, and the like, P. 138. " l. the last, and p. 139. " l. 1.

And speaking of the Ancient Fathers in the same Page, he tells us: " They " nicely distinguished be- " tween *Person* and *Hypo-* " *stasis*, and *Nature*, and " *Essence*, and *Substance*; " that they *were three Per-* " *sons*, but one *Nature*, *Es-* " *sence and Substance*: But " that when Men curiously " examined the significati- " on of these words, they " found that upon some ac- " count or other, *They were* " *very unapplicable to this* " *Mystery*.

Hereupon he asks the following Questions in an upbraiding manner, *viz.* " *under Scripture-Phrases.* " *But why must the School-* " *men bear all the blame of* " *this*? Why does he not " accuse the *Ancient Fa-* " *thers*, *and Councils*, *from* " *whom the School-men* " *learnt these Terms.* Why " does he let St. *Austin* e- " scape, from whom the " Master of the Sentences " borrowed most of his " Distinctions and Subtle- " ties? But suppose, these " unlucky Wits had used " some new Terms, have " they taught any new " Faith about the Trinity " in Unity, which the " Church did not teach? " And if they *have only* " *guarded the* Christian " *Faith with an Hedge of* " *Thorns*, *which disguised* " Hereticks *cannot break* " *through*, is this to wound " Christianity in its very " Vitals? No, no: *They* " *will only prick the Fin-* " *gers of* Hereticks, *and se-* " *cure Christianity from be-* " *ing wounded*; and this " is one great Cause, why " some Men are so angry

" *What is the Substance and* " *Nature of* God? " *How can three* " *distinct Persons* " *have but one* " *Numerical Sub-* " *stance?* And, " *What is the Distinction be-* " *tween Essence*, and *Perso-* " *nality*, and *Subsistence?*

See these empty Questions distinctly answered in my 7th. *Chapter.*

And Lastly, at the end of the same Page, " He " confesses, that some to- " lerable Account of the " School-Terms and Di- " stinctions might be gi- " ven, but that it would be " a work of *more difficulty* " than *use*. " with the School-Doctors; " though the more General " Cause is, because they " have not Industry enough " to Read, or understand " them. *Apology, P.*4,5.

I have (to prevent all Exceptions) given the Reader the whole Paragraph; in which the last Clause *strikes Home* indeed; tho' in such Cases, some think this Author would do well to take heed of striking *too Home* and *Hard*, for fear the Blow should *rebound* back again, and do execution where he least intended it.

Now here the Reader is desired to observe the Sovereign usefulness ascribed by our Author to those School-Terms: *Person, Nature, Essence, Subsistence, Consubstantiality*, &c. As, *That they will not suffer* Hereticks *to lie concealed under Scripture-Phrases.* That *the Schools learned all these Terms of the Ancient Fathers.* That *they have guarded the Christian Faith with an Hedge of Thorns, which disguised* Hereticks *cannot break through. That instead of wounding* Christianity *in its Vitals, they only prick the Fingers of* Hereticks, *and secure* Christianity *from being wounded.* All these great and good things he tells us have been done in behalf of Christianity by the *Schoolmen*, and their fore-mentioned *Terms*, here in this *Apology*; and now if the Reader will but look back into the

Vindication too, our Author will there tell him also, *How*, and by *what Way* and *means* the said *School-men* and their *Terms* have Atchieved all these worthy Feats, *viz. By their obscuring instead of explaining the Doctrine of the Trinity. By their mistaking the meaning of the Fathers, or clogging it with peculiar Niceties of their own.* Also *by confounding the Mystery of the Trinity, through a vain endeavour to reduce it to such Terms of Art, as* Essence, Substance, Subsistence, Nature, Person, *and the like.* As likewise *by the said Terms being found very* unapplicable *to this Mystery.* And lastly, *Because though some tolerable Account might possibly be given of their meaning, yet that it would be of little or* no use *to give any such Account, or Explication of them: So useful* (it seems) does he account them, to *secure* Christianity *against* Hereticks, that it is *of no use* at all to *explain* them. And now, I hope, when the Reader has considered, what this Author has said on both sides, he will acknowledge, that *Hand* and *Glove* cannot more exactly agree, than the *Vindication* and the *Apology*. And as for that *Melancholy Stander-by*, upon whose Account this *Apology* is pretended to have been written, if he will but read and compare the *Apology* and *Vindication* together, I dare undertake, that he will not be half so *Melancholy* as he was before.

But does this Author, in sober sadness, think that this is the way to *Confute Hereticks*, thus to play backwards and forwards, to say, and unsay, and only to set two Books together by the Ears? Let me tell him, *That* God *is not mocked*, nor the World neither; and that he owes an Account, of what he has wrote, to both. For my own part, so far as my Converse reaches, I meet with no serious and judicious Person, who does not reckon, that this Author, by his *Desultorious, Inconsi-*

stent,

ſtent, but withal *Impoſing* way of writing, will in all likelihood make twenty *Hereticks*, before he Confutes one.

It is indeed an amazing Thing to conſider, That any one Man ſhould preſume to Brow-beat all the World at ſuch a rate; and we may well wonder at the force of Confidence and Self-Conceit, that it ſhould be able to raiſe any one to ſuch a pitch. But *Naturaliſts* have obſerved, That Blindneſs in ſome *Animals*, is a very great Help and Inſtigation to Boldneſs. And amongſt Men, as *Ignorance* is commonly ſaid to be the *Mother* of *Devotion*, ſo in accounting for the Birth and Deſcent of *Confidence* too, (whatſoever other Cauſe ſome may derive it from) yet, certainly, He who makes *Ignorance the Mother of this* alſo, reckons its Pedigree by the *ſurer ſide*.

CHAP. III.

In which the Author's New Notion of Self-Consciousness *and* Mutual-Consciousness, *is briefly declared.* Self-Consciousness *made by him the formal Constituent Reason of* Personality *in all Persons, both Create and Uncreate; and on the contrary, proved against him in the first place, That it is not so in Persons Create.*

OUR Author not being satisfied with the Account given of the Mystery of the Blessed Trinity by the Schools, nor with those Notions about it, which have hitherto obtained in the World, till he came into it (no doubt as a Person peculiarly sent and qualified to rectifie all those Imperfect, and Improper Notions, which had been formerly received by Divines.) He, I say, with a Lofty Undertaking Mind, and a Reach beyond all *before*, and indeed *beside* him, and (as the Issue is like to prove) as much *above* him too, undertakes to give the World a much better, and more satisfactory Explication of this great Mystery, and that by two new Terms, or Notions (purely and solely of his own invention) called, *Self-Consciousness*, and *Mutual-Consciousness*; which, though still joyned together by our Author in his Explication of the *Blessed Trinity*, have yet

yet very different Effects, as we shall presently see.

For by *Self-Consciousness*, he means, a Mind's, or Spirit's being Conscious to its own Thoughts, Reasonings and Affections (and I suppose all other Internal Motions too) which no other finite Spirit is, or can be naturally Conscious to, but it self. And this (he says) makes a finite Spirit Numerically one, or *one with it self* (for he uses both Expressions) and withal separates and distinguishes it from all other Spirits; so that hereby every Spirit feels only its own Thoughts, Passions, or Motions, but is not Conscious to the Thoughts, Passions, or Motions of any other. And this (so far as his own words import) he means by *Self-Consciousness*.

As for *Mutual-Consciousness*. That takes place, when two or more Spirits, or Minds know all that of one another, which each Mind, or Spirit knows of it self, by a particular *Self-Consciousness* of its own. And this, I conceive to be a just Account of what this Man means by *Mutual-Consciousness*.

Now the Effects of these two (as I noted before) are very different.

For *Self-Consciousness*, (according to him) is the Constituent Principle, or formal Reason of Personality. So that *Self-Consciousness* properly Constitutes, or makes a Person, and so many *Self-Consciousnesses* make so many distinct Persons.

But *Mutual-Consciousness*, so far as it extends, makes an Unity, not of Persons, (for Personality as such imports distinction, and something personally Incommunicable;) but an Unity of Nature in Persons. So that after *Self-Consciousness* has made several distinct Persons, in comes *Mutual-Consciousness*, and sets them all at *one* again; and gives

gives them all but one and the ſame Nature, which they are to take amongſt themſelves, as well as they can. And this is a True and ſtrict Account of this Author's New Hypotheſis; and ſuch, as I ſuppoſe, he will not except againſt, becauſe juſtly, I am ſure, he cannot; howſoever I may have expreſſed the Novel Whimſey ſomething for the Reader's Diverſion.

Now, by what has been ſaid, it is evident, that the Author aſſigns *Self-Conſciouſneſs* as the formal Reaſon of Perſonality, in all Perſons Univerſally, whether Finite, or Infinite, Create, or Uncreate. For having firſt ſtated it ſo in Finite and Created Spirits, *Page* 48. *line* 26. &c. He afterwards applys it to Infinite and Uncreate, *viz.* the three Perſons of the *God-head.*

And therefore, that we may proceed fairly, and without any ground of Exception in the Caſe, we will examine,

I. Whether or no *Self-Conſciouſneſs* be the Reaſon of Perſonality in *Finite* Perſons? And,

II. Whether it be ſo in *Infinite*?

And Firſt, For *Finite*, or Created Spirits. I deny *Self-Conſciouſneſs* to be the formal Reaſon of Perſonality in theſe. And before I give my Reaſons againſt it, I ſhall premiſe this one Conſideration, *viz.* That whereſoever the formal Reaſon of Perſonality is, there is Perſonality. And again, That whereſoever Perſonality is, there is the formal Reaſon of Perſonality, *viz.* That they exiſt Convertibly, and that one Mutually and Eſſentially infers the other.

Now this premiſed and laid down, my Reaſons, why I deny *Self-Conſciouſneſs* to be the formal Reaſon of Perſonality in Finite, or Created Beings, are theſe.

1. *Argument.*

1. *Argument.* According to the natural order of Things, *Self-Consciousness* in Persons, pre-supposes their Personality, and therefore is not, cannot be the Reason of it. The Argument, I conceive, is very plain. For whatsoever pre-supposes a Thing, is in order of Nature Posterior and Subsequent to the Thing so pre-supposed by it; and again on the other hand the formal Reason of any Thing is in Order of Nature precedent to that thing, of which it is the Reason. We will therefore prove the Major Proposition. And we do it thus. Personality is the Ground and Principle of all Action, wheresoever it is. For where there is a *Suppositum*, whether it be *Rational* (which is another word for Person) or not, still it is the whole *Suppositum*, which Acts. So that there must be a Person before there can be an Act, or Action proceeding from, or Attributable to a Person. In a word, there must be a Person in Being, before any Action issues from him; and therefore the Act must essentially and necessarily pre-suppose the Person for the Agent. But now *Self-Consciousness* does not only do this; but (which is more) it also pre-supposes another Act Antecedent to it self. For it is properly and formally a *Reflex Act* upon the Acts, Passions, or Motions of the Person whom it belongs to. So that according to the Nature of the Thing, there is not only a Person, but also an Action (which is, and must be subsequent to a Person) that is Antecedent to *Self-Consciousness*; which being a *Reflex Act*, must needs in order of Nature be Posteriour to the Act reflected upon by it. And therefore *Self-Consciousness*, which is by two degrees Posterior to Personality, cannot possibly be the *formal Reason* of it. This I look upon as a Demonstration of the Point. And I leave it to our Author (who is better a great deal at

scorning

ſcorning the Schools, than at confuting them) to anſwer and overthrow it *at his leiſure.*

2. Our Second *Argument* is this. The Humanity, or Humane Nature of Chriſt, is perfectly Conſcious to it ſelf of all the Internal Acts, whether of Knowledge, Volition, Paſſion, or Deſire, that paſs in it, or belong to it; and yet the Humanity, or Humane Nature of Chriſt is not a Perſon, and conſequently *Self-Conſciouſneſs* is not the proper formal Reaſon of Perſonality; foraſmuch as it may be in that, which is no Perſon. That the Humane Nature of Chriſt is thus *Self-Conſcious*, is evident, ſince it has all the Principles and Powers of Self-reflexion upon its own Acts, whereby it intimately knows it ſelf to do what it does, and to be what it is, which are in any particular Man whatſoever; ſo that if any Man be Conſcious to himſelf of theſe things, the Humane Nature of Chriſt, which has the ſame Operative Powers in perfection (and thoſe eſſentially proper to, and inſeparable from it ſelf) which the reſt of Mankind are endued with, muſt needs be ſo too. And then, as for the Aſſumption, *That the Humane Nature of Chriſt is not a Perſon*, is no leſs evident. Since it is taken into, and ſubſiſts in and by the Perſonality of the ſecond Perſon of the Trinity, and therefore can have no diſtinct Perſonality of its own; unleſs we will with *Neſtorius* aſſert two Perſons in Chriſt, an Humane, and a Divine. And the Truth is, If *Self-Conſciouſneſs* were the formal Reaſon of Perſonality, ſince there are two diſtinct *Self-Conſciouſneſſes* in Chriſt, no leſs than two diſtinct Wills, an Humane, and a Divine, *viz.* One in each Nature, I cannot ſee how, upon this Author's Hypotheſis, to keep off the Aſſertion of *Neſtorius*, That there are *Two diſtinct Perſons* in him alſo.

3. My

3. My Third *Argument* against the same shall be taken from *the Soul of Man in a state of separation from the Body.* And it is this: The Soul in its separate Estate is Conscious to it self of all its own Internal Acts, or Motions, whether of Knowledge, Passion, or Desire, and yet the Soul in such an Estate is not a Person: And therefore *Self-Consciousness* is not the formal Reason of Personality; for if it were, it would and must constitute a Person, wheresoever it was. Now, that the Soul, in its separate Estate, is thus *Self-Conscious*, I suppose no body will pretend to deny, but such as hold a Psychopannychisme, *viz.* such a dormant Estate, as renders it void of all Vital Motion or Action, during its separation from the Body. But this being an errour which few now a-days think worth owning, neither shall I think worth the disproving.

But for the *Minor Proposition, That the Soul in its separate Estate is not a Person.* In this I expect to find some Adversaries, and particularly our Author himself, who expresly affirms, That *the Soul in such a separate state is a Person,* Page 262. *A Soul* (says he) *without a Vital Union to an Humane Body, is a Person.* Nor does he bestow the Name and Nature of a Person upon the Soul only as separate from, but also (as shall be afterwards made appear) as it is joyned with the Body; which Assertion of his, together with some others of near affinity with it, shall in due place be examined by themselves.

At present in Confirmation of my *Argument,* I shall produce my *Reasons* against the Personality of the Soul, held by this Author, and in order to it, shall lay down this Conclusion in direct opposition to his, *viz. That the Soul of Man is not a Person.* And ſince (as we have noted) he holds, that it is ſo, both in its Conjunction with the Body, and its ſeparation from it, I ſhall bring my *Arguments* againſt the Perſonality of it in both.

And Firſt, I ſhall prove, That the Soul while joyned to, and continuing in the Body, is not a Perſon; and as a ground-work of the Proof thereof, I ſhall only premiſe this one Thing, as a Truth acknowledged on all Hands, viz. *That the Soul and Body together conſtitute the Perſon of a Man*: The ſame being plainly aſſerted in the *Athanaſian Creed*, where it tells us, *That the Reaſonable Soul and Fleſh, is one Man*, [or one Human Perſon] for both ſignifie but the ſame Thing; which being thus laid down, as a Thing certain and confeſſed, I Argue thus: If the Soul and Body in Conjunction conſtitute the Perſon of a Man, then the Soul in ſuch a Conjunction is not a Perſon. But the former is true, and therefore the latter muſt be ſo too. The *Propoſition* is proved thus. Nothing which, together with the Body, Conſtitutes a Perſon, is, or can be it ſelf a Perſon. For if it be, then the Body muſt be joyned to it, either by being aſſumed into the Perſonal Subſiſtence of the Soul, as the Humane Nature of Chriſt is aſſumed into the Perſonal Subſiſtence of the λόγος. Whereupon the *Compoſition* and *Conſtitution* of a Man, will be an Hypoſtatick Union between Soul and Body; which, I ſuppoſe, no Body will be either ſo bold, or abſurd as to affirm; all Divines accounting an Hypoſtatical Union ſo peculiar to Chriſt's Perſon, as not to be admitted in any other Perſon or Being whatſoever. Or,

Secondly, The Body muſt be joyned with the Soul, as one part, joyntly concurring with another, to the Com-

Composition of the whole Person. And if so, then the Soul being a Part, cannot possibly be a *Person*. Forasmuch as a *Part* is an Incomplete Being, and therefore, in the very Nature of it, being designed for the Completion of something else, must subsist in and by the Subsistence of the whole. But a Person imports the most compleat Degree and Mode of Being, as subsisting wholly by it self, and not in or by any other, either as a Subject of Inherence, or Dependence. So that it is a direct Contradiction to the very Definition and Nature of the Thing, for the same Being to be a *Part* and a *Person* too. And consequently that which makes the Soul the former, does irrefragably prove it not to be the other.

Besides, if the Soul in the Composition of a Man's Person, were an entire person it self, and, as such, concurred with the Body towards the Constitution of the Man; then a Man would be an Imperfect, Accidental, and not a Perfect, Natural Compound. He would be that which Philosophy calls *Unum per Accidens*, that is, a thing made up of two such Beings, as cannot perfectly coalesce and unite into one. For a Complete Being (as every Person essentially is) having received the utmost degree of Subsistence, which its Nature can give it, if it comes afterward to be compounded with another Being, whether Complete, or Incomplete, it must necessarily make such a loose, unnatural Union and Composition. But to assert, That the Person of a Man is such a compound, would be exploded by all who understood any thing of Natural Philosophy. So that it would be a very idle thing to attempt any further Confutation of it. Let this Author overthrow these Reasonings, and support his Assertion against them if he can.

But having thus disproved the Personality of the Soul while in Conjunction with the Body, I go on to disprove it also while in a state of Separation from it: Which I do thus. If the Soul in such a state be a Person, then it is either the same Person, which the Man himself was, while he was living and in the Body; or it is another Person: But to Assert either of them, is extreamly Absurd, and therefore equally Absurd, that the Soul in such a state should be a Person.

And First, It is Absurd to affirm it to be the same Person. For a Person compounded of Soul and Body, as a Man is, and a simple uncompounded Person, as the Soul (if a Person at all) must needs be, can never be numerically one and the same. For that, differing from one another as *Simple* and *Compound*, they differ as two things, whereof one implys a Contradiction and Negation of the other. A Compound, as such, including in it several parts compounding it And a simple Being utterly excluding all Parts and Composition. So that if a Man, while alive, be one Person, and His Soul after his Death be a person too, it is impossible for the Soul to be one and the same Person with the Man.

And then for the other part of the Disjunction. To Assert, That they are two distinct Persons, is as Absurd as the other, as drawing after it this Consequence, *viz.* That it is one Person who lives well or ill in this World, to wit, The Man Himself while he was personally in the Body; and another Person, who passes out of the Body into Heaven, or Hell, there to be rewarded, or punished (at least till the Resurrection) for what that other Person had done well or ill here upon Earth. And does not this look mightily agreeable to all the Principles of Reason and Divinity? Nevertheless so much is certain,

tain, That whereſoever there are two diſtinct Perſons, we do, and muſt by all the Rules of Grammar and Logick, ſay, That one of them is not the other; and, where one is not the other, we cannot in Truth, or Juſtice ſay, That one ought to account for what was done, or not done by the other. But then, if it be intolerably Abſurd, (as no doubt it is) That the Soul in the other World ſhould not be reſponſible for what the Man himſelf in Perſon had done in this, then it is altogether as Abſurd and Intolerable, for any one to repreſent and ſpeak of theſe Things under ſuch Terms and Notions, as muſt neceſſarily throw all Diſcourſe and Reaſoning about them, into Paradox and Confuſion.

But 'tis needleſs to inſiſt any longer upon a thing ſo clear, or to add any other Arguments in ſo plain a Caſe. And indeed to me, the Soul's thus changing its ſtate forwards and backwards, from one *manner of Subſiſting* to another, looks very odd and unnatural. As, that from an *Incomplete ſtate in the Body*, it ſhould paſs to a *Perſonal and Complete ſtate* out of the Body, (which ſtate is yet preternatural to it) and then fall back into an *Incomplete ſtate* again by its re-union to the Body at the Reſurrection (which yet, one would think, ſhould rather improve our principal parts, in all reſpects, not merely relating to the *Animal Life*; as the bare *Subſiſtence* of them, I am ſure, does not.) Theſe Things, I ſay, ſeem very uncouth and improbable, and ſuch as ought not, without manifeſt Neceſſity, to be allowed of; which here does not appear; ſince all this Inconvenience may be avoided, by holding, That the Soul continues but *a Part of the whole Perſon*, and no more, in all its Conditions.

And thus having proved our Aſſertion againſt the *Perſonality of the Soul*, Whether *in the Body*, or *out of it*; let us now ſee what may be oppoſed to it.

And

And here, I suppose, some will object, That the Soul in a state of Separation, is not properly a Part, forasmuch as it exists not in any Compound, nor goes to the Composition of it. To which I Answer, That an Actual Inexistence in a Compound, is not the only Condition which makes a Thing a part, but its Essential Relation to a Compound; which Relation is founded partly upon its *Original Designation*, and partly upon its *Natural Aptitude* to be an Ingredient in the Constitution of a Compound. And this Relation to the Compound, I affirm the Soul to retain, even while it is separated from it; as is evident from what both Philosophers and Divines hold concerning the Soul, *viz.* That even in its Separation and Disjunction from the Body, it yet retains a strong Appetite and Inclination (as well as an Essential Aptitude) to return and be re-united to it: Which Reunion also we know will be effected at the great and last Day.

But you will say, Does not the Scripture, in *Heb.* 12. 23. speaking of Blessed Souls in a state of Separation from the Body, call them, *The Spirits of Just Men made perfect*, Πνεύματα τῶν ἁγίων τετελειωμένων; And if those Just Men were made *Perfect*, must it not have been in respect of *the Perfection* of *their Souls*, since their Bodies were then Rotting, or (rather) rotten under ground? And if they derived this *Perfection* from their Souls, must not their Souls have been eminently perfect themselves, which rendred them so? And if perfect, can we deny them the perfection of Personality, which (as we have shewn)in Rational Beings,carries in it the greatest Natural Perfection?

To all which I Answer, That the Perfection here spoken of, is not *Natural*, but *Supernatural*; and relates only to the Consummation of their *Graces*,and not to the

manner

manner of their *Subsistence*. Which being the only Thing now in dispute, This Scripture, which speaks only of the former, can make nothing at all to the present Purpose.

Having thus evinced, That the Soul, notwithstanding its *Self-Consciousness* is neither during its Conjunction with the Body, nor its Separation from it, properly a Person; and having withal shewn the grounds and Reasons upon which I conclude it impossible to be so, I shall however think it worth while something more particularly to examine (as I promised) this Author's extraordinary and peculiar Notions of *Person* and *Personality*, as he applies them to the Soul, even while it is joined with the Body also. And first in the 268th Page, he discourses of it in this manner. *All the Sufferings* (sayes he) *and Actions of the Body, are attributed to the Man, though the Soul is the* Person, *because it is the Superiour and Governing Power, and* Constitutes *the Person.* These are his words, and they contain a very pleasant way of arguing, though wholly contrary to the common known Rules of *Philosophy*. For according to these, one would, and must have concluded, That for this very Reason, *That all the Actions and Sufferings of the Body* (and he ought to have added of the Soul too) *are ascribed to the Man*, therefore the Man himself, to whom these Personal Acts are ascribed, must indeed be the Person, and that for the same reason also, the Soul cannot be so. But our Author has a way of Reasoning by himself. For (says he) *The Soul is the Person, because it Constitutes the Person.* But for that very Cause, say I, The Soul is not the *Person*. For whatsoever Constitutes a Person, must do it either efficiently, or formally. That is, either as a Principle producing it, or a Principle compounding it. As for the first way, whatsoever Conſtitutes a perſon efficiently, muſt do it either by Creation, or Generation; but this the Soul (as much a *Superiour Power as it is*) is not able to do. For will any one ſay, That the Soul can either Create or Generate the Perſon, or (to ſpeak more plainly) the Man who is the Perſon? And then, for the other way, by which it may be ſaid to Conſtitute a Perſon, to wit, *formally*. This it can do no otherwiſe than as it is a *Conſtituent Part*, and therefore only as a *Partial*, and not a *Total* Adequate Cauſe of the Conſtitution. That is, in other words, the Soul, as the *Form*, muſt concur with the Body as the *Matter*, to the Conſtitution of the whole Perſon of the Man. But then for that very Reaſon again, the Soul cannot poſſibly be a Perſon, ſince it contributes to the Conſtitution of the Perſon only as a *Part*; which, by reaſon of its *Incomplete Being*, can upon no Principle of Philoſophy be a *Perſon*. And I would fain have this profound *Philoſopher* give me but one allowed Inſtance, where one Perſon is the conſtituent Principle of another.

But to examine the forementioned Aſſertion yet more particularly, ſince this Man ſo peremptorily ſays, *That the Soul is the Perſon, becauſe it is the Superiour Power, and Conſtitutes the Perſon.* I muſt tell him, That the *Superiour Power* is not therefore the ſole Power, and conſequently cannot ſolely Conſtitute the Perſon, which yet this Author pretends it does. If indeed he had ſaid, That the Soul as the *Superiour Power* bears the chief and principal part in the Conſtitution of a perſon, this had been ſence, but by no means ſufficient for his purpoſe; for ſtill this would not prove the Soul to be a Perſon, (which he contends for) but on the contrary, by proving it to concur thereto only as a *Part*, demonſtrate it, upon the ſame Account not to be a *Perſon*.

But

But this is not all, for in *Page* 169. he calls the *Mind* of Man a *Person*, and thus Discourses about it. *Faculties*, (says he) *Vertues and Powers have Personal Acts and Offices ascribed to them only upon the Account of their Unity and Sameness with the mind in which they are, which is a Person, and Acts by them.* Now this also is very odd and strange (could any thing in this Author, which is *odd*, be *strange* too;) For the thing Asserted by him amounts to neither more nor less than this, That *Powers*, *Faculties*, and *Vertues* have *personal* Acts ascribed to them upon the account of their Unity and Sameness with that, which it self neither is, nor can be a *Person*; as we have abundantly proved, That the *Mind* of Man, (taking it in his sense for the *Soul*) cannot be. And for his further Conviction, I could tell him of something which has *personal* Acts very remarkably ascribed to it; and yet neither for being it self a *Person*, nor for its *Unity* and *Sameness* with the *Mind*, in which it is, and which sometimes acts by it. And that, if he pleases to turn to 1 *Corinth.* 13. he will find to be that notable Grace and Virtue, called *Charity*; which, being but an *Accident*, I believe, that even this Author himself will not affirm to be a *Person*; and, I am sure, as little can be said for any *Unity* or *Sameness* that it has with the Mind, which it is lodged in: Since, though it should be utterly lost, the Mind would nevertheless retain all the Essentials of a Mind, and continue as truly a Mind, as it was before: Which, I think, is but an ill *Argument* of any *Unity or Sameness* between the Mind and that; and this being indubitably true, all that this Author here discourses about *personal* Acts being ascribed to the Mind, and about their *Identity* with the Mind, as the Reason of it, is with equal mistake and impertinence alledged by him in this case. For he might and should have known, That *personal* Acts are often ascribed to *Faculties, Vertues, and Graces,* not in strict propriety of Philosophical speaking, but *Tropically* and Figuratively, by a Figure (which he shall hear further of hereafter) called *Prosopopœia*; which represents Things, that are not *Persons*, speaking and doing as if they were so.

But besides this, there are here two Things which this Author takes for granted, which yet such dull Mortals as my self will be apt a little to demurr to.

As First, That he takes the *Mind* and the *Soul* of Man for one and the same Thing; whereas very Learned Men, both *Grammarians* and *Philosophers* hold, That in Men there is a great difference between *Animus* and *Anima*; and that as *Anima* imports the Spiritual Substance which we call the Soul, so *Animus* signifies only a Power or Faculty, *viz.* The Supreme Intellectual, Reasoning, Governing Faculty of the Soul, or at least, the Soul it self considered, as exerting the forementioned Acts. But whether it be one or the other, we have sufficiently proved against this Authour, That neither of them can be a Person.

The other Thing here supposed by him, is the *Unity* or *Sameness* of the Powers or Faculties of the Soul, with the Soul it self; which yet the *Peripateticks* generally, and most of the *School-men* with *Thomas Aquinas* in the Head of them do positively deny, and think they give very good Reason for such their Denial. For if Substances and Accidents are Beings really distinct, and if Qualities be Accidents, and the Powers and Faculties of the Soul come under the second *Species* of Quality, as *Aristotle* reckons them, then it is manifest, that they are really distinguished, and that there is no Identity between them. Nor does there want a further Reason for the same. For, since the bare *Substance* or *Essence*

of

of the Soul, consider'd nakedly in it self, may rationally be supposed undetermined, and therefore indifferent to all those Acts or Actions that naturally proceed from it; and since withal, bare Objects can of themselves neither enable nor dispose the Agent to exert any Action, there seems a Necessity of asserting the Intervention of some Third Thing distinct from both, which may thus enable, dispose, and determine the Soul to exert it self in such a particular way of acting rather than another, suitably to the several Objects which shall come before it; which thing is properly that Quality residing in the Soul, which we call a *Faculty* or *Power*. And this to me seems the true Philosophy of the matter. But I need not here press the Decision of the Case one way or other; as not directly affecting the Point in debate between us. Only I thought fit to suggest these Remarks, to check this Author's bold unwary way of dictating and affirming in things disputable and dubious, and to remind him how much it becomes and concerns one that writes Controversies, to be more liberal in his Proofs, and less lavish in his Assertions.

But before I quit this Point about the *Personality of the Soul*. Since this Authour has so absolutely and expresly affirmed, *That the Soul, or Mind of Man is a Person*, and given this for the Reason of it, *That being the Superiour Governing Power* in Man, it does, as such, *Constitute the Person*, over and above the Arguments which have been already brought for the Confutation of it, I desire to leave with him two or three Questions, which seem naturally to rise from this Wonderful Position. As,

First, Whether the *Soul*, or *Mind* of Man be *one Person*, and the Man himself *Another*?

Secondly, Whether the aſſerting of the *Soul to be a Perſon,* becauſe it *Conſtitutes the Perſon,* does not infer ſo much, *viz.* That the *Soul* is *the Perſon that Conſtitutes,* and the *Man the Perſon that is Conſtituted*; unleſs we will ſay, That the *Soul Conſtitutes it ſelf a Perſon?* And then,

Thirdly, Whether to ſay, or aſſert this, does not infer *Two diſtinct Perſonalities* in the ſame *Soul,* one in order of Nature before the other, *viz.* That, by which it is it ſelf *formally a Perſon,* and that other, which by its Conſtituting it ſelf a Perſon, is *Conſtituted* and *cauſed by it?*

But ſince it is too hard a Task to drain any one Abſurdity (eſpecially a very great one) ſo, as to draw forth and repreſent all its naturally deſcending Conſequences, I deſire the Author with the utmoſt (if Impartial) ſtrictneſs to compare the foregoing Queſtions with his own Aſſertion and to ſee, Firſt, Whether they do not directly ſpring from it: And next, Whether the Matter couched under the ſaid Queſtions, if drawn out into ſo many Poſitive Propoſitions, would not afford as many Intolerable Defiances to Common Senſe, Reaſon and Philoſophy. But thus it is, when Men will be Writing at Thirty, and ſcarce Thinking till Threeſcore.

But to proceed and ſhew, That it is not only the *Soul, or Mind of Man* which our Authour dignifies with the Name and Nature of a *Perſon*; but that he has almoſt as free an hand in making every thing he meets with a *Perſon,* as K. *Charles the Second* had in making almoſt every *Perſon* he met with, a *Knight*; (So that it was very dangerous for any one who had an Averſion to Knighthood, to come in his way,) our Author, out of the like Over-flowing Communicative Goodneſs and Liberaberality, is graciously pleased, to take even the *Beasts* themselves into the Rank and Order of Persons; in some imitation, I suppose, of the Discreet and Humble *Caligula*, so famous in History for making his Horse *Consul*. And for this, Let us cast our Eyes upon *page* 262. where he has these words, worthy (*in sempiternam rei memoriam*) to be wrote in Letters of Gold. *A Beast* (says he) *which has no Rational Soul, but only an Animal Life* (*as a Man has together with an Humane Soul*) *is a Person, or* Suppositum, *or what you will please to call it*: But, by your favour, Good Sir, the Matter is not so indifferent; for *Person* and *Suppositum*, are by no means the same Thing; and I pity you with all my heart, that you should think so. For any single Complete Nature actually subsisting by it self, is properly a *Suppositum*, but not therefore a *Person*. For as *Subsistence* superadded to Nature, Constitutes a *Suppositum*, so *Rationality* added to *Suppositality*, Constitutes a *Person*; which is therefore properly defined *Suppositum Rationale*, or *Intelligens*, as we have sufficiently shewn already in our Second Chapter: So that to call a *Beast* a *Person*, is all one as to call it a *Rational Brute*: Which this Author, who can so easily reconcile Contradictions, or (which may serve him as well) *swallow them*, may do, if he pleases; *and so stand alone by himself* in this, as well as (he says) he had done in some other Things. But others, who think themselves obliged to use Philosophical Terms only as Philosophers intended them, dare not venture to speak thus, for fear *Aristotle* should bring an *Action of Battery* against them; who certainly has *a Pate* to break as well as *Priscian*, and is as sensible of hard usage, how patiently soever he has took it hitherto at this Author's hands. But to give the said Author his due, he is not so much *a Slave to his word*, as to speak the same Thing in all places of his Book. For, to quote his own Authority (though of little value, but when brought against himself) in *page* 62. of this very Tract, he has these words. *A Person* (says he) *and an Intelligent Substance are Reciprocal Terms.* And, are they so? Why, how then comes a *Beast*, in *page* 269. to be *a Person?* Is a *Beast* an *Intelligent Substance?* Or, can a *Beast* be a *Person*, and yet not an *Intelligent Substance*, when he affirms, That they are Terms Reciprocal? If I have not quoted this Author fairly and justly, let the Advantage be his, and the shame mine. But if I have, then let all the Learned and Impartial World (which I appeal to) judge, whether one who talks thus Ignorantly and Self-Contradictiously about the Nature of a *Person*, be fit to prescribe to the whole Church New Terms and Models never heard of before, to explicate the *Persons* of the *Sacred Trinity* by. But the Truth is, the distance between the 69. and the 262. *pages*, was so great, and the Contradictions which passed within that compass so Numerous, that how gross and bulky soever this one might be, yet with the help of a little good luck, it might well escape the Author's Eye in such a Crowd. And perhaps, it had been never the worse luck for the Author Himself, if it could as easily have escaped the Reader's Eye too.

And now, to sum up in short, the Chief Heads of what has been treated of in this Chapter, I have proved against this Authour, That *Self-Consciousness* is not the formal Reason of Personality in Created Beings. And that first by an Argument drawn from the very Nature of the Thing; For that, *Self-Consciousness* presupposes Personality, and therefore cannot be the formal Reason of it. As also from two Notable Instances, One of the Humanity, or Humane Nature of Christ.

The

The other of the Soul of Man in its ſtate of Separation from the Body: Both of which I have ſhewn to be perfectly *Self-Conſcious* of all the Internal Acts, Motions and Paſſions reſpectively belonging to each of them; and yet that they were, neither of them, *Perſons*. And purſuant to this Subject, I have, by clear, and ſolid Reaſons overthrown the pretended Perſonality of the Soul, both in a ſtate of Conjunction with the Body, and of Disjunction from it; which in both is aſſerted by this Author. And Laſtly, I have examined his Abſurd Unphiloſophical Aſſertions about theſe Matters; in one whereof, he aſcribes a Perſonality even to Beaſts themſelves. By all which, it is but too manifeſt againſt this Aſſuming big-talking Man, that, as loftily as he carries it, yet in very Deed and Truth he does not underſtand what thoſe Terms *Suppoſitum and Subſiſtence, Perſon and Perſonality* mean. So fit is he (as I have ſaid) to treat of the *Divine Perſons* of the *God-head*; whom yet he has made ſo bold with.

And here I ſhould judge it high time to conclude this Chapter; but that, methinks, it is pity to leave this fine Trim Notion of *Self-Conſciouſneſs* ſo; without taking a little further View of the Curious Artifice and admirable Contrivance of ſo rare a production. For if it were not ſuch, could this Authour vaunt of it at ſuch a rate as he does, pleaſing himſelf, and proclaiming his Ἕυρηκα, εὕρηκα, as upon an Invention (forſooth) which all Antiquity before him could never yet reach to?

Nevertheleſs to deal clearly and plainly amongſt Friends, ſuch a Cheating, Lurching thing does this Expectation uſually prove, that after all theſe Pompous Shews, and Glorious Boaſts of *Self-Conſciouſneſs, Self-Conſciouſneſs*, uſhered in with twenty *Encomium's* (at

leaſt)

least) like so many Heralds, or Tip-staves, or (rather) *Yeomen of the Guard* marching before it; yet, in Truth, after all this noise, it is, (like an Owl stripp'd of its Feathers) but a very Mean, Meagre, Ordinary Thing; being, in down-right Terms, neither more nor less than only *one Property of a Rational, or Intelligent Being*; by vertue whereof, the Soul is (as the Schools express it) *Supra se Reflexiva*, that is to say, Able by a Reflex Act of Knowledge, intimately to know and consider it self, and its own Being, together with its own Acts, Motions, and Operations. This is the Sum Total of the Matter, and all that *Self-Consciousness* is, or can truly pretend to be.

And, (which is yet a further Diminution to it) as poor and mean a Notion as it is, it is Borrowed too. But you will say, From whom? Why? Even from Honest *Des Cartes*, and his *Cogito ergo sum*. Only with this unhappy difference in the Application of it, That this Proposition, which *Des Cartes* lays as the Basis and Ground-work of his Philosophy, our Author places with its Heels upwards in his Divinity. For whereas *Des Cartes* insists upon *Cogitation*, only to prove and infer Being, as one would prove a Cause from its Effects, or rather an Antecedent from its Consequent: our Author on the contrary, makes *Cogitation* the very Cause and Principle of Being and Subsistence, by making it the formal Constituent Reason of Personality in the Person who Thinks, or Reflects; than which nothing can be more false, and ridiculous.

And this, according to the Truest, and most Philosophical Account of the Thing, is the very utmost which this New, and so much bragg'd of Notion amounts to. And I do hereupon Challenge this Author to prove these two Things if he can.

First,

First, That the *Self-Consciousness* hitherto spoken of by him is any Thing more than a bare *Property* of an Intelligent Being, whereby it reflects upon it self, and its own Thoughts and Actions.

And in the next place, That such a *Property* does, or can Constitute the Being or Nature which it flows from, and belongs to, properly *a Person*.

These two things, I say, I call upon him to prove; and if he does not by dint of *Argument* make them good, he exposes a poor, senceless, infant Hypothesis to the wide World, and then very unmercifully leaves it to shift for it self. In fine, I cannot but again and again own my Amazement at the Confidence of some bold presuming Men, who set up for Enlighteners of the Church, and new Modellers of Divinity in the strength of some odd upstart Notions, which yet are not able to acquit, or support themselves *upon*, and much less *against* the very first Elements and Principles of a long tryed, and never yet baffled Philosophy.

CHAP. IV.

In which is proved against this Author, That neither is Self-Consciousness *the formal Reason of* Personality *in the three Persons of the Blessed Trinity; nor* Mutual-Consciousness *the Reason of their Unity in one and the same Nature.*

HAving thus examined, and (as I think) overthrown our Author's Notion of *Self-Consciousness*, with reference to Created and Finite Persons, I shall now proceed to the Consideration of what he says of it with reference to the three Persons in the Glorious Godhead. And this I shall do under these following Heads, which shall be the Subjects of five distinct Chapters. As,

First, I shall treat of his two new Notions, *viz.* of *Self-Consciousness*, and *Mutual-Consciousness*, and shew, That *Self-Consciousness* is not the *formal Reason* of *Personality* in the three *Divine Persons*, nor *Mutual-Consciousness* the Reason of their Unity in one and the same Nature. And this we have here allotted for the business and Subject of this 4th Chapter.

Secondly, I shall prove, That the Three *Divine Persons* of the Godhead, are not Three *Distinct, Infinite Minds, or Spirits*, in the 5th Chapter.

Thirdly,

Thirdly, I ſhall Conſider, what this Author pretends to from the Authority of the *Fathers* and *School-men*, in behalf of his New invented Hypotheſis, and ſhew, That they ſpeak nothing *at all for it*, or *towards it*: And this ſhall make the 6th and 7th Chapters.

Fourthly, I ſhall ſet down the Ancient and generally received Doctrine of the Church and Schools concerning the Article of the *Trinity*, and Vindicate it from this Author's Exceptions, in the 8th Chapter.

And when I ſhall have diſcuſſed and gone over theſe Particulars, I cannot imagine what can be found Conſiderable in this his Book (ſo far as I have undertook it) but what will have received hereby a full and ſufficient Anſwer.

Though, when all is done, I confeſs I have ſome further Complements to make to this Author upon ſome other Accounts (though ſtill occaſioned by this Work of his) which, I ſhould be extremely wanting both to him and the Cauſe now before me, ſhould I not, with all due Addreſs, paſs upon him. And this will add three or four Chapters more to the former, and ſo conclude this Work.

And Firſt, To begin with the firſt of theſe, I ſhall endeavour to prove, That *Self-Conſciouſneſs is not the formal Reaſon of Perſonality in the Three Divine Perſons*.

In order to which, I ſhall premiſe and lay down theſe following *Conſiderations*.

Conſideration 1. That although the *Divine Nature* be one Pure, Simple, Indiviſible Act, yet in our Conceptions of it (which are always inadequate to it) there is a Natural Order of *Prius* and *Posterius* founded in the Universal Reason of Things (according to which, the Conception of one Thing presupposes, and depends upon the Conception of another) which, though it can make no *Prius* and *Posterius* in the *Divine Nature*, yet is by no means to be contradicted, or confounded in our discoursing of *God*; forasmuch as without our admitting this Rule it is impossible for any Humane Understanding either to Conceive, or Discourse consistently, or intelligibly of Him at all.

Consideration 2. (Which, I think, affords us a Rule safely and universally to be relied upon) is this, That in Things having a dependence between them, where we may form to our selves a clear and distinct Conception of one Thing, without implying, or involving in it the Conception of any other Thing, there that Thing is in Order of Nature precedent to all those Things which are not essentially included in the Conception of it. Thus, for instance, we may have a clear and distinct Conception of *Entity and Being*, and of *Unity* too, without entertaining in our Mind, at the same time, any Notion, or Conception of *knowledge* at all; and therefore the *Ratio Entitativa* of any Thing must needs in Nature precede the *Ratio Cognitiva*, or *rather Cognoscibilis* of the same.

Consideration 3. We must distinguish between the Affections, or *Modes* of Being (as they are strictly so called) and between the *Attributes* of it. The first sort are reckoned of the same Order with *Being* it self, and so precede whatsoever is consequent upon it, as the Attributes of it are accounted to be; which relate to the

Being

Being or Subject they belong to, as things in Order of Nature *Posterior* to it. Accordingly in the first rank are *Existence*, *Subsistence*, *Personality*, &c. and in the second are all Acts issuing from a *Nature*, or *Subject* so Subsisting; whether they be of *Knowledge*, *Volition*, *Power*, *Duration*, or the like: The *Denominations* derived from which, are properly called *Attributes*.

Consideration 4. Though there can be no Accidents inhering in God, yet there may be *Accidental* Predications belonging to him. And I call those *Accidental*, which are not *Necessary*, or *Essential*. Such as are all *Extrinsecal Denominations* of him founded on such Acts of God, as were perfectly free for him to do, or not to do; nothing in the *Divine Nature* obliging him thereto. Of which number are the *Denominations*, or *Predicates* of *Creatour*, *Redeemer*, and the like: Since there was nothing in God that made it necessary for him to be so.

Consideration 5. When the Terms [*Cause*, *Formal Reason*, *Constituent*, *or productive Principle*, and the like] are used about the *Divine Nature*, and *Persons*, they are not to be understood as applicable to them in the strict and proper signification of the said Terms, but only by way of Analogy; as really meaning no more than a Causal, or Necessary Dependence of one Notion, or *Conceptus objectivus* upon another; so that it is impossible for the *Mind* to Conceive distinctly of the one, but as depending upon, or *proceeding from* the other.

Consideration 6. That the *Divine Nature* may with all fair Accord to the Rules of Divinity and Philosophy be Considered as *Prescinding*, or *Abstracting* (*though* not as *divided*) from the *Divine Persons*.

Consideration

Consideration 7. That whatsoever is Essentially included in the *Divine Nature* thus Considered, is equally Common and Communicable to all the *Divine Persons.*

Consideration 8. That whatsoever is the proper *Formal Reason* of *Personality*, is utterly Incommunicable to any Thing, or *Person* beyond, or *beside the Person* to whom it belongs.

Consideration 9. That for any Absolute Perfection essentially included,or implyed in the *Divine Nature* to be *multiplyed* in the Three *Persons* belonging to it, is a manifest Multiplication of the *Divine Nature* it self in the said *Persons.* By which we are given to understand the difference between the *Multiplication*, and the *Communication* of the *Divine Nature* to those *Persons.*

These Rules, I thought fit to draw up and lay down before-hand, in order to the use which we shall have of them in the ensuing Disputation.

And so I proceed to my *Arguments* against this Author's New Notion of *Self-Consciousness*, with reference to the Persons of the *Blessed Trinity.* And the First is This:

Argument I. No *Personal* Act can be the formal Reason of *Personality* in the *Person*, whose Act it is. But *Self-Consciousness* is a *Personal* Act, and therefore *Self-Consciousness* cannot be the formal Reason of *Personality* in the *Person*, whose Act it is, and to whom *personally* it belongs. The Minor, I suppose, neither our Author Himself, nor any one else, can deny. For if *Self-Consciousness*

sciousness be not a *Personal* Act, let any one assign what else it is, or what it ought to pass for. It is certainly an Act of Knowledge, by which each *Person* knows and comprehends himself, and whatsoever belongs to him. The Major Proposition therefore is to be proved, *viz.* That no *Personal* Act can be the formal Reason of *Personality* in the *Person* whose Act it is. And I prove it thus: The formal Reason of every Thing, is in order of Nature, before the Thing of which it is the formal Reason; but no *Personal* Act is, in order of Nature, before the *Personality* of the *Person* whose Act it is, and therefore it cannot be the formal Reason of his *Personality*. The Major is Self-evident. And as for the Minor, That no *Personal* Act is before the *Personality* of the *Person* whose Act it is; This also is manifest; Because such an Act cannot be before the *Person* himself, and therefore not before his *Personality*: For as much as his *Personality* is that by which he is formally a *Person*; so that it is impossible to be before the one without being before the other too. And now, that it cannot be before the *Person* himself, is manifest from hence, that as every *Personal* Act in general bears a Relation of *Posteriority* to the *Person* to whom it belongs, as to the Cause or Productive Principle of all the Acts proceeding from Him; so this particular Act of *Self-Consciousness*, bears a Treble Relation of *Posteriority* to the *Person* whose Act it is, *viz.* as to the Agent or *Principle* producing it. 2. As to the *Subject* Recipient of it, and sustaining it. And Thirdly and Lastly, As to the *Object* which it is terminated to. All which Respects it sustains, not barely as it is an Act, but partly as it is an *Immanent Act*, and partly also a *Reflex Act*.

In the first place therefore, every *Person* being the Agent, or Productive Cause of all the *personal* Acts issuing

ing from Him, he must upon that Account, in Order of Nature, precede the said Acts; and consequently every *Divine Person* must in Nature be before that Act of *Self-Consciousness*, which *personally* belongs to him. And moreover since it is likewise an *Immanent* Act, it relates to him, as *the Subject in which it is*, as well as *the Cause from which it is*, and upon that Account also, must bear a *Natural Posteriority* to Him. And then lastly, as it is also *a Reflex Act*, by which the *Person* knows himself to be a *Person*, and is Conscious to Himself, what he is, and what he does, it terminates upon him as its Object also. So that the *Cause*, the *Subject*, and the *Object* of this Act being the same *Person*, in this last respect, no less than in the two former, it bears another and third Relation of *Posteriority* to Him; since every Act, not productive of something besides, and without the Agent, is in Order of Nature *Posterior* to the *Object* it terminates upon.

From all which I conclude, That that Act of *Self-Consciousness*, by which each *Divine Person* knows, or is *Conscious* to Himself of his own *Personality*, cannot be the *Formal Reason* of the said *Personality*, without being, in Order of Nature, *both before it*, and *after it* too, *viz.* Before it, as it is the *Formal Reason* of it, and yet *Posterior* to it, as it is an Act *proceeding from*, *lodged* and *received in*, and lastly, *Terminated upon* the *same Person*.

All which is so very plain, that hardly can any Thing be plainer: And indeed, the very word *Self-Consciousness* contradicts and overthrows its being the *ground*, or *Formal Reason* of *Personality*. For still *Self* must be before *Consciousness*; and *Self* imports *Personality*; as being that, by which a *Person* is said *to be, what he is*; and they both stand united in this one Word, as the *Act and the Object*, and therefore *Consciousness* cannot be the *Reason*

Reaſon of it. Or to expreſs the ſame Thing by other Terms, *Self-Subſiſtence* muſt precede *Self-Conſciouſneſs*, and *Self-Subſiſtence* here implys *Perſonality*; and therefore *Perſonality*, upon the ſame Account, muſt in Nature precede *Self-Conſciouſneſs*, and conſequently cannot be the *formal Effect*, or *Reſult* of it. For, ſurely, according to the moſt Eſſential Order of Things, *a Perſon muſt be what he is*, before he can *know what he is*.

And this *Argument*, I confeſs, being founded upon the *Priority* of *Subſiſtence* to all *Acts*, and particularly to thoſe of *knowledge* in every *Perſon Self-Conſcious*, does, and muſt Univerſally run through all Inſtances, in which *Perſonality* and *Self-Conſciouſneſs*, with reference to one another, come to be treated of. And as it affects *Self-Conſciouſneſs*, ſo it will equally take place in *Mutual-Conſciouſneſs* too.

What Allowances are to be here made for the abſolute *Simplicity*, *Eternity*, and *Pure Actuality* of the *Divine Nature* and *Perſons*, (when theſe Notions are applyed to them) we have already obſerved, in the firſt of thoſe Preliminary Conſiderations mentioned in this Chapter. The proper uſe and deſign of all which Notions, is to lead, guide, and direct our Apprehenſions about that *Great Object*, ſo much too big for our Narrow *Faculties*; ſo that whatſoever contradicts the Natural Order of theſe Apprehenſions ought upon no grond of Reaſon to be admitted in our Diſcourſes of the *Divine Nature*, how much ſoever it may and does tranſcend the ſaid Apprehenſions. And this muſt be allowed us, or we muſt ſink under the vaſt Diſproportion of the thing before us, and not diſcourſe of it at all. For I cannot think, that the Word *Self-Conſciouſneſs* has brought the *Deity* one jot lower to us, or raiſed our Underſtandings one degree higher and nearer to that.

Argument II. My Second *Argument* againſt *Self-Conſciouſneſs* being the *Formal Reaſon* of *Perſonality* in the *Divine Perſons*, is this: *Nothing* in the *Nature* of it *Abſolute and Irrelative* can be the *Formal Reaſon* of *Perſonality* in the *Perſons* of the *Bleſſed Trinity*; but *Self-Conſciouſneſs* is in the Nature of it *Abſolute and Irrelative*; and therefore it cannot be the Reaſon of *perſonality* in any of the ſaid *Perſons*.

Now the Major Propoſition is proved thus. Nothing in the *Nature* of it *Abſolute* can be the *Formal Reaſon* of any Thing in the Nature of it purely and perfectly Relative. But the *Perſonality* of every one of the *Divine Perſons* is purely and perfectly Relative; and therefore Nothing *Abſolute* can be the *Formal Conſtituent Reaſon* of their *Perſonality*. The Major of which Syllogiſm is alſo manifeſt. For Things Eſſentially different, and thereby uncapable of being affirmed of one another, cannot poſſibly be the *Formal Reaſon* of one another. And, that the Perſons in the *Bleſſed Trinity* are purely Relative to one another, and conſequently, that their Perſonalities are ſo many Relations, is no leſs evident from this, That Two of them relate to one another, as *Father and Son*, and the Third to Both, as proceeding from Both; and it is impoſſible for one Thing to proceed from another, eſpecially by a Continual Act of Proceſſion, without Importing a Relation to that from which it ſo proceeds; ſo that the very *perſonal Subſiſtence* of theſe *Perſons* implys and carries in it a Formal Relation. For the Father Subſiſts perſonally as a Father, by that Eternal Communication of his Nature to his Son; which Act, as proceeding from him, is called *Generation*, and renders him Formally a Father, and as Terminated in the Son, is called *Filiation*, and Conſtitutes him Formally

mally a Son; and in like manner the Holy Ghost Subsists personally by that Act of *Procession*, by which he proceeds from, and relates to both the Father and the Son. So that, that *proper Mode of Subsistence* (by which in Conjunction with the *Divine Essence* always included in it, each of them is rendred a *Person*) is wholly Relative, and so belongs to one of them, that it also bears a Necessary reference to another. From all which, it undeniably follows, That the Three *Persons* in the *Blessed Trinity*, are in the Formal Constitution of them Relative to one another; and consequently, That the Three *Personalities*, by which they become Formally Three *Persons*, and are so denominated, are Three *Eternal Relations*.

But now, for the Minor Proposition in the first Syllogism, viz. *That Self-Consciousness is a Thing in the Nature of it Absolute and Irrelative*, that, I think, can need but little Proof; it being that Act by which each *Person* intimately knows, and is Conscious to himself of his own *Being*, *Acts*, *Motions*, and every Thing *personally* belonging to him; so that, as such, it terminates within, and looks no further than that one *Person*, whom it is an Entire Survey and Comprehension of. And as it is an *Absolute* and *Irrelative* Term, so it may be Conceived distinctly and fully without Conceiving, or implying the Conception of any Thing, or *Person* besides. And now, what *Relation* does or can such an Act of *Self-Consciousness* imply in it? It is indeed on the contrary, a direct Contradiction to all that is *Relative*. For it incloses the *Person* wholly within himself; neither pointing nor looking further, nor referring to any one else.

If it be here said, That each *Person*, by an Act of *Self-Consciousness*, intimately knows the *Relation* which he stands in to the other Two Persons.

To this, I Answer Two Things.

1. That to know a *Thing* or *Person* to be Relative, or to be Conscious of the Relation belonging to it or him, does not make that Act of Knowledge to be either a Relation, or of a Relative Nature.

2. I Answer, That this very Thing proves *Self-Consciousness* not to be the Constituent Reason of *Personality*. For, if the Father knows himself to be a Father by an Act of *Self-Consciousness*, it is evident, That *Self-Consciousness* did not make him so: but that he was a Father, and had the Relation of a Father, and thereby a *Personality* belonging to him as such, in Order of Nature Antecedent to this Act of *Self-Consciousness*; and therefore that this *Self-Consciousness* cannot be the Reason of the Relation, nor of the *Personality* implyed in it. Forasmuch as it is in several respects Posterior to the Person whom it belongs to, as in the foregoing *Argument* we have abundantly shewn.

But to take a particular and distinct Account of this Notion, in the several *Persons* of the *Trinity*; Does the *Father* become a *Father* by being *Conscious to himself*, that he is so, or rather by that Act by which he Communicates his *Nature* to, and thereby generates a Son? Or does the *Son's Relation to the Father* consist in his being *Conscious to himself* of this *Relation*? Or Lastly, does the Holy Ghost *proceed from the Father and the Son*, and so *personally* relate to both by that Act of *Self-Consciousness*, by which he is Conscious to himself of this *Procession*? All this is *Absurd*, *Unnatural*, and *Impossible*. For

no

no *Perſon* is related to another by that Act of *Self-Conſciouſneſs*, by which he knows and reflects Perſonally upon himſelf. And yet it is certain, That *to be a Father*, is a *Relative Subſiſtence*, and to be a Son depending upon the Father by an Eternal Act of Generation perpetually begetting him, is alſo to have a *Relative Subſiſtence*; and Laſtly, to be *Eternally proceeding from Both*, as the Holy Ghoſt is, muſt likewiſe import *a Way or Mode of Subſiſting altogether as Relative* as the Two former. In which three ways of *Subſiſtence* conſiſt the Perſonalities of the Three Perſons reſpectively; and upon theſe *Self-Conſciouſneſs* can have no Conſtituting Influence at all; as being an Act quite of another Nature; to wit, *Abſolute and Irrelative*, and reſting wholly within the Perſon, whom it belongs to.

From all which, I conclude, That *Self-Conſciouſneſs* neither is, nor can be the *Formal Reaſon* of *Perſonality* in the Three *Perſons* of the *Bleſſed Trinity*. And this *Argument* I take to have the force and clearneſs of a *Demonſtration*.

Argument III. The Third *Argument* is this. If *Self-Conſciouſneſs* be the *Formal Reaſon* of *Perſonality* in the Three *Divine Perſons*, then there is no Repugnancy in the *Nature* and *Reaſon* of the Thing it ſelf, but that there might be Three Thouſand Perſons in the *Deity* as well as Three. But this is Abſurd, and therefore ſo muſt that be likewiſe from which it follows. The Conſequence appears from this, That there is no Repugnancy but that there might be ſo many *Self-Conſciouſneſſes*, or *Self-Conſcious Minds* or *Spirits*, for the *Deity* to Communicate it ſelf to: And therefore, if *Self-Conſciouſneſs* be the *Formal Reaſon* of *Perſonality*, there is no Repugnancy, but that there might be Three Thouſand Perſons in the God-head, as well as Three. The

The Propoſition is proved thus. Becauſe this Repugnancy (if there be any) muſt be either from the *Nature* of *Self-Conſciouſneſs*, in the ſeveral *Self-Conſcious Minds* or *Spirits* it belongs to, or from the *Nature* of the *God-head*, which is to be Communicated to them. But it is from neither of them, For

Firſt, there is nothing in the Nature of *Self-Conſciouſneſs* to hinder its Multiplication into never ſo great a Number of Particulars; but that there may be Three Thouſand, or Three Millions of *Self-Conſcious Minds* or *Spirits*, as well as Three. Nor, in the next place, is there any Repugnancy on the Part of the *God-head*, *That Three Thouſand Self-Conſcious Spirits* ſhould ſubſiſt in it any more than that Three ſhould: For the *Godhead* conſidered preciſely and abſtractedly in it ſelf (and not as actually included in any Perſon) is as able to Communicate it ſelf to the greateſt Number as to the ſmalleſt.

If it be here ſaid, That the Three *Perſons* are not only Three *Self-Conſcious Spirits*, but alſo Three diſtinct Infinite *Self-Conſcious Spirits* (as our Authour ſays they are, and of which, more in the next Chapter.) I Anſwer, That there may be as well Three Thouſand diſtinct *Infinite Spirits* as Three. For Infinity is as much inconſiſtent with the leaſt Plurality of Infinites, as with the greateſt; and therefore if it be no Repugnancy, that there ſhould be Three diſtinct *Infinite Minds*, neither is there that there ſhould be Three Thouſand. So that if *Self-Conſciouſneſs* be the *Formal Reaſon* of *Perſonality*, there appears no Repugnancy either from the Nature of *Self-Conſciouſneſs*, or the Number of the *Spirits* endued with it, nor from the [ſuppoſed] *Infinity* of the ſaid *Spirits*, no nor yet from the *Nature* of the *God-head* it ſelf, but that there might be Three Thouſand *Perſons* in it as well as Three.

But

CHAPTER IV.

But how then comes there to be only Three? Why, upon these grounds no other Reason can be assigned for it, but only that it was God's free Determination that there should be Three and no more. And then the *Trinity* of *Persons* must be an Effect of God's Will, and not a Necessary Condition of the Divine Nature; and the further Consequence of this must be, that the three *Persons* are Three *Created Beings*, as proceeding from the free Results of God's Will, by vertue whereof they equally might, or might not have been.

But on the contrary our Author himself holds *Page* 129. *line* 13. That the Three *Persons* are Essential to the Divine Nature, and so Essential to it, that they necessarily belong to it in this number, *and can be neither more nor fewer than Three*. And if this be so, I am sure it is a Contradiction that it should be otherwise: for it is a Contradiction, that that should not be, which necessarily is, and cannot but be. But now I have proved, that there is no Repugnancy or Contradiction to the Nature of Things considered barely according to their Nature, that three thousand *Self-Conscious Minds* or *Spirits* should subsist in the *Godhead* any more than that three such *Spirits* should so subsist. And therefore if it be Absurd, and Impossible, (as undoubtedly it is) that so many *Persons* should belong to the *Divine Nature*, then must the Reason of this Absurdity be fetched from some other Thing, than either from *Self-Consciousness*, with reference to the *Divine Nature*, or from the *Divine Nature*, (considered in it self abstractedly from all Actual *Personality*:) for these, as we have shewn, afford no sufficient Proof of this Absurdity. And therefore, I say, some other *Reason* must be found out, and assigned against it. And accordingly, let this Author produce such an one (whatsoever it be) as shall

solidly

ſolidly and concluſively prove, That there cannot be Three Thouſand *Self-Conſcious Perſons* belonging to the *Godhead*, and that from the Nature of the Thing it ſelf (as ſeveral ſuch *Reaſons* may be brought) and I will undertake to him to prove, by the very ſame *Reaſon* and *Argument* as Concluſively, That *Self-Conſciouſneſs* is not, cannot be the *Formal Reaſon* of *Perſonality* in the Three *Divine Perſons* of the *Trinity*. In the mean time, by that kind of Arguing, which is called *Deductio ad Abſurdum*, I have ſufficiently diſproved it, by ſhewing what an Intolerable Abſurdity muſt follow the Aſſerting it.

Argument IV. The Fourth and Laſt *Argument* ſhall proceed thus. If Three diſtinct *Self-Conſciouſneſſes* Formally Conſtitute Three diſtinct *Perſonalities*, then Three diſtinct *Self-Complacencies* will Conſtitute Three diſtinct *Perſonalities* too. But our Author, I ſuppoſe, will not allow of the latter, and therefore neither ought he to aſſert the former.

The Conſequence is plain. Becauſe there is no Reaſon alleagable (according to our Author's Hypotheſis) why *Self-Complacency* may not found a *Perſonality* as well as *Self-Conſciouſneſs*.

For they are both of them equally diſtinct *Internal* Acts in the Perſon whom they belong to; and as to the Formal Effect of each, an Act of *Self-Complacency* ſeems to have the Preheminence; ſince it is a greater Perfection to be *United* to an *Infinite Good*, that is, to the *Deity*, by way of *Love* and *Adheſion*, than barely by way of knowledge and Intellection. And *Self-Complacency* is the former, whereas *Self-Conſciouſneſs* riſes no higher than the latter. And conſequently ſince *Self-Complacency* is the more perfective Act of the two (knowledge of good being

being ſtill in order to the Love of it) and ſince withall *Perſonality* is the moſt perfect way of *Subſiſting*, which any *Nature* is capable of, it ſeems moſt rational to derive the perfecteſt way of *Subſiſtence*, belonging to an *Intelligent Being*, from the moſt *Perfective* Act of that *Being*; if from any *Act* at all.

And now if this Author ſhould Object, That *Self-Complacency* is in Order of Nature Subſequent to *Self-Conſciouſneſs*; and ſo, that there cannot be the ſame ground to make it the *Formal Reaſon* of *Perſonality*, that there is, to make *Self-Conſciouſneſs* ſo.

I Anſwer, That, according to my Principle, whereby I deny *Self-Conſciouſneſs* to be the *Reaſon* of *Perſonality*, becauſe it is poſtnate to *Self-Subſiſtence*, it is, indeed, a good Reaſon; but according to our Author's Hypotheſis, it is none at all. For if the Priority of *Self-Subſiſtence* to *Self-Conſciouſneſs* (according to him) hinders not but that *Self-Conſciouſneſs* may nevertheleſs be the *Principle* or *Reaſon* of *Perſonality*, why ſhould the precedency of *Self-Conſciouſneſs* to *Self-Complacency*, hinder *Self-Complacency* from being as proper a Reaſon or Principle to found *Perſonality* upon, as the other.

All this I alledge only as *an Argument ad Hominem*; and deſire this Author to conſider, if any one ſhould borrow ſome of that Boldneſs of him, by which he diſſents from all Antiquity, and confidently averr, That *Self-Complacency is the Proper formal Reaſon of Perſonality in each and every one of the Divine Perſons*, I would have him, I ſay, conſider by what Reaſon or Argument, conſiſtent with his New Opinion he could Confute this other New Aſſertion.

For my own part, ſince I think as much may be ſaid for the one as for the other, I am ready to ſet up for *Self-Complacency* againſt his *Self-Conſciouſneſs*, when he

P plea-

pleases; and will undertake to give as good Reasons for my Notion, as he can for his, and perhaps better; let him begin and enter into the Dispute, as soon as he will. And as I shall oppose my *Self-Complacency* to his *Self-Consciousness*, so I shall find out a *Mutual-Complacency* to Vye against his *Mutual-Consciousness* too. And if any one should here Object, That this and the like Disputes are of that Nature, that the World is not like to be much Edified by them; I, perhaps, think so as much as he: But that is no great matter; since our Author is of so very Benign a Temper, That he does not always Write only for the *Reader's Edification*, but sometimes *for his Diversion* too.

Having thus given my Reasons against this Author's New Notion of *Self-Consciousness*, both with reference to Persons Create and Uncreate, and proved, That it neither is, nor can be the *Formal Reason* of *Personality* in either of them: I shall now pass to his other New Notion of *Mutual-Consciousness*, whereby those *Persons*, who were distinguished from one another by their respective *Self-Consciousnesses*, are United and made one in Nature by vertue of this *Mutual-Consciousness*. Concerning which Notion also, I must profess my self in the number of those who are by no means satisfied with it, as of any such peculiar Efficacy to the use and purpose it is here brought for.

And there are sufficient Reasons against it. In giving of which, as I must acknowledge, That that one Consideration of the *Priority* of *Being* (whether *Essentially*, or *Personally* considered) together with the first Modes and Affections of it, to any *Act* of *Knowledge* Attributable to the said *Being*, is the Fundamental Principle upon which I impugn this Author's New Hypothesis; so it does and must (as I have noted) run through all, or

Consci-

most of the parts of this Disputation, both about *Self-Consciousness* and *Mutual-Consciousness* too. And accordingly, in the first place I Argue against it thus.

Argument I. No *Act of Knowledge* can be the *Formal Reason* of an Unity of Nature in the *Persons* of the *Blessed Trinity*: But an Act of *Mutual-Consciousness*, is an Act of *Knowledge*; And therefore no Act of *Mutual-Consciousness* can be the *Formal Reason* of an Unity of Nature in the Three *Divine Persons*. The Major I prove thus. Every *Act of Knowledge* supposes the *Unity* of a Thing, or *Being* from which that Act flows, as Antecedent to it, and therefore cannot be the *Formal Reason* of the said *Being*. For still I affirm, that *Being*, and consequently *Unity of Being* (which is the first Affection of it) must in Order of Nature precede *Knowledge*, and all other the like Attributes of *Being*. And if so, no *Attribute* Subsequent to a Thing, can be the *Formal Reason* of that Thing, which it is thus, in Order of Nature, Subsequent to. For neither can *Omniscience* it self (one of the greatest and most acknowledged Attributes of the *Divine Nature*) be said to be the Reason either of the *Being*, or of the *Unity* of the said *Nature*: And therefore neither can any *Act of Knowledge* whatsoever be so. This is my first *Argument*, which I think sufficient fairly to propose, without any farther Amplification.

Argument II. If Unity of Nature in the *Divine Persons* be the Cause, Reason, or Principle of *Mutual-Consciousness* in the said *Persons*, then their *Mutual-Consciousness* is not the Cause or Reason of the Unity of their *Nature*: But the former is true, and therefore the latter is so too.

As for the Consequence of the Major Proposition, it is as evident, as, that Nothing can be the Cause and Effect of the same Thing.

And for the Minor, *That Unity of Nature, or Essence in the Divine Persons is the Cause, Reason, or Principle of Mutual-Consciousness*, is proved from this, That we can no otherwise conceive of *Mutual-Consciousness*, than as of an Essential Property equally belonging to all the Three *Persons*: And all Properties, or Internal Attributes, are accounted to issue and result from the *Essence* or *Nature* of the Things which they belong to; and therefore can have no Antecedent Causal Influx upon the said *Nature*, so as to Constitute either the *Being*, or the *Unity* thereof. But the *Divine Nature* or *Essence* being one and the same in all the Three *Persons*, there is, upon this Account, one and the same *Knowledge* in them also. And they are not *one in Nature*, by vertue of their *Mutual-Consciousness*; but they are therefore *Mutually Conscious*, because the *perfect Unity and Identity of their Nature*, makes them so. And to Assert the contrary, is of the like import (still allowing for the Disproportion of an *Infinite* and a *Finite Nature*) as if we should make *Risibility* in a Man, the Principle of *his Individuation*, and affirm, That *Peter*'s having this Property, is that which Constitutes him this particular Individual Man; which is egregiously absurd in all the Philosophy I ever yet met with, whatsoever it may be in this Author's.

Argument III. To affirm *Mutual-Consciousness* to be the Cause of the *Union* of the Three *Divine Persons*, in the same *Nature*, is to confound the *Union* and *Communion* of the said *Persons* together: But such a confusion ought by no means to be allowed of: and therefore neither ought that to be Asserted, from whence it follows.

Now

Now certain it is, That all Acts of several Persons upon one another (as all that are *Mutual* must needs be) are properly Acts of *Communion*, by which the said Persons have an Intercourse amongst themselves, as acting interchangeably one upon the other. But then, no doubt, both their *Essence* and *Personality* must still go before this *Mutual-Consciousness*, since the Three *Persons* must needs be really one in Nature before they can know themselves to be so. And therefore *Union* of *Knowledge* (as I think *Mutual-Consciousness* may properly be called) cannot give an *Union* of *Nature*. It may indeed suppose it, it may result from it, and upon the same Account may infer and prove it, but it can never give or cause it, nor be that Thing or Act, wherein an *Unity of Nature* does properly consist, whatsoever this Author Asserts to the contrary.

But the Truth is, all that he has said both of *Self-Consciousness* and *Mutual-Consciousness* (and he has no more than said it, as never offering at the Proof of any Thing) is founded in a manifest Perversion of that Natural Order, in which Humane Reason Conceives and Discourses of Things: Which Order (to give an Instance of it in our discoursing of any particular Person, or Compleat Being) proceeds by these steps. First we conceive of this Person as possessed of a certain *Essence* or *Nature* Constituting or rendring him what he is. Then we conceive of this Nature *as one*, which is the first Affection resulting from *Being*. After this we consider this *Being*, as stepping forth, or exerting it self in *some Acts*, whether of *Intellection*, *Volition*, *Power*, or the like. In which whole process the Order of these Conceptions is such, That it cannot, with any Accord to *Reason*, be transposed, so as to have the second or third put into the place of the first.

But

But now let us see how contrary to this Order our Author's Hypothesis proceeds. For whereas *Nature or Being* should be *first*, *Unity next*, and the *Acts issuing* from thence obtain the *Third place*, and then those Acts stand in their due Order amongst themselves. This Author, on the contrary, makes *Mutual-Consciousness*, which is by two Degrees, or Removes posterior to Unity of Nature (in the Persons whom it belongs to) to be the Cause or *Formal Reason* of the *said Unity*. For first *Self-Consciousness* is posterior to this *Unity*, and then *Mutual-Consciousness* is posterior to *Self-Consciousness*, as being an Act supervening upon it. For *Mutual-Consciousness* is that Act by which each *Person* comprehends, or is Conscious of the *Self-Consciousness* of the other two; and therefore must needs presuppose them, as the Act must needs do its *Object*. And therefore to make (as this Author does) *Mutual-Consciousness* the Constituent Reason of the *Unity* of the Three *Persons*, when this *Unity* is by two degrees, in Order of Nature, before it, runs so plainly counter to all the Methods of true Reasoning, that it would be but time lost to pursue it with any further Confutation.

Argument IV. Our 4th and last *Argument* proceeds equally against *Mutual-Consciousness* and *Self-Consciousness* too; and is taken from that known Maxime in Philosophy, That *Entities, or Beings, are not to be multiplied without manifest Necessity*: That is, we are not to admit of New Things, nor to coin new Notions, where such as are known and long received are sufficient to give us a true and full Account of the Nature of the Things we discourse of, and to answer all the Ends and Purposes of Argumentation.

Accordingly

Accordingly I affirm, That the Notions of *Mutual-Consciousness* and *Self-Consciousness* in the Subject now before us ought to be rejected not only as New and Suspicious, but as wholly Needless. For what can be signified by those, which is not fully, clearly, and abundantly signified by that one plain Word, and known Attribute, the *Divine Omniscience?* And what are *Mutual-Consciousness* and *Self-Consciousness* else (if they are any thing) but one and the same *Omniscience* exerting it self several ways, and upon several *Objects?* As to apply it to the Matter before us; does not every one of the *Divine Persons*, by vertue of the *Divine Nature*, and of this *Omniscience* therewith Communicated to him, Perfectly, Intimately, and Intirely know himself as a *Person*, and all the *Actions*, *Motions*, and every thing else belonging to him? No doubt he does; for that otherwise he could not be *Omniscient*. And does not the same *Person* again, by the very same *Omniscience*, know all that is known by the other Two *Persons*, and the other Two *Persons* by the same Mutually know all that is known by him? No doubt they may and do: Forasmuch as *Omniscience* knows all things that are knowable, and consequently all that is or can be known of, or in any one or all of the *Divine Persons* joyntly or severally considered.

But to argue the Matter yet more particularly. Either *Self-Consciousness* and *Mutual-Consciousness* are one and the same with the *Divine Omniscience*, or they are distinct sorts of knowledge from it. If they are the same, then they are useless and superfluous Notions, as we affirm they are; but if they import distinct sorts of knowledge, then these two Things will follow.

1. That

1. That in every one of the *Divine Persons* there are three distinct sorts of *Knowledge, viz.* A Knowledge of *Omniscience*, a Knowledge of *Self-Consciousness*, and a Knowledge of *Mutual-Consciousness* too; which, I think, is very absurd and ridiculous.

2. And in the next place: If we affirm them to be distinct sorts of Knowledge from that of *Omniscience*, then they must also have *Objects* distinct from, and not included in the *Object* of *Omniscience*; since all such difference, either of sorts or Acts of Knowledge is founded upon the difference of their *Objects*. But this is impossible; since the *Object* of *Omniscience* comprehends in it all that is knowable; and consequently if *Mutual-Consciousness* and *Self-Consciousness* have *Objects* distinct from, and not included in the *Object* of *Omniscience*, those *Objects* must be something that is not knowable; for that *Omniscience* (as we have shewn) claims all that is knowable, or possible to be known, for its own *Object*. From all which it follows, That *Self-Consciousness* and *Mutual-Consciousness* considered as distinct from *Omniscience* are two empty Chimerical Words, without any distinct Sense, or Signification.

In a word, Every Person in the *Trinity*, by one and the same Act of *Omniscience*, knows all the Internal Acts, Motions, and Relations proper both to himself, and to the other Two Persons besides. And if so, what imployment or use can there be for *Self-Consciousness*, or *Mutual-Consciousness*, which *Omniscience* (that takes in the Objects of both) has not fully answered and discharged already?

If it be here said, That *Omniscience* cannot give *Personality*; forasmuch as the Personality of each *Person* distinguishes him from the other two; which *Omniscience* (being common to them all) cannot do. This I grant, and

and own it impoſſible for any Thing Eſſentially involved in the *Divine Nature*, to give a Perſonal Diſtinction to any of the Three *Perſons*; but then I add alſo, That we have equally proved, that neither was *Self-Conſciouſneſs* the *Formal Reaſon* of this *Perſonal* Diſtinction, by ſeveral *Arguments*; and more eſpecially, becauſe that *Self-Conſciouſneſs* being a Thing Abſolute and Irrelative, could not be the *Formal Reaſon* of any thing in the Nature of it perfectly Relative, as the *Divine Perſons* certainly are. For this is a received Maxime in the Schools, with reference to the *Divine Nature* and *Perſons*, *Repugnat in Divinis dari Abſolutum Incommunicabile*, Greg. de Valen. 1 Tom. p. 874. And it is a ſure Rule, whereby we may diſtinguiſh in every one of the *Divine Perſons*, what is *Eſſential*, from what is *Perſonal*. For every Attribute that is Abſolute, is Communicable, and conſequently Eſſential, and every one that is purely Relative, is Incommunicable, and therefore purely Perſonal, and ſo *è converſo*: Upon which Account *Self-Conſciouſneſs*, which is a Thing Abſolute and Irrelative, cannot be Incommunicable, nor conſequently the *Formal Reaſon* of *Perſonality* in any of the *Perſons* of the *Bleſſed Trinity*; as we have already at large demonſtrated.

So that ſtill our Aſſertion ſtands good, That all that can be truly aſcribed to *Self-Conſciouſneſs* and *Mutual-Conſciouſneſs* with reference to the *Divine Nature* and *Perſons*, may be fully and fairly accounted for from that one known Attribute, the *Divine Omniſcience*. And therefore, that there is no uſe at all either of the Term *Self-Conſciouſneſs* or *Mutual-Conſciouſneſs*, to contribute to the plainer or fuller Explication of the *Bleſſed Trinity*; as this Author, with great fluſter of Oſtentation pretends, but has not yet by ſo much as one ſolid *Argument* proved.

But when I conſider how wonderfully pleaſed the Man is with theſe two new-ſtarted Terms ſo high in ſound, and ſo empty of ſence, inſtead of one ſubſtantial word, which gives us all that can be pretended uſeful in them, with vaſt overplus and advantage, and even ſwallows them up, as *Moſes*'s Rod did thoſe pitiful Tools of the *Magicians*; This (I ſay) brings to my Mind (whether I will or no) a certain Story of a Grave Perſon, who Riding in the Road with his Servant, and finding himſelf ſomething uneaſie in his Saddle, beſpoke his Servant thus. John (ſays he) *a-light; and firſt take off the Saddle that is upon my Horſe, and then take off the Saddle that is upon your Horſe; and when you have done this, put the Saddle that was upon my Horſe, upon your Horſe, and put the Saddle that was upon your Horſe upon my Horſe:* Whereupon the Man, who had not ſtudied the Philoſophy of Saddles (whether *Ambling* or *Trotting*) ſo exactly, as his Maſter, replys ſomething ſhort upon him; *Lord! Maſter, What needs all theſe words? Could you not as well have ſaid, Let us change Saddles?* Now I muſt confeſs, I think the Servant was much in the right; though the Maſter having *a Rational Head of his own*, and being withal wiſhing to make the Notion of *changing* Saddles more *plain, eaſie, and intelligible*, and to give a clearer Explication of that word, (which his Fore-Fathers, how good *Horſe-men* ſoever they might have been, yet were *not equally happy in the explaining of*) was pleaſed to ſet it forth by that more full and accurate Circumlocution.

And here it is not unlikely but that this Author, who, with a ſpight equally Malicious and Ridiculous, has reflected upon one of his Antagoniſts, and that for no Cauſe, or Provocation that appears (unleſs for having Baffled him) may tax me alſo, as one Drolling upon

See Chapter II.

Things

Things ſacred, for repreſenting the vanity of his Hypotheſis by the forementioned Example and Compariſon. But I hope the World will give me leave to diſtinguiſh between Things *Sacred*, and his Abſurd Phantaſtick way of treating of them; which, I can, by no means look upon as *Sacred*, nor indeed any Thing elſe in his whole Book, but the bare *Subject* it treats of, and the *Scriptures* there quoted by him. For to ſpeak my thoughts plainly, I believe this Sacred Myſtery of the *Trinity*, was never ſo ridiculed and expoſed to the Contempt of the Profane Scoffers at it, as it has been by this New-faſhioned Defence of it.

And ſo I diſmiſs his two ſo much *Admired* Terms (by himſelf I mean) as in no degree anſwering the Expectation he raiſed of them. For I cannot find, That they have either heightned or ſtrength'ned Men's Intellectual Faculties, or caſt a greater light and clearneſs upon that Object which has ſo long exerciſed them; but that *a Trinity in Unity* is as Myſterious as ever; and the Mind of Man as unable to graſp and comprehend it, as it has been from the beginning of Chriſtianity to this day. In a word, *Self-Conſciouſneſs* and *Mutual-Conſciouſneſs* have rendred nothing about the *Divine Nature* and *Perſons*, *plainer*, *eaſier*, and more *Intelligible*; nor indeed, after ſuch a mighty ſtreſs ſo irrationally laid upon two ſlight empty words, have they made any thing (but the Author himſelf) *better underſtood than it was before.*

CHAP. V.

In which is proved against this Author, That the Three Persons *of the* Blessed Trinity, *are not Three Distinct* Infinite Minds, *or* Spirits.

IT being certain both from *Philosophy* and *Religion*, that there is but one only *God*, or *God-head*, in which *Christian Religion* has taught us, That there are Three *Persons*; Many Eminent Professors of it have attempted to shew, how one and the same Nature might Subsist in Three *Persons*, and how the said Three *Persons* might meet in one, and make no more than one simple, undivided *Nature*. It had been to be wished, I confess, that Divines had rested in the bare Expressions delivered in Scripture concerning this Mystery, and ventured no further by any particular, and bold Explications of it. But since the Nature, or rather Humour of Man has been still too strong for his Duty, and his Curiosity (especially in things Sacred) been apt to carry him too far; those, however, have been all along the most pardonable, who have ventured least, and proceeded upon the surest grounds both of Scripture it self, and of Reason discoursing upon it. And such I affirm the Ancient Writers and Fathers of the Church, and after them the Schoolmen to have been; who with all their Faults (or rather Infelicities, caused by the Times and Circumstances they

they lived in) are better Divines, and Soberer Reasoners than any of those Pert, Confident, Raw Men, who are much better at Despising and Carping at them, than at Reading and Understanding them: Though Wise Men Despise nothing, but they will know it first; and for that Cause very rationally despise them.

But among those, who leaving the Common Road of the Church have took a By-way to themselves, none (of late Years especially) have ventured so boldly and so far as this Author; who pretending to be *more happy* (forsooth) *in his Explication of this Mystery than all before him* (as who would not believe a Man in his own Commendation?) and to give a more satisfactory Account of this long received, and Revered Article by Terms perfectly New, and peculiarly his own, has advanced quite different Notions about this Mystery, from any that our Church was ever yet acquainted with; Affirming, (as he does) *That the Three Persons in the God-head, are Three Distinct Infinite Minds, or Spirits*, as will appear from the several places of his Book, where he declares his Thoughts upon this great Subject. As, First in *Page* 50. he says, The Three *Divine Persons*, Father, Son, and Holy Ghost, *are Three Infinite Minds really distinct from each other*. Again, in *Page 66*. The *Persons* (says he) are perfectly distinct; *for they are Three distinct and Infinite Minds, and therefore Three distinct Persons:* For a *Person is an Intelligent Being; and to say, they are Three Divine Persons, and not Three distinct Infinite Minds, is both Heresie and Nonsence*. For which extraordinary Complement passed upon the whole Body of the Church of *England*, and perhaps all the Churches of *Christendom* besides, as I have paid him part of my thanks already, so I will not fail yet further to account with him before I put an end to this Chapter. In the mean-

time,

time, he goes on, in *Page* 102. *I plainly assert* (says he) *That as the Father is an Eternal and Infinite Mind, so the Son is an Eternal and Infinite Mind distinct from the Father*, and the *Holy Ghost* is an *Eternal and Infinite Mind distinct both from Father and Son*: Adding withall these words; *Which* (says he) *every Body can understand without any skill in Logick, or Metaphysicks.* And this, I confess, is most truly and seasonably remarked by him: For the want of this Qualification is so far from being any hindrance in the Case mentioned, that I dare undertake, that nothing but want *of skill* in *Logick and Metaphysicks*, can bring any Man living, who acknowledges the *Trinity*, to own this Assertion. I need repeat no more of his Expressions to this purpose; these being sufficient to declare his Opinion; save only that in *Page* 119. where (he says) *That Three Minds, or Spirits, which have no other difference, are yet distinguish'd by Self-Consciousness, and are Three distinct Spirits.* And that other in *Page* 258. where speaking of the Three *Persons, I grant* (says he) *that they are Three Holy Spirits.* By the same Token, that he there very Learnedly distinguishes between *Ghost* and *Spirit*, allowing *the said Three Persons* (as we have shewn) to be *Three Holy Spirits*, but at the same time denying them to be *Three Holy Ghosts*,and this with great scorn of those who should hold,or speak otherwise. To which at present I shall say no more but this,That he would do well to turn these two Propositions into *Greek*, or *Latin*; and that will presently shew him what difference and distinction there is between a *Ghost* and a *Spirit*,and why the very same things which are affirmed of the one (notwithstanding the difference of those words in *English*) may not, with the same Truth, be affirmed of the other also. But the Examination of this odd Assertion will fall in more naturally towards the latter end of

this

this Chapter, where it ſhall be particularly conſidered.

I have now ſhewn this Author's Judgment in the Point, and in oppoſition to what he has ſo boldly Aſſerted, and laid down, I do here deny, *That the Three Perſons in the Bleſſed Trinity, are Three diſtinct Infinite Minds or Three diſtinct Infinite Spirits.* And to overthrow his Aſſertion, and evince the Truth of mine, I ſhall trouble neither my Reader nor my ſelf, with many *Arguments.* But of thoſe, which I ſhall make uſe of, the firſt is this.

Argument I. *Three diſtinct Infinite Minds, or Spirits, are Three diſtinct Gods.*
But the Three Perſons of the Bleſſed Trinity, are not Three diſtinct Gods.
And therefore the Three Perſons of the Bleſſed Trinity, are not Three diſtinct Infinite Minds, or Spirits.

The Minor, I ſuppoſe, this Author will readily concur with me in; howbeit his Hypotheſis (as ſhall be ſhewn) in the certain Conſequences of it Contradicts it, and, if it ſhould ſtand, would effectually overturn it. For by that he Aſſerts a perfect *Tritheiſme*, though I have ſo much Charity for him, as to believe, that he does not know it.

The Major Propoſition therefore is that which muſt be debated between us. This Author holds it in the Negative, and I in the Affirmative: and my Reaſon for what I affirm, *viz.* That Three *diſtinct Infinite Minds, or Spirits, are Three diſtinct Gods*, is this, That *God* and *Infinite Mind,* or *Spirit*, are Terms Equipollent, and Convertible. *God* being truly and properly an *Infinite Mind, or Spirit*, and *an Infinite Mind or Spirit* being as truly

truly and properly *God.* And to ſhew this Convertibility and Commenſuration between them yet further: Whatſoever may be affirmed or denied of the one, may with equal Truth and Propriety be affirmed or denied of the other. And to give an Inſtance of this with reference to the Three *Perſons* of the *Bleſſed Trinity*; As it is true, that one and the ſame *God*, or *God-head* is Common to, and Subſiſts in all and every one of the Three *Perſons*; ſo is it true, *That one and the ſame Infinite Mind, or Spirit*, is Common to, and Subſiſts in the ſaid Three *Perſons*: And conſequently, as it is falſe, That one and the ſame *God*, or *God-head*, by being Common to, and Subſiſting in the Three *Perſons*, becomes Three *Gods*, or Three *God-heads*; ſo is it equally falſe, That one and the ſame *Infinite Mind*, or *Spirit*, by being Common to, and Subſiſting in the ſaid Three *Perſons*, becomes Three *Infinite Minds* or *Spirits*. This is clear Argumentation, and craves no Mercy at our Author's Hands.

If it be here Objected, That we allow of Three *diſtinct Perſons* in the *God-head*, of which every one is *Infinite*, without admitting them to be Three diſtinct *Gods*; and therefore, why may we not as well allow of Three *diſtinct Infinite Minds* or *Spirits* in the ſame *God-head* without any neceſſity of inferring from thence, That they are Three diſtinct *Gods?*

I Anſwer, That the Caſe is very different, and the Reaſon of the difference is this, Becauſe Three *Infinite Minds*, or *Spirits* are Three Abſolute, Simple *Beings*, or *Eſſences*, and ſo ſtand diſtinguiſhed from one another, by their whole *Beings* or *Natures*. But the *Divine Perſons* are Three Relatives, (or one ſimple *Being*, or *Eſſence*, under three diſtinct Relations) and conſequently differ from one another, not wholly, and by all that is in them,

them, but only by ſome certain *Mode*, or *reſpect* peculiar to each, and upon that Account cauſing their Diſtinction. And therefore to Argue from a *Perſon* to a *Spirit* here is manifeſtly Sophiſtical, and that which is called, *Fallacia Accidentis*, or (ſince ſeveral Fallacies may concur in the ſame Propoſition) it may be alſo *à dicto ſecundùm quid ad dictum ſimpliciter*. For ſo it is to conclude, That Three *Perſons* are Three *diſtinct Gods*; ſince the difference of Perſons is only from a *diverſe reſpect* between them; but Three *Gods* import Three abſolutely *diſtinct Natures or Subſtances*. And whereas we ſay, That the Three *Perſons* are all and every one of them *Infinite*, yet it is but from one and the ſame Numerical Nature Common to them all that they are ſo, the Ternary Number all the while not belonging to their *Infinity*, but only to their *Perſonalities*. The Caſe therefore between *a Mind, or Spirit*, and *a Perſon*, is by no means the ſame. Foraſmuch as [*Perſon*] here imports only a Relation, or Mode of *Subſiſtence* in Conjunction with the Nature it belongs to: And therefore a Multiplication of *Perſons* (of it ſelf) imports only a Multiplication of ſuch *Modes*, or *Relations*, without any neceſſary Multiplication of the Nature it ſelf to which they adhere. Foraſmuch as one and the ſame Nature may ſuſtain ſeveral diſtinct Relations, or Modes of Subſiſtence. But now on the other ſide, a *Mind*, or *Spirit*, is not a Relation, or Mode of *Subſiſtence*, but it is an Abſolute *Being*, *Nature*, or *Subſtance*; and conſequently cannot be multiplyed without a Multiplication of it into ſo many Numerical Abſolute *Beings*, *Natures*, or *Subſtances*; there being nothing in it to be *multiplyed* but it ſelf. So that Three *Minds*, or *Spirits*, are Three Abſolute *Beings*, *Natures*, or *Subſtances*, and *Three diſtinct Infinite Minds, or Spirits*, are accordingly *Three diſtinct*

Infinite Abſolute Beings, Natures, or Subſtances. That is, in other words, *They are Three Gods*; which was the Thing to be proved; and let this Author ward off the Proof of it as he is able.

Argument II. My Second *Argument* againſt the Three *Perſons* in the *Bleſſed Trinity* being *Three diſtinct Infinite Minds, or Spirits, is this.*

Three diſtinct Minds, or Spirits are Three diſtinct Subſtances.
But the Three Perſons in the Bleſſed Trinity are not Three diſtinct Subſtances.
And therefore they are not Three diſtinct Minds, or Spirits.

The Major Propoſition is proved from the Definition of a *Mind*, or *Spirit*, That it is *Subſtantia Incorporea Intelligens*, an Intelligent, Incorporeal, [or Immaterial] Subſtance; and therefore Three *diſtinct Minds*, or *Spirits*, muſt be Three ſuch *diſtinct Subſtances*. And beſides, if a *Mind*, or *Spirit*, were not a *Subſtance*, what could it be elſe? If it be any Thing, it muſt be either *an Accident*, *or Mode of Being*. But not an Accident, ſince no Accident can be in *God*; nor yet *a Mode of Being*, ſince a *Spirit* (not deſigned to concur as a part towards any Compound) is an Abſolute, Entire, Complete Being of it ſelf, and has it's proper Mode of Subſiſtence belonging to it; and therefore cannot be *a Mode* it ſelf. From whence it follows, That a *Spirit* is, and muſt be a *Subſtance*, and can be nothing elſe.

As for the Minor, viz. *That the Three Perſons in the Bleſſed Trinity are not Three diſtinct Subſtances*; this is evident both from Authority, and from Reaſon.

And

And first for Authority, *Tertullian* against *Praxeas* affirms, *Semper in Deo una Substantia*. And St. *Jerom* in his Epistle to *Damasus*, *Quis ore sacrilego Tres Substantias prædicabit?* And St. *Austin* in his 5th Book *de Trinitate*, Chap. 9. and in Book 7. Chap. 4. And *Ruffinus* in the 10th Book of his History, Chap. 29. All affirm One Substance in *God*, and deny Three, and yet the same Writers unanimously hold Three *Persons*, which shews, That they did not account these Three *Persons*, Three *Substances*. And *Anselmus* in his Book *de Incarnatione*, Chap. 3. says, That the Father and the Son may be said to be Two *Beings*, provided that by Beings we understand Relations not Substances. And *Bellarmine*, a Writer Orthodox enough in these points, and of unquestionable Learning otherwise, in his 2d *Tome*, *page* 348. about the end, says, That to assert, that the Father and the Son differ in Substance, is *Arianism*: And yet if they were Two *distinct Substances*, for them not to differ in Substance, would be impossible. And as for the *Greek* Writers, they never admit of Three οὐσίαι in the *Deity*, but where οὐσία is used to signifie the same with ὑπόστασις, as sometimes it was used: And by reason of this Ambiguity it was, that the *Latine* Church was so long fearful of using the word Hypostasis, and used only that of *Persona*, answering to the *Greek* Πρόσωπον, lest they should hereby be thought to admit of *Three Substances*, as well as Three *Persons* in the *God-head*.

Nor, in the next place, is the same less evident from Reason, than we have shewn it to be from Authority. For if the Three *Persons* be Three *distinct Substances*, then Two *distinct Substances* will concur in, and belong to each Person; to wit, *That Substance* which is the *Divine Essence*, and so is Communicable or Common to all the *Persons*, and *that Substance* which Constitutes each

R 2 Person,

Person, and thereby is so peculiar to him as to distinguish him from the other, and consequently to be incommunicable to any besides him to whom it belongs: Since for one and the same Substance to be Common to all Three *Persons*, and withal to belong incommunicably to each of the Three, and thereby to distinguish them from one another, is Contradictious and Impossible. And yet on the other side to assert Two *distinct Substances* in each *Person*, is altogether as Absurd; and that, as upon many other Accounts, so particularly upon this; That it must infer such a Composition in the *Divine Persons*, as is utterly Incompatible with the Absolute Simplicity, and Infinite Perfection of the *Divine Nature*. And therefore the Three *Persons* in the *Blessed Trinity*, can by no means be said to be Three *distinct Substances*, but only one *Infinite Substance*, equally Common to, and Subsisting in them all, and diversified by their respective Relations. And moreover, since Three *distinct Minds*, or *Spirits* are Essentially Three *distinct Substances*, neither can the Three *Persons* of the *Trinity* be said to be Three *distinct Minds, or Spirits*; which was the Point to be made out.

Argument III. My Third *Argument* against the same shall proceed thus.

If it be truly said, That one and the same Infinite Mind, or Spirit is Father, Son, and Holy Ghost, (I mean all Three taken together) and it cannot be truly said, That one and the same Infinite Mind, or Spirit is Three distinct Infinite Minds, or Spirits; then it follows, That Father, Son, and Holy Ghost are not Three distinct Infinite Minds, or Spirits.

But

But it may be truly ſaid, That one and the ſame Infinite Mind, or Spirit is Father, Son, and Holy Ghoſt; and it cannot be truly ſaid, That one and the ſame Infinite Mind, or Spirit is Three diſtinct Infinite Minds, or Spirits.

Therefore the Three Perſons in the Trinity, viz. *Father, Son, and Holy Ghoſt are not Three diſtinct Infinite Minds, or Spirits.*

This is the *Argument.*

Now the Conſequence of the Major appears from this, That the ſame Thing, or Things, at the ſame time, and in the ſame reſpect, cannot be truly affirmed and denied of the ſame Subject: And therefore ſince [*Father, Son;* and *Holy Ghoſt*, taken joyntly together] are truly predicated of one and the ſame *Infinite Mind*; and [Three *diſtinct Infinite Minds*, or *Spirits*] cannot be truly affirmed or predicated, and conſequently may be truly denied of the ſame; it follows, That [*Father, Son,* and *Holy Ghoſt*] and [Three *diſtinct Infinite Minds*, or *Spirits*] neither are, nor can be accounted the ſame, nor be truly affirmable of one another.

As for the Minor, it conſiſts of two parts, and accordingly muſt be proved ſeverally in each of them.

And Firſt, That it is, and may be truly ſaid, *That one and the ſame Infinite Mind is Father, Son, and Holy Ghoſt* (*viz.* joyntly taken) as I noted before. This, I ſay, may be proved from hence, That *God* is truly ſaid *to be Father, Son*, and *Holy Ghoſt* (ſtill ſo taken.) And it having been already evinced, That [*one Infinite Mind, or Spirit*] and [*one God*] are terms convertible and equipollent, it follows, That whatſoever is truly affirmed or denied of the one, may be as truly affirmed or denied of the other. And this is too evident to need any further proof.

And

And therefore in the next place, for the proof of the other part of the Minor, viz. *That one and the same Infinite Mind, or Spirit, cannot be truly said to be Three distinct Infinite Minds, or Spirits*; This is no less evident than the former, because in such a Proposition both Subject and Predicate imply a Mutual Negation of, and Contradiction to one and another; and where it is so, it is impossible for one to be truly affirmed, or predicated of the other.

And now, after this plain proof given both of the Major and the Minor Proposition, and this also drawn into so little a compass, I hope this Author will not bear himself so much above all the Rules which other Mortals proceed by, as, after the Premises proved, to deny the Conclusion, viz. *That the Three Persons in the Blessed Trinity, Father, Son, and Holy Ghost, are not Three distinct Infinite Minds, or Spirits.* The Affirmation of which, is that which I undertook to confute.

But before I dismiss this *Argument*, I cannot but take notice, That the same Terms, with a bare Transposition of them, *viz.* by shifting place between the Predicate and the Subject (which in Adequate and Commensurate Predications, may very well be done) will as effectually conclude to the same Purpose, as they did in the way in which we have already proposed them. And so the *Argument* will proceed thus.

If it be truly and properly said, That the Three Persons in the Blessed Trinity, are one Numerical Infinite Mind, or Spirit; then they cannot be truly said to be Three distinct Infinite Minds, or Spirits.

But they are truly and properly said to be one Numerical Infinite Mind, or Spirit.

And

And therefore they neither are, nor can be truly ſaid to be Three diſtinct Infinite Minds, or Spirits.

The Conſequence of the firſt Propoſition is manifeſt, becauſe (as we have ſhewn before) *one and the ſame Infinite Mind* cannot be Three *diſtinct Infinite Minds* without a Contradiction in the Terms.

And for the Minor, viz. *That the Three Perſons are truly ſaid to be one Infinite Mind, or Spirit*; That alſo is proved by this, That all and every one of them, are truly and properly *ſaid to be God*; *and God is truly and properly one Numerical Infinite Mind, or Spirit*: And therefore if the Three *Perſons* are ſaid to be the Firſt, they muſt be ſaid to be this Latter alſo; and that (as I ſhew before) becauſe of the Reciprocal Predication of thoſe Terms. But as to the Matter before us, *That God is truly and properly one Numerical Infinite Mind, or Spirit*, even this Author himſelf allows, who in *Page* 69. poſitively ſays, *That we know nothing of the Divine Eſſence, but that God is an Infinite Mind.* Very well; and if he grant him to be an *Infinite Mind*, let him prove *this Infinite Mind* to be *three diſtinct Infinite Minds*, if he can. The Truth is [*Infinite Mind or Spirit*] is an Eſſential Attribute of the *Divine Nature*, and Convertible with it, and whatſoever is ſo, belongs equally to all the Three *Perſons*, and conſequently cannot be aſcribed to them *plurally* any more than the *Deity* it ſelf; it being as uncapable, as that, of being multiplied. Upon which Account, if the Three *Perſons* are with equal Truth ſaid to be [*one Infinite Mind, or Spirit*] and to be [*one God*] they can no more be ſaid to be Three *diſtinct Infinite Minds*, than they can be ſaid to be Three *diſtinct Gods*.

So

So that which way ſoever the *Argument* be propoſed, either, *That one Infinite Mind is Father, Son, and Holy Ghoſt*; or, *That Father, Son, and Holy Ghoſt, are one Infinite Mind*, it ſtill overthrows this Author's Hypotheſis, That the ſaid Three *Perſons* are Three *diſtinct Infinite Minds*, or *Spirits*.

Argument IV. My Fourth and Laſt *Argument* againſt the ſame, ſhall be this.

Whatſoever Attribute may be truly predicated of all and each of the Divine Perſons in the Athanaſian *Form, ſo belongs to them all in Common, that it can belong to none of them under any Term of diſtinction from the reſt.*

But the Attribute [Infinite Mind, or Spirit] *may be truly predicated of all and each of the Divine Perſons in and according to the* Athanaſian *Form.*

And therefore it can belong to none of them under any Term of diſtinction from the reſt.

The Major is as evident; as that no Attribute can be Common to ſeveral Subjects, and yet peculiar and appropriate to each of them.

And the Minor is proved by Inſtance thus; The *Father* is an *Infinite Mind*, the *Son* is an *Infinite Mind*, and the *Holy Ghoſt* is an *Infinite Mind*; and yet they are not Three *Infinite Minds*, but one *Infinite Mind*.

And this I affirm to be as good Divinity as any part in the *Athanaſian Creed*, and ſuch as I ſhall abide by, both againſt this Author, and any other whatſoever.

But now let us ſee how his Aſſertion caſt into the *Athanaſian* Model, ſhews it ſelf, as thus.

The

The Father is a distinct Infinite Mind, the Son is a distinct Infinite Mind, and the Holy Ghost is a distinct Infinite Mind; and yet they are not Three distinct Infinite Minds, but one distinct Infinite Mind.

And this is so far from being true, that it is indeed neither *Truth* nor *Sence*. For what Truth can there be in denying, That Three *Persons*, of which every one is said to be a *distinct Infinite Mind, are Three distinct Infinite Minds?* And what sence can there be in affirming, or saying, *That they are but One distinct Infinite Mind?* Whereas the Term [*distinct*] is never properly used or applyed, but with respect had to several Particulars each discriminated from the other; but by no means where there is mention made only of *one* Thing and no more, as it is here in this Proposition.

But to make what allowances the Case will bear, and for that purpose to remit something of the strictness of the *Athanasian Form*, by leaving out the word [*distinct*] in the last and illative Clause, we shall then see that our Author's Hypothesis will proceed thus.

The Father is a distinct Infinite Mind, the Son is a distinct Infinite Mind, and the Holy Ghost is a distinct Infinite Mind; and yet they are not Three Infinite Minds, but one Infinite Mind.

Thus, I say, it must proceed in the *Athanasian* way with the word [*distinct*] left out of the Conclusion. Nevertheless even so, the Inference is still manifestly and grosly false in both the branches of it. For it is absolutely false [That *Three distinct Infinite Minds, are not Three Infinite Minds*] and altogether as false [*That Three Infinite Minds, are but One Infinite Mind*.]

The Author's Hypothesis put into the *Athanasian* Model, must needs fall in with that Fallacy sometimes urged against us by the *Socinians*, viz. The *Father is a Person, the Son a Person, and the Holy Ghost a Person, and yet they are not Three Persons, but one Person*; which is manifestly Sophistical, by arguing *ab imparibus tanquam paribus*, viz. Concluding that of an Attribute *Relative*, and *Multiplicable*, which can be concluded only of such as are not So.

For the *Athanasian* Inference holds only in Attributes *Essential* and *Common* to all the Three *Persons* joyntly, or severally taken, and not in such as are *Proper*, *Personal*, and Peculiar to each. As also in such as are *Absolute* (as the Attribute of *Mind*, or *Spirit* without the word [*distinct*] is) and not in such as are *Relative*. For those Attributes, which agree to the *Divine Persons*, Personally, Peculiarly, and Relatively, can never Unite, or Coincide into *one* in the Inference, or Conclusion. In a word [*Infinite Mind, or Spirit*] is a Predicate perfectly Essential, and so in its Numerical Unity Common to all the Three *Divine Persons*, and for that cause not to be affirmed of, or ascribed to, either all or any of them with the Term [*distinct*] added to it, or joyned with it. For that would *multiply* an Attribute that cannot be *multiplyed*.

And now, what I have here discoursed upon, and drawn from the *Athanasian* Creed with respect to this particular Subject, I leave to our Author's strictest Examination. For my own part, I rely upon this *Creed*, as a sure Test, or Rule to discover the falshood of his Hypothesis by. So that as long as it is true, that *God is one* numerical *Infinite Mind or Spirit*, and as long as the *Athanasian* Form duely applied is a firm and good way of Reasoning, this Author's Assertion, *That the Three Divine Persons, are Three distinct Infinite Minds, or Spirits*, is thereby irrefragably overthrown.

And

And therefore I ſhall not concern my ſelf to produce any more Arguments againſt it. Only by way of *Overplus* to, and *Illuſtration* of thoſe, which have already been alledged, I cannot but obſerve the Concurrent Opinion of the Philoſophers, and moſt Learned Men amongſt the Heathens about *God's being One Infinite Mind, or Spirit*, as a neceſſary deduction (no doubt) made by Natural Reaſon from the Principles thereof concerning the *Divine Nature*. For moſt of thoſe Philoſophers looked upon *God* as the *Soul of the World*, as *One Infinite Mind*, *or Spirit*, that animated and preſided over the Univerſe. For ſo held *Pythagoras*, as *Cicero* in his firſt Book, *de Naturâ Deorum*, and *Lactantius* in his Book *de irâ Dei*, tells us, *Pythagoras quoque unum Deum confitetur dicens Incorpoream eſſe* mentem *quæ per omnem Naturam diffuſa & intenta vitalem ſenſum tribuit*. In like manner the Great *Hermes* being asked, *What God was*, anſwered, ὁ τῶν ὅλων δημιουργὸς σοφώτατος νοῦς καὶ ἀΐδιος, The Maker of all Things, a moſt Wiſe and Eternal Mind. *Thales* called him, νοῦν τοῦ κόσμου Θεὸν, God, the Mind of the World. *Diogenes*, *Cleanthes*, and *Oenipides*, τὴν τοῦ κόσμου ψυχὴν, The Soul of the World. *Plato* in *Phædone*, ſays of God, That he is νοῦς ὁ διακοσμῶν τε καὶ πάντων αἴτιος, a Mind that is the Cauſe and orderer of all Things. And *Plato* the Son of *Ariſton* ſays, ὁ γὰρ Θεὸς νοῦς ἐστι τοῦ κόσμου, God is the Mind of the World. And *Lactantius* gives this Teſtimony of *Ariſtotle*, That, *Quamvis ſecum ipſe diſſideat, ac repugnantia ſibi & dicat, & ſentiat*, (by which one would think our Author better acquainted with him than he is) *in ſummum tamen unam mentem mundo præeſſe teſtatur*. Lact. de falſâ Relig. Lib. 1. Cap. 5. Agreeably to all which, *Seneca* in the Preface to his Natural Queſtions, putting the Queſtion, *Quid eſt Deus?* What is God? Anſwers, *Mens Univerſi*, The Mind of the Univerſe. As the Learned

Emperour *Antoninus* after him, expresses God the same way, and by the same word in *Greek*, ὁ τοῦ ὅλου νοῦς, *Lib.* 5. *p.* 148. *Oxon. Edit.* And that Passage in *Virgil's* 6. *Æneid* is famous; where speaking of God, as the *Great Soul of the World*, running through all the Parts of that vast Body, he expresses it in those known Verses:

> ----- *Cœlum, ac Terras, Camposq; liquentes,*
> *Lucentemq; Globum Lunæ, Titaniaq; Astra,*
> *Spiritus intus alit, totamq; infusa per artus*
> *Mens agitat molem, & magno se corpore miscet.*

And the same was the Opinion of *Cato* before him, a great Man, though but a small Author, who tells us from the Ancient Poets (who were accounted the Philosophers of the first Ages) That *Deus est animus*, God is a Mind, or Spirit.

And the Truth is, I reckon that these Learned Men, all along, *by an Infinite* Mind, or Spirit, understood as truly and certainly *One* Infinite Mind, or Spirit, as if the Term of Unity had been added by them. For besides that the Particles *a*, or *the*, (which we use in translating any single word into our own Language) import so much, the very condition also of the Subject spoken of, as being *Infinite*, must needs infer the same. So that we see here how the Judgment of Natural Reason in these Eminent Philosophers amongst the Heathens falls in with what God himself revealed by the Mouth of our Saviour concerning his own Nature, in *John* 4. 24. viz. *That God is a Spirit*. For we have them expressing him by these words, *Animus*, *Mens*, & *Spiritus*. So that had they all lived after St. *John*, (as one of them did,) their Sentences might have passed for so many Paraphrases upon

upon the Text, all declaring God to be *One Infinite Soul, Mind, or Spirit.*

But perhaps our Author will here ſay, What is all this to the purpoſe, ſince we found our knowledge of the Three *Divine Perſons*, wholly upon *Revelation?* And I grant, we do ſo: Yet nevertheleſs I ſhall, by his good favour, ſhew, That what I have alledged is very much to the purpoſe. And to this end, premiſing here what we have already proved, *viz.* That *to be One Infinite Mind, and to be Three diſtinct Infinite Minds*, involve in them a Mutual Negation of, and Contradiction to one another: (Foraſmuch as to be *Unum*, is to be *Indiviſum in ſe*; that is to ſay, Indiviſible into more things, *ſuch* as it ſelf.) This, I ſay, premiſed,

Firſt, I deſire this Author to produce that Revelation, which declares the Three *Perſons* of the *Bleſſed Trinity*, to be Three *diſtinct Infinite Minds*, or *Spirits*. For I deny that there is any ſuch.

Secondly, I affirm, That whatſoever is a Truth in Natural Reaſon, cannot be contradicted by any other Truth declared by Revelation; ſince it is impoſſible for any one Truth to contradict another.

Upon which grounds, I here ask our Author, Is it a Contradiction *for One God to be One Infinite Mind*, or *Spirit, and to be alſo Three Infinite Minds*, or *Spirits?* If he grant this (as I have proved it, whether he does or no) then I ask him in the next place, Whether it be a Propoſition true in Natural Reaſon, [*That God is one Infinite Mind*, or *Spirit?*] If he grants this alſo, then I infer, That it cannot be proved true from Revelation, [*That God is Three Infinite Minds, or Spirits*,] ſince the certain Truth of the firſt Propoſition ſuppoſed and admitted muſt needs diſprove the Truth of that *Revelation*, which pretends to eſtabliſh the ſecond.

But

But ſome again may perhaps ask, Suppoſe it were revealed in *expreſs Terms*, [*That God is Three diſtinct Infinite Minds, or Spirits*,] would you in this caſe throw aſide this Revelation in ſubmiſſion to the former Propoſition declared by Natural Reaſon? I Anſwer, No: But if the Revelation were *expreſs* and undeniable, I would adhere to it; but at the ſame time, while I did ſo, I would quit the former Propoſition, and conclude, That Natural Reaſon had not diſcourſed right when it concluded, *That God was one Infinite Mind, or Spirit*: But to hold both Propoſitions to be True, and to aſſent to them both as ſuch, This the Mind of Man can never do.

So that, in a word, I conclude, That if it be certainly true from Reaſon, *That God is One Infinite Mind, or Spirit*. No Revelation can, or ought to be pleaded, *That he is Three diſtinct Infinite Minds, or Spirits*: And if Revelation cannot, or ought not to be pleaded for it, I am ſure, we have no ground to believe it. And yet at the ſame time I own and aſſert a Revelation of the truth of this Propoſition, [*That God is Three Perſons*,] or, which is all one, [*That God is Father, Son, and Holy Ghoſt*,] ſince it does not at all contradict the forementioned Propoſitions founded upon Natural Reaſon, [viz. *That God is One Infinite Mind, or Spirit*,] nor could it yet ever be proved to do ſo, either by *Arrians*, or *Socinians*. But on the contrary, theſe two Propoſitions, viz. [*God is One Infinite Mind, or Spirit*] and that other, [*God is Three diſtinct Infinite Minds, or Spirits*] (which he muſt be, if the Three *Divine Perſons* are Three *diſtinct Infinite Minds, or Spirits*) are Groſs, Palpable, and Irreconcileable Contradictions. And becauſe they are ſo, it is demonſtratively certain, *That the ſaid Three Perſons are not Three diſtinct Infinite Minds, or Spirits*: As this Author againſt all

all Principles of Philosophy and Divinity has most erroneously affirmed them to be.

I have said enough, I hope, upon this Subject. But before I quit it, it will not be amiss to observe what work this Man makes with the *Persons* of the *Blessed Trinity*, (as indeed he seldom almost turns his Pen, but he gives some scurvy stroke at it or other,) particularly in *Page* 89. he affirms, That the Expression of [*the One true God*, and *the only true God*] *cannot properly be attributed to the Son*, *nor to the Holy Ghost*. From whence I infer, That then neither can the Expression of [*God, or the True God*] be properly attributed to the *Son*, or to the *Holy Ghost*. Forasmuch as the Terms [*One God*] and [*One True God, or one only True God*] are equivalent. The Term [*One God*] including in it every whit as much as the Term [*One True God, or One only True God*] and the Term [*One True God, or One only True God*] including in it no more than the Term [*One God*;] and consequently if he asserts, That these Terms cannot with equal Propriety be attributed to, and predicated of the *Son* and the *Holy Ghost*, we have him both *Arrian* and *Macedonian* together in this Assertion.

And I believe his Adversary the *Author of the Notes* could hardly have desired a greater Advantage against him, than his calling it (as he does) *a Corruption of the* Athanasian *Creed*, to joyn the Term [*One True God*] to every *Person* of the *Trinity*; adding withal, That upon the doing so, *it would sound pretty like a Contradiction to say in the close* [*That there was but One True God.*] These are our Author's words, but much fitter to have proceeded from a *Socinian*, than from one professing a belief, and (which is more) *a defence* of the *Trinity*. But in answer to them, I tell him, That the repeated Attribution of [*The One True God, or only True God*] to each of the

the Three *Persons* is no Corruption of that Creed at all. Forasmuch as these Terms [*The One True God, and the only True God*] import, an Attribute purely Essential,and so equally, and in Common belonging to all the Three *Persons*, and not an *Attribute properly Personal*, and so appropriate to some one or other of the said *Persons*. And if this Author would have duly distinguished between *Essential* and *Personal* Attributes, he could not have discoursed of these Matters at so odd a rate, as here he does. And therefore I deny it to be any *Contradiction* (let it sound in his Ears how it will) to conclude, That the said Three *Persons* (notwithstanding this Repetition) *are not Three True Gods, but only One True God.* But he says, *That such a Repeated Application implies as if each Person considered as distinguished and separated from the other were the One True God.* To which I Answer,

1. *That to imply as if a thing were so*, and to imply, *that really it is so*, makes a very great difference in the case; indeed so great, that this Author must not think from words implying only the former to conclude the latter; which yet must be done,or what he here alledges is nothing to his purpose. But

2. I Answer yet farther, That the forementioned words do indeed *imply*, and (which is more) plainly declare, That the Three *Persons* who are said to be [*the One, or only True God*] are,while they sustain that Attribute, really distinct from one another, but it does not imply, That this is said of them under that peculiar *Formality, as they are distinct*, and much less, *as separated*; which latter they neither are, nor can be. The truth is, what he has said against the repeated Application of this Term to every one of the Three *Persons*, may be equally objected

objected against all the repeated Predications in the *Athanasian* Creed; but to as little purpose, one as the other; since, albeit all these Predications do agree to *Persons really distinct*, yet they agree not to them under that formal and precise consideration *as distinct*: For nothing but their respective Personal Relations agree to them under that Capacity; and this effectually clears off this Objection.

But here I cannot but wonder, that this Man should jumble together these two Terms [*distinguished* and *separated*] as he does twice here in the compass of eight Lines; when the signification of them, as it is applyed to the Three *Divine Persons*, is so vastly different, that one of these Terms [viz. *distinguished*] necessarily belongs to them, and the other which is [*separated*] neither does nor can take place amongst them: Nay, and when this Author himself has so earnestly and frequently contended for the difference of them; as all along asserting the *distinction of Persons*, and as often denying their *separation*.

But he proceeds, and says, That this Expression of [*The One* [*or only*] *True God*] *is never (that he knows of) attributed to Son, or Holy Ghost, either in Scripture, or any Catholick Writer*. Which words, methinks, (as I cannot but observe again) do not look, as if a Man were writing against the *Socinians*. Nevertheless admitting the Truth of his Allegation, *That this Term* [*the One True God*] *is not to be found expresly attributed to the Son, or the Holy Ghost*, will he infer from hence, that therefore it neither can, nor ought to be so? For if that be attributed to them both in Scripture and Catholick Writers, which necessarily and essentially implys [*The one True God*] and does, and must signifie the very same Thing, is it not all one, as if *in Terminis* it had been aſcribed to them? Doubtleſs there are ſeveral other Expreſſions in the *Athanaſian* Creed, as hardly (as this) to be found elſewhere: However, the Thing being certain from other words equivalent, this exception is of no force at all; nor by any one, who underſtands theſe Matters, is, or ought to be accounted ſo; and much leſs can I ſee to what end it ſhould be inſiſted upon by any one, while he is encountring the *Socinians:* And therefore, whereas he ſays, This Attribute, or Title, *viz.* [*The One True God*] *cannot* ſo properly *be aſcribed to any one Perſon*, *but only to the Father*; (whom, he tells us, the Fathers call *the Fountain of the Deity*) what he here deſigns by the words *ſo properly* (which ſeem to import degrees of Propriety) I cannot well tell: But this I ask, in ſhort, May it be *properly* attributed *to the Son,* and *to the Holy Ghoſt*, or may it not? If not; then they are not properly [*The One True God*] nor conſequently are they properly [*The True God*:] For whatſoever any *one properly is*, that he may be *properly ſaid to* be.

And as for [the Father's being *the Fountain of the Deity*,] I hope he looks upon this Expreſſion only as Metaphorical, and ſuch as ought not to be ſtretched to the utmoſt of its Native Sence, for fear the Conſequences of it may engage him too far, to be able to make an handſome Retreat; which I aſſure him, if he does not take heed, they certainly will. But, in a word, I demand of him, Whether [*the Father's being the Fountain of the Deity*] does appropriate and reſtrain the Thing expreſſed by the [*One True God*] to the *Father* in contra-diſtinction to the other Two *Perſons*, or not? If it does, then the ſame Abſurdity recurs, *viz.* [That neither *is the Son*, *nor the Holy Ghoſt*, *the One True God*] and conſequently, neither ſimply, really and eſſentially [*God.*]

But

But on the other ſide, if [*the Father's being the Fountain of the Deity*] does not appropriate the Thing ſignified by [*the One True God*] to the Father, then it leaves it common to the other Two Perſons with Himſelf, and to each of them. And whatſoever is ſo, may with the ſame Propriety and Truth of Speech be aſcribed to, and affirmed of them, as it is often aſcribed to, and affirmed of the *Father* Himſelf. The Truth is, this Man's adventurous and unwary way of expreſſing himſelf in this ſacred and arduous Subject, (to give it no worſe word, whatſoever it may deſerve) affords the *Arrians* and *Socinians* no ſmall Advantages againſt this Doctrine; ſhould it ſtand upon the ſtrength of His Defence, as (thanks be to *God*) it does not.

But I muſt not here omit that Paſſage, which, in the former part of this Chapter, I promiſed more particularly to conſider; a Paſſage, which indeed looks ſomething ſtrangely. It is that in *P.*258. *line* 27. where he tells us, that he allows, *That in the Bleſſed Trinity there are Three Holy Spirits*, but denys, *That there are Three Holy Ghoſts*; ſo natural is it for falſe Opinions to force Men to abſurd Expreſſions. But my Anſwer to him is ſhort and poſitive, That neither are there *Three Holy Spirits nor Three Holy Ghoſts* in the *Bleſſed Trinity* in any ſenſe properly belonging to theſe words. However, the Thing meant by him (ſo far as it is reducible to Truth and Reaſon) is, and muſt be this, *viz.* That when the Third *Perſon* of the *Trinity* is called the *Holy Ghoſt*, there the word *Holy Ghoſt* (which otherwiſe ſignifies the ſame with *Holy Spirit*) muſt be taken *Perſonally*, and conſequently *Incommunicably*; but when the *Father*, or *Son*, is ſaid to be a *Spirit*, or *Holy Spirit*, there *Spirit* muſt be underſtood *Eſſentially*, for that *Immaterial*, *Spiritual*, and *Divine Nature*, which is common to, and

Predicable of all the *Divine Persons.* All which is most true. But then, for this very Reason, I must tell our Author withal, That as *Holy Ghost* taken *Personally* is but *Numerically one*; so *Spirit*, or *Holy Spirit*, as it is understood *Essentially*, is but *Numerically one* too. And therefore, though the *Father* may be called a *Spirit*, or *Holy Spirit*, and the two other *Persons* may each of them be called so likewise, yet they are not therefore *Three distinct Spirits*, or *Holy Spirits*, nor can be truly so called (as this Author pretends they ought to be, and we have sufficiently disproved) but they are all one and the same *Holy Spirit Essentially* taken; and which so taken, is as much as *one and the same God.* And moreover, though *Spirit* understood *Personally* distinguishes the *Third Person* from the other two, yet taken *Essentially*, it speaks him *one* and the *same Spirit*, as well as *one* and the *same God* with them, and can by no means distinguish him from them, any more than the *Divine Essence*, or *Nature*, (which *Spirit*, in this sence, is only another word for) can discriminate the Three *Persons* from one another. So that upon the whole Matter, it is equally false and impossible, That in the *Blessed Trinity* there should be *Three Holy Spirits*, or *Holy Ghosts*, (Terms perfectly Synonymous) either upon a *Personal*, or an *Essential* account; and consequently that there should be so at all. For, as the word *Spirit* imports a peculiar Mode of *Subsistence*, by way of *Spiration* from the *Father* and the *Son*, so it is *Personal* and *Incommunicable*; but as it imports the *Immaterial Substance* of the *Deity*, so indeed (as being the same with the *Deity* it self) it is equally Common to all the Three *Persons*; but still, for all that, remains *Numerically one* and no more; as all must acknowledge the *Deity* to be. And this is the true state of the Case. But to state the difference between the *Holy Ghost*,

and

and the other Two *Perſons*, upon ſomething ſignified by *Holy Ghoſt*, which is not ſignified by *Holy Spirit*, (as the words of this Author manifeſtly do; while *he affirms Three Holy Spirits*, but *denies Three Holy Ghoſts*) this is not only *a playing with words* (which he pretends to ſcorn) but *a taking of words for things*; which, I am ſure, is very ridiculous.

And now, before I conclude this Chapter, (having a Debt upon me declared at the beginning of it) I leave it to the Impartial and Diſcreet Reader to judge, what is to be thought or ſaid of that Man, who in ſuch an Inſolent, Decretorious manner, ſhall in ſuch a point as this before us, charge *Nonſence* and *Hereſie*, (two very vile words) upon all that Subſcribe not to this his New (and before unheard of) Opinion. I muſt profeſs, I never met with the like in any Sober Author, and hardly in the moſt Licentious Libeller: The Nature of the Subject, I have, according to my poor Abilities, diſcuſſed, and finding my ſelf thereupon extremely to diſſent from this Author, am yet by no means willing to paſs for a Nonſenſical Heretick for my pains. For muſt it be Nonſence not to own Contradictions? viz. *That One Infinite Spirit is Three diſtinct Infinite Spirits?* Or muſt it be *Hereſie* not to Subſcribe to *Tritheiſme*, as the beſt and moſt Orthodox Explication of the Article of the *Trinity*? As for *Non-ſence*, it muſt certainly imply the aſſerting of ſomething for true concerning the Subject diſcourſed of, which yet in Truth is contradictory to it (ſince there can be no Non-ſence but what contradicts ſome Truth.) And whereas this Author has elſewhere, *viz.* *P.* 4. declared it *unreaſonable to charge a contradiction in any Thing, where the Nature of the Thing diſcourſed of is not throughly* comprehended *and underſtood*, I deſire to know of him, whether he throughly underſtands and comprehends

hends the Article and Mystery of the *Trinity?* If he says, he does, I need no other Demonstration of his unfitness to write about it. But if he owns that he does not, let him only stick to his own Rule, and then he may keep the Charge of *Non-sence* to himself.

But what shall we say to the Charge of Heresie, (in which St. *Austin* would have no Person, who is so charged to be silent?) Why, in the first place we must search and enquire, whether it be so, or no? And here, if my Life lay upon it, I cannot find either in *Ireneus adversùs Hæreses*, or in *Tertullian*'s *Prescriptions contra Hæreticos*, Cap. 49. Nor in *Philastrius*'s Catalogue, nor in *Epiphanius*, nor in St. *Austin*, nor in *Theodoret*, nor in *Johannes Damascenus*'s Book *de Hæresibus*; nor in the latter *Hæresiologists*, such as *Alphonsus à Castro & Prateolus*, with several others: I cannot, I say, find in all, or in any one of these the Heresie *of not asserting the Three Persons of the Blessed Trinity to be Three distinct Infinite Minds, or Spirits*; no, nor yet the Heresie *of denying them to be so.* But where then may we find it? Why, in this Author's Book. And therefore look no further; it is enough, that so great a *Master* has said it; whose Authority in saying a Thing, is as good as another Man's in proving it, at any time: And he says it (as we see) positively, and perhaps (if need be) will be ready to take his *Corporal Oath* upon it, That such as deny his Hypothesis are *Hereticks.*

Now in this case our Condition is, in good earnest, very sad; and I know nothing to comfort us, but that the Statute *de Hæretico comburendo* is Repealed. And well is it for the Poor Clergy and Church of *England*, that it is so; for otherwise this Man would have kindled such a Fire for them, as would have torrified them with a vengeance. But as he has stocked the Church with such plenty

plenty of New *Hereticks* (and all of his own making) ſo could he, by a ſway of Power, as *Arbitrary* as his *Divinity*, provide for them alſo ſuch a *Furnace* as that of *Nebuchadnezzar* (whom in his Imperious Meen and Humour he ſo much reſembles) yet he muſt not think, That the *Sound* and *Jingle* of *Self-Conſciouſneſs* and *Mutual-Conſciouſneſs* (how melodiouſly ſoever they may tinkle in his own Ears) will ever be able to Charm Men over to the Worſhip of his *Idol* ; or make them Sacrifice their Reaſon and Religion either to *Him*, or to the *New Notions* which he *has ſet up*. And indeed I cannot but here further declare, that to me it ſeems one of the moſt prepoſterous and unreaſonable things in Nature, for any one firſt to aſſert Three *Gods*, and when he has ſo well furniſhed the World with *Deities*, to expect that all Mankind ſhould fall down and Worſhip *Him*.

CHAP. VI.

In which is Considered, what this Author pretends to from the Authority of the Fathers *and* School-men, *in behalf of his Hypothesis; and shewn, in the first place, That neither do the* Fathers *own the Three* Divine Persons *to be Three Distinct* Infinite Minds, *nor* Self-Consciousness *to be the* Formal Reason *of their Distinction.*

I Have in the foregoing Chapters debated the Point with this Author, upon the Reason and Nature of the Thing it self. But that is not all, which he pretends to defend his Cause by; endeavouring to countenance it also with great Authorities; and that in these positive and remarkable words.

This is no New Notion (says he) *but the constant Doctrine both of the Fathers and the Schools*, Page 101.

These are his very words; and I desire the Reader carefully to consider, and carry them along with him in his Memory. For as they are as positive, as Confidence can make them: so if they are not made good to the utmost, they ought severely to recoil upon any one, who shall presume to express himself at such a Rate.

And

And now, that we may do him all the right that may be, The way to know, whether this Author's Hypothesis be the Constant Doctrine of the *Fathers* and *Schools*, is in the first place truly and fairly to set down, what this Author's Doctrine is, and wherein it does consist; as we shall declare, what the received Doctrine of the *Fathers* and *Schools* is, in our Eighth Chapter.

Now we shall find, That the whole Doctrine delivered by him concerning the *Blessed Trinity*, is comprehended under, and reducible to these four Heads.

First, That the Three *Persons* in the *Blessed Trinity*, are *Three distinct Infinite Minds*, or *Spirits*.

Secondly, That *Self-Consciousness* is the *Formal Reason* of *Personality*; and consequently that each of the *Divine Persons* is such by a *distinct Self-Consciousness* properly and peculiarly belonging to him.

Thirdly, That the Three *Divine Persons* being thus distinguished from one another by a *distinct Self-Consciousness* proper to each of them, are all United in one and the same Nature, by one *Mutual-Consciousness* Common to them all. And

Fourthly and Lastly, That a *Trinity in Unity*, and *an Unity in Trinity*, by this Explication and Account given of it, is a very *Plain*, *Easie and Intelligible Notion*.

These four Heads, or Particulars, I say, contain in them a full and fair representation of this Author's whole Hypothesis concerning the Oeconomy of the *Blessed Trinity*: And I am well assured, That the knowing and impartial Reader, neither will, nor can deny, that they do so.

In the next place therefore, that we may see how far our Author makes good all the said Particulars by the Authority of the *Fathers*, as he has peremptorily promised and undertook to do, I think it requisite to consider, how the *Fathers* expressed themselves upon this Subject, and how this Author brings the said Expressions to his purpose. For surely the natural way of knowing any Writer's Mind is by the Words and Expressions, which he pretends to deliver his Mind by. But concerning these we have our Author declaring,

First, That he has not troubled his Reader with the signification of *Essence, Hypostasis, Substance, Subsistence, Person, Existence, Nature,* &c. Pag. 101. and some of his Readers could give him a very good Reason why, though I fear too true for him to be pleased with. But the Reasons which he himself alledges for his not troubling his Readers either with these Terms, or the Explication of them, are,

First, *That they were very differently used by the Fathers themselves*, Page 101. And be it so; yet still for all that, *used by them* they were; and that not so very differently neither; the chief difference having been about the words οὐσία and ὑπόστασις, which yet was fairly accorded, and well nigh setled between the *Greeks* and the *Latines*, before the end of the 6th Century, as shall be further made to appear in our Eighth Chapter. And his next Reason for *his not troubling his Reader* (forsooth) with these Terms is, Because they have (as he tells us) *very much obscured the Doctrine of the Trinity, instead of explaining it*, Page 101. which being one of the Chief Things, which, he might conclude, would assuredly be disputed with Him; for Him thus to presume it, before he had proved it, is manifestly to beg the Question. In the mean time, certain it is, That these, and these only

were

were the Terms which the *Fathers* uſed in their Diſputes about the *Trinity*, and by which they mannaged them; and conſequently, were they never ſo *Ambiguous*, *Faulty*, or *Improper* (as they are much the contrary) yet, whoſoever will pretend to give the Sence of the *Fathers*, muſt have recourſe to them, and do it by them; and to do otherwiſe would be to diſpute at Rovers, or (as the word is) *to ſpeak without Book*; which may much better become our Author in the Pulpit, than in the mannagement of ſuch a Controverſie.

And now let the Reader (whom he is ſo *fearful of troubling* with any Thing that is to the Purpoſe) judge, Whether this Man has not took a moſt extraordinary *way of proving his Doctrine the very ſame with the Fathers*. For neither in the firſt place does he ſet down, what the Doctrine of the *Fathers* concerning the *Trinity* was; which yet, one would have thought, was abſolutely neceſſary for the ſhewing how his own Doctrine agreed with it, which he profeſſed to be his deſign: Nor, in the next place, does he either *uſe*, *or regard*, or offer to explain thoſe Terms, which the *Fathers* all along delivered that their Doctrine in; but is ſo far from it, *That he reproaches*, *explodes*, *and utterly rejects them*, *as ſerving only to obſcure this Doctrine*, *inſtead of explaining it*: Which, in my poor Judgment, is ſuch a way of proving the *Fathers* on his ſide, as perhaps the World never heard of before, and will be amazed at now. But it is *his way*, and it will not be long before we find him beſtowing a like caſt of his kindneſs upon the *School-men* too.

But ſince, notwithſtanding all this, He allows the *Fathers* (good Men) to have *meant well*, and taught right; albeit, by reaſon of a certain Infelicity and Awkwardneſs they had in repreſenting *what they meant*, *by what they wrote*, their *meaning* ought, by no means, to be gathered from their *own words* (as, possibly also for the introducing a new and laudable Custom amongst the *Fathers* and *Sons* of the Church, that the *Sons* must teach the *Fathers* to speak) our Author has, for these and the like Reasons, in great Charity and Compassion to their Infirmities, provided two other and better words of his own Invention, viz. *Self-Consciousness*, and *Mutual-Consciousness*, by which alone the True Sense and Doctrine of the Fathers, in all their Writings about this Article of the *Trinity*, may, or can be understood.

Nevertheless how kind soever this design of his may be, yet to me it seems very unreasonable. For, in the first place, it is, (upon the most allowed grounds of Reason) a just, and a sufficient Presumption, that the *Fathers* were wholly Strangers to what our Author intends by these two words, for that they never so much as mention, or make use of the words themselves: Whereas, *to be Self-Conscious, and Mutually-Conscious*, were things (no doubt) easie enough, not only for the *Fathers*, but for any Man else of Common Sense to find out and understand; and they might also, without much difficulty, have been applyed to the *Divine Nature*, as well as other Acts *of Knowledge*; and therefore since the *Fathers* never used them in this case, it is but too plain, that they never thought them fit, or proper for this purpose. For the *Arrian* Controversie was then, *viz.* in the 4th and 5th Centuries (in which also the most Eminent of the *Fathers* wrote against it) at the Highest. Among which Writers, *Gregory Nyssen* (whom this Author so often quotes) has a Passage, which, in this case, is to me very remarkable, and a Rational ground to conclude, that he knew nothing of *Mutual-Consciousness*, as it is here applyed by this Author. For that, speak-

speaking of the Unity of the *Divine Persons*, in respect of one *Common* (though *Single*) Nature, he expresses it by κοινότης κατὰ τὴν οὐσίαν, instead of which, certainly he could not have chosen a more apposite and proper place to have expressed the same by a κοινότης κατὰ τὴν Συνείδησιν, had that *Father* had the same Notion of it, which this Author so much contends for. But it seems, he was either *less Happy*, or more judicious in this Particular. And besides all this, it is most worthy to be Noted, That the very Terms in which the Orthodox Writers expressed themselves about the *Trinity*, and whatsoever related to it, were severely canvased and examined, and some of them settled by Councils; which is a fair Proof, that the said Terms were fixed and authentick, and exclusive of all others, and consequently of those of this Author, as well as of the Notion signified by, and couched under them, which he would here with such Confidence obtrude upon the World, by and from the Credit of the *Fathers*, tho' their Writings demonstrate, that they were wholly unconcerned, both as to his Doctrines, and his Expressions.

— οὔτε τὸ κατὰ τὴν οὐσίαν κοινότητος τὸ ἰδιάζον τῶν γνωρισμάτων ἀναχέεσθαι. Greg. Nyssen. de differentiâ οὐσίας καὶ ὑποστάσεως. Tom. 2. P. 455. Edit. Paris. 1515.

Nor can any Want, or Penury of words be here pleaded for their silence in this Matter, since the *Greek* being so happy, above all other Languages, in joyning and compounding words together; in all probability had *the Fortunes of Greece* (as the word is) been concerned in the case, we might have heard of some such words, as, αὐτοσυνείδησις, and κοινοσυνείδησις. Or since most such words, as in *English* terminate in *-ness*, usually in the *Greek* terminate in -μος, possibly we might have met with some such made-words, as, αὐτοσυνειδησμὸς, and κοινοσυνειδησμὸς, since these do more properly import *Consciousness* than the former; which rather signifie *Self-*

Conscience

Conscience and *Mutual-Conscience*, and so in, strictness of Speech, differ something from the other. But he who seeks in the *Greek Fathers* for these words, or any thing like them (as applyed to the *Trinity)* may seek longer than his Eyes can see.

Nor will his Inquest succeed at all better amongst the *Latines*. For although that Language be extremely less copious than the other, and so affords no one *Latine* word either for *Self-Consciousness*, or *Mutual-Consciousness*, but what we must first *make*, and being *made* would sound very barbarously; yet, no doubt, there were ways and words enough to have otherwise expressed the same thing, had they found it the fittest and best Notion to have expressed this great Article by. But no such thing or word occurs in any of their Writings.

But why do I speak of the *Greek* and *Latine Fathers?* When the very *School-men*, the boldest Framers and Inventors of Words and Terms, of all others, where they think them necessary to express their Conceptions by, notwithstanding all their *Quiddities*, *Hæcceities*, and *Perseities*, and the like, have yet no word for *Self-Consciousness* and *Mutual-Consciousness*: which is a sufficient Demonstration, that either the thing it self never came into their Heads; or (which is most likely) that they never thought it of any use for the explication of this Mystery, which yet they venture further at, than any other Writers whatsoever.

But after all; though this Author is very much concerned to ward off the charge of Novelty and Singularity from his Notions, (for which I cannot blame him; this being a charge sufficient to confound and crush any such Notion applyed to so Sacred and received an Article as the *Trinity)* and for this cause is not a little desirous to shelter it with the Authority of the *Fathers*; yet I assure

ſure the Reader, That he is no leſs careful and concerned to keep the Glory of the Invention wholly to himſelf,and would take it very ill either of *Fathers*, *School-men*, or any one elſe, ſhould they offer to claim the leaſt ſhare in it. For he roundly tells us, That the *Fathers were not ſo happy as to hit upon his way of explaining this Myſtery*, Page 126. Line 5. nay, and that, how right a Judgment ſoever they might have of it, yet in down-right Terms, *That they knew not how to explain it*, Page 126. Line 18. which, I confeſs, is no ſmall Complement paſſed upon himſelf (a thing which he is ſeldom or never failing in) but, in good earneſt, a very courſe one upon the *Fathers*. In ſhort, he would appropriate the *Credit* of the *New Invention* entirely to himſelf, but with admirable, and more than Metaphyſical Abſtraction, at the ſame time clear himſelf of the *Novelty of it*; and ſo, in a word, prove it of at leaſt 12 or 13 hundred years ſtanding in the World; when yet the Author of it was Born ſince *Conventicles* began in *England*, as is well known. But I frankly yield him the Invention, as perfectly his own; and ſuch an one too, as he is more like to be known by, than ever admired for; and ſo, much happineſs attend him with it.

But as little ſucceſs as we have had in ſeeking for his Darling and peculiar Notion of *Self-Conſciouſneſs* and *Mutual-Conſciouſneſs*, in the Ancient Writers of the Church, we are like to find no more in ſeeking for his other equally eſpouſed Notion and Opinion there, *viz.* That the Three *Perſons* of the *Bleſſed Trinity are Three diſtinct Infinite Minds, or Spirits*: We find indeed the Terms πρόσωπα, ὑποστάσεις, ἰδιότητες, γνωρίσματα, &c. but not one Tittle of τρία πνεύματα, or τρεῖς οὐσίαι, except where οὐσία (as I hinted before) is ſometimes uſed in the ſame ſenſe and ſignification with ὑπόστασις. And in this

caſe

caſe (I am ſure) no difficulty of framing Words, or Terms (as might poſſibly in ſome meaſure be pretended in the Caſe of *Self-Conſciouſneſs*) can with any colour of Reaſon be alledged for our not finding this Notion in the *Fathers*, had the thing it ſelf been at all there. For can there be any words more Obvious, and Familiar than τρία πνεύματα, or τρεῖς Νόες, in the *Greek*, or than *Tres Spiritus*, or *tres Mentes*, in the *Latine?* But neither one nor the other are to be met with any where amongſt them, as applyed to the Subject now before us.

But in Anſwer to this, I expect that our Author will reply, That they are not the words [*Three diſtinct Infinite Minds, or Spirits*] or thoſe other [of *Self-Conſciouſneſs* and *Mutual-Conſciouſneſs*] but the Things meant and ſignified by them, which he affirms to be found in the *Fathers*. But this is the very Thing which I inſiſt upon againſt him, *viz.* That the Non-uſage of theſe words, (nor any other equivalent to them) in the Works of thoſe Ancient Writers, (while they were ſo particularly, and nicely diſputing this Matter) is a ſolid Argument, That neither are the things themſelves there. For that all thoſe Great and Acute Men ſhould mean the very ſame thing with this Author, and not one of them ever light upon the ſame words, is not rationally to be imagined. For, What Reaſon can be given of this? Was either the Thing it ſelf (as I noted before) of ſuch deep, or ſublime Speculation, as not to be reached by them? Or the Language, they wrote in, too ſcanty to expreſs their Speculations by? Or can we think that the *Fathers* wrote *Things* without *Words*, as ſome do but too often write *Words* without *Things?* So that to me it is evident to a Demonſtration, That the *Fathers* never judged, nor held in this Matter, as this Author pretends they did: And beſides all this, there is yet one Conſideration more, and that

that of greater weight with me, than all that has been, or can be objected against this Man's pretensions, *viz.* That it seems to me, and I question not but to all Sober Persons else, (and that upon good reason) wholly unsutable to the wise and good Method of *God's Providence*, That a clear Discovery of such a Principal Mystery of the *Christian Religion, as the Trinity* is, should now at length be owing to the Invention, or lucky Hit of any one Man's single Mind, or Fancy; which so many Pious, Humble, as well as Excellently Learned Persons, with long and tedious search, and the hardest study, (and these, no doubt, joyned with frequent and fervent Prayers to *God,* to enlighten and direct them in that search) have been continually breathing after, but could never attain to for above Sixteen Hundred Years together. This, I freely own and declare, That I judge it morally impossible for any serious, thinking Person, ever to bring himself to the belief of; and much less for any one, not Intoxicated with intolerable Pride, to arrogate to Himself. To which sort of Persons *God* never reveals any thing extraordinary for the good of the World, or of themselves either.

But, since I am now upon *Disputation*, which has its proper Laws, and that this Author may have no ground of Exception, I will proceed to examine his Quotations out of the *Fathers*, and try whether his *Hypothesis* may be found there, where, it is certain, that we can find none of his Terms.

And here, he first begins with the Distinction of the *Divine Persons*, where I must remind him, That it is not the bare proving a *Distinction of Persons* (which none, who acknowledges a *Trinity*, either doubts of, or much less, denies) which will here serve his turn; but He must prove also, That they stand distinguished as

Three diſtinct Infinite Minds, or Spirits, and that this Diſtinction is owing to Three *diſtinct Self-Conſciouſneſſes* belonging to them; otherwiſe all his Proofs will fall beſide his *Hypotheſis.*

This premiſed, I will conſider what he alledges. And in the firſt place he poſitively tells us, *Page* 101. *That no Man who acknowledges a Trinity of Perſons, ever denied, That the Son and Holy Spirit were Intelligent Minds, or Beings.* To which I Anſwer,

Firſt, That it is not ſufficient for him, who advances a Controverted Propoſition, that none can be produced, who before denied it; but it lies upon him the Advancer of it, to produce ſome who have affirmed it. Foraſmuch as a bare non-denial of a Thing, never before affirmed, can of it ſelf neither prove nor diſprove any Thing. But

Secondly, I Anſwer further, That if none of the Ancient Writers did ever, in expreſs Terms, deny this, it was becauſe none had before in expreſs Terms aſſerted it. But then I add alſo, That the *Ancients* have expreſly aſſerted that, which irrefragably infers a Negation of the ſaid Propoſition: For they have affirmed, *That the Son and Holy Spirit are one ſingle Intelligent Mind,* and conſequently that being ſo, they cannot poſſibly *be more.* And this is a full Anſwer to this ſorry ſhift; for an Argument, I am ſure, it deſerves not to be called.

But he proceeds from Negatives to Poſitives, and tells us, Page 101. *That it is the Conſtant Language of the Fathers* (for it ſeems, he has read them all) *That the Son is the Subſtantial Word and Wiſdom of the Father, and that this can be nothing elſe, but to ſay, That he is an Intelligent Being, or Infinite Mind.* And he is ſo, I confeſs. But does this infer, That He is therefore *a diſtinct Intelligent Mind, or Being from the Father?* This we deny, and

and it is the very Thing, which he ought to prove. And it is not come to that pass yet, that we should take his bare affirmation for a Proof of what he affirms.

He comes now to Particulars, and tells us, That *Gregory Nyssen* (though since he neither mentions Book nor Page, this ought not to pass for a Quotation) calls the Son νοερόν τι χρῆμα, which this Author renders *Mind, or Intellect*: And I will not deny, but that it may, by consequence, import so much; but I am sure it does not by direct Signification. Νοερόν τι χρῆμα, signifies properly, *Res quædam Intellectualis*, or *Intellectu prædita*: And since nothing is so, but a *Mind*, or *Spirit*, it may (as I have said) imply a *Mind*, but it does not directly signifie it. But admitting that it does both; does this expression prove, That the Son is a νοερόν τι χρῆμα, *distinct* from the *Father*? By no means: For not only the *Son*, but the *Father* may be called, Νοερόν τι χρῆμα, and the *Holy Ghost*, Νοερόν τι χρῆμα, and yet they are not Three Νοερὰ χρήματα, but ἓν νοερὸν χρῆμα. And the Reason of this is, because Νοερὸν χρῆμα, is an *Essential Attribute* following the *Divine Nature*, and therefore common to all the Three *Persons*, and not a *Personal Attribute* peculiar to any one of them. So that granting the *Son* to be as truly and properly νοερόν τι χρῆμα, as this Author would have him, yet we absolutely deny, That he is a *distinct* νοερὸν χρῆμα, from the *Father*. And this Expression, I am sure, is far enough from proving him to be so.

From *Nyssen*, he passes to St. *Athanasius*, who (he tells us) observes out of these words of our Saviour, *John* 10. 30. ἐγὼ καὶ πατὴρ ἕν ἐσμεν, that our Saviour does not say, ἐγὼ καὶ πατὴρ ἕν εἰμι, but ἕν ἐσμεν, and that, by so speaking, he gave us a perfect *Duality of Persons* in the word ἐσμεν, and an *Unity of Nature* in the word ἕν.

All which is very true, and that this distinction of *Persons* overthrows the *Heresie* of *Sabellius*; and the Unity of their Nature, the *Heresie* of *Arius*. But then this is also as true, that all this is nothing at all to our Author's Purpose. For how does this prove, either that the Three *Divine Persons* are *Three distinct Infinite Minds, or Spirits?* Or, that *Self-Consciousness* is the proper ground, or Reason of their distinction? Why, yes, (says He) *If the Father be an Eternal Mind and Wisdom, then the Son is also an Eternal, but begotten Mind and Wisdom.* Very true; but still I deny, that it follows hence, *That the Eternal Mind, or Wisdom, Begetting, and the Eternal Mind, or Wisdom Begotten, are Two distinct Minds, or Wisdoms,* but *only one and the same Mind, or Wisdom,* under these *Two distinct Modifications of Begetting* and *being Begot.*

But he pretends to explain and confirm his Notion of a *distinct Mind, or Wisdom,* out of those words of the *Nicene Creed,* in which the *Son is said to be God of God, Light of Light, very God of very God.*

By which words, I cannot imagine, how this Author thinks to serve his turn; Unless that by *Light* must be meant *Infinite Wisdom,* or *Infinitely Wise Mind,* and that this must also infer the *Father* and *Son* to be *Two distinct Infinitely wise Minds, or Wisdoms,* one issuing from the other.

But if so; then the same words will, and must infer them also to *be Two distinct Gods, and very Gods.* For all these words stand upon the same level in the same Sentence; and then, if we do but joyn the Term [*Distinct*] equally with every one of them, we shall see what Monstrous Blasphemous Stuff will be drawn out of this Creed.

In

In the mean time let this Author know once for all, *That Light of Light* imports not here *Two distinct Lights*; but *one Infinite Light under Two different ways of Subsisting*, viz. either *of* and *from it self*, as it does in the *Father*, or of and from another, as it does *in the Son*. All which is plainly and fully imported in and by the Particle [*of*] signifying properly *Derivation*, or *Communication* in the thing which it is applyed to. And this is the clear undoubted sense of the Word, as it is used here. In the mean time, I hope the *Arrians* and *Socinians* will joyn in a Letter of Thanks to this Author, for making such an Inference from the *Nicene Creed*.

In the next place, he comes to St. *Austin*; where, though I am equally at a loss to find how he proves his Point by him, any more than by those whom he has already produced; yet I will transcribe the whole Quotation into the Margin, that so both the Reader may have it under his Eye, and the Author have no cause to complain, that he is not fairly dealt with.

Quæ ratiocinatio ad id cogit, ut dicamus Deum Patrem non esse sapientem nisi habendo sapientiam quam genuit non existendo per se pater sapientia. Deinde si ità est, Filius quoque ipse, sicut dicitur, *Deus de Deo*, *Lumen de Lumine*, videndum est utrùm possit *Sapientia de Sapientiâ* dici, si non est Deus pater ipsa sapientia, sed tantùm Genitor sapientiæ. Quod si tenemus, cur non & magnitudinis suæ, & bonitatis, & æternitatis, & omnipotentiæ suæ Generator sit? ut non ipse sit sua magnitudo, & sua bonitas, & sua æternitas, & sua Omnipotentia, sed eâ magnitudine magnus sit, quam genuit, & eâ bonitate bonus, &c. Aug. Tom. 3. Lib. 6. de Trinitate.

Now that which he would infer from thence, seems to be this, That *God the Father* is *Infinitely Wise*, by a Wisdom of his own distinct from that Wisdom by which the *Son* is called *The Wisdom of the Father*; and consequently, that they are *Two distinct Infinite Wisdoms*, or *Infinitely Wise Minds*. This, I say, is that, which he would infer, and argue from St. *Austin*, or I know not what else it can be.

But

But this is by no means deducible from his words: for the *Father* is wise by one and the same *Infinite Wisdom* equally belonging both to the *Father* and the *Son*, but not by it under that peculiar Formality, *as it belongs to the Son.* For it belongs to the *Son*, as *Communicated to Him*; whereas it belongs to the *Father*, as *Originally in and from Himself.*

And whereas it is objected, *That if the Father should be Wise by the Wisdom which he Begot, then he could not be said to be Wise by a Wisdom of his own, but only by a Begotten Wisdom proper to the Son.* I Answer, That neither does this follow; since it is but one and the same *Essential Wisdom* in both, *viz.* in him who Begets, and in him who is Begotten: Though [*as*] *it is in him* who is Begotten, it is not *after the same way* in Him who Begets: So that it is this determining Particle [*as*, or *Quatenus*] which by importing a distinction of the *manner*, causes a quite different application of the Term, while the Thing is still the same. For the *Father* himself is not denominated *Wise*, even by that very *Wisdom* that is *Essential* to *Him*, considered as *Personally determined* to the *Son*; for so it must be considered as *Derived* and *Communicated*, and no *Divine Perfection* can agree to the *Father* under the Formal Consideration of [*Derived* and *Communicated*] albeit the Thing it self, *which is Derived* and *Communicated*, absolutely considered, may and does. In a word, the *Father* is Wise by one and the same Wisdom, which is both in himself and in his Son, but not by it, *as it is in the Son.*

But, by the way, it is worth observing, That this Man who here in the 102 and 103 Pages denies *the Father to be Wise by this Begotten Wisdom*, which the Son is here called (and which, in the Sense we have now given of it, is very true) and alledges St. *Austin* and *Lombard* to abett

abett him in it. This very Man, I ſay, *Page* 131. *Line* 24. affirms, That the Son is that *Wiſdom* and *Knowledge, wherewith his Father knows himſelf.* Where, *If for the Father to be Wiſe and to know himſelf* be formally the ſame Act, and as much the ſame as his *Wiſdom* and *Knowledge* can be, as it is manifeſt, they are; then, I leave it to this Author to tell us, which of theſe two Aſſertions is falſe; for both of them, I am ſure, cannot be true. But he who makes nothing to contradict himſelf within the compaſs of two or three Pages (and ſometimes as many Lines) may do it *cum Privilegio* at the diſtance of near Thirty.

And whereas it is urged again from the ſame place in St. *Auſtin, That if we ſay the Father begets his own Wiſdom, we may as well ſay, That he Begets his own Goodneſs, Greatneſs, Eternity,* &c.

I Anſwer, No doubt but we may ſay one as well as the other, but that in Truth and Propriety of Speech, we can ſay neither. For *God* cannot properly be ſaid *to beget Wiſdom,* and much leſs *his own Wiſdom,* nor indeed any of his other Attributes, or Perfections *Eſſentially* taken and conſidered; he may indeed be ſaid to *Communicate them,* and by ſuch *Communication* to *Beget a Son.* But ſtill, though theſe are thus ſaid to be *Communicated,* it is the *Perſon only,* who is, or can be properly ſaid to be *Begotten.*

But our Author tells us, *Page* 103. out of the next Chapter of St. *Auſtin* (the words of which he ſhould have done well to have quoted) that he there calls *God the Father, Sapientia Ingenita,* and the *Son, Sapientia Genita,* and are not theſe *Two diſtinct Infinite Wiſdoms?*

I Anſwer, No: For that the Wiſdom here ſpoken of, is not taken *Abſolutely and Eſſentially,* but *only Perſonally:* That is, for *Wiſdom* under two ſeveral Modifications; which

which Modifications, though they *diversifie* and *distinguish* the Thing they belong to, yet do not *multiply* it. For still it is one and the same *Wisdom*, which is both *Genita*, and *Ingenita*, though *as it is one*, it is not the *other*. *Sapientia*, or *Wisdom*, considered *Absolutely* and *Essentially* in it self, belongs in Common to all the *Three Persons*; but with the Term *Genita*, or *Ingenita* joyned with it, it imports a peculiar *Mode* of *Subsistence*, which determines it to a particular *Personality*: So that *Sapientia quatenus Genita* properly and only denotes the *Person* of the *Son*. In like manner when the *Third Person* of the *Trinity* is called the *Spirit*, The Term *Spirit* is not there taken *Essentially* for that *Infinite Immaterial Incorporeal Nature*, *Absolutely* considered (for so it is common to all the Three *Persons*) but for that *Infinite Incorporeal Nature*, *Quatenus procedens aut spirata*, and under that peculiar *Mode* of *Subsistence*, it belongs not to the other Two *Persons*, but stands appropriate only *to the Third*. Nevertheless this makes them not *Three distinct Infinite Spirits* (as we have already shewn) but only one *Infinite Spirit* under *Three distinct Modalities*. Accordingly, when the *Son* is here called *the Wisdom of the Father*, that very Term [*of the Father*] imports a Modification of it peculiar to the *Son*, but yet this Modification does not make it *another Wisdom*, from that which is in the *Father*; since one and the same *Wisdom* may sustain several determining *Modes*.

Our Author's next Quotation is out of *Peter Lombard*, *Page* 103. whom (for the Credit of what he Quotes from him) he styles *the Oracle of the Schools* (though he, who shall read *Lambertus Danæus* upon the first Book of his Sentences, will quickly find what a Doughty Oracle he is.) The Passage quoted, proceeds upon the same Notion which we find in the foregoing Citation out of

St. *Austin*,

St. *Austin*, whom he also alledges for it. Nevertheless, I shall Transcribe this also, as I did the other, both for the Choice Stuff contained in it, as also that the Reader may have it before him, and thereby see, what use our Author is able to make of it for his purpose.

——Sed absit ut ità sit; [viz. *That the Father should be wise only by the Wisdom he Begets*] quia si hoc est ibi *esse* quod *sapere*, non per illam sapientiam quam genuit sapiens dicitur Pater, alioquin non ipsa ab illo sed ille ab ipsâ est. Si enim sapientia quam genuit causa est illi ut sapiens sit, etiam ut *sit* ipsa illi causa est; quod fieri non potest nisi gignendo eum, aut faciendo: Sed nec genitricem nec conditricem Patris ullo modo quisquam dixerit Sapientiam. Quid enim insanius? &c. Lib. 1. *Dist.* 32. *Cap.* 3.

First of all then, he tells us, *That in God* to be, *and* to be *Wise, is the same thing*. And I grant it, with respect to the Absolute Simplicity of the *Divine Nature*: but, for all that, I must tell him, That *to Be, and to be Wise*, fall under two formally distinct Conceptions, of which the former does not include the latter; and that for this Reason, such as treat Scholastically of these Matters, do always allow *a formal difference* between them, and never treat of them, but as so considered. And let me tell him also, that this Consideration looks yet something further; as inferring, That Things *formally* distinct, must have *formally* distinct Effects; so that the *formal* effect of one cannot be ascribed to the other. And moreover, that it is a very gross Absurdity to confound the *Formal Cause with the Efficient*, and so, to argue from one, as you would do from the other.

Which Observations being thus laid down, let us see how this Man and his Oracle argue in the Case. And it is thus.

If the Wisdom which He [*viz.* God the Father] *Begets, be the cause of his being wise, then it is the cause also of his very Being.*

In Answer to which, I deny the Consequence. For that, Wisdom is the cause of one's being Wise only *by a formal Causality*, viz. by Existing in Him, and affecting him in such a particular way; and this it does without being the Cause also of his *Existence*, that being a Thing formally distinct from his *Being Wise*: And therefore, though Wisdom, I grant, must presuppose the Existence of the Subject, where it has this effect: Yet it does not *formally* cause it; or rather indeed, for this very reason, cannot possibly do so.

But he proceeds and argues further, viz. *That supposing the Wisdom Begotten by the Father were the Cause both of his* Being, *and of his* being Wise, *then it must be so either by Begetting, or Creating him* (for so I Interpret *Conditricem*) but for *one to say, That Wisdom is any way the Begetter, or Maker of the Father, would be the heighth of Madness.*

It would be so indeed. And so on the other side to attempt to prove the *Father* and the *Son* to be Two *distinct Infinite Minds* by such strange, odd, uncouth Notions as these, which St. *Austin* himself (particularly treating of them in his 7 and 15 Books *de Trinitate*) confesses to be *Quæstiones inextricabiles*, this, I say, (whatsoever may *be the height of Madness*) is certainly not *the height of Discretion.* Nevertheless, as to the Argument it self, I deny the Consequence. And that because the *Begetting*, or any otherwise *Producing* a Thing imports a Cause operating by a proper Efficiency, or Causality; whereas Wisdom, being only the *formal Cause* of one's being Wise, (as it would be no other, could it be the Cause of one's very Being also) operates only by an Internal, Improper Causality, *viz.* in a word, *Wisdom* makes one *Wise*, as Whiteness makes a Thing White, not by producing any Thing in him, but by Existing in

him,

him, and affecting him by it self, after such a certain manner, and thereby giving him such a certain Denomination.

Now from hence let any one judge how forcibly and Philosophically this Man Disputes; the Truth is, were the whole Argument Conclusive, it were nothing to his purpose. But I was willing to shew, That his way of arguing is as defective, as the Thing he Argues for is Absurd.

Neverthelefs let us see, what the main Conclusion is, which he would draw from the Premisses. Why, it is this, *That the Father is Eternal Wisdom, or Mind, and the Son Eternal Wisdom and Mind.* I give you his very Terms. And who denies this? Or what does it conclude for him? For still I ask, Does he who says, That the *Father is Eternal Wisdom, or Mind*, and the *Son Eternal Wisdom and Mind*, by saying so, affirm, That the *Father* and the *Son* are *Two distinct Eternal Wisdoms*, or *Minds?* Any more than he who says, That the *Father* is *God*, and the *Son God*, affirms them to be *Two distinct Gods?* Let him say it if he can; and he shall not fail of a through Confutation as soon as it can be Printed off.

But to give the *Reader* an Account of the whole matter in short. This Author has espoused a very Heterodox and dangerous Notion, viz. *That the Three Persons of the Blessed Trinity, are Three distinct Infinite Minds, or Spirits*; and, in order to the proof of this, would perswade us, That there are *Two distinct Wisdoms*, one in the *Father*, and the other in the *Son*; and that, for this *Reason*: Because the *Father*, who is *Essentially Wise*, cannot be said to be *Wise* by *that begotten Wisdom, which is in the Son* (albeit the *Son* be yet said to be *the Wisdom of the Father*) but that the *Father* must have one *distinct*

Wisdom of his own, and the *Son* another *distinct Wisdom* of his own. This, I am sure, is the full Account of his Argument from top to bottom. In Answer to which, I have plainly and undeniably shewn, That the *Father* is Wise by one and the same *Essential Wisdom*, common to *Father*, *Son*, and *Holy Ghost*, though not under that particular Modification, as it Subsists in the other Two *Persons*, but by that peculiar Modification, by which it is appropriated to, and Subsists in his own. And that those different Modifications do not, for all that, make it any more than one single Numerical Wisdom, but only one and the same under so many *distinct Modes* of *Subsistence*, determining it to so many *distinct Personalities*.

This is the Sum both of his Opinion and of mine, and I refer it to the Judicious Reader to arbitrate the Case between us, with this profession and promise, that if in all, or any one of the Quotations alledged by him he can shew, That it is either expresly affirmed, or necessarily implyed, *That the Father and the Son are Two distinct Infinite Minds*, I will, without further proof of any sort, forthwith yield him the Cause, and withal renounce all my poor share in Common Sense and Reason; nay, and all belief of my own Eyes for the future.

But there is one Clause more, which he brings in as one part of his main Conclusion, *Page* 103. *Line* 33. viz. *That if we confess this of the Father and the Son*, to wit, That they are each of them *Eternal Mind*, or *Wisdom*, *there can be no dispute about the Holy Ghost who is Eternal Mind, and Wisdom, distinct both from Father and Son.*

Now this is perfectly *gratis dictum*, without either proof, or pretence of proof; and that whether we respect the Orthodox, or the Heterodox and Heretical. And,

First,

First, For the Orthodox, they utterly deny the *Holy Ghost* to be an *Eternal Mind*, or *Wisdom* distinct both from the *Father* and the *Son*; and I challenge this Author to produce me but one reputed *Orthodox Writer*, who affirms it. In the mean time, it argues no small Confidence (to give it the mildest Term) in this Man to Assert that *as certain, and without Dispute*, which is neither granted on one side, nor so much as pretended to be proved on the other. But

Secondly, If we respect the Heterodox and Heretical, who (no doubt) *can dispute* as much as others, will this Man say, That these also grant this his Assertion about the *Holy Ghost without any dispute*? No, it is certain, that they neither do, nor will. For this Author may be pleased to observe, That as some in the *Primitive Times*, allowed the Son to be only *like the Father*; so they made the *Holy Ghost* a downright *Creature*, and an inferiour Agent to Both. Such were the Πνευματομάχοι under their Head and Leader *Macedonius*; as we see in St. *Austin de Heresibus*, Cap. 52. hereby placing him as much below the *Son*, as they had placed the *Son* below the *Father*; or rather more. Whereupon, I appeal even to this Author Himself, whether those, who did so, would *without all dispute* have allowed the *Holy Ghost* to be an *Eternal Infinite Mind, or Wisdom*, distinct both from the *Father* and the *Son*; and, upon that Account, Essentially and Necessarily equal to them Both? Let this Author rub his Fore-head, and affirm this if he can; and for the future take notice, That it becomes a True and Solid Reasoner, where a Thing is disputed, fairly to prove it, and not boldly and barely to presume it.

In the last place he alledges the Judgment of *all* the *Fathers* indefinitely in the Case. And truly where he cannot cite so much as one of them to the purpose, I think

think he does extremely well to make ſhort work of it, and with one bold Impertinent ſtroke to alledge them *all* together.

His Allegation is this, *That it is uſual with the Fathers to repreſent the Three Perſons in the Bleſſed Trinity as diſtinct as* Peter, James, *and* John. Well; and what then? Why; *That then the ſaid Three Perſons are Three diſtinct Infinite Minds, or Spirits.* I deny the Conſequence, and to give a particular Anſwer to his general Allegation, I tell him, That it is a Fallacy of the *Homonomy of the Word*, and that the Term [*as diſtinct*] is Ambiguous. For it may either ſignifie,

1. *As Real.* Or,

2. *As Great* a Diſtinction.

As for the firſt, I grant, That the *Three Perſons* in the *Bleſſed Trinity differ as really* as *Peter*, *James*, and *John*; Foraſmuch as they differ by ſomething in the Thing *it ſelf*, or, *ex parte rei*, antecedent to, and independent upon any Apprehenſion, or Operation of the Mind about it; which is a *Real difference*, and whatſoever is ſo, is altogether *as Real* as the Difference between one Man and another can be. But,

Secondly, If by *Real* diſtinction be meant as *great a diſtinction*, ſo we utterly deny that the *Three Divine Perſons* differ as much as *Peter*, and *James*, and *John* do, or that the *Fathers* ever thought they did ſo. For this would infer a greater difference, or diſtinction between them, than even our Author himſelf will allow of; even ſuch a difference, as reaches to a *Diviſion*, or *Separation* of the *Perſons* ſo differing. And ſince it is impoſſible for the *Perſons* of the *Trinity* to differ ſo, it is hard to imagine upon what bottom of Reaſon our Author ſhould meaſure the Diſtinction, or Difference of the *Three Divine Perſons*, by the Diſtinction, or Difference, that is between

between *Peter*, *James*, and *John*. For though the *Three Divine Persons* differ *as really*, yet it is certain, that they do *not differ as much*. But what the *Fathers* alledged only as an Illustration of the Case, this Man is pleased to make a direct proof of his Point; which, by his favour, is to stretch it a little too far: For, if he would make the foregoing Example a Parallel Instance to the Thing which he applies it to, it would prove a great deal too much,(as has been shewn) and therefore.as to the Thing, which it is brought for, does indeed prove nothing at all. Now the Thing it is brought to prove, is, *That the Three Divine Persons are Three distinct Infinite Minds, or Spirits*; but since we have shewn, That a *Real Difference*, or *Distinction*, may be much short of such an one as is between *two or more Minds, or Spirits*, (which we own to be as great, as between two or more Men) it follows, That the *Real Difference*, which is between the *Three Divine Persons*, cannot prove them to *be so many distinct Minds, or Spirits*. In short, our Author's whole Argument amounts to no more but this (which, though it may sound somthing jocularly, is really and strictly true) *viz.* That because *Peter*, *James*, and *John are so many Men*, therefore *Father*, *Son*, *and Holy Ghost are so many Minds*. A pleasant way of Arguing certainly.

I have now examined all, that this Author has alledged about the *distinction of the Three Divine Persons*, and I have done it particularly and exactly, not omitting any one of his Quotations. But how comes it to pass all this while, that we have not so much as one Syllable out of the *Fathers*, or *School-men*, in behalf of *Self-Consciousness?* Which being, according to this Author, the *Constituent Reason* of the *Personality* and *Personal Distinction* of the *Three Divine Persons*, will he pretend to prove the Distinction it self from the *Fathers*, and at the

same

ſame time not ſpeak one Tittle of the Principle, or Reaſon of this Diſtinction? Or will he profeſs to prove his whole Hypotheſis by the Authority of the *Fathers*, and yet be ſilent of *Self-Conſciouſneſs*, which he himſelf makes one grand and principal part of the ſaid Hypotheſis? Certainly, one would think, that the very ſhame of the World, and that Common Awe and regard of Truth, which Nature has imprinted upon the Minds of Men, ſhould keep any one from offering to impoſe upon Men in ſo groſs and ſhameleſs a manner, as to venture to call a Notion or Opinion, the *Conſtant Doctrine both of the Fathers and the Schools*; nay, and to profeſs to make it out and ſhew it to be ſo, and while he is ſo doing, not to produce *one Father*, or *School-man*, I ſay again, not ſo much *as one of either* in behalf of that, which he ſo confidently and expreſly avows to be the joynt Sentiment of Both. This ſurely is a way of *proving*, or rather of *impoſing* peculiar to Himſelf. But we have ſeen how extremely fond he is of this new Invented Term and Notion: And therefore ſince he will needs have the Reputation of being the ſole *Father* and *Begetter* of the *Hopeful Iſſue*, there is no Reaſon in the World that Antiquity ſhould find other *Fathers* to maintain it.

CHAP.

CHAP. VII.

In which is shewn, That the Passages alledged by this Author out of the Fathers *do not prove* Mutual-Conſciouſneſs *to be that, wherein the* Unity *of the* Divine Nature *in the* Three Perſons *of the* Bleſſed Trinity *does Conſiſt: But that the* Fathers *place it in ſomething elſe.*

OUR Author having undertook to make good his Doctrine about the *Bleſſed Trinity*, from the *Fathers*; and that both as to the Diſtinction of the *Divine Perſons*, and alſo as to their Unity in the ſame Nature; And having ſaid what he could from thoſe Ancient Writers, for that new ſort of Diſtinction which he aſcribes to the ſaid *Perſons*, in the former part of his 4th Section, which I have confuted in the preceding Chapter; he proceeds now, in the following, and much longer part of the ſame Section, to prove the Unity of the *Three Perſons* in one and the ſame Nature, according to his own Hypotheſis.

And the Proofs of this we ſhall reduce under theſe Two following Heads, as containing all that is alledged by him upon this point of his Diſcourſe, *viz.*

First, That it is one and the same *Numerical Divine Nature*, which belongs to all the *Three Divine Persons*. And,

Secondly, That the Thing, wherein this *Numerical Unity* of the *Divine Nature* does consist, is that *Mutual-Consciousness*, by which all the *Three Persons* are intimately *Conscious* to one another of all that is known by, or belongs to each of them in particular.

And here the Authority of the *Fathers* is pleaded by him for both of these, and I readily grant it for the *first*, but however shall examine what this Author produces for the one, as well as for the other.

But before I do this, I must observe to him, That if that Distinction Asserted by him between the *Divine Persons*, whereby they stand distinguished as Three *Infinite Minds*, or *Spirits*, holds good, all his proofs of the Unity of their Nature will come much too late. For he has thereby already destroyed the very Subject of his Discourse; and it is in vain to seek, wherein the *Numerical Unity* of the *Divine Nature* (as it belongs to the *Three Persons)* does Consist, after he has affirmed that, which makes such an *Unity* utterly impossible. And it has been sufficiently proved against him in our 5th Chapter, That *Three Infinite Minds, or Spirits*, can never be one *Numerical Infinite Mind, or Spirit*, nor consequently one *God*. Three *distinct Spirits* can never be otherwise *One*, than by being United into one Compound, or *Collective Being*, which, (could such a Thing be admitted here) might be called indeed *an Union*, but *an Unity* properly it could not. And hereupon I cannot but observe also, That this Author very often uses these Terms promiscuously, as if *Union* and *Unity*, *being United into One*, *and being One*, signified the very same Thing; whereas, in strictness and propriety of Speech, whatsoever Things are *United into One*, cannot be Originally *One*; and *è Converso*, whatsoever is Originally *One*, cannot be so, by being *United* into *One*: For as *Suidas* explains the word, ἕνωσις εἴρηται διὰ τὸ εἰς ἓν συνωθεῖσθαι τὰ πράγματα, that is to say, *Union* is so called from the pressing [or thrusting] together several Things into one. But our Author, who with great profoundness, tells us *of the same Nature in Three Distinct Persons being United into One Numerical Essence*, or *God-head*, Page 118. Lines 9, 10. has certainly a different Notion of *Union* from all the World besides. For how one and the same Nature (though in never so many *distinct Persons*; since it is still supposed the same in all) can be said to be *United* into any *one* Thing, I believe surpasses all Humane Apprehension to conceive; *Union* in the very Nature of it, being of *several Things*, *not of one and the same*. I desire the Reader to consult the place, and to extract the best sense out of it that he can.

And thus having presented our Author with this Preliminary Observation, I shall now proceed to consider how he acquits himself in the *first Thing* undertook by him, *viz.* The proving a *Numerical Unity* of *Nature* in the *Three Divine Persons*, *out of the Fathers*; which tho' I do as readily grant, and as firmly believe, as this Author does, or can; yet I think it worth while to shew, with what Skill, Decency, and Respect he Treats the *Fathers* upon this Subject.

And here in the first place he tells his Reader, *That this being a Mystery so great*, *and above all Example in Nature*, *it is no wonder if the Fathers found it necessary to use several Examples*, *and to allude to several kinds of Union to form an adequate Notion of the Unity of the God-head.* And withal, *That they take several steps towards the Explication of this great Mystery,* viz. of an *Unity of Nature* in a *Trinity of Persons,* Page 106. In our Examination of which Passages (reserving his former words to be considered elsewhere) we will first consider the *steps* which (he says) the *Fathers* made towards the Explication of this Mystery.

And these, he tells us, are Two.

First, The τὸ ὁμοούσιον, or ὁμοουσιότης, (*i. e.*) the *Coessentiality* of the *Divine Persons,* whereby all the *Three Persons* of the *God-head* have the same *Nature,* Page 106.

Secondly, The other is a *Numerical Unity* of the *Divine Essence,* or *Nature,* Page 121. Line 6. which (to answer one *Greek* word with another) we may call the τὸ ἕν, or the ἑνότης τῆς οὐσίας, or φύσεως, St. *Cyril* Authorizing the Expression, whom we find speaking of an ἑνότης φυσικὴ καὶ οὐσιώδης ἐν τῷ πατρὶ καὶ υἱῷ καὶ πνεύματι ἁγίῳ, as *Ammonius* Cites him in his *Catena* upon *John* 17. 11, 21.

Now as this ὁμοούσιον, or *Sameness of Nature,* and this *Numerical Unity of Nature,* lying fifteen whole Pages, in this Author's Book, distant from one another, must be confessed to make a very *large stride*; so, for all that, they will be found to make but an insignificant *step*; as setting a Man not one jot further than he was before. For as touching those Words and Terms, which the *Fathers* used to express the Unity of the *Divine Nature* by, I do here, without any demur, affirm to this Author, That *Coessentiality, Sameness of Nature, and Sameness of Essence,* all signified by the τὸ ὁμοούσιον, or ὁμοουσιότης, as also, *Unity of Nature, and Unity of Essence,* expressed by the τὸ ἕν, or ἑνότης τῆς οὐσίας, or φύσεως, do all of them, in the

the ſenſe of the *Fathers*, denote but one and the ſame Thing, viz. *A Numerical Unity of the Divine Nature*, only, I confeſs, with ſome Circumſtantial Difference, as to the way, or manner of their ſignification. For,

1. The τὸ ὁμοούσιον, ſignifies *Unity of Nature*, with a Connotation of ſome Things, or Perſons to whom it belongs. Upon which Account it is, that St. *Ambroſe* (whom this Author cites) ſpeaking of this word in his 3d Book, Chap. 7. tells us, That ὁμοούσιον *aliud alii, non ipſum eſt ſibi:* Nor indeed is any Thing ſaid to be the *ſame*, but with reſpect to ſome Thing, or Circumſtance beſides it ſelf. And therefore no wonder if the μονούσιον was anciently rejected, ſince the τὸ μόνον, relating to the *Perſon*, whom the ὀσία belongs to, muſt import an *Unity* in *Perſonality*, as well as in *Eſſence*, which would be contrary to the *Catholick Faith*. But,

2. The τὸ ἓν, or the ἑνότης τῆς οὐσίας, or φύσεως, ſignifies *Unity of Nature*, or *Eſſence*, without Connotation of any to whom it belongs: Not but that it does really and indeed belong to the *Three Divine Perſons*, but that according to the ſtrict and proper ſignification and force of the word, it does not connote, or imply them, but abſtracts, or preſcinds from them.

And this is a true Account of theſe words, by which the *Fathers* (without making more ſteps than one) intended and meant the ſame Thing, *viz.* a *Numerical Unity* of the *Divine Nature* belonging to all the *Three Perſons*, only with this difference, That the ὁμοουσιότης ſignifies the *Unity* of the *Divine Nature*, with a Connotation of the *Perſons* in whom it is; which alſo gives it the Denomination of *Sameneſs*; and that the τὸ ἓν, or the ἑνότης, ſignifies the *Unity* of the ſame *Nature* abſolutely and abſtractedly, without implying, or co-ſignifying any reſpect to thoſe in whom it is, and to whom it belongs.

So

So that theſe words (as much *Two* as they are) yet in the ſenſe and meaning of the *Fathers*, import but one and the ſame *Unity*.

But our Author tells us, That though indeed the *Fathers* own *an Unity of Nature* in the *Divine Perſons*, yet, ſince there is a *Specifick*, as well as a *Numerical Unity*, the Diſpute is here, which of theſe two *Unities* we ſhall aſſign to the *Divine Nature*, with reference to the *Divine Perſons*.

And for this; He tells us, That *Petavius* and Dr. *Cudworth* have abundantly proved, That the *Nicene Fathers did not underſtand the word ὁμοουσιότης of a* Numerical, *but of a* Specifical Sameneſs *of Nature, or the agreement of Things Numerically different from one another in the ſame Common Natrre*, Page 106. about the end.

In Anſwer to which, I muſt confeſs my ſelf very unfit to take ſuch Great and Truly Learned Perſons to task, and that upon comparing this Author and *Petavius* together (if there can be any compariſon between them) I find much more Reaſon to believe that he miſtook the meaning of *Petavius*, than that *Petavius* could miſtake the meaning of the *Fathers*.

But however, I ſhall lay down this as a Concluſion, which I take to be undoubtedly true, *viz.* That the *Ancient Fathers*, as well the *Nicene*, as thoſe after them, held only a *Numerical Unity* of the *Divine Nature* in the *Perſons* of the *Bleſſed Trinity*: That is, in other words, They held and acknowledged one *Numerical God*, and no more. This Concluſion I hold, and have good reaſon to believe, That neither *Petavius*, nor Dr. *Cudworth* ſhall be able to wreſt it from me. For the chief Reaſon of ſome Men's charging the *Fathers* with holding a *Specifick Unity of Nature* amongſt the *Divine Perſons*, is drawn from this, That ſome of them, and particularly

Maximus

Maximus and *Nyſſen* (cited by this Author) ſeem to argue from that *Specifick Unity of Nature* which is found in ſeveral Individual Men, to an *Unity of the Divine Nature* in the *Perſons* of the *Bleſſed Trinity*.

To which I Anſwer, That the *Fathers* never uſed the Example of Three or more Individual Men, agreeing in the ſame *Nature* as a Parallel Inſtance of the ſame ſort, or degree of *Unity* with that which is in the *Three Divine Perſons*; but always alledged it, *one*, or (perhaps ſometimes) *both* of theſe two ways.

Firſt, By way of Alluſion, or Illuſtration (as I have already noted in the foregoing Chapter) and as it is the neareſt Reſemblance of, and Approach to this *Divine Unity* of any that could be found in *Created Beings*. For ſtill their Argument proceeds only by the οἷος and the οἵως on the one ſide, and the οὕτως on the other, (as appears from that place quoted out of *Maximus*, P. 107.) which Terms ſurely do not of neceſſity import an *Identity* of the Caſe, but only ſome *Similitude* in the parts of the Compariſon.

Secondly, The *Fathers* uſed the forementioned Example as an Argument *à minore ad majus*, viz. That if ſeveral Individual Men could not properly be ſaid to have more than one *Nature* (upon which *Nyſſen*'s whole Argument turns) much leſs could this be ſaid of the *Three Divine Perſons*. Foraſmuch as it is not only certain, but evident, That Perſons merely diſtinguiſhed from one another and no more, muſt have a greater *Unity of Nature*, than ſuch as are not only *diſtinguiſhed*, but alſo *divided* from one another by a ſeparate Exiſtence. And let any one ſtretch this Argument of the *Fathers* further if he can.

I do not in the least deny, but several Expressions may have dropped from the *Fathers*, which, if we look'd no further, might be drawn to a very inconvenient sense. But then also it is as little to be denied, That the same *Fathers* professedly and designedly treating of the same Points, have declared themselves in such Terms, as are very hardly, if at all reconcileable to those Occasional and Accidental Expressions. And therefore since their meaning cannot be taken from Both, it ought much rather to be taken from what was Asserted by them designedly, than what was Asserted only occasionally.

To which I shall add this further Remark, That a due consideration of the Circumstances, under which those *Fathers* wrote, may very well Apologize for the Defects of some of their Arguments. For the Grand Controversie which exercised the *Orthodox Writers* of the fourth and part of the fifth Century, was that with the *Arrians*. So that we have the less cause to wonder if some of their Reasonings about the *Trinity* seem to look no further than the Proof of a *Specifick Unity of Nature in the Divine Persons*, while they had to deal with Adversaries who would not allow so much as this between the *Father* and the *Son*, but instead of an ὁμοούσιον, or *Sameness*, held only an ὁμοιούσιον, or *Likeness of Nature* between them; which, together with the foregoing Considerations, may serve as a Key to let us into the true Explication of several Passages of the *Fathers*; about the meaning of which we might otherwise possibly be something at a loss. And the same likewise may serve to give a fair Account of what has been alledged by *Petavius*, and mistook by this Author upon the present Subject. For to traverse and examine all *Petavius*'s Allegations particularly would require a full and distinct Work by it self.

But

Chapter VII.

But still our Author seems extremely set upon making good his first step of a *Specifick Unity* of the *Divine Nature* from the *Fathers*; and to that purpose he tells us, *Page* 107. *Line* 23. *That one Thing wherein the Fathers place the Unity of the God-head is, that all the Three Persons have the same Nature*, by which he means (as shall be shewn presently) Specifically the same *Nature*; and a few Lines after, he tells us again, *That some of the Fathers went further than this, and plac'd the Essential Unity of the Divine Nature in the Sameness of Essence*, Lines 30, 31, 32. of the same Page.

Now here I would desire this Author to inform me of Two Things.

First, By what rule of speaking, or upon what Principle of Divinity, Logick, or Philosophy, *Sameness of Nature* ought to signifie one Thing, and *Sameness of Essence* to signifie another; and withal to be so contra-distinguished to each other, that in the degrees of *Unity*, this latter must be a step beyond the former? For the *Fathers*, I am sure, make no such Distinction, but use the words *Sameness of Nature*, and *Sameness of Essence*, as well as the words οὐσία and φύσις themselves promiscuously; so that neither by their Native signification, nor yet by their use, do they import any more than one sort of *Unity*.

Secondly, Whereas in *Page* 106. *Lines* 23, 24. he makes the *first step* towards this *Unity* to consist in the ὁμοουσιότης, or *Coessentiality*, (which also in the next Page, *Line* 23. &c. he explains by *Sameness of Nature*); And whereas, in *Page* 121. he makes *a Numerical Unity of the Divine Essence*, the *next step* (introducing it with the word *Secondly*) and telling us, That the *Fathers* added it to the ὁμοουσιότης, which he had before made the *firſt ſtep*; And whereas, notwithſtanding this, having in *Page* 107. told us, *That Sameneſs of Nature was one Thing wherein the Fathers placed the Unity of the Divine Nature*, within ſeven Lines after, he tells us, *That ſome of the Fathers went further, and placed it in the Sameneſs of Eſſence*, (which, yet it is manifeſt all along, that he reckons not the ſame thing with *Numerical Unity of Eſſence*,) I deſire to know of him, whether there be *Two ſecond ſteps* in this *Unity?* or, whether there be *one between the firſt and the ſecond?* For he makes ὁμοφυΐα, *or Sameneſs of Nature one step*, Page 106, 107. *And Sameneſs of Eſſence a further ſtep*, Page 107. Line 30. *&c.* And then *Numerical Unity of Nature another ſtep*, calling it alſo *the Second*, Page 121. Line 5. Theſe Things, I muſt confeſs, I am utterly unable to give any Conſiſtent Account of, and I ſhrewdly ſuſpect, that our Author himſelf is not able to give a much better. But it is ſtill his way to forget in one place what he has ſaid in another; and how kind ſoever he may be to himſelf, I ſhould think it very hard for another Man to *forget* himſelf ſo often, and to *forgive* himſelf too.

Nevertheleſs our Author, without mincing the Matter, roundly Aſſerts a *Specifick Unity of Nature in the Divine Perſons*, telling us, *Line* 23. *&c.* of the fore-cited *Page* 107. *That this is abſolutely neceſſary to make the Three Perſons one God, and that it is impoſſible that they ſhould be ſo without it*; where it is evident, that he means a *Specifick Unity*, both from this, that it was the *Subject*, which he had been there treating of, as alſo from this, that immediately after he mentions another ſort, or degree of *Unity*, as a *ſtep further* than this; which, ſince nothing can be *but a Numerical Unity*, it follows, That that which was *one ſtep* ſhort of a *Numerical*, muſt needs be a *Specifical*. And now is it not ſtrange, that in *Page* 109.

which is but the next ſave one after this, this Man ſhould poſitively ſay, (as he does) *That the Fathers never ſo much as Dream'd of a Specifick Unity of Nature in the Divine Perſons*, having here in *Page* 107. affirmed it *to be no leſs than abſolutely neceſſary to make the Three Perſons one God?* And that certainly is a neceſſity with a witneſs. But he, who exacts of this Author a conſiſtency with himſelf for five Pages together, deals very ſeverely with him.

And accordingly, the more I conſider of this Matter, I cannot but think, That what he ſays of the *Nicene Fathers holding a Specifick Unity of Nature in the Divine Perſons*, Page 106. And his affirming that *Gregory Nyſſen*, St. *Cyrill*, *Maximus* and *Damaſcen never ſo much as Dream'd of any ſuch Unity*, Page 109. Line 22. will by no means conſiſt together.

For Firſt, If by the *Nicene Fathers* be meant not only thoſe who were preſent at that Council, but thoſe *Fathers* alſo, who about thoſe Times held the ſame Faith which was Eſtabliſhed in that Council, then his two fore-cited Paſſages contain a groſs, manifeſt, fulſome Contradiction; even as groſs as the *poſitive aſſerting of a thing*, and the *never ſo much as dreaming of it*, can import. But if by the *Nicene Fathers* he means only thoſe who ſat and acted in that Council, he will hardly however perſwade any underſtanding Man, That *Gregory Nyſſen*, who Wrote and flouriſhed between fifty and Sixty Years after the Council, and *Maximus* about Sixty, and St. *Cyrill* about Ninety, could be ſo groſly ignorant of, and Strangers to the Sentiments of thoſe *Fathers*, as not ſo much *as to Dream of that wherein they had placed the Unity of the God-head*. This to me ſeems Incredible and morally Impoſſible: ſince it is not to be imagined, that *Nyſſen*, *Cyrill*, and *Maximus* could ſo ſoon forget, or knowingly dare to relinquiſh the Doctrine of the fore-mentioned *Fathers*, whose Authority was so great and Sacred all the *Christian World* over. And therefore since this Author allows these *Fathers* not to have *Dreamt* of a *Specifick Unity of the Divine Nature*; I conclude, That neither did the *Nicene Fathers Dream* of it any more than they, howsoever they might express themselves upon some occasions.

And thus having (as well as he could) made *his first step*, by Asserting a *Specifick Unity*, or *Sameness of Nature* in the *Three Divine Persons* from the *Fathers*, that is to say, partly from what *Petavius* and Dr. *Cudworth* had told him of the *Nicene Fathers* holding such a *Specifick Unity* between them, and partly from the other *Fathers never so much as dreaming of it*, he proceeds now to his other *step*, or rather *Counter-step*; which is to shew, That the *Unity* between the *Divine Persons*, held by the *Fathers*, was no other than a *Numerical Unity of Nature*, or *Essence* belonging to them: For since *to be one only Specifically*, and to be *one only Numerically*, are by no means consistent with one another, in respect of the same *Persons*, what can this be so truly and properly called as *a Counter-step to* that which he had made before? His Method being plainly this. First he tells us, That the *Nicene Fathers* by the ὁμοουσιότης understood only a *Specifick Unity*, or *Sameness of Nature* in the *Divine Persons*, Page 106. And then, that the *Fathers* [mentioning them indefinitely] *held this Sameness of Nature* absolutely necessary to make the said *Three Persons one God*, Page 107. And now at length he tells us, Page 121. Lines 27, 28, 29. *That though several of the Fathers attempted several ways of explaining that Unity of Nature that is in the Divine Persons, yet they all agree in the Thing, That Father, Son, and Holy Ghost, Three distinct Divine Persons are united in one Numerical Nature and Essence.* So that the Sum of all

must

must be this (as appears also from his own words in the latter end of *Page* 120. and the four first Lines of the 121.) that, according to him, the *Fathers* held a *Specifick Unity of Nature necessary* to make the *Three Divine Persons one God*, but not *sufficient* without the Completion of it by a *Numerical Unity* superadded to it.

This, I say, is the Sum of what he delivers; and in direct opposition to which, I do here deny, That there is any such Thing as a *Specifick Unity of Nature* belonging to the *Divine Persons*, or that the *Fathers* ever held, that there was.

And to prove this, I shall premise this Assertion both as certain in it self, and withall affirmed by this Author in those fore-cited words, *viz. That all the Fathers held, That Father, Son, and Holy Ghost, Three distinct Persons are United in* (or rather *are One, by*) One Numerical *Nature and Essence.*

Which being so premised, I have these *Considerations* to oppose to the Admission of any *Specifick Unity* in the *Divine Nature* as it belongs to the *Divine Persons*. As,

First, If a *Numerical Unity* in the same *Divine Nature* be sufficient to make the *Three Divine Persons* to whom it belongs, *One God*, then a *Specifick Unity* of the same is not necessary; but a *Numerical Unity* in the same *Divine Nature* is sufficient to make the said *Three Persons One God*, and therefore a *Specifick Unity* is not necessary. The Consequence is evident, because nothing can be *necessary* to any Thing, or Effect, beyond, or beside what is *sufficient* for the same; since this would imply a manifest Contradiction, by making the same Thing, in the same respect, both *sufficient* and *not sufficient*. And as for the Minor, That an Agreement in one and the same *Numerical*

rical Divine Nature is sufficient to make the *Persons* so agreeing *One God.* I suppose this carries with it so much Self-Evidence, that no Man of Reason will pretend to doubt of, and much less to deny it.

Secondly, A greater degree of *Unity*, and a less degree of *Unity* are not to be admitted in the *Divine Nature.* But a *Numerical Unity* and a *Specifical Unity*, are a greater and a less degree of *Unity*, and therefore they are not both to be admitted in the *Divine Nature.* The Major is proved thus, Because two such *Unities* would overthrow the simplicity of the *Divine Nature*; forasmuch as they must be either two *degrees* of the same kind of *Unity*, or they must be two different *kinds* of *Unity*: Either of which would infer a Composition by no means to be endured in the *Divine Nature.* As for the Minor, it is evident in it self, and needs no Proof.

Thirdly, Such a degree, or sort of *Unity of Nature*, as may agree to Ten Thousand Individuals, neither can nor ought to be admitted in the *Divine Nature*, with reference to the *Divine Persons.* But a *Specifick Unity of Nature* may agree to Ten Thousand Individuals, as well as to Two or Three; since (upon a *Specifick* Account) it has no Stint or Limitation, but may be every whit as well and properly in the former Number, as in the latter; and therefore it neither can nor ought to be admitted in the *Divine Nature.*

Fourthly, Such an *Unity* as is principally, if not absolutely *Notional* and depends upon the Operation of the Intellect drawing one common Notion from the agreement, which it observes in several Individuals, is by no means necessary to make the *Three Divine Persons One God*, nor can any way properly belong to them. But a *Specifick Unity* is such an one. And therefore it neither is, nor

nor can be neceſſary to the making the *Three Divine Perſons One God*; as this Author moſt abſurdly Aſſerts, *P.* 107. *Line* 23, 24. The Major is evident. For that, if ſuch an *Unity* could be neceſſary upon that Account, then there would be ſome ſort or degree of *Unity* in the *Divine Nature* ſo depending upon the Operation of ſome Intellect, or other (forming one common Notion out of ſeveral Particulars,) that, had not ſuch an Operation paſſed upon the ſaid Particulars, ſuch an *Unity* could not have been; nor conſequently could the *Three Divine Perſons* have been one *God* without it; which to affirm, would certainly be both a Monſtrous and Blaſphemous Aſſertion.

Fifthly and Laſtly, If a *Specifick Unity of Nature* conſiſts with, and indeed implys a *Multiplication* of the ſaid *Nature*, in every one of the Particulars, to which it belongs; then ſuch a *Specifick Unity* can by no means be admitted in the *Divine Nature*. But a *Specifick Unity of Nature* imports a *Multiplication* of the ſaid *Nature* in every one of the Particulars to which it belongs; And therefore ſuch an *Unity* cannot be admitted in the *Divine Nature*. The Reaſon of the Conſequence is evident; becauſe the *Divine Nature* is uncapable of any *Multiplication*: And herein conſiſts the difference of the *Divine Nature*'s belonging to the *Divine Perſons*, and of any other *Nature's* belonging to its proper Individuals; That this latter is by a *Multiplication of it ſelf in them*, and the other by a bare *Communication of it ſelf to them*, ſo as that the ſame *Numerical Nature exiſts in*, and becomes thereby common to all the *Three Perſons*. As for the Minor Propoſition, That a *Specifick Unity of Nature* conſiſts with and implies a *Multiplication* of the ſaid *Nature* in the ſeveral Individuals which it belongs to;

I refer him to all the *Logicians* and *Metaphyſicians* who have wrote of *Species*, and *Specifick Unity*, of *Idem*, & *Diverſum*, whether they do not give this Account of it.

But I fancy this Author has a reach of Cunning (tho' but a ſhort one) in the caſe. For that having made the *Three Divine Perſons Three diſtinct Infinite Minds, or Spirits*, which can never be *One* by a *Numerical Unity*; he is willing to provide them a *Specifical Unity*, and to ſee whether that will ſerve the turn; but as the *Nature of the Thing* unhappily falls out to be, that will not do it neither.

Theſe are the *Conſiderations* which I thought fit to advance againſt the Admiſſion of a *Specifick Unity* in the *Divine Nature*, with reference to the *Divine Perſons*. And the Concluſion, which I draw from them all, is this, That ſince the *Fathers* (and that even by this Author's own Confeſſion) held a *Numerical Unity of Nature in the Three Divine Perſons*, we can by no means grant that the ſaid *Fathers* admitted alſo a *Specifick Unity* in the ſame, without making them guilty of a groſs Abſurdity and Contradiction. Foraſmuch as theſe Two ſorts, or degrees of *Unity* are utterly incompatible in the *Divine Nature*.

I hope by this time the Judicious Reader ſees how fit this Man is to be truſted with the *Fathers*, whoſe Judgment about ſo weighty an Article he dares miſrepreſent in ſuch a manner. For to ſum up briefly what he has ſaid upon this Point.

Firſt, he tells us, *That the Fathers agree very well in the Account they give of a Trinity in Unity*, Page 106. and the four firſt lines. Next he tells us, *That the Nicene Fathers aſſerted a Specifick Unity of the Divine Nature in the*

the

the Persons of the Blessed Trinity, and understood the word ὁμοούσιον *only of such an Unity, and not of a Numerical,* Page 106. and the five last Lines. And Thirdly, *That this Specifick Unity, or Sameness of Nature, was absolutely Necessary to make the Three Divine Persons One God, and that it was impossible they should be so without it,* Page 107. Lines 23, 24. And Fourthly, That the other *Fathers* (of which he there names four) *never so much as Dream'd of a Specifick Unity of the Divine Nature,* Page 109. Lines 22, 23. And Lastly, *That the Fathers do not stop in this Specifick Unity and Identity of Nature, but proceed to shew how the* ὁμοούσιον *proves a true Numerical and Essential Unity of the God-head in the Three Divine Persons,* Page 114. Lines 30, 31, 32, 33.

From all which Assertions, which lie plain and open in the forecited Pages, I desire this Author to resolve me these following Queries.

1. Whether those *Fathers* who Assert a *Specifick Unity of the Divine Nature,* and *those who never Dreamt of such an Unity*; And those again, who by the ὁμοούσιον understood only a *Specifick,* and not a *Numerical Unity of Nature*; and those who by the same ὁμοούσιον proceed to prove a *Numerical Unity of Nature* in the *Divine Persons,* can be said to agree so very well in the Account they give of a *Trinity in Unity?*

2. Whether those could give a true and right Account of a *Trinity* in *Unity,* who never so much as *Dreamt* of that, which was so absolutely necessary to make the *Three Divine Persons One God,* that they could not possibly be so without it?

3. Whether a *Specifick Unity,* or *Sameness of Nature* in several *Persons,* is or can be a direct and proper proof of a *Numerical Unity* and *Identity of Nature* in the said *Persons?*

These Questions, I say, being the Natural and Immediate Results of this Author's Positions, I hope he will graciously vouchsafe, sometime or other, to give the World a Satisfactory Resolution of.

In the mean time I will tell him what it was, that imposed upon him so, as to make him talk thus Absurdly and Unphilosophically of a *Specifick Unity of the Divine Nature*, and traduce the *Fathers* also, as if they held the same. And that in one word is, That in the Subject before us, he takes *Specifick Nature* and *Common Nature* to signifie one and the same Thing; whereas, though every *Specifick Nature* be a *Common Nature*, yet every *Common Nature* is not *a Specifick Nature* (no nor a *Generical* neither.) And that this was his mistake appears from those words of his in Page 106. where he says, That Petavius *and Dr.* Cudworth *have abundantly proved, That the* Nicene Fathers *did not understand the word* ὁμοούσιον *of a Numerical, but of a Specifical Sameness of Nature, or the agreement of Things Numerically differing from one another, in the same* Common *Nature.*] In which words it is evident, That he makes *Specifick Sameness of Nature, and the Agreement of Things numerically different, in one and the same* Common *Nature*, to signifie Convertibly the same Thing; and when he has done so, he opposes them Both to a *Numerical Sameness of Nature*; as appears from the Adversative Particle [*But*] placed between them. In which, let me tell him he is guilty of a very great mistake, both by making those Things the same, which are not the same, and by making an Opposition where there is a real Coincidence. For, by his favour, *one and the same Numerical Divine Nature is a* Common *Nature too*; forasmuch as without any Division, or Multiplication of it self, it *belongs in Common* to the *Three Divine Persons*. The Term [*Deus*] indeed is neither a *Genus*, nor a *Spe-*

cies,

ties. Neverthelefs all *Divines* and *School-men* allow it to be a *Terminus Communis*, as properly predicable of, and Common to *Father*, *Son*, and *Holy Ghoft*; and in this very Thing confifts the Myftery of the *Trinity*, That one and the fame *Numerical Nature* fhould be *Common* to, and Exift in *Three Numerically diftinct Perfons.* And therefore for one (who pretends to teach the whole World Divinity) while he is Difcourfing of the *Divine Nature* and *Perfons*, to oppofe *Common Nature*, to *Nature Numerically One*, and from the *Commonnefs of it*, to make the *Fathers* Argue againft *its Numericalnefs* (whereas the fame *Divine Nature* may be, and really is both) it is a fhrewd fign of the want of fome thing or other in that Man, that muft needs render him extremely unfit to prefcribe,and dictate in thefe Matters.

In fine, the fole Point driven at all along by the *Fathers*, as to the Queftion about the *Unity* of the *Divine Nature* (for their Arguments to prove the Coequality of the *Three Divine Perfons* againft the *Arrians* are not now before us) is an Affertion of a Real Numerical Exifting *Unity* of the faid *Nature* in the faid *Perfons.* I fay, a *Numerical Unity*, without making any more *fteps*, or *degrees* in it than *One*,or owning any diftinction between *Samenefs of Nature*, and *Samenefs of Effence.* And much lefs by making (as this Author does) a *Specifick Samenefs of Nature*, one thing wherein they place the *Unity* of the *Divine Nature*, and then making *Samenefs of Effence another and further degree* in the *Unity* of the faid *Nature*; and when they have done fo, by a return back explaining this *Samenefs of Effence*, by the *Samenefs of Nature* newly mentioned; as, he fays, they do, in thefe words, immediately following (by way of Exegefis of the former) viz. *That there is but one God, becaufe all the Three Divine Perfons have the fame Nature*, Page 107. and the two last Lines. All which is a Ridiculous Circle, and a Contradiction to boot, making *Sameness of Nature* one *step*, and *Sameness of Essence* another, and then making this *Sameness of Essence* no more than *a Sameness of Nature*, again; so that according to him the *Fathers* must be said to go *further*, by resting in the very same *step* which they first made: Which way of Reasoning, I confess, may serve well enough for one, who can forget in one Page, what he had said in the other just before; But (by his favour) the *Fathers* were a little more Consistent, and understood themselves better than to run Divisions in such a senseless manner upon a Thing that admitted none.

And thus having shewn how he has dealt with the *Fathers* in the Account given by him of their Opinion about *the Unity of the Divine Nature in the Persons of the Blessed Trinity*, (which was the *first Head*, under which I reduced his Allegations from them,) I come now in the

2d Place, to the other and Principal Head; under which he undertakes to prove the chief and more peculiar part of his Hypothesis from the said *Fathers*, viz. *That the Unity and Identity of Nature belonging to the Three Divine Persons, consists in the* Mutual-Consciousness *which is between them*, That is in Truth, That they are therefore *One God*, because they are *Conscious* to themselves, that they are so.

And here I shall begin with shewing how this Author overthrows the Point undertook by him before he produces any Arguments from the *Fathers* for it. And to this Purpose I shall resume those words of his before cited by me out of Page 106. In which he reminds his Reader, *That Trinity in Unity being so great a Mystery, and of which we have no Example in Nature, it is no wonder*

der if it cannot be explained by any one kind of Natural Union, and that therefore it was necessary to use several Examples, and to allude to several kinds of Union, to form an adequate Notion of the Unity of the God-head. Now here, since our Author's Notion, and the *Fathers* too (as he says) of this *Unity* is nothing else but *Mutual-Consciousness*, I desire to Learn of him, what necessity there was, or is of *using several Examples, and alluding to several kinds of Union to explain, or form an adequate notion of that?* And I wonder what kind of *Thing he would make of his Mutual-Consciousness*, should he come to explain and describe it by several Examples, and several Kinds of Union? But this is not all, for he tells us likewise (as we also observed before) that there are several *steps* to be taken towards the Explication of this Mystery. Whereupon I would again learn of him how many *steps* are necessary to explain *Mutual-Consciousness*; for one would imagine one single *step* sufficient to represent and declare a Thing which every Body understands. This Author indeed confidently enough Asserts, That *the Fathers give no other Account of a Trinity in Unity, than the same which he gives of it*, Page 101. Line 2. But certainly if the *Fathers* thought *several Examples*, Steps *and Kinds of Union absolutely necessary to explain the Notion they had of this Unity*, and if these cannot be necessary to explain the Notion of *Mutual-Consciousness*, then it must follow, That the *Fathers* neither did, nor possibly could by that *Unity* mean *Mutual-Consciousness.* And if this Author doubts of the force of this Reasoning, let him try his skill, and see what Learned stuff he is like to make of it when he comes to explain his Notion of *Mutual-Consciousness by several Examples, Steps, and Sorts of Union, and out of them all to form one adequate Notion of this so much admired Thing.* Wherefore

I conclude, and, I think, unanſwerably, That the *Fathers* by this *Unity* between the *Divine Perſons*, mean one Thing, and this Man quite another; and conſequently that they have given a very different Account of it, from what he gives, contrary to his equally bold and falſe Aſſeveration, affirming it to be *the very ſame.*

And now I am ready to ſee what he has to offer us from the *Fathers* in behalf of his *Mutual-Conſciouſneſs*; but becauſe I am extremely deſirous, that the Reader ſhould keep him cloſe to the Point, and not ſuffer him to wander from it (which, in diſpute, he is as apt to do as any Man living) I ſhall preſume to hint this to him, That the Point to be proved by this Author, is not that the *Three Divine Perſons* have one and the ſame *Numerical Nature*, or *Eſſence*, nor that they are *Mutually Conſcious* to one another of whatſoever each of them *is*, or *knows*; no, nor yet that this *Mutual-Conſciouſneſs* infers an *Unity of Nature* in them, as a Thing inſeparable from it. But he is to prove, That this *Unity of Nature*, and this *Mutual-Conſciouſneſs* are Convertibly one and the ſame Thing, or that this latter is to the former what the *Eſſence*, or *Form* of any Thing is to that Thing: That is to ſay, That the *Unity* of the *Divine Nature* formally *Conſiſts in*, and is, what it *is*, *by* that *Mutual-Conſciouſneſs* which belongs to the *Three Divine Perſons*. This, I ſay, is the Thing to be proved by Him.

And ſo I proceed to his Arguments (which I aſſure the Reader, he ſhall find very ſtrange ones) nevertheleſs to give him as eaſie and diſtinct a view of them, as I can, I will ſet down the ſeveral Heads of them before I particularly diſcuſs them.

1. The Firſt of them is from the μία ἐνέργεια aſcribed, by the *Fathers*, to all the *Three Divine Perſons* joyntly.

2. The

2. The Second from the *μία κίνησις καὶ διακόσμησις τοῦ ἀγαθοῦ βουλήματος.*

3. The Third from the *περιχώρησις*, or Circuminceſſion attributed likewiſe by the *Fathers* to them.

4. The Fourth from the Repreſentation, which St. *Auſtin* makes of the *Trinity*, by the *Mind*, and its *Three diſtinct Faculties of Underſtanding, Memory, and Will.* And,

5. The Fifth and laſt from the *Unity* of the *Original Principle*, or *Fountain of the Deity*, or rather (ſay I) of the ſecond and third *Perſons* of the *Trinity.*

All which I ſhall examine diſtinctly, and in their order. But before I do ſo, I think fit to give the Reader an Account in one word of this Author's whole deſign in all the Particulars above ſpecified. And that is, to prove, That the *Unity* of the *Divine Nature* conſiſts in *Unity of Operation*, and then to ſuppoſe (for he does not ſo much as go about to prove it) that this *Unity of Operation is Mutual-Conſciouſneſs.* This is the Sum Total of the Buſineſs; but I now come to Particulars. And

Firſt, For the *μία ἐνέργεια*, quoted by him out of *Greg. Nyſſen.* Where, before we ſee how far it may be formed into an Argument, I think it requiſite to give ſome Account how this Author Diſcourſes of it. I muſt confeſs, I have ſometimes wondred, what deſign he could have in ſo zealouſly exploding thoſe commonly received Terms of *Subſtance, Eſſence and Nature* from any application of them to God: which here he does again afreſh, telling us in *Page* 115. *lines* 24, 25, 26, 27. *That it confounds our minds when we talk of the Numerical Unity of the Godhead to have the leaſt Conception or Thought about the Diſtinction and Union of Natures and Eſſences.* And that therefore we are to ſpeak of God only in words importing *Energy or Operation:* And accordingly for this reaſon

Gr.

Gr. Nyſſen expreſſes God by Θεατὴς and ἔφορος, words not ſignifying *Nature* or *Eſſence*, but only *Sight* and *Inſpection*; Nay and this Author has gone *a ſtep* much beyond this, plainly telling us, *That the Father and the Son are Energy or Operation*, Page 132. Line 13. And *that Nature and Energy are the ſame in God*, P. 133. L. 20. and conſequently, That we are to entertain no other Conception of God, but as *of a pure ſimple Operation.* And thus, when we have degraded the *Divine Nature* from *Subſtance* to *Operation*, it is but *one ſtep* more to degrade it to bare *Notion.* This conceit of this Author, I ſay, at firſt I could not but wonder at, but am ſince pretty well aware of what he drives at by it. And that is in ſhort, That he thinks it a much eaſier Matter to make *Action*, or *Operation*, than *Subſtance*, *Eſſence*, or *Nature* paſs for *Mutual-Conſciouſneſs*: And this upon good Reaſon, I am ſatisfied, is the Thing he deſigns: But I believe he will fall ſhort of fetching *his Mutual-Conſciouſneſs* out of either of them. And therefore firſt to Correct that Crude Notion of his, *That we muſt not ſpeak of God in Terms importing Nature, but Operation*; I deſire this Bold Man (as I urged before in Chap. 2.) to tell me whether the Names of *Jah* and *Jehovah*, and *I am that I am*, by which *God* revealed himſelf to his People, were not Names of *Nature* and *Eſſence?* and whether *God* revealed them for any other purpoſe than that he might be *known* and *underſtood* by them? But for all this he will have us to know from *Gr. Nyſſen*, That the *Divine Nature* is *quid* ἀκατωνόμαστον καὶ ἄφραστον, a Thing above Name or Expreſſion. And it is ſo, I confeſs, as to an adequate complete Conception or Deſcription of it. But then, I ask him, are not the *Divine Operations ſo too?* Are we able to comprehend them perfectly, and to the utmoſt of *what*, and *how* they are? When the Pſalmiſt tells us, that *God has put darkneſs under*

der

quite spoils all his fine Notion about expressing *God* only by Terms of *Energy* and *Operation*, in exclusion of those of *Nature*, *Essence* and *Substance*. This I thought fit to premise, as throwing up the very foundation of all his Arguments, and indeed of his whole Hypothesis.

And so I come to his Argument, the Sum of which, is this.

That the *Divine Nature* is *Divine Energy*, or *Operation*; And therefore, That the *Unity* of *Divine Operation*, is *Unity* of *Divine Nature*; And Lastly, That this *Unity* of *Divine Nature* is *Mutual-Consciousness*.

Now it is certain, That there is not one of all these Three Propositions true; but that is no fault of mine: since if they were cast into a Syllogism, that would not mend the Matter; for the Syllogism must proceed thus.

> *Unity of Divine Energy, or Operation is Mutual-Consciousness.*
>
> *Unity of Divine Nature is Unity of Divine Energy, or Operation.*
>
> And therefore, *Unity of Divine Nature is Mutual-Consciousness.*

Every one of which *Propositions* is still false. And yet I shall refer it to this Author himself, or to any one, who has Read and Considered his Book, to form a better Argument from what he has said of a μία ἐνέργεια, with reference to the present Subject, if he can.

Nevertheless whether it be an Argument, or no Argument, my Answer to his Allegation of the μία ἐνέργεια, with relation to the *Unity of the Divine Nature*, and to *Mutual-Consciousness*, is thus.

First, That it is one Thing to be a *Proof* of a Thing, and another to be that wherein the *Nature of the Thing* proved, does consist. Thus actual Ratiocination is a certain Proof of a Principle of Reaſon, yet nevertheleſs it is not that wherein a Principle of Reaſon does conſiſt; ſince that may be and continue when actual Ratiocination ceaſes. In like manner I will allow the μία ἐνέργεια; to be a Proof of the μία οὐσία. But I abſolutely deny, That the ἑνότης of the *Energy*, is that wherein the ἑνότης of the *Nature* is, or ought to be placed; or that the *Fathers* ever accounted it ſo, how truly and ſtrongly ſoever it might, in their judgment, infer it.

What the *Fathers* deſigned to prove by *Unity of Operation in the Three Divine Perſons*, is evident from the following Paſſages; (to which Twenty times as many might be added.) *Gregory Nyſſen* tells us, *That thoſe whoſe Energy is the ſame, have their Nature altogether the ſame.* And St. *Baſil*, *That thoſe who have the ſame Operations, have alſo the ſame Eſſence* [or Subſtance.] *But the Operation* [or Energy] *of the Father and the Son is one, as appears in that Expreſſion,* Let us make Man. *And again,* Whatſoever the Father does, that likewiſe does the Son, *and therefore there is but one Eſſence of the Father and the Son.* And again, *The Sameneſs of Operation in the Father, Son, and Holy Ghoſt, evidently ſhews, That there is no difference in their Eſſence, or Subſtance.* And accordingly St. *Auſtin*, *The Operation cannot be diverſe, where the Nature is not only equal, but alſo undivided.* From all which, it is moſt clear, That the *Fathers* alledge this *Unity of Operation* only as a Proof or Argument of this *Unity of Nature, or Eſſence*: And therefore, ſince nothing can be a Proof of it

Ὧν δὲ ἡ ἐνέργεια μία καὶ ἡ φύσις πάντως ἡ αὐτὴ τούτων ἐστίν. *Greg. Nyſſen in Orat. Dom. Nu. 3.*

Ὧν αἱ αὐταὶ ἐνέργειαι τούτων καὶ ἡ οὐσία μία· ἐνέργεια δὲ πατρὸς καὶ υἱοῦ μία ὡς τὸ ποιήσωμεν ἄνθρωπον. καὶ πάλιν, ἃ γὰρ ἂν ὁ πατὴρ ποιῇ καὶ ὁ υἱὸς ὁμοίως ποιεῖ· ἄρα καὶ οὐσία μία πατρὸς καὶ υἱοῦ. *Baſil. lib 4. contra Eunomium.* οὐκοῦν ἡ τῆς ἐνεργείας ταυτότης ἐπὶ πατρὸς καὶ υἱοῦ καὶ ἁγίου πνεύματος δείκνυσι σαφῶς τὸ τῆς οὐσίας ἀπαράλλακτον. *Baſil Epiſt. ad Euſtathium.* Non poteſt operatio eſſe diverſa ubi non ſolùm æqualis, verùm etiam indiſcreta Natura. *Auguſt. Serm. de Verbo Dom. 63. Cap. 3.*

But I must confess, it is a very pleasant Thing (as was in some measure hinted before) to prove the *Divine Nature to be Energy*, because the Name [*God*] does not *signifie Nature, but Energy, or Operation*; whereas in Truth (if it proves any thing) it proves that *Nature* and *Energy* (applyed to *God*) do by no means signifie the same Thing.

And so I have done with his Argument from the μία κίνησις βελήματος, and effectually demonstrated, That there is not so much as the least shew, or semblance of any proof from this, *That Mutual-Consciousness is properly that wherein the Unity of the Divine Nature in the Three Persons of the Blessed Trinity does consist.*

3. His Third Argument is from the Word περιχώρησις, commonly Translated *Circumincession*, and signifying a *Mutual-Inexistence*, or *In-dwelling* of each *Person* in the other Two. The Word was first used in this sense (so far as I can find) by *Damascen*, a *Father* of the 8th Century. But the Thing meant by it, is contained in those words of our Saviour in *John* 14. 11. 21. *Believe me that I am in the Father, and the Father in me*, which, I confess, are a solid and sufficient proof of the *Unity* and *Identity* of the *Divine Nature*, both in the *Father* and the *Son*; and withal a very happy and significant Expression of the same.

But what is this to our Author's Purpose? And how does he prove this περιχώρησις to be *Mutual-Consciousness?* Why truly, by no Argument, or Reason produced, or so much as offered at by him, but only by a confident, Over-bearing Affirmation, *That there is no other Account to be given of that Mutual-In-being of the Divine Persons in each other, (which the Fathers call περιχώρησις) but by Mutual-Consciousness*, Page 125. Lines 6, 7, 8.

But, by his leave, I must debate the case a little with him, before he carries it off so. And in order to this, I must tell him in the first place, That the Question is not whether *Mutual-Consciousness best explains this* περιχώρησις, but whether it be the περιχώρησις it self, and that περιχώρησις be the *Unity* of the *Divine Nature* in the *Three Persons?* And in the next place, I demand of him, Whether our Saviour's Words do not plainly and expresly signifie the *Mutual-In-being*, or *In-existence* of the *Persons* in one another, without any signification of their *Mutual-Consciousness at all?* And if so; let me hear a Reason, Why we should not take our Saviour's meaning from the Native signification of his own Words, rather than from those of this Author. For will he venture to affirm, That the *Father* cannot be in the *Son*, and the *Son* in the *Father* by a *Mutual-Inexistence* in one another, but only by a *Mutual-Knowledge* of one another? Let him take heed what he says, and how he ventures beyond his Depth. Or will he say, That our Saviour meant the same Thing with himself, but was *not so happy in expressing it?* For no other Reason, but one of these Two can be assigned, That when our Saviour expresses himself in Terms importing *Mutual-In-existence*, this Man shall dare to say, That he means nothing by them but *Mutual-Consciousness.* I refer it to the Serious and Impartial Reader to judge of the Horrible Boldness of this Man: and withal, to observe how extremely he varies from himself about this περιχώρησις and *Mutual-Consciousness.* For

First, He sometimes says, That *Mutual-Consciousness is the only Thing wherein both the Unity of the Divine Nature, and this Mutual-In-dwelling of the Three Divine Persons does Consist*, Page 124. Lines 4, 5. And

Secondly,

Secondly, He ſays, *That Mutual-Conſciouſneſs is the only thing that can explain, or give an Account of this Mutual-In-dwelling, or περιχώρησις*, Page 125. Lines 6, 7.

To which I Anſwer, That when he ſpeaks of giving an Account of this περιχώρησις, if he means only *an Account that there is ſuch a Thing belonging to the Divine Perſons*, Our Saviour's Words have given a ſufficient Account of that already. But,

Secondly, If he means ſuch an Account of it, as explains and makes clear to us the *Nature* of it, by ſhewing *what it is*, and *how it is*. I deny that any ſuch Account can be given (or perhaps *underſtood)* by Humane Reaſon; and much leſs, that his *Mutual-Conſciouſneſs* does or can give it.

Concerning which, I ſhall ask him this one Queſtion, *viz*. Whether the *Three Perſons of the Bleſſed Trinity* are not *Mutually-Conſcious* to one another of their *Mutual-In-exiſtence* in one another? I ſuppoſe he will not (becauſe he dares not) deny it. And if he grants it, then it manifeſtly follows, That their *Mutual-In-exiſtence* in one another, is in Order of *Nature* before their *Mutual-Conſciouſneſs*; and conſequently cannot be the ſame with it, nor Conſiſt in it. For certainly thoſe *Divine Perſons* muſt *Exiſt Mutually* in one another, before they can know, or be *Conſcious* to themſelves that they do ſo.

So that we ſee here, that nothing is, or can be concluded from this περιχώρησις for his *Mutual-Conſciouſneſs*, whether we conſider the *Uſe* of the Word, or the *Nature* of the Thing. But let us ſee, how he makes good his Point from the Authority of the *Fathers*, which was the grand Thing undertook by him in this his 4th Section. And here as for the *Fathers*, he both Deſpiſes and Reproaches them, and that very groſſly too. For firſt he tells us, *That such an Union amongst the Divine Persons* (as is expressed by the word περιχώρησις) *they all agree in, but how to explain it they knew not*, Page 125. Lines 17, 18. And why then, in the Name of *God*, does he refer to the *Fathers* to justifie his Explanation of that, which in the very same Breath he says, *They knew not how to Explain?* And the Truth is, the *Fathers* never owned themselves able to explain it; and that for a very good Reason; *viz.* because they held it unexplicable and unconceivable; and not for that Scandalous Reason given by him, *viz.* That they *had gross Material Conceptions of the Deity*, by conceiving of it as of a *Substance*, Page 125. Lines 27, 28. For, says he, within Two Lines after, *Had they Contemplated God as a pure Mind, it had been easie to explain this περιχώρησις, or Indwelling of the Divine Persons in each other. Good God!* That any *Professor of Divinity* should call *that easie to explain*, which the Reason of all Mankind has hitherto bent under, as a Thing too great, and mysterious for it to comprehend, or to grapple with! So that if ever we have cause to cry out ὦ βάθος, it is here: Or that he should tax all those, who own themselves at a loss about it, *for not Contemplating God as a pure Mind!* But to him, I confess, who can Conceive *of such a Pure Mind, as is no Substance*; that is to say, in other words, *No Being*. (For I am sure he will not so much as pretend it to be *an Accident*) to Him, I say, I cannot wonder, if nothing seem difficult, or mysterious. In the mean time, it is shameless and insufferable in this Man to say, as he does Page 100, 101. *That his Explication of the Trinity is* not new, *but* the same *with that of the Fathers*, and afterwards in pursuance of this Assertion, to say, *That the Fathers knew not how to explain it*, and to give this as a Reason of their not knowing how to do so, viz. *That they had such*

gross

groſs Notions of God, that they could not conceive rightly of this Myſtery. For this he has roundly affirmed; and therefore ought in all Reaſon, either to prove this Charge upon the *Fathers*, or to give the World, and the Church of *England* in particular, ſatisfaction for ſpeaking ſo falſely and ſcandalouſly of ſuch glorious Lights and principal Pillars of the *Christian Church*; and ſuch as, I dare ſay, never Preached nor Prayed in any Conventicle.

But what the Doctrine of the *Fathers* is concerning this περιχώρησις, and how they underſtood thoſe words of our Saviour (expreſſed by this Term) is manifeſt from the Teſtimony of two or three of them, which I ſhall ſet down, as (in ſo known a caſe) abundantly ſufficient. St. *Cyrill* of *Alexandria*, ſays expreſly, *Chriſt's ſaying*, that he is in the Father, and the Father in him, *ſhews the Identity of the Deity, and the Unity of the Subſtance, or Eſſence.* And ſo likewiſe *Athanaſius*: *Accordingly therefore* (ſays he) *Chriſt having ſaid before*, I and my Father are one: *He adds*, I am in the Father, and the Father in me, *that he might ſhew both the Identity of the Divinity, and the Unity of Eſſence.* And ſo again St. *Hilary*: *The Father is in the Son, and the Son in the Father, by the Unity of an inſeparable [Undivided] Nature.* By which Paſſages, I ſuppoſe any Man of ſenſe will perceive, That the Thing which the *Fathers* meant and gathered from thoſe words of

Ἵνα διὰ μὲν τοῦ, τοῦτον ἐν ἐκείνῳ κἀκεῖνον ἐν τούτῳ φαίνεσθαι τὴν ταυτότητα τῆς Θεότητος καὶ τῆς οὐσίας ἑνότητα, δείξῃ. *Cyril. Theſaur. lib.* 12. p. 109.

Διὰ τοῦτο γοῦν, καὶ εἰκότως εἰρηκὼς πρότερον, Ἐγὼ καὶ ὁ πατὴρ ἕν ἐσμεν, ἐπήγαγε τὸ Ἐγὼ ἐν τῷ πατρὶ καὶ ὁ Πατὴρ ἐν Ἐμοὶ ἵνα τὴν μὲν ταυτότητα τῆς Θεότητος, τὴν δὲ ἑνότητα τῆς οὐσίας δείξῃ. *Athanaſius Oratione quarta contra Arianos.*

Pater in filio eſt & filius in Patre per inſeparabilis Naturæ Unitatem, *Hilarius de Trinitate, lib.* 8.

of our *Saviour* (since expressed by this περιχώρησις) was no *Unity of Mutual-Consciousness* (which they never mention) but an *Unity of Essence, or Nature* (which they expresly and constantly do.) Nor does this very Author deny it, as appears from his own words, though he quite perverts the sence of the *Fathers*, by a very senceless Remark upon them, *Page* 125. Lines 20, 21. *This Sameness* [or Unity] *of Nature* (says he) *might be the Cause of this Union* [in the *Divine Persons*] viz. by a περιχώρησις, *but not explain what this Intimate Union is.* Now this Author has been already told, That the Question here is not, what *explains this Union*, but what *this Union is?* But besides this his mistake of the Question, I desire him to declare, what he means *by the Cause of this Union?* (as he here expresses himself.) For will he make an *Union* (as he calls an *Unity*) in the *Divine Persons by Sameness of Nature a Cause of their Intimate Union by a* περιχώρησις, *or Mutual-In-being of them in each other*, and affirm also this περιχώρησις to be the same Thing *with Mutual-Consciousness?* If he does so, he makes the same Thing the Cause of it self. For the *Sameness of Nature in the Three Persons*, and their *Mutual-In-being, or In-dwelling*, are the very *same Thing*, and the *same Unity*, though differently expressed. But however, if we take him at his own word, it will effectually overthrow his Hypothesis. For *if the Sameness of the Divine Nature* in the *Three Persons*, be (as he says) the cause of this περιχώρησις, and this περιχώρησις be the same with *Mutual-Consciousness*; it will and must follow, That this *Sameness, or Unity of Nature* can no more consist in *Mutual-Consciousness*, than the *Cause* can consist in its *Effect*, or the Antecedent in its Consequent. And this Inference stands firm and unanswerable against him.

But

But as to the Truth of the Thing it ſelf, though we allow and grant *the Unity of the Divine Nature* in the *Three Perſons*, and *the Mutual In-being, or In-dwelling* of the ſaid *Perſons* in each other, to be the ſame Thing, yet we deny, That this their *Mutual In-being* is the ſame with their *Mutual-Conſciouſneſs*. But that their *Mutual-Conſciouſneſs* follows and *reſults from it*, and for that cauſe cannot be *formally the ſame* with it. And ſo I have done with his 3d Argument, which he has drawn from the περιχώρησις, and is indeed nothing elſe, but a bold downright *Perverſion of Scripture, and a* groſs Abuſe of the *Fathers.*

4. His fourth Argument is from an Allegation out of St. *Auſtin*, who, though he does not (as our Author confeſſes) *Name this Mutual-Conſciouſneſs, yet he explains a Trinity in Unity* (as he would perſwade us) *by Examples of Mutual-Conſciouſneſs*; particularly by *the Unity of the Three Faculties of* Underſtanding, Memory *and* Will *in the ſame Soul, all of them Mutually Conſcious to one another of the ſeveral Acts belonging to each of them.* And his 9th Book is ſpent upon this Argument; In which he makes *the Mind*, conſidered *with its knowledge of it ſelf, and its love of it ſelf* (all three of them (as he ſays) but one and the ſame Thing) *a faint Reſemblance of the Trinity in Unity.* And this is, what he Argues from St. *Auſtin.*

To which I Anſwer.

Firſt, That *Faint Reſemblances* are far from being ſolid Proofs of any Thing; and that, although ſimilitudes may ſerve to illuſtrate a Thing otherwiſe proved, yet they prove and conclude nothing. The *Fathers* indeed are full of them both upon this and ſeveral other Subjects, but ſtill they uſe them for Illuſtration only, and nothing elſe. And it is a ſcurvy ſign that Proofs and Arguments run very low with this Author, when he passes over those Principal Places in which the *Fathers* have plainly, openly and professedly declared their Judgment upon this great Article, and endeavours to gather their sence of it only from Similitudes and Allusions; which looks like a design of putting his Reader off with *something like an Argument, and not an Argument*, and *of which the Tail stands where the Head should*: For according to the True Method of proving Things, the *Reason* should always go first, and the *Similitude* come after; but by no means ought the *Similitude* ever to be put instead of the *Reason*. But

Secondly, To make it yet clearer, how unconclusive this Author's Allegation from St. *Austin* is, I shall demonstrate, That this *Father* does not here make use of *an Example of Mutual-Consciousness*, by shewing the great disparity between the Thing alledged, and the Thing which it is applyed to, and that, as to the very Case, which it is alledged for. For we must observe, That *the Mutual-Consciousness* of the *Persons* of the *Blessed Trinity* is such, as is fully and entirely in each *Person*, so that by vertue thereof every one of them is truly and properly *Conscious* of all that belongs to the other Two. But it is by no means so in those three Faculties of the Soul, *Understanding*, *Memory*, *and Will*. For though the *Understanding* indeed be *Conscious* to all that passes in the *Will*, yet I deny the *Will* to be *Conscious* to any Thing, or Act that passes either in the Understanding, or the Memory, and it is impossible it should be so, without exerting an Act of Knowledge, or Intellection; which to ascribe to the Faculty of the *Will*, would be infinitely absurd. It is true indeed, That one and the same Soul is *Conscious* to it self of the Acts of all these Three Faculties: But still it is by vertue of its Intellectual Faculty alone,

alone, that it is ſo. And the like is to be ſaid of its *Knowledge* and of its *Love* of it ſelf: For though it be the ſame Soul which both Knows and Loves it ſelf, yet it neither Knows it ſelf by an Act of *Love*, nor Loves it ſelf by an Act of *Knowledge* any more, than it can *Will* by an Act of the *Memory*, or *Remember* by an Act of the *Will*; which is impoſſible: and amongſt other proofs that it is ſo, it ſeems to me a very conſiderable one, that, if a Man could *remember* by his *Will*, this Author in all likelyhood, would not *forget* himſelf ſo often as he does. It is clear therefore on the one ſide, That the *Acts* of *Underſtanding*, *Memory, and Will*, neither are nor can be *Acts* of *Mutual-Conſciouſneſs*; and on the other, that *Father*, *Son*, and *Holy Ghoſt* do every one of them Exert *Acts* of *Mutual-Conſciouſneſs* upon one another, and conſequently, that, as to this thing, there is a total entire difference between both ſides of the Compariſon. For which cauſe it is to be hoped, that this Author himſelf will henceforth Conſult the Credit of his own Reaſon ſo far, as to give over proving, *That the Unity of the Divine Nature in the Three Bleſſed Perſons conſiſts wholly and ſolely in the Mutual-Conſciouſneſs of the ſaid Perſons*, by Examples taken from ſuch Created Things as are by no means *Mutually-Conſcious* to one another.

But to manifeſt yet further the Vanity of this his Allegation out of St. *Auſtin*, I ſhall plainly ſhew, wherein this *Father* placed the *Unity* of the *Three Divine Perſons*. And that, in ſhort, is *in the Unity of their Nature, Eſſence, and Subſtance. This is the Catholick Faith* (ſays he) *that we believe Father, Son, and Holy Ghoſt to be of one and the ſame Subſtance.*

Patrem Filium & Spiritum Sanctum, unius ejuſdemque Subſtantiæ, *Lib.* 1. *de Trinitate*, *Cap.* 4.

And again, *Let us believe in the Father, Son, and Holy Ghost. These are Eternal and Unchangeable*, that is, *One God, of One Substance, the Eternal Trinity*. And moreover, ſpeaking of ſuch as would have *Three Gods* to be Worſhipped, he adds, *That they know not what is the meaning of One and the ſame Subſtance, and are deceived by their own Fancies*; *and, becauſe they ſee Three Bodies ſeparate in Three Places, they think the Subſtance of God is ſo to be underſtood.*

Credamus ergo in Patrem & Filium & Spiritum Sanctum: Hæc æterna ſunt & incommutabilia, id eſt, Unus Deus, Unius Subſtantiæ, Trinitas æterna. Ibid.

Neſciunt enim quid ſit Una eademque Subſtantia, &c. *Lib. de Agone Chriſtiano.*

I think it very needleſs to add the like Teſtimonies from other *Fathers* (how numerous and full ſoever they may be) for our Author having here quoted only St. *Auſtin*, I ſhall confine my Anſwer to his Quotation, and think it enough for me to over-rule an Inference from a *Similitude* taken out of St. *Auſtin* by a *Plain, Literal, Unexceptionable* Declaration of St. *Auſtin*'s Opinion.

The Sum of the whole Matter is this, That the Thing to be proved by this Author, is, *That the Three Divine Perſons are One, only by an Unity of Mutual-Conſciouſneſs*: And to prove this, he produces only a Similitude out of St. *Auſtin*, and that alſo, a *Similitude* taken from Things, in which no ſuch Thing as *Mutual-Conſciouſneſs* is to be found. By which it appears, That his Argument is manifeſtly Lame of both Legs, and, as ſuch, I leave it *to ſhift for it ſelf*.

5. In the fifth and laſt place, He tells us, *That the Fathers alſo reſolved the Unity of the God-head in the Three Divine Perſons into the* Unity of Principle; *meaning thereby, That though there be Three Divine Perſons in the God-head,*

head, Father, Son and Holy Ghost; yet the Father is the Original and Fountain of the Deity, who begets the Son of his own Substance; and from whom, and the Son, the Holy Ghost eternally proceeds of the same Substance with the Father and Son; so that there is but one Principle and Fountain of the Deity, and therefore but one God, Page 128. Line 6.

Now all this is very true; but how will our Author bring it to his purpose? Why, thus, or not at all, *viz.* That the *Numerical Unity of Nature* in the *Three Divine Persons*, by being founded in, and resolved into this *Unity of Principle*, does therefore properly consist in *Mutual-Consciousness*. This, I say, must be his Inference, and it is a *large step*, I confess, and larger than any of the *Fathers* ever made: Nevertheless without making it, this Author must sit down short of his Point. And yet if he really thinks, that his Point may be concluded from hence; why, in the Name of Sence and Reason might he not as well have argued from *Gen.* 1. 1. *That God Created the Heavens and the Earth*, and that therefore the *Three Divine Persons* are and must be one, only by an *Unity* of *Mutual-Consciousness?* For it would have followed every whit as well from this as from the other. But, since the Creation of both, I believe, never Man disputed as this Man does, while he pretends to prove his *Mutual-Consciousness* from *the Unity of Principle* in the *Oeconomy* of the *Divine Persons*: And yet, if he does not design to prove it from thence, to what purpose is this *Unity of Principle* here alledged, where the only Point to be proved is, That the *Unity* of the *Divine Nature* in the *Three Persons* is only an *Unity* of *Mutual-Consciousness?*

But to come a little closer to him. If this Author can make it out, That the *Father* Communicates his Subſtance to the *Son*, and the *Father* and the *Son* together Communicate the ſame to the *Holy Ghoſt* by one *Eternal Act* of *Mutual-Conſciouſneſs*, Common to all *Three Perſons*, then his Argument from *Unity of Principle to an Unity of Nature, conſiſting in Mutual-Conſciouſneſs*, may ſignifie and conclude ſomething; but this he attempts not, nor if he ſhould, would he or any Man living be ever able to prove it.

But he is for coming over this Argument again, and tells us, *That (as* Petavius *well obſerves) it does not of it ſelf prove the Unity (that is to ſay, the Numerical Unity) of the God-head, but only the* ὁμοουσιότης, *or Sameneſs of Nature*, i. e. as he elſewhere explains himſelf [*the Specifick Sameneſs of Nature.*] *And that therefore the Fathers thought fit to add,* That God begets a Son, not without, but within Himſelf, *Page* 128. *Line* 17, &c.

In Anſwer to which Obſervation, though it affects the Point of *Mutual-Conſciouſneſs* (the only Thing now in hand) no more than what he had alledged before; yet in vindication both of the *Fathers* and of *Petavius* himſelf, I muſt needs tell this Author, That it is equally an Abuſe to both. For as to the *Fathers*; it has been ſufficiently proved to him, That neither is there any ſuch Thing as a *Specifick Unity, or Sameneſs of Nature* in the *Divine Perſons*, nor that the *Fathers* ever owned any ſuch, but ſtill by the ὁμοούσιον held only a *Numerical Unity of Nature*, and no other; ſo that their ſaying, That *God begot a Son within himſelf*, was rather a further Explication of the ὁμοούσιον, than any *Addition* at all to it. And as for *Petavius*, whereas this Man ſays, That he has obſerved, *That this Argumentation of the Fathers, does not of it ſelf prove the Numerical Unity of the God-head in the Three Perſons*; I averr, That *Petavius* obſerves no ſuch Thing. He ſays indeed; *If this Reaſoning (viz.* from

from Unity of Principle) *were considered Absolutely and Universally, it would prove rather a Specifick than a Numerical Unity of Nature*, and gives a Reason for it from *Humane Generation:* But then he does by no means say, That the *Fathers Arguments* in this Case ought to be so considered, but plainly limits them to the *Divine Generation*, as of a peculiar kind, differing from all others. And thereupon no less plainly Asserts, *That when the Father begets the Son, he Communicates to him the same Numerical Substance and Nature*, and says expresly, *That the force and strength of the Fathers Argumentation is taken from the proper Condition and Nature of the Divinity, and the Divine Generation, from whence they collect, not any kind of Unity of Essence, but only a Singular and Numerical Unity in the Three Divine Persons*: Which he makes good by Instances from St. *Athanasius* and St. *Hilary*. And this is the true state of the Case, and shews, That *Petavius* understood the *Fathers*; whether he, who takes upon him to be his Corrector and Confuter, does or no. In the mean time it is shameless to insinuate in this manner, that *Petavius* represented these Arguments of the *Fathers*, as proving only the [*Specifick*] *Sameness of Nature*, and *not the Numerical Unity of the God-head*, when he plainly shews, That they designed thereby to prove a *Numerical Unity of Essence* in the *Divine Persons*, and nothing else.

Ex *propria* Divinitatis divinæque Generationis Conditione ac natura Vis & robur Argumentationis istius petitur, quatenus non qualemcunque Essentiæ Unitatem sed Singularem & Numeralem inesse Tribus Personis colligit. *Petav. Dog. de Trinitate. Lib. 4. Cap.* 15.

But this Author seems to assume to himself a peculiar Priviledge of saying *what he will, and of whom he will.* In which nevertheless I cannot but commend his Conduct, as little as I like his Arguing. For that, as he makes so bold with so Learned and Renowned a Person as *Peta-*

vius; So he wiſely does it now that he is laid faſt in his Grave. For had *Petavius* been living, and this Man wrote his Book in the ſame Language in which *Petavius* wrote his (which, for a certain Reaſon, I am pretty well ſatisfied he never would) there is no doubt but *Petavius* would have toſſed him and his *New Notion* of *Three diſtinct Infinite Spirits*, long ſince, in a Blanket, and effectually taught him the difference of Inſulting over a Great Man when his Head is low, and when he is able to defend himſelf.

We have ſeen how little our Author has been able to ſerve himſelf of the fore-mentioned *Reſolution of the Unity of the Divine Nature, into an Unity of Principle*, by way of Argument in behalf of his *Mutual-Conſciouſneſs*. Nevertheleſs, though it fails him, as an *Argument*, yet, that he may not wholly loſe it, he ſeems deſirous to cultivate it as a *Notion*; and upon that ſcore tells us, That it needs ſomething further both to *Complete* and *Explain* it, (which, with reference to his own Apprehenſions of it, I eaſily believe) but however, I ſhall take ſome Account of what he ſays, both as to the *Completion, and Explication of it*. And

Firſt, For the *Completion*. He tells us, *That Father, Son, and Holy Ghoſt, are Eſſential to One God*, and that upon this Account there muſt be neceſſarily *Three Perſons in the Unity of the Godhead, and can be no more*. As to which laſt Clauſe he muſt give me leave to tell him, That it is not the *bare Eſſentiality* of the *Three Perſons* to the *God-head*, which proves that there can be no more than *Three* belonging to it: but it is the *Peculiar Condition* of the *Perſons*, which proves this; without which the *Eſſentiality* of the *Three*, would no more hinder the *Eſſentiality* of a *Fourth* or *Fifth*, than the *Eſſentiality* of *Two* could take away the *Eſſentiality* of a *Third*. And therefore though the

the Propoſition laid down by him be true, yet his Reaſon for it will not hold.

But one choice Paſſage quoted by him out of a great *Father*, I muſt by no means omit, *viz*. That upon Account of this *Unity of Principle*, St. *Auſtin* calls the *Trinity*, *Unam quandam ſummam Rem*, Page 123. Line 8. Concerning which, I deſire any Man living (except this Author) to declare freely, whether he thinks that St. *Auſtin*, or any one elſe of Sence and Learning would call *Three diſtinct Infinite Minds, or Spirits* (which are neither *Numerically*, nor *Specifically*, nor ſo much as *Collectively One) Unam quandam ſummam Rem*. But in the

Second Place: As for his *Explication* of the ſaid *Notion*, he tells us, *That he ſhall proceed by ſeveral ſteps*, and thoſe (as he would perſwade us) *very plain, and Univerſally acknowledged by all*, Page 126. Lines 16, 17, *&c*.

Nevertheleſs, by his good leave, I ſhall and muſt demur to Two of them, as by no means fit to be acknowledged by any, and much leſs *ſuch as are acknowledged by all*. And they are the *Third* and *Fourth*. In which he tells us, That, in the firſt place, *Original Mind and Wiſdom*, and in the ſecond, *That Knowledge of it ſelf*, and laſtly, *Love of it ſelf*, are all of them *diſtinct Acts, and ſo diſtinct, that they can never be one Simple Individual Act*. And withal, that theſe Acts being thus diſtinct, muſt be *Three Subſtantial Acts in God*, That is to ſay, *Three Subſiſting Perſons*: By which *Three Subſtantial Acts* he muſt of neceſſity mean *Three ſuch Acts, as are Three Subſtances*. Foraſmuch as he adds in the very next words, *That there is nothing but Eſſence and Subſtance in God*, Page 130. Lines 7, 8, 9. to the middle of the Page.

Now againſt theſe ſtrange Poſitions, I Argue thus.

First, If the Three fore-mentioned *Acts* are so distinct in *God*, that they can never be *One Simple Individual Act*, then I infer, That the said *Three Acts* cannot possibly be *One God*. Forasmuch as to be *One God*, is to be *One Pure Simple Indivisible Act*. And thus we see how at *one step*, or stroke, he has *Ungodded* the *Three Persons* of the *Blessed Trinity*. For *these Three Acts* (he tells us) *are the Three Persons in the Godhead*. Though I believe no *Divine* before him, ever affirmed a *Person to be an Act, or an Act a Person*; with how great Confidence soever (and something else) this Man affirms it here.

Secondly, If those *Three Acts* in the *God-head* are *Three distinct Infinite Substances* (as he plainly says they are, by telling us, Page 130. Line 19. *That there is nothing but Essence and Substance in God)* then in the *Godhead* there are and must be *Three distinct Gods*, or *Godheads*. Forasmuch as an *Infinite Substance* being properly God, every *distinct infinite Substance*, is and must be a *distinct God*.

These I affirm to be the direct unavoidable Consequences of those two short Paragraphs in *Page* 130. which he makes his *Third* and *Fourth Explanatory Steps*.

But because he may here probably bear himself upon that Maxim, *That there is nothing but Essence and Substance in God*, (which yet by the way might better become any one to plead than himself) let me tell him, That that *Proposition* is not absolutely, and in all Sences true. If indeed he means by it, That there is no *Being*, whether *Substance*, or *Accident* in *God*, besides his own most *Pure, Simple, Indivisible Substance*, or *Essence*, (which is the commonly received sence of it) it is most true. But if he therefore affirms, That neither are there any

Modes,

Modes, or *Relations* in *God*, this will not be granted him. For in *God*, besides *Essence*, or *Substance*, we assert, That there is that, which we call *Mode*, *Habitude*, and *Relation*: And by one or other of these in Conjunction with *Essence*, or *Substance*, we give account of all the *Acts*, *Attributes*, and *Personalities* belonging to the *Divine Nature*, or *Godhead*. This is the constant, unanimously received Doctrine of *Divines*, *School-men*, and *Metaphysicians*, in their Discourses upon *God*, and without which, it is impossible to Discourse intelligibly of the *Divine Acts*, *Attributes*, or *Persons*. And as it stands upon a firm bottom, so it may well be defended: And if this Author has ought to except against it, I shall be ready to undertake the defence of it against him at any time.

But still, that he may keep up that Glorious, standing Character of *Self-Contradiction*, (which, one would think to be the very *Ratio formalis*; or, at least, the *Personal Property* of the Man.) Having here, in *Page* 130. made a very bold *step*, by Asserting *the Three Divine Persons, to be Three distinct Acts, and so distinct, that they can never be one Simple, Individual Act*. In the very next Page but one, *viz.* 132. Line 13. he roundly affirms, *That the Father and the Son are one single Energy and Operation*. Now, how safe and happy is this Man, that no Absurdities, or Contradictions can ever hurt him! Or at least, that he never feels them, let them *pinch* never so close and hard.

What remains, is chiefly a Discourse about the different way of the *Son*'s issuing from the *Father*, and the *Holy Ghost*'s issuing from both: As that the former is called *Generation*, because the *Son* issues from the *Father* by a *Reflex Act*, and the latter termed *Procession*, because the *Holy Ghost* issues from both by a *direct Act*. But why a *Reflex Act* must needs be termed properly a *Generation*, and a *direct Act* not be capable of being properly so accounted, this our Acute Author very discreetly says nothing at all to; though (under favour) all that he says besides, leaves us as much in the Dark as we were before. And for my own part, I cannot think my self concerned to clear up a Point wholly foreign to that, which alone I have undertook the Discussion of.

And thus I have finished my Dispute with Him, concerning the Authorities of the *Fathers* alledged in behalf of his *Notion* of *Mutual-Consciousness*, as that, wherein he places the *Unity* of the *Divine Nature* belonging to the *Three Blessed Persons*. The Sum of which whole Dispute is resolved into this single Question, viz. *In what the Fathers placed the Unity in Trinity?* And if they placed it in the *Sameness*, or *Unity* of *Nature*, *Substance*, or *Essence*, (words applyed by them to this Subject at least a Thousand Times, and still used *to signifie one and the same Thing*) then it is plain that they did not place it in an *Unity of Mutual-Consciousness*. For, I suppose, no Man (this Author himself not excepted) will say, That *Essence*, or *Substance*, and *Mutual-Consciousness* are Terms *Synonymous*, and of the same signification. And as the whole Dispute turns upon this single Question; so in the management of it, on my part, I have with great particularity gone over all the Proofs by which this Author pretends to have evinced his Doctrine from the *Fathers*. The utmost of which Proofs amounts to this, That the *Fathers* proved an *Unity of Nature* in the *Divine Persons*, from the μία ἐνέργεια, the μία κίνησις βουλήματος, and the περιχώρησις Common to them all: And moreover, sometimes illustrated the said *Unity* by the *Three Faculties* of the *Understanding*, *Memory*, and *Will* being one with the Soul which they belonged to. And Lastly,

That

That they reſolved *the Unity of the Trinity* into *an Unity of Principle*; the *Father* being upon that account ſtyled, *Principium & fons Deitatis*, as Communicating the *Divine Subſtance* to the *Son* and together with the *Son* to the *Holy Ghoſt*. And what of all this, I pray? Do all, or any of the fore-mentioned Terms ſignifie *Mutual-Conſciouſneſs*? Why, No: But this Author with a *non obſtante* both to the proper ſignification and common uſe of them all, by abſolute Prerogative declares them to mean *Mutual-Conſciouſneſs*: And ſo his Point is proved, viz. *That Mutual-Conſciouſneſs is not only an Argument inferring the Unity of the Divine Nature in the Three Bleſſed Perſons*, (which yet was all, that the *Fathers* uſed the fore-mentioned Terms for) but, (which is more) *That it is that very Thing wherein this Unity does Conſiſt*. This, I ſay, is a True, though a ſhort Account of all his *Arguments* upon this *Subject*; and (according to my cuſtom) I refer it to the Judicious Reader, to judge impartially, whether it be not ſo, and withal to improve and carry on the aforeſaid *Arguments* in his behalf to all further advantage that they may be Capable of.

But in the iſſue, methinks the Author himſelf ſeems to review them with much leſs Confidence of their Puiſſance, than when at firſt he produced them. For if we look back upon the Triumphant Flag hung out by him at his *Entrance* upon this part of his Work (the only proper time for him to Triumph in) and when he declared, *That his Explication of the Trinity was the Conſtant Doctrine of the Fathers and the Schools*, Page 101. Lines 24, 25. who could have imagined but that he then foreſaw, that he ſhould prove his Point with all the ſtrength and evidence which his own Heart could deſire? And yet alas! Such, for the moſt part, is the vaſt diſtance between Promiſes and Performances, that we have him bringing up the Rear of all with this sneaking Conclusion, Page 138. Line 22, &c. *It must be confessed*, (says he) *That the Ancient Fathers did not express their sence in the* same Terms *that I have done. But I leave it to any Indifferent and Impartial Reader, whether they do not* seem to have intended *the same Explication which I have given of this Venerable Mystery.* These are his words; and I do very particularly recommend them to the Reader, as deserving his peculiar Notice. For is this now the Upshot and Result of so daring a Boast, and so confident an Undertaking, to prove his Opinion *the Constant Doctrine of the Fathers?* viz. *That though the Fathers speak not one word of it*; nay, *though they knew not how to express themselves about it*, Page 125. Line 18. Yet *that to an Indifferent Reader* (and a very *indifferent* one indeed he must needs be in the worst sence) they may *seem to intend the same Explication he had given of it?* So that the Sum of his whole Proof and Argument amounts to this and no more, *viz.* That to some Persons *videtur quòd sic*, and to others, *videtur quòd non.* For see, how low he sinks in the issue. First of all from the *Fathers positive saying, or holding* what he does, it is brought down to their *Intending* it; and from their *Intending* it, it falls at last to their *seeming to Intend it*; and that is all. And now, is not this a worthy Proof of so high a Point? And may it not justly subject this Author to the same *Sarcastical Irony* which he passed upon his *Socinian Adversary?* Page 92. Line 17, &c. *Right, very Right, Sir, a plain Demonstration!*

But still there is one half of his Promise to be yet accounted for, viz. *The proving his Opinion to have been the constant Doctrine of the Schools.* And how does he acquit himself as to this? Why, in a very extraordinary manner too. For, first, instead of alledging the Authority

of

of the *School-men*, he tells us, Page 138. *That they are of no Authority at all, but as they fall in with the Fathers.* And withal, That instead of doing so, *They use to mistake, and clog the sence of the Fathers with some peculiar Niceties and Distinctions of their own.* And *that, the Truth is, the vain Endeavours of reducing this Mystery to Terms of Art, such as Nature, Essence, Substance, Subsistence, Hypostasis, Person, and the like,* (which (he says) some of the *Fathers* used in a very *different sence from each other) have wholly confounded this Mystery.*

And here I cannot but desire the Reader to judge, whether this be not a new and wonderful way of procuring Credit to an Hypothesis, upon the score of its being *the constant Doctrine of the Schools*, by telling the World (as this Man here does) that the *School-men* are a Company of *Impertinent Fellows*, of little or no Authority in themselves, and who have by their useless absurd Niceties, confounded this whole Mystery? For if they are of no Authority but what they derive from the *Fathers*, (as he avers) why does he quote them upon the same level with the *Fathers*, and plead them both as *two distinct Authorities?* And if they do nothing but pervert and confound this Mystery, why, instead of alledging them, does he not earnestly caution his Reader against them, and disswade him from having any Thing to do with their dangerous and absurd Writings? This certainly is a way of proving a Point by *Testimony* and *Authority*, so beyond all Example ridiculous, that unless the Reader will vouchsafe to read these Passages in the Author himself, and so take his Conviction from his own Eyes, I can hardly blame him, if he refuses to believe my bare Affirmation in a Thing so Incredible.

As for the Terms *Essence, Substance, Subsistence, Person, and the like,* which he so explodes, I hope I have given

given my Reader a satisfactory Account both of their Usefulness, and of the uselesness of such as this Author would Substitute in their room, in *Chap.* 2. at large, to which I refer him. And whereas he says, Page 139. Line 25. &c. *That the Deity is above Nature, and above Terms of Art; and that there is nothing like this Mysterious Distinction and Unity; and therefore, no wonder, if we want proper words to express it by; at least, that such Names as signifie the Distinction and Unity of Creatures, should not reach it.* If by all this he means, That there are no *Terms of Art* Comprehensive, and fully expressive of the *Divine Nature*, and the *Mysterious Distinction* and *Unity* of the *Persons* belonging to it, none that I know of thinks otherwise. But if he means that no *Terms of Art* can be of any use to aid us in our inadequate imperfect Conceptions of those great Things, so as thereby we may conceive of them in some better degree, and clearer manner, than we could without such *Terms*, pray then, of what use are his *Self-Consciousness* and *Mutual-Consciousness* in this Matter? For I suppose he will allow these to be *Terms of Art* too; and such (I am sure) as he has promised the World no small Wonders from. But if he will allow any Usefulness in those two *Terms of Art* (of his *own Inventing)* towards our better Apprehension of the *Divine Nature* and *Persons*, the same and greater has the constant use of all *Church-Writers* proved to be in the *Terms Essence, Substance, Hypostasis, Person*, &c. as the properest and most significant, the fittest and most accommodate to help and methodize Men's Thoughts in discoursing of *God*, and *Immaterial Beings*, of all or any other *Terms of Art*, which the Wit of Man ever yet invented, or pitched upon for that purpose. And I hope, the known avowed use and experience of such great Men, and those in so great a number,

is

is an abundant overpoise to the contrary Affirmation of this, or any other *Novel* Author whatsoever.

But all this (it seems) he endeavours to overthrow and dash with *Three* Terrible Confounding Questions, *Page* 139. Lines 22, 23, *&c.* Which yet I can by no means think so very formidable, but that they may be very safely Encountered, and fairly Answered too. As,

Qu. 1. *What* (says our Author) *is the Substance, or Nature of God?*

I Answer. It is a *Being* existing of, and by it self, Incorporeal, Infinite, Eternal, Omniscient, Omnipotent, *&c.*

Qu. 2. *How can Three distinct Persons have but One Numerical Substance?*

I Answer. Every whit as well as they can be said to have but one *Numerical Godhead*, or *Divine Nature*; or as they can have one *Numerical Mutual-Consciousness* common to them all.

Qu. 3. *What is the Distinction between Essence, and Personality, and Subsistence?*

I Answer. The same, that is between a *Thing*, or *Being, and the Modes of it.* And he, who neither knows, nor admits of a difference between these, is much fitter to go to School himself, than to sit and pass judgment upon the *School-men.* And as for the Terms *Subsistence* and *Personality*, they import the last and utmost Completion of the Existence of Things, by vertue whereof, they exist by themselves so, as neither to be *Supported* by, nor *Communicable* to any Subject. Of which Two *Modes*, *Personality* belongs only to *Intelligent Beings*, but *Subsistence* to all others, to whom the aforesaid Definition does agree. And this is the True, Proper Difference and Distinction between these Two. And

this

this Author may take Notice of it, if he pleases.

However, having thus answered his Questions (tho' to what purpose he proposed them, I cannot imagine) yet that he may see how ambitious I am to follow his great Example, I shall, in requital of his Three Questions, propose these Four to him: As

First, Since in *Page* 139. he affirms *the Deity to be above Nature, and all Terms of Art*; *so that we want proper Words and Names to express the Distinction and Unity of the Divine Persons by, and that such, as signifie the Distinction and Unity of Creatures, cannot reach it.* I desire to know of him upon what ground of Reason it is, That speaking of this same *Mysterious Unity and Distinction* in *Page* 106. *Lines* 11, 12, &c. He says, That *the Fathers used several Examples, and alluded to several kinds of Union, thereby to form an adequate Notion of the Unity of the Godhead?* For if the Deity be so far above *Nature* and all *Terms of Art*, that there is an utter want of words, or Names to express the *Unity* of it by, *How could any Examples, or Allusions drawn from Nature* (though never so many) form in us *an Adequate Notion thereof?* Hitherto both *Divines* and *Philosophers* have judged the *Divine Nature* absolutely Incomprehensible by any *Adequate*, or *Complete Conception* of it. And for my own part, I account *the Unity of it in Trinity*, much less capable of having an *Adequate Notion* formed of it, than the *Deity* considered barely in it self is, and consequently that it is as much as Humane Reason can reach to, to have a *true* and *certain* Notion of it, though very *Imperfect* and *Inadequate*. But as for an *Adequate Notion of the Unity of the Godhead in Three Divine Persons*, if this Author can form to himself such an one, let him enjoy it as a Priviledge peculiar to himself, and not obtainable by any other

Mortal

Having thus followed this Author both in his Reasonings and Quotations, and found him equally Impertinent in both, I must again desire my Reader to joyn with me in admiring the strange Confidence of the Man. I have already noted, with what a daring Assurance he vouched his New Opinion *for the constant Doctrine both of the Fathers and the Schools*, Page 101. Line 24. *&c.* After which Peremptory Asseveration, who could have expected, but that he would have appeared in the Head of Thirty, or Twenty *Fathers* at least (*Greek* and *Latin* together) to have rescued his beloved *Hypothesis* from the Imputation and Charge and Novelty, which he seems so desirous to Ward off? *P.* 100. *L.* 22. And that besides *Gr. Nyssen, Athanasius, Maximus, Nazianzen, Damascen* (and these for the most part quoted upon an Account not at all relating to his *Hypothesis*) and St. *Cyrill*, (who is not so much as Quoted, but only Named) we should have had *Justin Martyr, Irenæus, Origen, Clemens Alexandrinus*, St. *Basil, Theodoret, Epiphanius*, with several more, all alledged in his behalf? And amongst the *Latins* that we should besides St. *Austin*, whom alone he quotes, and St. *Ambrose*, whom he only mentions about the ὁμοούσιον, *Page* 107. *Line* 10. have heard also of *Tertullian, Lactantius*, St. *Cyprian*, St. *Jerome*, and St. *Hilary*, with a great many others? And then lastly for the *Schoolmen*, who could have expected fewer of them also, than Ten, or Twenty? And that we should have seen *Alexander Alensis* (the first who Commented upon the *Oracle*) with *Durandus, Aquinas, Scotus, Major. Biel, Soto, Vasquez, Cajetan, Gr. de Valentiâ, Estius*, and many more of the *Scholastick Tribe*, all drawn forth in Rank and File, to have fought his Battels? But when after all, none but poor *Peter Lombard* comes forth like a *Doughty Captain*, with none to follow him, this methinks looks more like the Despair of a Cause, than the Defence of it. For though our Author calls *Peter Lombard the Oracle of the Schools*, and all know his Sentences to be the Text which the *School-men* undertake to Explain and Comment upon: Yet Experience has told us, That the *Responses of this Oracle* (as well as of those heretofore) are often found very *Dubious and Ambiguous*. Witness *Thomas* and his Followers expounding them one way, and *Scotus* and his Disciples understanding them another; and several, (amongst whom *Durandus* and *Greg. Ariminensis*) going a different way from both. So that sometimes there is but too much need of a good Interpreter to fix the sence of this *Oracle*, (as great a Veneration as the *Schools* may have for him.) And therefore since his Text is not always so very plain and easie as to make an Explication of it superfluous, this Author having quoted *Peter Lombard* in such, or such a sence, ought in all Reason to have produced the Major and more eminent part of the *School-men* and *Writers* upon him, and shewn their Unanimous Concurrence in the same Sence and Notion, which he took him in, and quoted him for. And this indeed would have been to his Purpuse, and look'd like proving his Opinion to have been *the Doctrine of the Schools*. Otherwise I cannot see how the *Master of the Sentences* can be called, or pass for all the *School-men*, any more than the *Master of the Temple* can pass for all the *Divines* of the *Church of England*. Unless we should imagine, that this *Peter Lombard* had by a kind of *Mutual-Consciousness* gathered all his Numerous Brood into Himself, and so United them all into one Author. So that the Sum of all is this, That this Author, having declared his Opinion, *the constant Doctrine both of the Fathers and the Schools*, to make his words good, has produced for it Three or Four *Greek Fathers*, and Two

Latin (though even these no more to his purpose than if he had quoted *Dod* and *Cleaver*, or τὸν δ' ἀπαμειβόμενος, out of *Homer*) and lastly, *One* Sentence out of *one School-man*. Which if it be allowed to pass for a good, just, and sufficient Proof of any Controverted Conclusion, let it for the future, by all means, for this our Author's sake, be an Established Rule in Logick from a Particular, to infer an Universal.

And now that I am bringing my Reader towards a close of this long Chapter, I must desire him to look a little back towards the beginning of the foregoing Chapter, wherein, upon this Man's Confident Affirmation, That *his Opinion was the Constant Doctrine both of the Fathers and the Schools*, I thought it necessary to state what his Opinion was, and accordingly I shew'd, that it Consisted of Four Heads.

1st. That the *Three Persons of the Blessed Trinity were Three distinct Infinite Minds, or Spirits*; which how far he was from being able to prove from the Authority of any of the *Fathers* cited by him, was sufficiently shewn by us in the preceding Chapter. The

2d. Was, *That Self-Consciousness was the formal Reason of Personality in the said Three Persons, and consequently That, whereby they were distinguished from each other*; which (in the same Chapter) I shew'd he was so far from proving from the Authority of those *Ancient Writers*, that he did not alledge one Tittle out of any of them for it, nor indeed so much as mention it in any of the Quotations there made by him. And as for the

3d. Member of his said *Hypothesis*, viz. *That the Unity of the Divine Nature in the Three Blessed Persons, Consisted in the Mutual-Consciousness belonging to them*, This we have Examined at large, and Confuted in this Chapter. But still there remains the

4th. And

4th. And last to be spoken to, as completeing his whole Hypothesis, and resulting, by direct Consequence, from the other Three, viz. *That a Trinity in Unity, and Unity in Trinity, explained by the Three forementioned Terms, or Principles, is a very plain, easie, and Intelligible Notion*; which having been in a most Confident, Peremptory manner, affirmed by him all along, (as I shew in *Chap.* 1.) and upon that Score, making so great a part of his *Hypothesis*, ought in all reason to be be proved to have been the Sence and Doctrine of the *Fathers* concerning this Article.But not one word does he produce upon this Head neither. Nor, for my own part, do I expect ever to find the least *Sentence* or *Syllable* in any *Ancient Writer* tending this way. And I challenge this Author to produce so much as one to this purpose.

In the mean time, how, and with what kind of words I find these *Ancient Writers* expressing themselves about this Venerable Mystery, I shall here set down. Only I shall premise a Sentence or two out of this Author himself; and which I have had occasion to quote more than once before, from *Page* 106. *Line* 7. viz. *That the Unity in Trinity being* (as he confesses) *so great a Mystery, that we have no Example of it in Nature, it is no wonder if it cannot be explained by any one kind of Natural Union*; *and that therefore it was necessary to use several Examples, and to allude to several Kinds of Union, to form an Adequate Notion of the Godhead*; and moreover, *Page* 139. *Line* 26. &c. *That there is nothing like this Mysterious Distinction and Unity, and that we want proper words to express it by.*

All which Passages lying clear, open, and express in the fore-cited places of this Author, I must needs ask him, Whether all these are used by Him to prove *the Unity*

Unity in Trinity a plain easie and Intelligible Notion, as he has frequently elsewhere asserted it to be? As, to go over each of the Particulars;

First, Whether we must account it *Plain*, because he says, *It is a Great Mystery, of which we have no Example in Nature?* And

Secondly, Whether we must reckon it *easie*, because he says, *That it cannot be Explained by any one kind of Natural Union, but that several Examples must be used, and several sorts of Union alluded to for this purpose?* And

Lastly, Whether it must pass for *Intelligible*, because he tells us, *That we want proper words to express it by*, that is, in other Terms, to make it *Intelligible?* since *to express a Thing*, and *to make it Intelligible*, I take to be *Terms* equivalent.

In fine, I here appeal to the Reader, Whether we ought from the forementioned Passages of this Author, to take the *Unity in Trinity, and Trinity in Unity for a plain, easie, Intelligible Notion*, according to the same Author's affirmation so frequently inculcated in so many Parts of his Book?

But I shall now proceed to shew, (as I promised) how the *Fathers* speak and declare themselves upon this great Point. And here we will begin first with *Justin Martyr*. *A Singularity, or Unity* (says he) *is understood by us, and a* Trinity in Unity *is acknowledged. But how it is thus, I am neither willing to ask others, nor can I perswade my self, with my Muddy Tongue and Polluted Flesh, to attempt a Declaration of such*

Μονὰς ἐν τριάδι νοεῖται, καὶ τριὰς ἐν μονάδι γνωρίζεται. Καὶ πῶς τοῦτο, ἢ διερωτᾷν οὔτ' ἄλλους ἐθελόμην, οὔτ' αὐτὸς ἐμαυτὸν δυνάμην πείθειν τοὺς περὶ τῶν ἀποῤῥήτων λόγους γλώσσῃ πηλίνῃ καὶ σαρκίῳ ῥυπῶντι κατατολμᾷν. *Justin. Martyr. Exposit. Fidei de rectâ Confessione. Pag. 379. Edit. Colon.* 1686.

Ineffable

Οἰκονομίας τῆς θείας Τριάδος ἄρρητος ὁ λόγος. *Justin. Mar.* ibid. p. 381.

Ineffable Matters. And again, ſpeaking of the *Oeconomy* of the *Bleſſed Trinity*, The *Nature* and *Manner* (ſays he) of this *Oeconomy is unutterable.* And yet again, ſpeaking of this Myſterious *Oeconomy* of the *Deity* and the *Trinity*, as one of the greateſt *Myſteries* of the *Chriſtian Faith: I cry out* (ſays he) *O wonderful! For that the Principles and Articles of our Religion ſurpaſs, and tranſcend the Underſtanding, Reaſon, and Comprehenſion of a Created Nature.* In the next place, *Dionyſius* the *Areopagite* (or ſome very *Ancient Writer* under that Name) calls it the *Tranſcendent*, *Supereſſential*, and *Superlatively Divine Trinity.* In like manner *Gregory Nyſſen*, *We apprehend* (ſays he) *in theſe* (viz. the *Three Divine Perſons*) *a certain Inexpreſſible, Inconceivable Unity (or Communication) and Diſtinction*, &c. St. *Baſil* alſo, Writing againſt ſuch as would derogate from the Equality of the *Divine Perſons*, ſpeaks of the *Trinity* thus, *Either let theſe Inexpreſſible Things be ſilently Reverenced, or Religiouſly and Becomingly Repreſented.* And again, in a Diſcourſe againſt ſuch as uſed Contumelious Words of the *Trinity*, ſpeaking there of the *Holy Ghoſt* as *Eſſentially* one with the *Father*

Ἀναφωνῶ ὦ θαῦμα, ὅτι ὑπὲρ νοῦν, ὑπὲρ λόγον, ὑπὲρ κατάληψιν τῆς κτιστῆς φύσεως τὰ ἡμέτερα. *Juſtin. Mart.* ibid. p.387, 388.

Τριὰς ὑπερούσιος καὶ ὑπέρθεος. *Dionyſius Areopagita in Myſticâ Theologiâ*, cap. 1. pag. 271. *Pariſ. Edit.* 1615.

Ἄρρητός τις καὶ ἀκατάληπτος ἐν τούτοις καταλαμβάνεται καὶ ἡ κοινωνία καὶ ἡ διάκρισις, &c. *Greg. Nyſſen.* Pag.465. Tom.2. *Edit. Pariſienſ.* 1615.

Ἢ γὰρ σιωπῇ τιμάσθω τὰ ἄρρητα, ἢ εὐσεβῶς ἀριθμείσθω τὰ ἅγια. *Baſilius libro de Spiritu Sancto ad Amphilochium*, cap. 18. p. 332. Tom. 2. *Edit. Pariſ.* 1637.

ther and the *Son*, he says, *The Intimate Conjunction between him and them is hereby declared* (viz. by the *Scripture* there quoted by him, and applyed to them) *but the* Ineffable Manner *of his Subsistence hereby Inviolably preserved.* So that still (we see) with this *Father* the *Oeconomy of the Three Divine Persons in the Blessed Trinity*, is a Thing *Ineffable*, and above all Description, or Expression. *Nazianzen* also speaks of the *Trinity* under these Epithetes, styling it *the Adorable Trinity*, Above, and before the World, before all Time, of the same Majesty, of the same Glory, Increate, and Invisible, above our Reach, and Incomprehensible. And the same Epithetes are given it by *Nicephorus* Patriarch of *Constantinople*, in the *Acts* of the *Council* of *Ephesus*, declaring the *Trinity* to be of *One and the same Essence, Transcendent in its Substance, Invisible, and Inconceivable.* And Lastly, *Eulogius*, Archbishop of *Alexandria*, sets it forth thus. *We divide not* (says he) *what is but One, we part not the Singularity, nor distract the Unity; but so Assert this* Unity,

Τῆς μὲν οἰκειότητος δηλουμένης ἐντεῦθεν, τοῦ δὲ τρόπου τῆς ὑπάρξεως ἀῤῥήτου φυλαττομένου. ibid. pag. 333.

Τριὰς προσκυνητὴ, ὑπερκόσμιος, ὁμόθρονος, ὁμόδοξος, ὑπέρχρονος, ἄκτιστος, ἀόρατος, ἀναφὴς, ἀπερίληπτος. *Greg. Nazianzen. Oratione* 12. P. 204. *Edition. Parisiens. Anno Dom.* 1630.

Τριὰς ὁμοούσιος, ὑπερούσιος, ἀόρατος, ἀκατάληπτος. *Nicephorus Constantinopolitanus in Actis Synodi Ephesinæ*, Pag. 307. *Editionis Commelianæ* 1591.

Οὐ γὰρ διαιροῦμεν, οὐ τὴν μονάδα μερίζομεν, οὐ τὴν ἑνάδα διασπῶμεν, ἀλλὰ τῇ ἀϊδίῳ μονότητι θεολογοῦντες ταύτην, ἐν τρισὶν αὐτὴν συνθεολογοῦμεν ὑποστάσεσιν, οὐ διαθρυπτοῖς λογισμοῖς τὰ ὑπὲρ νοῦν ὑπερβάλλοντες, οὔτε περινοοῦντες ταῖς ἐρευναῖς τὰ ὑπὲρ εὕρεσιν συμβιβάζοντες. *Eulogius Archiepiscopus Alexandrinus in Bibliothecâ Photii.* Cod. 230. Pag. 865. *Rothomagi Anno Dom.* 1653.

Unity, in an Eternal Singularity, as to ascribe the same to Three distinct Hypostases; *by no means subjecting things* above our Understanding, *to Human Reasonings, nor by an Over-curious Search undervaluing Things so much* above all Search, or Discovery.

Having given this Specimen of what the *Greek Fathers* and *Writers* thought and spoke of the *Trinity*, let us now pass to the *Latines*. And amongst these, we have in the first place, St. *Hilary* expressing himself thus. *The Mystery of the Trinity is Immense and Incomprehensible, not to be express'd by Words, nor reach'd by Sence, Imperceivable, it blinds our Sight, it exceeds the Capacity of our Understanding. I understand it not. Nevertheless, I will comfort my self in this, That neither do the Angels know it, nor Ages apprehend it, nor have the Apostles enquired of it, nor the Son himself declared it. Let us therefore leave off complaining*, &c.

Trinitatis Mysterium est immensum,& Incomprehensibile, extra significantiam sermonis, extra sensûs intentionem, Imperspicabile, Lumen occæcat, Intelligentiæ Capacitatem excedit. Ego nescio ; sed consolabor me tamen : Angeli nesciunt, sæcula non tenent, Apostolus non interrogavit, Filius ipse non edidit. Cesset ergo dolor querelarum, &c. *Sanctus Hilarius Libro secundo de Trinitate*.

After him, let us hear St. *Ambrose*, *The Divinity of the Holy Trinity* (says he) *is to be believed by us to be without beginning or end*; *albeit, hardly possible to be comprehended by the Mind of Man.*

Absque ullo Principio aut fine credenda est Sanctæ Trinitatis Divinitas. Licèt humanæ sit menti ipsa comprehensione difficilis. Unde non incongrue dicitur quòd hoc solum ex eâ comprehendimus, quia prorsus comprehendi non potest. *Ambrosius Tract. in Symbolum Apostolicum*. Tom. 4. p. 43. col. 1. *Edit. Colon.* 1616.

Upon

Upon which Account it may be not improperly said concerning it, That we comprehend this only of it, That in truth it cannot be comprehended.

To St. *Ambrose* succeeds St. *Austin*. *In this Trinity* (says this Learned Father) *is but One God, which is indeed wonderfully unspeakable, and unspeakably wonderful.*

In illâ Trinitate, Trinitas est unus Deus, quod sanè est mirabiliter ineffabile, vel ineffabiliter mirabile, *Aug. de Trinitate Lib.* 15.

To the same purpose *Fulgentius*. *So far as I can judge, only the Eternal and Unchangeable Trinity ought to be looked upon by us, as worthy to be esteemed Incomprehensibly Miraculous; and as much exceeding all that we can think or imagine of it, as it surmounts all that we are.*

Sola (quantùm arbitror) immutabilis illa sempiternitas Trinitatis reperietur Incomprehensibilitatis digna miraculo, quæ sic excedit omne quod cogitare vel sapere possumus, sicut superat omne quod sumus. *Fulgentius ad Thrasymundum Regem*, lib. 2. cap. 1.

After him we shall produce *Hormisda* Bishop of *Rome*, in a Letter to *Justinian* the Emperour, about the beginning of the Sixth Century, speaking thus. *The Holy Trinity* (says he) *is but One, It is not multiplyed by Number, nor grows by any Addition, or Encrease: Nor can it either be comprehended by our Understanding, nor in respect of its Divinity be at all Divided.* And a little after. *Let us Worship Father, Son, and Holy Ghost, distinct in*

Unum est Sancta Trinitas, non multiplicatur Numero, non crescit Augmento; nec potest aut Intelligentiâ comprehendi, aut hoc quod Deus est discretione sejungi. *Ac paulò pòst.* Adoremus Patrem & Filium & Spiritum Sanctum Indistinctum distinctè Incomprehensibilem & inenarrabilem substantiam Trinitatis. *Atque iterum*, Magnum est sanctæ & incomprehensibile Mysterium Trinitatis, *Crabb. Concil.* Tom. 1. Pag. 1034, 1035.

themselves, but with one indistinct Worship, That is to say, *The Incomprehensible and Unutterable Substance of the* Trinity. And presently again, *Great and Incomprensible is the Mystery of the* Holy Trinity.

In the last place St. *Bernard* delivers himself upon the same Subject thus. *I confidently affirm* (says he) *that the Eternal and Blessed Trinity, which I do not understand, I do yet believe, and embrace with my Faith, what I cannot comprehend with my Mind.*

Fidenter dixerim æternam beatamquè Trinitatem, quam non intelligo, credo, & fide teneo, quod non capio mente, *Bernardus Sermone 76. super Cantic.*

I have here, as I said, given a Specimen of what the *Ancient Writers* of the *Church*, both *Greek* and *Latin*, thought and said of the *Blessed Trinity*, and it is, I confess, but a Specimen; since I think that enough for an Universally acknowledged, and never before contradicted Proposition: Whereas had it but in the least seemed a Novelty, (as this Author's *Hypothesis* not only *seems*, but unquestionably *is*) I should have thought my self obliged to have brought as many Quotations for it from Antiquity, as would have filled a much larger Book than I intend this shall be.

But as for those which I have here produced, I do solemnly appeal to any Man living, *Christian*, or not *Christian* (who does but understand these Languages) whether the *Fathers* now Quoted by me (and all the rest upon the same Subject speak agreeably to them) looked upon *Trinity in Unity, and Unity in Trinity, as a Plain, Easie, and Intelligible Notion?* So that if the Judgment of the *Fathers*, and of this Author, be in this point *one* and the *same*, it must unavoidably follow, That either the *Fathers* have not yet declared their Judgment and Doctrine, or that this Author has not yet declared his: Since

as precedent to the *Relation:* Forasmuch as Humane Reason considers Things simply as *Subsisting*, before it can consider them as *Relating* to one another.

But for the further Explication of the Point before us, it will here be necessary to premise what is properly a *Mode of Being.* And this the *School-Divines* do not allow to be either a *Substance*, or an *Accident* (which yet makes the adequate Division of *Real Beings*; since there is no such *Being* but what is contained under one of them) but a *Mode* is properly a certain *Habitude* of some *Being*, *Essence*, or *Thing*, whereby the said *Essence*, or *Being* is determined to some particular State, or Condition, which, barely of it self, it would not be determined to. And according to this account of it, a *Mode* in Things Spiritual and Immaterial seems to have much the like reference to such kind of *Beings*, that a Posture has to a Body, to which it gives some difference, or distinction, without superadding any new *Entity*, or *Being* to it. In a word, a *Mode* is not properly a *Being*, either *Substance*, or *Accident*, but a certain affection cleaving to it, and determining it from its *common general Nature* and *indifference* to something more particular, as we have just now explained. As for Instance, in *Created Beings*, *Dependence is a Mode* determining the *general Nature* of *Being* to that particular State, or Condition, by vertue whereof it proceeds from, and is supported by another; and the like may be said of *Mutability*, *Presence*, *Absence*, *Inherence*, *Adherence*, and such like, *viz.* That they are not *Beings*, but *Modes*, or *Affections of Being*, and inseparable from it so far, that they can have no Existence of their own, after a separation, or division from the Things, or *Beings* to which they do belong.

And thus having explained, in General, what *a Mode* is, we are to know, That the *Personalities*, by which the *Deity* ſtands diverſified into *Three diſtinct Perſons*, are by the Generality of *Divines*, both *Ancient* and *Modern*, called and accounted *Modes*, or at leaſt ſomething Analogous to them (ſince no one Thing can agree both to *God* and the *Creature*, by a perfect *Univocation*.) And moreover, as every *Mode Eſſentially* includes in it the *Thing*, or *Being* of which it is the *Mode*, ſo every *Perſon* of the *Bleſſed Trinity*, by vertue of its proper *Mode* of *Subſiſtence*, includes in it the *Godhead* it ſelf, and is properly *the Godhead as ſubſiſting with and under ſuch a certain Mode, or Relation.* And this I affirm to be the Current Doctrine both of the *Fathers* and the *Schools*, concerning the *Perſons* of the *Bleſſed Trinity*, and the conſtantly received Account given by them of a *Divine Perſon*, ſo far as they pretend to Explain what ſuch a *Perſon* is.

And accordingly, as theſe *Relations* are *Three*, and but *Three*, ſo the *Perſons* of the *Godhead*, to whom they belong, are ſo too, viz. *Father*, *Son*, and *Holy Ghoſt*. But then, we muſt obſerve alſo, That the *Relations* which the *Godhead* may ſuſtain, are of Two ſorts.

1ſt. *Extrinſecal*, and founded upon ſome *External Act* iſſuing from *God*; of which ſort are the *Relations* of *Creator*, *Preſerver*, *Governor*, and the like, to the *Things Created*, *Preſerved*, and *Governed* by him. Which, though they leave a real effect upon the Things themſelves, yet derive only an *External Habitude*, and denomination conſequent from it upon the *Deity* it ſelf. The

2d. Sort of *Relation*, is *Intrinſecal*, and founded upon thoſe *Internal Acts*, by which one *Perſon produces* another, or *proceeds* from another: For to *produce* and to *proceed* (whether by *Generation*, or *Spiration*) is that which makes, or Conſtitutes a Plurality of *Perſons* in the *Godhead*.

From

From all which it follows, That the *Relation*, by which *God* as a *Creator*, or *Preserver*, respects his Creatures, is extremely different from that by which *God* as a *Father* respects *his Son*. The former adding only to the *Deity* an *Extrinsecal denomination*, but the latter leaving upon it an *Internal Incommunicable Character, Essentially Inseparable* from the *Deity*. So that although it may well enough be said, That *God* might never have been a *Creator*, yet it cannot be said of Him, That he might never have been *a Father*; the former being only an effect of his Will, but this latter the Necessary Result of his *Nature*.

Now these *Internal Acts*, upon which the *Divine Relations* are founded, and from which they flow, are,

First, That *Eternal Act*, by which the *Father* Communicates his *Divine Nature* to the *Son*, which accordingly is called *Generation*.

And that by which the *Son* receives his *Divine Nature* from the *Father*, which is called *Filiation*. And

Thirdly, The *Act of Spiration*, by which the *Father* and the *Son* together, eternally breath forth the *Holy Spirit*. And,

Lastly, The *Act of Procession*, by which the *Holy Ghost proceeds*, and receives his *Divine Nature*, joyntly from them both. These, I say, are those *Internal*, *Incommunicable* and *distinguishing Acts*, from which the *Personal Relations* belonging to the *Three Divine Persons* are derived.

But you will say: *Does not this infer Four Persons in the Godhead?* viz. That as *Generation* and *Filiation* make two, so *Spiration* and *Procession* should make two more?

I Answer, No: Because the same *Person* may sustain several *Personal Relations,* and Exert, and receive several *Personal Acts,* where those *Acts,* or *Relations* are not *opposite to,* or inconsistent with one another in the same Subject. As for instance, The *Person* of the *Father* may Exert both an *Act* of *Generation and of Spiration*, and so sustain the *Relations* resulting from both without any Multiplication of his *Person*; and the *Son* likewise may receive and sustain the *Act* of *Filiation,* and withal Exert an *Act* of *Spiration,* without any Multiplication of *Personality.* And this, because neither are the *Acts* of *Generation* and *Spiration* inconsistent in the *Father,* nor the *Acts* of *Filiation* and *Spiration,* incompatible in the *Son.* Though indeed the *Acts* of *Generation* and *Filiation,* and the *Relations* springing therefrom, would be utterly inconsistent (because opposite) in any one *Person,* as likewise upon the same Account would the *Acts* of *Spiration* and *Procession.*

From whence by plain and undeniable Consequence it follows, That *Generation* and *Filiation, Spiration* and *Procession* Constitute only *Three Persons* in the *Eternal Godhead* and no more. For *Relations* merely *disparate,* do not Constitute several distinct *Persons,* unless they be *opposite* too. That Maxime of the *Schools* being most true, That *Sola Oppositio multiplicat in Divinis.* So that albeit, *Filiation* and *Spiration* are Terms opposite to their respective Correlates, yet being only *disparate* with reference to one another, and as both of them meet and are lodged in one and the same Subject, (*viz.* the *Person* of the *Son*) they neither cause, nor infer in him any more than one *Single Personality.*

But now if any one should ask me, What this *Generation* and *Filiation,* this *Spiration* and *Procession* are?

I Answer,

all concur in the same use and design; which is to express something proper and peculiar to the *Divine Persons*, whereby they are rendred distinct from, and Incommunicable to one another.

But these few general Remarks I think fit to lay down concerning them. As,

1. That albeit most of these Terms, as to the Form of the Word, run *Abstractively*, yet they are for the most part to be understood *Concretively*, and not as simple Forms, but as Forms in Conjunction with the Subject, which they belong to. In the former abstracted sence they are properly *Personalities*, or *Personal Properties*, viz. Those *Modes*, or *Forms* by which the *Persons*, whom they appertain to, are formally constituted and denominated what they are; but in the Latter and Concrete Sence, they signifie the *Persons* themselves.

2. The Second Thing, which I would observe, is, That there has been in the first Ages of the Church some Ambiguity in the use of the words ὀυσία and ὑπόστασις, Πρόσωπον, or *Persona*. For neither would the *Latines* at first admit of *Three Hypostases* in *God*, as taking ὀυσία and ὑπόστασις for the same Thing; for that they had no other *Latin* Word, to Translate ὑπόστασις by, but *Substantia*, by which also they Translated ὀυσία; (the Word *Subsistentia* being then looked upon by them as Barbarous, and not in use) so that they refused the Term τρεῖς ὑποστάσεις, for fear of admitting of *Three distinct Substances*, or *Essences* in the *Trinity*, which they knew would lead them into the Errour of *Arius*. Nor on the other side would the *Greeks* acquiesce in a μία ὑπόστασις, nor admit of the πρόσωπα, for fear of falling thereby into the contrary Errour of *Sabellius*; for that they thought the Word πρόσωπον imported no *real Internal difference*, but only a difference of *Name*, or *Attribute*, or at most

of *Office*; and for them to allow no more than such an one amongst the *Divine Persons*, they knew was *Sabellianisme*. And this Controversie of Words exercised the Church for a considerable time; to appease and compose which (amongst other Matters) a Council was called and held at *Alexandria* about the Year of *Christ*, 362. in which amongst many other Bishops Convened from *Italy*, *Arabia*, *Ægypt* and *Lybia*, was present also *Athanasius* himself. And in this Council both sides having been fully heard, and found to agree in sence, though they differ'd in words, it was ordained, That they should thenceforth Mutually acknowledge one another for *Orthodox*, and for the future cease contending about these words to the disturbance of the Church. By which means, and especially by the Explication given of these words by *Athanasius*, (whereby (as *Gregory Nazianzen* tells us in his Panegyrick upon him) he satisfied and reconciled both *Greeks* and *Latines* to the indifferent use of them, and indeed that Oration made by *Nazianzen* himself in the Council of *Constantinople* (*viz*. the second General) before 150 Bishops, not a little contributing to the same;) the sence of these Terms from that time forward came generally to be fixed, and the Ambiguity of them removed, and so the Controversie by degrees ceased between the *Greeks* and *Latines*, and the Words πρόσωπα, or *Personæ*, and ὑποστάσεις, or *Subsistentiæ* grew at length to be promiscuously used without any Jealousie or Suspicion, and to be accepted on all hands (though not presently) in the same signification.

3. The Third Thing which I would observe, is, That some of the forementioned Terms signifie *Causally*, and some only *Declaratively*, that is to say, some import the *Ground and Reason* of the Distinction of the *Divine Persons*,

Persons, and some import only *Marks, Notes, and Signs* of such a Distinction. Of the first sort amongst the *Greeks*, are ὑποστάσεις, τρόποι ὑπάρξεως, and ἰδιότητες; and amongst the *Latines*, *Subsistentiæ*, *Modi Subsistendi*, *Proprietates & Relationes*. Of the Latter sort amongst the *Greeks* are χαρακτῆρες and γνωρίσματα: and amongst the *Latines*, *Notiones*. But for the fuller and further illustration and improvement of this Note, I cannot but add the Observation of the solid and exactly Learned *Forbesius*, *viz*. That of these *Modes*, called by the *Greeks*, τρόποι ὑπάρξεως, there is a four-fold Use, or Effect, as they sustain four several Considerations. *viz*. That

First, As *Modes of Subsistence*, they *Constitute the Persons*. And

Secondly, That by the *Relations*, which they imply and include, they cause the said *Persons* to be referred to one another. And

Thirdly, That as they are *Properties* they distinguish the Persons from each other. And

Lastly, That, as *Notions*, they are Means, and (as it were) Instruments whereby we are enabled in some measure to apprehend and conceive of the *Divine Persons*. *Forbesius Instruct. Hist. Theolog*. Lib. 1. Cap. 35. Sect. 16.

By all which it appears, That the several forementioned Terms do really import but one and the same Thing, differently considered, according to the several Uses and Effects ascribed to it, in respect of the *Oeconomy* of the *Three Divine Persons* amongst themselves.

4. In the Fourth and Last place, we may observe, That the words most commonly and frequently used by *Writers* in treating of the *Divine Persons*, are the forementioned ὑποστάσεις, τρόποι ὑπάρξεως, and ἰδιότητες amongst

mongst the *Greeks.* And the Terms *Personæ, Relationes, Proprietates,* and (in the latter Ages especially) *Subsistentiæ,* and *Modi Subsistendi* amongst the *Latines.*

These Observations I thought fit to lay down for our clearer and readier Apprehension of the Expressions used by the *Fathers,* and other *Church-Writers* in their Discourses about this great Article of the *Christian Faith.*

And so I proceed now to my Authorities, shewing both from the Ancient and Modern use of the Terms aforesaid, and more especially of the ὑποστάσεις, and τρόποι ὑπάρξεως, the *Subsistentiæ & Modi Subsistendi,* that the Church has all along placed the respective *Personalities of the Three Divine Persons in Three distinct Modes of Subsistence,* according to the Doctrine Asserted by us. And here I shall begin with the *Greek Writers,* setting them down according to the Order and Age in which they Lived.

Justin Martyr. And first with *Justin Martyr,* who in his ἔκθεσις τῆς πίστεως, or Exposition of Faith, speaks thus. Ὀυ ταυτὸν τῷ πατρὶ ὁ υἱὸς καὶ τὸ πνεῦμα ἅγιον, ὅτι τὸ μὲν ἀγέννητον καὶ γεννητὸν καὶ ἐκπορευτὸν οὐκ οὐσίας ὀνόματα ἀλλὰ τρόποι τῆς ὑπάρξεως. *The Son* (says he) *and the Holy Ghost, are not the same with the Father; for the Terms Unbegotten, Begotten, and Proceeding, are not the Names of Essence, but Modes of Subsistence, Justin. Exposition. fidei.* p. 373. *Colon. Edition.* 1686. Again, speaking of the same Terms, he tells us, *That they are not* οὐσίας δηλωτικὰ, but σημαντικὰ τῶν ὑποστάσεων, that is to say, *not denoting the Essence, but signifying the Hypostases, or Subsistences;* adding withal, ἱκανὰ γὰρ ἡμῖν διακρίνειν τὰ πρόσωπα, καὶ τὴν τοῦ πατρὸς καὶ υἱοῦ, καὶ ἁγίου πνεύματος ἰδιαζόντως δεικνύειν ὑπόστασιν, *That they are sufficient for us to distinguish*

stinguish the Persons, and to shew the proper and peculiar Subsistence of *Father, Son, and Holy Ghost by.* Pag. 374. And again, Ἕνα Θεὸν προσῆκεν ὁμολογεῖν ἐν πατρὶ καὶ υἱῷ, καὶ πνεύματι ἁγίῳ γνωριζόμενον, ᾗ μὲν πατὴρ καὶ υἱὸς, καὶ πνεῦμα ἅγιον τῆς μιᾶς Θεότητος τὰς ὑποστάσεις γνωρίζοντας, ᾗ δὲ Θεὸς τὸ κατ' οὐσίαν κοινὸν τῶν ὑποστάσεων νοοῦντας. That is, *we ought to own, or Confess One God, expressed to us in Father, Son, and Holy Ghost, hereby acknowledging, as they are Father, Son and Holy Ghost, Three Subsistences of one and the same Godhead; but as they are God, understanding thereby one Essence, or Substance common to all the Subsistences,* p. 379. *ibid.* By all which Expressions we see *Personality* stated upon *Subsistence.*

Our next Testimony shall be from *Athanasius*, who in his Treatise *de Sanctissimâ Virgine Deiparâ*, gives this Account of his Faith. Πιστεύομεν εἰς Πατέρα, καὶ υἱὸν, καὶ ἅγιον πνεῦμα, τριάδα ὑποστάσεων ἀδιάσπαστον ἐχόντων τὴν διαίρεσιν, καὶ τὴν ἕνωσιν ἀσύγχυτον. That is, *We believe in Father, Son, and Holy Ghost, a Trinity of Hypostases, or Persons, having amongst them such a Distinction, as admits of no Division, and such an Union, or Unity, as is without all Confusion. Athan. Tom.* I. *p.* 1029. *Colon. Edit.* 1686. *Athanasius.*

The Author called *Dionysius* the *Areopagite* (though by a false Title, for the *Areopagite* lived in the first Century, but this *Writer* in the fourth) in his Book *de Divinis Nominibus* cap. I. sets forth the Trinity thus. Τριὰς δὲ διὰ τὴν τρισυπόστατον τῆς ὑπερουσίου γονιμότητος ἔκφανσιν. *The Trinity* (so called) *because of its manifestation of a Divine, or Superlative Fecundity shewn in Three Subsistences, or Persons.* *Dionysius Areopagita.*

Epiphanius also in the 62d. Heresie, and 3d. Paragraph, gives the like account of the same, Τριὰς ἀριθμουμένη Πατὴρ, καὶ υἱὸς, καὶ πνεῦμα ἅγιον, οὐχ ὡς ἕν τι τρισὶν ὀνόμασιν *Epiphanius.*

κε-

κεκλημένον, ἀλλ' ἀληθῶς τέλεια τὰ ὀνόματα, τέλειαι ὑποστάσεις. *The Trinity is numbred by Father, Son, and Holy Ghost, not as one Thing called only by Three Names, but as being in Truth Three perfect Subsistences, [or Persons] as well as Three perfect Names.*

Gregory Nazianzen. In like manner *Gregory Nazianzen* speaks much the same Thing in his 29th Oration. Χρὴ καὶ τὸν ἕνα Θεὸν τηρεῖν καὶ τὰς τρεῖς ὑποστάσεις ὁμολογεῖν, εἴτ' οὖν τρία πρόσωπα, καθ' ἑκάστην μετὰ τῆς ἰδιότητος. *We ought* (says he) *to hold one God, and to confess Three Subsistences, or Three Persons, each with his respective Property according to his Subsistence, Greg. Nazianz. Tom.* 1. *P.* 490. *Edit. Paris.* 1630.

Gregory Nyssen. *Gregory Nyssen*, upon those words in the first of *Genesis, Let us make Man*, expresses himself thus. Ἐποίησεν ὁ Θεὸς ἄνθρωπον ἵνα ἑνώσῃς τὴν Θεότητα, ἑνώσῃς δὲ οὐ τὰς ὑποστάσεις, ἰδία γὰρ ὑπόστασις Πατρὸς, ἰδία υἱοῦ καὶ πνεύματος ἁγίου. *God* (says he) *made Man* (laying the stress upon the Word ἐποίησεν of the Singular Number) *that you may reckon, or account the Godhead to be but One: But not so the Subsistences*; for there is a *proper Subsistence* of the *Father*, a *proper Subsistence* of the *Son*, and a *proper Subsistence* of the *Holy Ghost. Greg. Nyssen Tom.* 1. *p.* 141. *Edit. Paris.* 1615.

St. Basil. St. *Basil* in his Book de *Spiritu Sancto*, Chap. 18. speaks thus of the Second *Person* of the *Trinity*. Δεύτερον δὲ Θεὸν οὐδέπω καὶ τήμερον ἀκηκόαμεν. Θεὸν γὰρ ἐκ Θεοῦ προσκυνοῦντες καὶ τὸ ἰδιάζον τῶν ὑποστάσεων ὁμολογοῦμεν καὶ μένομεν ἐπὶ τῆς μοναρχίας. *We* (says he) *never to this Day heard of a Second God; but Worshipping the Son as God of God, we both acknowledge the Property of the Hypostases [or Persons] and insist upon one Supreme Governor, or Lord of all Things. Bas. Tom.* 2. *p.* 332. *Edit. Paris.* 1637.

Likewise

Likewise St. *Cyrill* of *Alexandria* declares himself much the same way in his third Dialogue *de Trinitate.* St. Cyrill of Alexandria. Ἔνεστι γὰρ δὲ ἰδεῖν τὸ ἐν μιᾷ τῇ θεότητι τριπλοῦν καθ' ὑπόστασιν. *We may observe* (says he) *in one Deity, a Ternary, or Triplicity according to* [*or in respect of*] *Subsistence.*

The same we find also in *Isidorus Pelusiota*, *Lib.* 1. Isidorus Pelusiota. *Epist.* 247. Μία γὰρ ἐστὶν ἡ Θεότης, τρεῖς δὲ αἱ ὑποστάσεις· τοῦτο τήρει, τοῦτο ἔχε. *There is* (says he) *One Godhead, but Three Hypostases, or Subsistences. This keep, this hold,* &c.

Theodoret also speaks very fully upon the same Subject, Theodoret. in his first Dialogue *contr. Anomæos.* Τὰ μὲν τῆς οὐσίας ἴδια ὁμοίως εἰσὶ κοινὰ τοῦ πατρὸς καὶ τοῦ υἱοῦ καὶ τοῦ ἁγίου πνεύματος· τὸ δὲ Πατὴρ οὐ κοινόν. Οὐκ ἄρα τῆς οὐσίας ἴδιον τὸ Πατὴρ, ἀλλὰ τῆς ὑποστάσεως, εἰ δὲ ἄλλο τῆς ὑποστάσεως τὸ ἴδιον καὶ ἄλλα τῆς οὐσίας ἰδιώματα, οὐ ταυτὸν ἐστι σημαινόμενον οὐσία καὶ ὑπόστασις. That is to say, *Such Things as belong properly to the* [*Divine*] *Essence, or Substance, are in like manner common to Father, Son, and Holy Ghost.* But the Term [*Father*] *is not common to them; and therefore* [*Father*] *is no Property of the Essence, but of the Subsistence, or Person: But now, if one Thing be proper to the Hypostasis, or Subsistence, and there be other Properties of the Essence,* it follows, That *Essence* and *Hypostasis do not signifie one and the same thing.* And again, a little after: Ἡ δὲ οὐσία πατρὸς καὶ υἱοῦ καὶ ἁγίου πνεύματος κοινή· ὁμοίως γὰρ ἀθάνατος, ὁμοίως ἄφθαρτος, ὁμοίως ἁγία καὶ ὁμοίως ἀγαθή. καὶ διὰ τοῦτο λέγομεν μίαν οὐσίαν, τρεῖς ὑποστάσεις. That is, *the Essence, or Substance of the Father, and the Son, and the Holy Ghost is common, being equally and alike Immortal, Incorruptible, Holy and Good. And for this Reason we affirm One Essence, and Three Hypostases, Auctarium sive Tom.* 5. *Theodoret. p.* 286. *Edit. Paris.* 1684. Certainly

tainly nothing could, with greater Evidence, state the Personalities of *Father*, *Son*, and *Holy Ghost* upon Three several *Selfsistences*, than the Words here quoted out of this *Father*. And I quote them out of him, though I know the same Dialogues are inserted into *Athanasius*'s Works; but I am convinced by the reasons given by *Garnerius* the Learned Editor of this *Auctarium*, that the said Dialogues cannot belong to *Athanasius*.

Next to him let us hear *Basilius Seleuciensis* speaking the same Thing in his first Oration, upon the first Verse of the first Chapter of *Genesis*, where, upon these words, *Let us make Man after our own Image and Likeness*, he discourses thus. Μία μὲν εἰκὼν ἡ πλαττομένη, οὐχ ἑνὸς δὲ προσώπου μνήμη, ἀλλὰ τριῶν ὑποστάσεων· κοινὸν γὰρ τῆς Θεότητος δημιούργημα τὸ πλαττόμενον, τριάδα μὲν ἐμφαίνει τὴν πλάττουσαν, μίαν δὲ εἰκόνα τῆς τριάδος ὑπάρχουσαν, εἰ δὲ μία τῆς τριάδος ἡ εἰκὼν μία τῶν ὑποστάσεων ἡ φύσις. Τὸ γὰρ ταὐτὸν τῆς οὐσίας ἡ τῆς εἰκόνος ἑνότης κηρύττει. That is to say, *The Image here formed is but One, but the mention here made is not of One Hypostasis, or Person only, but of Three. For the Thing formed being the common Work of the whole Deity, shews the Trinity to have been the Former thereof, and so gives us one Image, or Resemblance of the Trinity: But if the Image of the Trinity be but One, the Nature of the Hypostases* [*or Persons*] *must be One too. For the Unity of the Image, proclaims the Unity of the Substance, or Essence. Basil. Seluciens. Orat.* 1. *p.* 5. Printed at *Paris* with *Gregorius Thaumaturgus*, &c. *Anno Dom.* 1622.

Zacharias Sirnamed *Scholasticus*, and sometime Metropolitan of *Mitylene* (of the Sixth Century) in his Disputation against the *Philosophers* who held the *Eternity of the World*, to a certain *Philosopher*, asking him, How the *Christians* could acknowledge the same both a *Trinity*

Trinity and an *Unity* too? Makes this Answer. Τριάδα φαμὲν εἶναι ἐν μονάδι καὶ μονάδα ἐν τριάδι, τῷ τὰς μὲν ὑποστάσεις τρεῖς εἶναι, τὴν δὲ οὐσίαν μόνην. That is, *We affirm a Trinity in Unity, and an Unity in Trinity; hereby affirming the Subsistences* [or *Persons*] *to be Three, and the Essence, or Substance to be only One.*

Johannes Damascenus, a Writer of the Eighth Century, in his third Book *de Orthodoxâ fide*, Chap. 11. about the end of it speaks thus. Θεότης μὲν γὰρ φύσιν δηλοῖ, τὸ δὲ πατὴρ τὴν ὑπόστασιν, ὥσπερ ἀνθρωπότης τὴν φύσιν, Πέτρος δὲ τὴν ὑπόστασιν. Θεὸς δὲ καὶ τὸ κοινὸν τῆς φύσεως σημαίνει, καὶ ἐφ' ἑκάστης τῶν ὑποστάσεων τάττεται παρωνύμως. That is, *The Godhead declares the Nature, but the Term* [*Father*] *the Subsistence; as Humanity does the Humane Nature, but* Peter *the Subsistence, or Person. For the Term* [*God*] *denotes the Divine Nature in Common, and equally denominates, or is ascribed to each of the Hypostases, or Subsistences. Damascen. Page* 207. *Edit. Basil.* 1575.

I shall close up these particular Testimonies with some Passages in the Creed, commonly called the *Athanasian*; which I place so low, because it is manifest, that *Athanasius* was not the Author of it, it being not so much as mentioned in any *Ancient Writer* (as the very Learned Dr *Cave* affirms) till it occurs in *Theodulphus Aurelianensis*, who lived about the latter end of the Eighth Century. Now the Passages are these, Μήτε συγχέοντες τὰς ὑποστάσεις (in some Copies πρόσωπα) μήτε τὴν οὐσίαν διαιροῦντες, ἄλλη γὰρ ἐστὶν ἡ τοῦ πατρὸς ὑπόστασις, ἄλλη τοῦ υἱοῦ, καὶ ἄλλη τοῦ πνεύματος τοῦ ἁγίου, ἀλλὰ Πατρὸς καὶ υἱοῦ καὶ πνεύματος ἁγίου μία Θεότης, &c. That is, *Neither confounding the Hypostases* [or *Persons*] *nor dividing the Substance. For there is one Hypostasis of the Father, another of the Son, and another of the Holy Ghost, but the Godhead of the Father, Son, and Holy Ghost is One*, &c. And again, ὅλαι αἱ τρεῖς ὑποστάσεις συνδιαιωνίζουσαι ἑαυταῖς εἰσι καὶ ἴσαι. That is, *The whole Three Hypostases* [or *Persons*] are *Coeternal together, and Coequal.* These Passages are full and plain, and the *Creed* it self may well claim the Antiquity at least of the Eighth Century.

My next *Authorities* shall be those of the *Councils*. But before I pass to them, I cannot but observe and own to the Reader concerning some of the first of my Quotations, *viz.* those out of *Justin Martyr*, and that out of St. *Athanasius*; that it has been very much questioned by some Learned Men, Whether those Books, from whence they are taken, do really belong to the Authors to whom they are ascribed, and among whose Works they are inserted, or no. This, I say, I was not ignorant of, nevertheless I thought fit to quote them by the Names under which I found them placed; since many very Learned Persons, and much more acquainted with the *Writings* of the *Ancients* than I pretend to be, have upon several Occasions done so before me. And the said Tracts are certainly of a very early date, and though the Authors of them should fall a Century or two lower, yet they still retain Antiquity enough to make good the Point for which I alledged them. Nevertheless I must and do confess it very probable, That the more distinct and exact use of the Terms ὑποστάσεις, and τρόποι ὑπάρξεως, as applyed to the *Divine Persons*, did not generally and commonly take place, but as by degrees the Discussion of the *Arian* and other the like Controversies, through frequent Disputes, grew to still a greater and greater Maturity. And that the use of these Terms did obtain then, and upon that Account, I think a very considerable Argument to authorize, and recommend them to all Sober and Judicious Minds.

And

And so I pass to the Testimonies of Councils concerning the same. Amongst which, we have here, in the first place, the Council of *Chalcedon*, making a Confession, or Declaration of their *Faith*, concerning the *Person* of our *Saviour*, and that, both as to the Absolute undivided *Unity* of his *Person*, and as to the Difference and Distinction of his Two *Natures*, part of which Confession runs thus. Ὁμολογοῦμεν ἕνα καὶ ταυτὸν Ἰησοῦν Χριστὸν, κύριον, υἱὸν μονογενῆ, ἐν δυο φύσεσι ἀσυγχύτως, ἀτρέπτως, ἀδιαιρέτως, καὶ ἀχωρίστως γνωριζόμενον· οὐδαμοῦ τῆς τῶν φύσεων διαφορᾶς ἀνῃρημένης διὰ τὴν ἕνωσιν, σωζομένης δὲ μᾶλλον τῆς ἰδιότητος ἑκατέρας φύσεως, καὶ εἰς ἓν πρόσωπον καὶ μίαν ὑπόστασιν συντρεχούσης. That is, *We confess One and the same Lord Jesus Christ, the only Begotten Son of God in Two Natures, without Confusion*, &c. *the difference of the said Natures, being by no means destroyed by their Union, but rather the Property of each Nature being thereby preserved, and both concurring to* [*or meeting in*] *One Person, or Hypostasis.* This Account of the *Chalcedon*-Confession we have in the 2d Book of *Evagrius*, towards the latter end of the 4th Chapter; and a lively Instance it is of the *Council*'s expressing the *Personality* of *Christ* by, and stating it upon, *Subsistence*. [illegible]

In the next place, upon *Justinian*'s calling the second *Council* of *Constantinople* (being the Fifth General one, in the Year 553, for Condemning of the *Tria Capitula*, we have a large and Noble Confession of Faith made by that Emperor, and owned and applauded by all the *Council*, and inserted amongst the *Acts* of it: And in this we have the *Three Divine Persons* several times expressed by so many ὑποστάσεις, as a Term equivalent to πρόσωπα, and indeed importing withall the *Personality*, or *Formal Reason* of the same; and that so fully and plainly, that nothing could, or can be more so. Ὁμο- [illegible] Confession.

λογȣ̃μεν τοινυν πιςεύειν εἰς Πατέρα, καὶ Υἱὸν, καὶ ἅγιον Πνεῦμα, Τριάδα ὁμοούσιον, μίαν Θεότητα, ἤτοι φύσιν καὶ ȣ̓σίαν, καὶ δύναμιν, καὶ ἐξȣσίαν ἐν τρισὶν ὑποςάσεσιν, ἤτοι προσώποις, δοξάζοντες, &c. That is, *We profess to Believe One Father, Son, and Holy Ghost, Glorifying thereby a Consubstantial Trinity, One Deity, or Nature, or Essence, and Power and Authority in Three Subsistences, or Persons.* And again to the same purpose, Μονάδα ἐν τριάδι καὶ τριάδα ἐν μονάδι προσκυνȣ̃μεν, παράδοξον ἔχȣσαν τὴν διαίρεσιν καὶ τὴν ἕνωσιν, μονάδα μὲν κατὰ τὸν τῆς ȣ̓σίας ἤγȣν Θεότητος λόγον, τριάδα δὲ κατὰ τὰς ἰδιότητας ἤγȣν ὑποςάσεις ἤτοι πρόσωπα. *We Worship* (says he) *an Unity in Trinity, and a Trinity in Unity, having both a strange and wonderful Distinction and Union,* that is to say, *an Union, or Singularity in respect of the Substance or Godhead, and a Trinity in respect of Properties, Subsistences, or Persons*; with several more such Passages to the same Purpose and Signification.

Fifth *General Council.* And then, as for the *Council* it self, the first Canon of it speaks thus; Εἴ τις ȣ̓χ ὁμολογεῖ Πατρὸς, υἱȣ̃, καὶ ἁγίȣ πνεύματος μίαν φύσιν, ἤτοι ȣ̓σίαν, καὶ μίαν δύναμιν, καὶ ἐξȣσίαν, τριάδα ὁμοȣ́σιον, μίαν Θεότητα ἐν τρισὶν ὑποςάσιν, ἤτοι προσώποις προσκυνητὴν, τοιȣ̃τος Ἀνάθεμα ἔςω. That is, *If any one Confess not One Nature, or Substance, One Power and Authority of Father, Son, and Holy Ghost, a Coessential Trinity, and One Deity to be Worshipped in Three Subsistences, or Persons, Let such an one be Accursed.*

The Sixth *General Council.* In the next place, we have the Sixth *General Council*, and the Third of *Constantinople*, called by *Constantinus Pogonatus* against the *Monothelites* in the Year 681. In the *Acts* of which *Council*, Article 6. we have the *Council* owning the same Thing, and in the same words, which a little before we quoted out of the *Council* of *Chalcedon*: And moreover in the Tenth Article, the *Council* declares it self thus. Τὸν κύριον ἡμῶν Ἰησȣ̃ν Χριςὸν

ςὸν

Concerning which I dare and do affirm, That for the Five or Six last Centuries, the said Terms have been Universally received and used by *Divines* in their Writings and Discourses about the *Trinity*; all stating the *Personalities* and *distinction* of the *Divine Persons* upon so many *distinct Subsistences*, or *Modes* of *Subsistence*; therein following the *Greek Fathers*, who were much more versed in this Controversie, and mannaged it much better and more exactly than the Ancient *Latines* did.

Accordingly, I shall proceed now to the *School-men*; Lombard.
amongst whom I shall begin with the Father of them, *viz. Peter Lombard*, who in *Book* 1. of his Sentences, *Distinct.* 25. and *Point*, or *Sect.* 9. speaks thus. *Cùm dicitur alia est Persona Patris, alia Filii, alia Spiritûs Sancti, utique id sanè intelligi potest, ut sit sensus talis; Alia est Subsistentia, vel Hypostasis Patris, alia Subsistentia Filii, alia Subsistentia Spiritûs Sancti*; & *alia Subsistentia Pater, alia Filius, alia Spiritus Sanctus.* By which surely it is plain, That he states the *Divine Persons* and their *Personalities* upon *Subsistence*, if any thing can be so.

Next to *Lombard*, I shall produce *Alensis*, who in *Vol.* 1. Alexander
and *Book* 1. *de Divinis nominibus in speciali*, has these Pas- Alensis.
sages. *In Divinis non dicitur una subsistentia, sicut una substantia.* Quæst. 57. Memb. 3. And *Tres sunt Hypostases unius Essentiæ*, Quæst. 58. Memb. 3. And *Persona est Hypostasis proprietate suâ distincta.* Quæst. 58. Memb. 4. By all which he manifestly Asserts the thing here contended for.

After him, let us see what *Durandus* says, who un- Durand.
dertaking to give the signification of *Substantia*, *Subsistentia*, *Essentia* and *Persona*, with reference to *God*, in order to the Explication of the Term *Subsistentia*, first tells us, What it is to *Subsist*, in these Words. *Subsistere dicit determinatum essendi modum, prout scilicet aliquid est*

Ens

Ens per se, & non in alio. A little after which, he tells us, That *Nomen Personæ dicit suppositum Intellectualis Naturæ, cui omnia Prædicta conveniunt*, scil. *Essentia, Substantia* & *Subsistentia*. By which he gives us a most exact Account and Definition of a *Person*; which (in *Intelligent Beings*) is nothing else but an *Essence*, or *Substance* (Terms Synonymous in *God*) *under a Subsistence peculiarly belonging to it*. And in the end of this Question, he further explains the *Personalities* of the *Divine Persons* by so many *distinct Relations*, in these Words. *Persona, quæ multiplicatur in Divinis, includit in eo, de quo dicitur, aliquid, quod non est omnino idem secundùm rem vel ex naturá rei cum Essentiâ vel Substantiâ, scilicet Relationem; ratione cujus plurificatur Persona in Divinis, & non essentia.* Durandus Lib. 1. Distinct. 23. Quæst. 2.

Aquinas. *Thomas Aquinas* also we shall find giving his Judgment to the same purpose, and that very fully and clearly. *Dicendum* (says he) *quòd quamvìs hoc Nomen* [*Substantia*] *in Latino respondere videatur huic Nomini* [*Hypostasis*] *in Græco, non tamen omninò idem significat secundùm usum utriusque linguæ. Nam hoc nomen* [*Hypostasis*] *apud Græcos significat tantùm Substantiam particularem quæ est substantia prima; sed Latini utuntur Nomine Substantiæ tam pro primâ quàm pro secundâ. Substantia autem particularis nihil aliud videtur, quàm quid distinctum Subsistens. Cùm ergo in Divinis invenitur aliquid distinctum subsistens, rectè ibi Nomen* [Hypostasis] *dici potest,* ☞ secundùm quod Divina verbis humanis significari contingit. And again, *Dicendum quòd hoc Nomen* [*Persona*] *non differt ab hoc nomine* [*Hypostasis*] *nisi quòd addit determinatam Naturam; quod patet ex hoc, quòd Hypostasis est Individua substantia. Persona verò Individua substantia Rationalis Naturæ. Hypostasis ergo in Rationali Naturâ accepta nihil aliud est, quàm Persona, sicut Animal cum Rationali*

Actu

Actu nihil aliud est quàm Homo. Unde cùm Divina Natura sit Rationalis, (largo modo accipiendo Rationale pro quolibet Intellectuali) oportet quòd Hypostasis Divina sit idem quod Persona Divina. And presently after, as to the *Relative Nature* of this *Hypostasis*, he adds this at the end of the Article. *Sicut ergo hoc Nomen* [*Persona*] *in Divinis significat Relationem per modum rei Subsistentis, sic & hoc Nomen* [*Hypostasis.*] Thomas in Scripto 2. in Sentent. Lib. 1. Distinct. 26. Quæst. 1. Artic. 1, 2. And again in his Comment upon the Epistle to the *Romans*, Cap. 1. *Nihil aliud est Persona quàm Hypostasis aut suppositum Rationalis Naturæ.*

Next to *Thomas*, let us hear *Cajetan*, one of the most Eminent Commentators upon him, who defending *Bonaventure* against *Scotus*, speaks thus as to this particular. *Substantia dupliciter sumitur, & pro Essentiâ & pro Hypostasi* (i. e.) *Subsistentiâ. Atque hoc secundo modo Substantia*, id est, *Hypostasis dicitur formaliter de Personâ Divinâ, & quòd simul ac semel Persona Divina est Hypostasis & tamen Relatio.* Adding these Words immediately hereupon. *Hæc omnia communia sunt omnibus Theologis.* Cajetan in 1m Thomæ, Quæst. 40. Artic. 2. *Cajetan.*

From *Cajetan* I shall pass to *Greg. de Valentiâ*, who discourses of the *Divine Persons* and *Personalities* thus. *Ex hoc consequenter apparet, debere concedi in Divinis Tres Subsistentias respectivas, non solùm ut Subsistentia accipitur pro Totâ Personâ, ut definitio Ecclesiæ declarat; sed etiam ut accipitur pro gradu illo ultimo Substantiali constituente Personam & reddente illam incommunicabilem, quem Theologi appellare solent Subsistentiam, & est ipsa Personalitas.* G. de Valentiâ Tom. 1. Disputat. generali 2. Quæst. 3. Artic. 2. p. 741. *Greg. de Valentiâ.*

To *Gregory de Valentiâ*, we will subjoin *Estius*, who speaking of the Words *Persona* and *Hypostasis* as they *Estius.*

were used by the *Greeks* and *Latines*, and of the sence of the *Fathers* about them, speaks thus. *Horum Authoritatem posteriores Græci ità sunt secuti, ut Hypostasim in Divinis non aliud intelligant, quàm quod Latini Personam vocant, maximè cum in promptu non esset aliud Vocabulum, quo Subsistentiam illam personalem, quâ inter se distinguuntur Pater, & Filius, & Spiritus Sanctus, commodè atque inoffensè exprimerent.* Estius in sentent. lib. 1. Distinct. 23. Articulo 3. By which Words it appears, That according to this Author, it is this *Personalis Subsistentia*, by which the *Three Divine Persons* are distinguished, and consequently in which the proper *Personality* of each of them does consist.

Suarez. After *Estius* let us cast our Eye upon *Suarez*, speaking much the same Thing with those before mentioned. *Advertendum est* (says he) *hoc nomen [Subsistentia] apud Antiquos Patres frequentiùs accipi in Vi concreti ad significandam Hypostasim seu Personam. In quo sensu nulla est Quæstio inter Catholicos, nam de fide est, dari in Trinitate Tres Subsistentias realiter distinctas, id est Tres Hypostases.* Suarez in 1m Thomæ de Trinitatis Mysterio lib. 3. cap. 4. And then again for the *Relative Nature* of the said *Subsistences*, he gives this Account of the *Divine Persons* and their *Personalities. Ex his quæ hactenus diximus*, &c. *concluditur Relationem Personalem esse etiam proprietatem constituentem Personam [seu quâ constituitur Persona.]* De Trinit. lib. 7. cap. 7. in the beginning.

Ripalda. To all which I shall add, *Martinez Ripalda*, a short, but Judicious Writer upon the Sentences, speaking of the Term [*Hypostasis*] in these Words. *Hæretici* (says he) *referente Hieronymo, eà voce abutebantur ad decipiendum fideles; jam eà significantes Essentiam, jam Personalitatem & incommunicabilem Subsistentiam.* By which last Expression this Author manifestly shews, That he takes

Personality

Personality and *Incommunicable Subsistence* for Words Synonymous; and consequently that such a *Subsistence* is and must be that, by which a *Divine Person* is constituted formally, what he is.

I cannot think it necessary to quote any more of this sort of Writers, nor am I sollicitous to alledge many of them, because I am well assured (according to the forecited Saying of *Cajetan)* that *these are the Terms, and this the Language of them all upon this Subject.* Only I think fit to remark this: That, whereas I have alledged some of the *School-men* (and particularly *Durandus, Thomas,* and *Suarez)* expressing the *Divine Personalities* by *Relations,* as well as by *Hypostases,* or *Subsistences,* as they do in both these mean but one and the same Thing, *viz.* a *Relative Subsistence,* or a *Subsisting Relation*; so by both of them they equally overthrow this Author's *Hypothesis,* deriving the *Divine Personalities* from *Self-Consciousness.* Forasmuch as *Subsistence* is in *Nature* before it, and *Relation* is opposite to it; it having been demonstrated by me in Chap. 4. That *Self-Consciousness* is a Thing wholly *Absolute* and *Irrelative,* and therefore cannot possibly be the *Formal Reason* of that which is *Essentially Relative.* In a word, *Self-Consciousness* is neither an *Hypostasis,* nor a *Relation*; and therefore can have nothing to do here, whatsoever other Employment this Author may have for it.

And now I shall at last descend to the Testimony of several *Modern Divines,* and all of them Men of Note in the Times in which they lived. And amongst these, let us first hear *Philip Melancthon* in his common places *Melancthon*
speaking thus upon this Head. *Satis constat* (says he) *veteres Scriptores Ecclesiæ solitos hæc duo vocabula discernere* οὐσίαν *&* ὑπόστασιν, *& dicere unam esse* οὐσίαν, id est, *Es-*

ſentiam æternam Patris, & Filii, & Spiritûs Sancti, ſed tres ὑποςάσεις.

Chemnitius From him we will paſs to *Chemnitius* who Wrote upon *Melancthon*'s Common Places: He in the firſt Chapter of his Book *de duabus in Chriſto Naturis*, gives his Opinion thus. *Hypoſtaſes ſeu Perſonæ Trinitatis omnes unum ſunt propter Identitatem Eſſentiæ ſuæ, atque adeò non differunt Eſſentialiter, nec ſeparatim una extra aliam & ſine aliâ ſubſiſtit.* And preſently after this, *Relatione autem ſeu τρόπῳ ὑπάρξεως, modo ſcilicet Subſiſtendi realiter differunt.*

Calvin. After *Chemnitius* let us conſider what *Calvin* ſays; in Book 1. of his *Inſtitutions*, Chap. 13. Sect. 2. *Filium Dei Apoſtolus characterem Hypoſtaſeos Patris nominans, haud dubiè aliquam Patri Subſiſtentiam aſſignat in quâ differat à Filio. Nam pro Eſſentiâ accipere (ſicuti fecerunt quidam Interpretes,* &c.) *non durum modò ſed abſurdum quoquè eſſet.* And again in *Sect.* 6. of the ſame Chapter. *Perſonam voco Subſiſtentiam in Dei eſſentiâ, quæ ad alios relata proprietate incommunicabili diſtinguitur. Subſiſtentiæ nomine aliud quiddam intelligi volumus quàm Eſſentiam.*

Peter Martyr. In the next place *Peter Martyr* gives us the ſame Account of the ſame Subject. *Multò rectiùs* (ſays he) *& veriùs intelligemus ex iſto loco (*nempe 2 Samuelis Cap. 7. Commate 23.) *Tres Perſonas in Unâ Naturâ Divinâ, Patrem, inquam, Filium & Spiritum Sanctum, quæ cum ſint Tres Hypoſtaſes, tamen concluduntur in Unam Eſſentiam.* Petrus Martyr Loc. Com. p. 50. col. 2. Loco de Dei Attributis & Sacro-Sanctâ Trinitate.

Wolfg. Muſculus. Likewiſe *Wolfgangus Muſculus* in his Common Places under the particular Head or common Place *de Deo*, declares the Matter thus. *Eſt itaque Deus Eſſentiâ Unus quemadmodum & Naturâ & Divinitate, Hypoſtaſi verò Trinus.* And a little after, *Hæc ſunt manifeſtâ ſide tenendâ,*

Deum,

Deum, viz. *Esse Unum Essentiâ, Naturâ, Divinitate, sententiâ, motione, & Operatione, Trinum verò Tribus Personis, quarum singulis sua est Hypostasis & Proprietas.* Musc. Loc. Comm. cap. 6. p. 7. And a little before speaking of the difference of ὐσία and ὑπόστασις, and in what sence the *Ancients* understood these Words. *Voce Essentiæ* (says he) *id expresserunt (nempe Veteres) quod commune est in Sacra Triade: per Hypostasim verò quod Unicuique Personæ proprium in illâ est, significârunt.* p. 6. ibid.

Piscator also in his *Theological Theses*, speaks after the same manner. *Quum igitur* λόγος *semper fuerit filius Dei, quis non videt* λόγον *de quo loquitur Johannes, semper fuisse Personam seu Hypostasim, rem scilicet per se Subsistentem*, Loc. 2. de Deo. p. 57, 58. *Piscator.*

Agreeably to this, *Tilenus* an Eminent *Divine* expresses himself in his Body of Divinity, ὑποστάσεις (says he) *sive Personæ sunt illa ipsa* ὐσία *quæ in singulis Personis est Tota; ipsæ verò Relationibus sive Proprietatibus* χαρακτηριστικαῖς *sunt distinctæ.* And again, *Simpliciter dicimus Proprietates istas* διακριτικὰς *esse diversos* τρόπυς ὑπάρξεως *hoc est, modos Subsistendi.* Tilen. Syntag. par. 1. cap. 20. p. 129. *Tilenus.*

The Learned *Ursinus* in his *Theological Treatises* under the Head *De tribus Personis in Unâ Deitate* declares the same. *Tenendum est, nequaquam eandem esse Patris, Filii & Spiritûs Sancti Personam; sed Tres esse Personas seu Hypostases Divinitatis reipsâ distinctas, nec plures nec pauciores.* Ursini Oper. Theol. Quæst. 4. Thesi 2. By which we see that this great Divine reckons *Subsistence* to be so much the Ground and Reason of *Personality*, that he uses *Persona* and *Hypostasis* as Terms perfectly equivalent. *Ursinus.*

But there would be no end of Particulars should I quote all that might be quoted, and therefore I shall conclude

conclude all these single Testimonies with that of *Turretinus*, late Professor of Divinity at *Geneva*, who gives us this full and Judicious Account, in his common Places, of the Point here before us. *Fides Orthodoxa haec est, in Unica & Simplicissima Dei Essentia Tres esse distinctas Personas, quae Proprietatibus Incommunicabilibus sive Modis Subsistendi ita inter se distinguuntur, ut una non sit alia, licet per ineffabilem περιχώρησιν maneant semper & existant in se invicem.* Turretinus part. 1. Loco 3. Quaest. 28.

In the last place to confirm the Testimonies of particular Persons, with the joynt Suffrage and Concurrence of whole *Churches* in their *Publick Confessions*, I shall mention some of them. And amongst these, the *Augustan*, or *Ausburg Confession*, gives this Account of the *Trinity*. *Ecclesiae scilicet Reformatae, magno consensu docent Decretum Synodi Nicenae credendum esse*, viz. *Quod sit Una Essentia Divina, & tamen sint Tres Personae ejusdem Essentiae*, &c. *Et Utuntur nomine Personae ea significatione qua usi sunt Scriptores Ecclesiastici, ut significet non partem, aut qualitatem, sed quod proprie Subsistit.* Confessio Augustana in Articulo fidei 1.

Next to this we have the *Wirtemberg* Confession declaring the same in the very beginning of it. *Credimus & confitemur Unum solum Deum*, &c. *Et in hac una & Aeterna Deitate Tres esse per se Subsistentes proprietates seu Personas, Patrem, Filium & Spiritum Sanctum.* This Confession was made and given forth in the Year 1552.

Likewise the *Gallican Reformed Churches* in their Confession made in the Reign of *Charles* the IX. and in the Year 1561. declare themselves much the same way upon this Article. *Sancta Scriptura nos docet in illa singulari & simplice Essentia Divina Subsistere Tres Personas, Patrem, Filium, & Spiritum Sanctum.*

Add

Add to these the *Belgick* Confession also, recognized, approved, and ratifyed in the Synod of *Dort*: which in its eighth Article speaks of the *Divine Persons* in the *Blessed Trinity* thus. *Hæc distinctio* [viz. *Personarum*] *non efficit ut Deus in Tres sit divisus, quandoquidem Scriptura nos docet Patrem, Filium, & Spiritum Sanctum singulos distinctam habere suis Proprietatibus Hypostasin*, which Words are extremely expressive and full.

But as touching these Confessions, the Reader ought not in Reason to be dissatisfied that I produce no more of them to the present purpose, (out of those many which are extant) since it has been still the Custom of most Churches to draw up their Confessions in Terms as general and short as they well could. So that we are the less to wonder if we seldom meet with such Words in them as are Explicatory and Particular.

And now after all these Authorities thus alledged by me, I would desire this Confident Man (whom I am here disputing with) to look back upon the fore-mentioned *Greek* and *Latin Fathers*, *Councils*, *School-men*, and all those Eminent *Modern Divines*, together with the *Clergy* of whole *Countreys* and *Nations*, Solemnly and Unanimously declaring themselves in their Publick Avowed *Confessions of Faith*, upon this great Article and Mystery; I say, I desire him to look all these in the Face, and to tell them, That they have hitherto abused the whole World with false Notions of the *Trinity*, by expressing the *Divine Persons* and *Personalities* by *Hypostases*, *Subsistences*, and *Modes of Subsistence*, Words (as he says) importing *little better than Sabellianism*, and serving for nothing else but to *obscure*, *perplex*, and *confound* the Minds and Thoughts of Men in conceiving, or discoursing of this Weighty and Sacred Point of our *Christian Faith*. This, I require him, in defence of what

what he has ſo expreſly, peremptorily, and Magiſterially affirmed all along in his Book, to do; if his *Heart* and *Forehead* will ſerve him for it.

In the mean time I have here delivered in all the Teſtimonies both *Greek* and *Latin*, *Ancient* and *Modern*, which I think fit to offer in behalf of the Point pleaded for: Though, ſhould I have repreſented all that occurrs in the fore-cited Authors (beſides many others not mentioned) to the ſame purpoſe, I ſhould not ſo much have *quoted*, as (upon the Matter) *Tranſcribed* them.

And now, if any one ſhould ask me, Whether I look upon theſe Teſtimonies as ſufficiently repreſenting the Doctrine of the *Catholick Church* upon this Head of *Divinity*?

I Anſwer, That barely by way of *Induction* they do not; ſince an *Induction* ought to conſiſt of a greater Collection of Particulars. Nevertheleſs I avouch this number of Teſtimonies to be a full and ſufficient Repreſentation of the ſence of the Church herein, if we conſider them as joyned with, and ſupported by theſe Three following Conſiderations. As

Firſt, That it is morally impoſſible, that the *Perſons* above quoted, being of ſuch Eminent Note in the Church, both for Orthodoxy and Learning, and Living (moſt of them) at ſuch great diſtance both of Time and Place, (rendring all Communication between them impracticable) ſhould, or could preſume to expreſs themſelves upon ſo Sacred an Article, and ſo Tender a Point, but in ſuch Terms as were generally received, uſed, and approved of by the Church.

Secondly, That theſe Terms were never yet Condemned, nor the Uſers of them Cenſured by any *Church*, or *Council*, accounted Orthodox; which in ſo great, and ſo revered an Article they would infallibly have been,

had

had they been judged *unfit* for, or *unapplicable* to, the Things to which they were actually applyed, as this bold Author with great Confidence affirms them to be.

Thirdly and Lastly, That hardly any Church-Writer of considerable Remark and Name can be produced, who ever treated of this great Subject in any other Terms than those expressed by us, or particularly made use of the Terms *Self-Consciousness* and *Mutual-Consciousness* to explain it by. All being wholly silent of them in all those Writings in which they do most particularly and exactly design a Discussion of these Matters.

These Three Considerations, I say, added to the fore-alledged Quotations irrefragably prove them to be a true, just, and sufficient Representation of the Sence and Doctrine of the *Catholick Church* in this Matter ; and that it is utterly inconsistent with the Common Reason, Principles and Practice of Mankind, that it should be otherwise. And as for what concerns this Author, whom I am disputing with, I dare affirm yet further, that any one or two of the Passages quoted by me, are more full and clear to the purpose I quote them for, than all that he has produced from the several *Fathers* alledged by him for his *Self-Consciousness* and *Mutual-Consciousness* put together; and much more than his forlorn νοερόν τι χρῆμα cited out of *Gr. Nyssen* to prove the *Son an Infinite Mind distinct from the Father*, Page 102. That is to say, than Three vagrant Words applyed by him , *to he knows not what*, and to be found (for ought appears) *he knows not where*.

All which being manifestly so, I desire any Sober Person to shew me something but like a Reason to prove, That the *Fathers* and other *Church-Writers* (from whom all these Quotations were drawn) placed the *Personal*

Distinction of the *Divine Persons* in *Self-Consciousness*, *and their Unity only in Mutual-Consciousness*. On the contrary, as these Words were never so much as mentioned by them, so I affirm, That, whensoever, in speaking of the *Trinity* they proceed beyond the bare Word and Name of *Person*, so as to give any Account of the Thing signified thereby, and the Reason thereof, they do it constantly by *Subsistences*, *Modes of Subsistence*, and *Relations*. This I am positive in; and withal, that, as they never mention the Terms *Self-Consciousness* and *Mutual-Consciousness* upon this Subject, so I averr moreover, That when they use the Words *Subsistences*, *Modes of Subsistence* and *Relations* on the one side, and of *Unity*, *or Identity of Nature*, *Essence*, *or Substance* on the other, (which they always do) they neither do, nor can mean *Self-Consciousness* by the former, nor *Mutual-Consciousness* by the latter, nor yet the Things signified by either of these Terms. And that for these Reasons.

First, Because all *Modes of Being* importing *Existence*, are in Order of *Nature* antecedent to the other Attributes of *Being*; such as are *Knowledge*, *Wisdom*, *Power*, and the like. And *Self-Consciousness* is no more; as being but a branch, or sort of *Knowledge*, and nothing else. And

Secondly, Because nothing *Absolute* can give *Distinction* and *Incommunicability* to the *Divine Persons*, the Rule of the *Schools* being undeniably true, *Non dari in Divinis Absolutum Incommunicabile*, Gr. Valent. Tom. 1. Pag. 874. But such a Thing I affirm *Self-Consciousness* to be, and in *Chap*. 4. have abundantly proved it so. So that it is evident, That all the *Fathers* and *Ancient Writers* in all the Terms which they used to express the *Trinity* and *Divine Persons* by, had no regard to *Self-Consciousness*, either *Name* or *Thing*, and consequently ly that it is a Term wholly forcign and unapplicable to this purpose. And what is said of their silence about *Self-Consciousness* extends to *Mutual-Consciousness* too.

And the Truth is, the other forementioned Terms asserted by us against this Innovator, are to be looked upon by all Sober Intelligent Men as a set of stated Words, or Forms of Expression first pitched upon by the Ablest *Divines* and *Writers* of the *Church*, then countenanced and owned by *Councils*, and lastly established by a kind of Prescription founded upon a long continued use of the same throughout the several Ages of the Church, as the best and fittest helps to guide Men in their Conceptions of, and Discourses about this great Mystery; and such as the *Church*, in treating of so arduous a Point, never yet would, nor durst go beyond. So that the Question now is, Whether they ought to be abandoned and made to give place to a New, Mushrom, unheard of Notion, set up by one Confident Man preferring himself before all Antiquity? A Notion, (no doubt) long before he was Born, throughly considered, canvased and laid aside, as not only insufficient, but Impertinent to give any tolerable Account of the *Trinity* by.

Well; but having declared this for the *Catholick, Orthodox*, and *Received Doctrine* about the *Blessed Trinity*, viz. *That it is one and the same Divine Nature, Essence, or Substance diversified into Three distinct Persons by Three distinct Modes of Subsistence, or Relations, so that by vertue thereof God is truly and properly said to be Three Persons, and Three Persons to be One God.* Having, I say, vouched this for the Doctrine of the Church, let us in the last place see what this Author has to object against it. And here his

First Reason (to put it into Form for him for once) may run thus: Whatsoever constitutes and distinguishes the *Divine Persons*, is really and truly in *God*, but *Modes of Subsistence* are not really and truly in *God*, and therefore *Modes of Subsistence* do not constitute, or distinguish the *Divine Persons*. The Major is evident, and shall be readily granted him. And the Minor he positively asserts, by denying any *Modes to be in God*, as particularly in *Page* 47. in these Words. *All Men grant* (says he) *that there are no Accidents, Qualities, or* Modes *in God*. And again, *Pag*. 84. *There are no* Modes, *no more than there are Qualities and Accidents in the Deity*. So that we see here what this Author holds concerning all *Modes* with reference to *God*.

In Answer to which Argument, as I have formed it (and I challenge him to shew that I have at all wronged him in it, if he can) I deny the Minor, viz. *That Modes of Subsistence are not in God*: And as for his Two forecited general Assertions: *That Modes are no more to be allowed in God than Qualities and Accidents* (which by the way are so put together, as if *Qualities* were not *Accidents*) I have these Two Things to remark upon those Two Assertions so positively laid down by him.

First, That it is a gross Absurdity, and no small proof of Ignorance, to reckon things so vastly different as *Modes* and *Accidents* are, upon the same Range, or Level, and then to argue and affirm the same thing of both. And therefore I do here with the same Positiveness tell him, That *Modes* and *Accidents* do extremely differ; and that none of any skill either in *Logick*, or *Metaphysicks* ever accounted them the same. For an *Accident* affects the Subject, it belongs to, so, that it is also a *distinct Being* it self. But a *Mode* affects it so, that it is not a *distinct Being* it self. I will not deny but *Accidents* may sometimes in a large and loose sence be called *Modes*: But I deny, That *Modes* are either *Accidents*, or ever so called,

where

where they are particularly and distinctly treated of by themselves. *School-men* and *Metaphysicians* may speak very differently of *Modes* when they mention them *occasionally*, and when they discourse of them *professedly*, and under a certain and peculiar Head. And whensoever they do so, if this Author can bring me any one *Logician*, *Metaphysician*, or *School-man* who takes *Accidents* and *Modes* promiscuously for the same Things, I dare undertake to forfeit to him a greater Sum, than ever yet he received for Copy-money in his Life.

Secondly, My next Remark upon his foregoing Assertion is this: That as it is grosly absurd to confound *Modes of Being* with *Accidents*; so it is equally absurd to deny *Modes of Being* to belong to *God*. And this I shall prove both from the manifest Reason of the Thing, and from Unquestionable Authority. And

First, For the Reason of the Thing. If *Modes of Being* should not be allowed in *God*, then I affirm it to be impossible for any Distinction, and consequently for any *Persons* to be in *God*. Which I prove thus. If there be any distinction in *God*, or the *Deity*, it must be either from some distinct *Substance*, or some *Accident*, or some *Mode of Being*, (for I defie him or any Mortal breathing to assign a fourth Thing besides these.) But it cannot be from any distinct *Substance*, for that would make a manifest Composition in the *Divine Nature*; nor yet from any *Accident*, for that would make a worse Composition: And therefore it follows, That this *Distinction* must unavoidably proceed from one or more *distinct Modes of Being*. This I affirm, and (according to my promise made to this Author in the foregoing Chapter) I shall be ready to defend the Truth of this Assertion against him, whensoever he shall think fit to engage in the Dispute.

Secondly,

Secondly, In the next place, for the proof of this from Authority, I affirm, that all *Metaphysicians*, *School-men* and *Divines* (at least, all that I have yet met with) do unanimously concurr in these Two Things.

1. That they utterly deny any *Accidents* in *God*. And

2. That they do as universally affirm *Modes of Being* to be in *God*, and to belong to him. Nay, and (which is more) That they do in these very *Modes* state the Ground and Reason of the *Personalities*, and the distinction thereof respectively belonging to the *Three Persons* of the *Godhead*.

And for a further proof of what I have here affirmed, and withal to shew how unable this Man's *Memory* is to keep pace with his *Confidence*, whereas in the fore-mentioned *page* 47. he affirms, *That all Men* (mark this Word) *deny Accidents*, *Qualities and Modes to be in God*. He himself afterwards, in *page* 48. owns, That the *School-men* hold these different *Modos Subsistendi* in the *Godhead*, and accordingly there sets himself (as well as he is able) to confute them for it. Now how shall we reconcile these blind Assertions, that so cruelly butt and run their Heads against one another? For will he say, That the *School-men* do not grant such *Modes* to be in *God*, after he himself has done his poor utmost to confute them for holding it? Or having said, *That all Men deny these Modes to be in God, and yet that the School-men grant and hold it*, will he say, That the *School-men are not Men*, and so come not under that Universal Appellative? What the *School-men* hold and assert in this Matter, has been sufficiently shewn already. But I must needs tell this Author upon this occasion, That he seems to have something a *bad Memory*, and withal to have more than ordinary need of a very *good one*.

There

There is one Thing more which I think fit to obſerve, and it is ſomething pleaſant, *viz.* That our Author having exploded all *Modos Subſiſtendi* in *God*, and Chaſtiſed the *School-men* for holding them, even to a forfeiture of their very *Humanity*; he yet vouchſafes afterwards, by a kind of Correctory Explication, to allow them in this ſence, viz. *That the ſame Numerical Eſſence is whole and entire in each Divine Perſon,but in a different* Manner, P. 84. Lines 12, 13, 14. By which Words it appearing that he grants that of the *Manner*, which he had before denied of the *Modus*, it is a ſhrewd Temptation to me to think, That certainly this Acute Author takes *Modus* for one Thing, and *Manner* for another.

In fine, I appeal to the Judicious and Impartial Reader, Whether a Man could well give a more convincing Argument of his utter Unacquaintance with the True Principles of Philoſophy and Theology, than by a Confident Aſſertion of theſe Two Poſitions.

1. That *Accidents* and *Modes of Being* are the ſame Things. And

2. That ſuch *Modes are not at all to be* allowed of, or admitted in *God.*

Secondly, His Second Objection againſt our ſtating the *diſtinction* of the *Divine Perſons* upon *Three different Modes of Subſiſtence*, is, That *theſe Modes are little better than Three Names of One God.* Which was the Hereſie of *Sabellius*. P. 83.

To which, I Anſwer Two Things.

Firſt, In direct and abſolute Contradiction to what he aſſerts, I affirm, That the difference between *Three Modes of Subſiſtence* in the *Godhead*, and only *Three diſtinct Names* applyed to it, is very great. For Names and Words depend only upon the Will and Pleaſure of the Impoſer, and not upon the *Nature* of the Thing it ſelf,

ſelf, upon which they are impoſed, and for that cauſe neither do nor can *Internally* affect it. But on the contrary, all *Modes of Subſiſtence* ſpring from the *Nature* of the *Thing*, or *Being*, which they affect, both antecedently to, and (by conſequence) independently upon the Apprehenſion, or Will of any one. So that altho' neither Man nor Angel had ever conſidered, or thought of, or ſo much as known that there were ſuch or ſuch things; yet the *Modes of Subſiſtence* proper to them, would have belonged to them, as really and as much as they do now. And if this Author cannot by this ſee a vaſt difference between theſe, and ſo many bare *Names*, (thanks be to God) others can both ſee, and defend it too. But

Secondly, Whereas he ſays, *That theſe Three Modes are but little better than Three Names.* I Anſwer, That his very ſaying ſo is a Conceſſion that they are ſomething at leaſt *more and better.* To which, I add further, That *this ſomething* (as ſmall a Difference as it makes) is yet ſufficient to diſcriminate things, which are only *Diſtinguiſhable*, and no more. For *ſeparable*, or *diviſible* from one another, I am ſure they are not. Nay, this is ſo far from being a juſt and rational Exception againſt placing the difference of the *Divine Perſons* in ſo many different *Modes of Subſiſtence*, that, in the Judgment of very Great and Learned Men, it is no ſmall Argument for it: For St. *Cyril* ſays, *That the difference between the* Divine Perſons *(by reaſon of the perfect Unity of their Nature (*as it were) blotting out, *or taking away all Diverſity between them) is ſo very* ſmall *as but juſt to diſtinguiſh them,*

Ὁμοούσιον τοίνυν τῷ Θεῷ καὶ πατρὶ τὸν υἱὸν ὁμολογοῦντες ὑπάρχειν ἐν ἰδίᾳ τε ὑποστάσει συνιστῶς τε ἅμα καὶ διῃρημένως ἑνῶσθαί φαμεν· τοῖς τῆς ταυτότητος λόγοις ἀναγκαιοτάτως εὖ μάλα συνάπτοντες τῶν προσώπων ἤτοι

them, and no more; and to cause that One of them cannot be called the other; the Father not the Son, nor the Son, upon any Account, the Father, &c. I thought fit to Transcribe the whole Passage, tho' the latter part, *viz.* from the Words ἵνα μὴ ταύτης, *&c.* is most immediately and directly to the Purpose, which I here alledge the whole for.

And *Thomas Aquinas* tells us, *That the Divine Persons ought to be distinguished by that, which makes the least distinction.*

In like manner *Durandus* affirms, *That the first Instance of Plurality* [or remove from Unity] *ought to be the least. And therefore that the distinction of the Divine Persons, since it is the first, ought to be by distinct Relations compatible in the same Essence: Which for that cause, is a less distinction than any that can be made by Things Absolute.*

And Lastly, *Bellarmine* averrs positively, *That the distinction of the Divine Persons ought to be the least that is possible.* Supposing all along, that it must still be *Real*, and not barely *Nominal*, or *Imaginary*. This was the Judgment of these

τῶν ὀνομάτων διαστολὴν καὶ τὴν τῶν ὑποστάσεων ἑτερότητα, τῆς ὡς ἐν Πατρὶ καὶ υἱῷ· κατ' αὐτὸ δὴ τοῦτο καὶ μόνον ἵνα μὴ ταύτης οὐσίας εἰς πᾶν ὁτιοῦν ἐμφερές, καὶ τὸ κατὰ τὰ αὐτὰ καὶ ὡσαύτως ἔχον ἀπαραλλάκτως ἔν τε τῷ Πατρὶ καὶ τῷ υἱῷ, καταλεαίνῃ τρόπον τινὰ τὴν διαφορὰν καὶ δυσδιάκριτον κομιδῇ τὸ ἀναμέρος ἴδιον ἑκατέρου κατεργάσαιτό πως. Ὁ μὲν γὰρ ἐστι Πατὴρ καὶ οὐχ υἱός· ὁ δὲ αὖ υἱὸς καὶ ὅτι που Πατήρ. &c. *Cyril. Dial.* 1. *de Trinit. p.* 4c9. *Edit. Lutet.* 1638.

Distinctio Personarum non debet esse nisi per id, quod minimùm distinguit, hoc est, per Relationem. *Aquin. primâ parte. Quæst.* 40. *Articulo* 2. *prope finem.*

Prima pluralitas debet esse minima; & ideo distinctio Personarum, quæ est prima, debet esse per Relationes compossibiles in eâdem Essentiâ: Et ob hoc, est minor aliâ quâcunque distinctione, quæ fit per Absoluta. *Durandus Lib.* 1. *Distinct.* 16. *Quæst.* 1. *in fine.*

Distinctio inter Divinas Personas debet esse minima. *Bellarminus Tom.* 1. *P.* 337. *Lutetiæ Paris.*

Learned Men; who as they were far from being *Sabellians*, so they very well knew both what to assert and how to express themselves without giving any ground for their being thought so.

From all which it follows, That for this very cause, that *Modes of Subsistence* import the least *Real difference* that can be, they are therefore the fittest to state the *Distinction* of the *Divine Persons* upon. So that our Author here relapses into a fault which he has been guilty of more than once, *viz.* in alledging that as an Argument against a Thing, which is indeed a most *Effectual Reason for it*. And so I come to his

Third and Last Objection against our making these *Modes of Subsistence* the ground, or *Formal Reason* of the *Distinction* between the *Persons* of the *Blessed Trinity*, which is, *That it makes the Three Divine Persons only Three Modes of the Deity, or only Modally distinguished*; whereas (according to his Doctrine) there are no *Modes in the Deity, and much less can a Mode be God.* And that, *As all must grant, that the Father is not a Mode of the Deity, but Essentially God; so no Man can think that the Father begot only a Modus, and called it his Son; whereas a Son signifies a Real Person of the same Nature, but distinct from the Father.* Thus he discourses, *pag.* 83, 84. And is not this close and profound reasoning? But as profound as it is, if it be at all to his Purpose, his Argument must lie in this, That all the forementioned Absurdities unavoidably follow from deriving the *Distinction* of the *Three Divine Persons* from *Three distinct Modes of Subsistence* belonging to one and the same *Divine Nature*. But this consequence I utterly deny, and to make out the Reason of this denial, I shall consider what he has said particularly.

And

Chapter VIII.

And here, first of all, I would fain know, Whether this Man will never leave confounding things perfectly different, and taking them for the very same? For to affirm the *Three Divine Persons* to be only *Three Modes* of the *Deity* is one Thing; and to affirm them to be only *Modally distinguished*, is quite another. The former we absolutely deny, and as positively hold the latter. And yet this wretched Fallacy would he impose upon his Reader all along, *viz.* That the Assertors of these *Modes of Subsistence* in the *Trinity*, make a *Person* to be only a *Modus Subsistendi*. But that is his own Blunder. For we do not say, That a *Person is only a Modus*, but that it is the *Divine Nature*, or *Godhead* Subsisting under such a *Modus*; so that the *Godhead* is still included in it, joyned to it, and distinguished by it. This is what we affirm and abide by, and what sufficiently overthrows his pitiful Objection.

And as for his Absurd Denial of all *Modes* in *God*, that has been throughly confuted already; so that we have nothing more to do, but to admire that Invincible and Glorious Ratiocination of his in these Words, *p.* 84. *No Man* (says he) *can think that the Father begot only a Modus, and called it his Son.* No, good Sir, No; none that I know of is in any danger of thinking, or saying so; no more, than that *Socrates* begot only the Shape and Figure of a Man, and then called it his *Son*; or (to turn your own blunt Weapon upon your self) no more than *God* the *Father* begot another *Self-Consciousness* besides his own, and called that his *Son*. Nevertheless I hope it will be granted me, That *Socrates* might beget *one* of such a Shape and Figure, and (by this Author's and *Xantippe*'s good leave) call that his *Son*; and that *God* the *Father* might beget a *Person* endued with such a *Self-Consciousness* (amongst other Attributes) and call that his *Son* too. But I perceive this Author and the *Fallacy of the Accident* are such fast Friends, that it is in vain to think of parting them.

In the mean time, as I told him what we do not hold concerning the *Father's* Generation of the *Son*, so for his better Information I shall tell him, what the Assertors of these *Modes of Subsistence* do hold concerning it, *viz.* We do hold and affirm, That the *Father* Communicates his Nature under a different *Mode of Subsisting*, from what it has in himself, to another, and that such a Communication of it, in such a peculiar way, is properly called his begetting of a *Son.* In which we do not say, *That the Father begets a Modus*, no nor yet an *Essence, or Nature*, but that he Communicates his own *Essence*, or *Nature* under such a *distinct Modus* to another, and by so doing begets a *Person*, which *Person* is properly his *Son.* This, Sir, is the true Account of what the Assertors of the *Personal Modes of Subsistence* hold concerning the *Eternal Generation.* And if you have any thing to except against it, produce your Exceptions, and they shall not fail of an Answer.

I am now come to a close of this Chapter, and indeed of the whole Argument undertook by me against this Author. In which I have Asserted the commonly received Doctrine about this great Article of the *Trinity*, both from the *Ancient Writers* of the *Church*, and against this Author's particular Objections; and in both fully shewn, That the *Three Persons* of the *Blessed Trinity* are one and the same *undivided Essence, Nature*, or *Godhead*, diversified only by *Three distinct Modes of Subsistence*, which are sometimes called *Properties*, and sometimes *Relations. So that a Divine Person is formally and properly the Divine Nature, Essence, or Godhead with, and under such a distinct Mode, Property, or Relation.* And this I averr to be the common, current, generally received

Doctrine

Doctrine of the *Church* concerning the *Trinity*. For *Councils* and *Fathers* hold it, the *School-men* teach it, the Confessions of *Churches* (where they are any thing particular upon this Subject) declare it; and all *Divines* both *Papist* and *Protestant*, in the several Bodies of Divinity wrote by them, do Assert it; only this Author, who yet (forsooth) owns himself a *Protestant* of the *Church of England*, denies and explodes it. To whom therefore (if he were not too great in his own Eyes to be Counselled and Advised) I would give this Charitable piece of Counsel for once, *viz. That for the future he would not presume at such a rate to contradict the whole World, till he has learn'd not to contradict himself.*

Animadverſions, &c.

C H A P. IX.

In which this Author's Paradoxes, *both* Philoſophical *and* Theological, *as they occurr in this his Diſcourſe, are drawn together, Examined, and Confuted.*

I Am ſenſible, that I am now engaged in a Subject that would threaten the Reader with a very long Chapter, ſhould I follow it, as far as it would carry me: For I am entered into a large Field, *viz.* this Author's *Paradoxical Aſſertions*: In the traverſing of which, I ſhall obſerve no other Method, but juſt to take them in that order in which they offer themſelves throughout his Book; ſave only, that I ſhall give my Reader this premonition, That ſuch of them as I have particularly examined, and laid open in the foregoing Animadverſions, I ſhall now ſet down without any further Deſcant, or Enlargement upon them, or at leaſt with very little.

But as for thoſe, which I there paſſed over without any Notice, or Remark, (as I did it all along with full purpoſe to treat of them by themſelves, ſo) I ſhall particularly inſiſt upon them now. And the Reader may pleaſe to take them as they follow.

P A R A D O X.

It is a vain and arrogant preſumption (ſays this Author) *to ſay, What is, or what is not a Contradiction, when we*

confeſs

confess we do not understand, or comprehend *the thing we speak of*, p. 4. And again, *I know nothing in the World that we do* perfectly understand, p. 7. line 19.

Answer. According to these Two Assertions taken together, I affirm, That though a Man discourses never so falsly and inconsistently of *God*, or indeed of any thing in the World besides, yet he cannot justly be charged as guilty of a Contradiction. And moreover, since this Author affirms, *page* 97, That for any one to say, *That Three Divine Persons who are divided and separated from each other, are each of them God, and yet that they are not Three Gods, but one God,* is a direct *Contradiction*; I desire to know of him, *Whether he* comprehends *what the Godhead, and what the Divine Persons are?* And if not, *Whether* (according to his own Rule) *it is not a vain and arrogant Presumption in him to say what is a Contradiction, when he professes himself not to* comprehend *the thing he is speaking of, and about which the Contradiction is said to be?*

PARADOX.

This Author having declared the *Intimate* and *Essential Unity* between the *Father* and the *Son* from those Words of our *Saviour*, John 14th. Chap. 10th. Ver. *I am in the Father, and the Father in me*: Subjoyns, *That this Oneness between them is such an Union, as there is* nothing in Nature like it; *and we cannot long doubt what kind of Union this is, if we consider that there is* but one possible *way to be thus United, and that is by this Mutual-Consciousness*, p. 57.

Answer. These Words I charge with Contradiction, and consequently with Absurdity upon two Accounts.

First, because they Contradict our Saviour's Words. And

Secondly, Because they Contradict the Author's own Words.

1. And

1. And first concerning those of our *Saviour*. Whereas this Author says, *That this Oneness between the Father and the Son, is such an Union, as there is nothing in Nature like it.* Our *Saviour* in *John Ch.* 17. (where this whole Passage is repeated twice) affirms something to *be like it*; *viz.* in *ver.* 11. where he prays to his *Father*, *That they* (viz. Believers) *may be One, as We* (viz. his *Father* and *Himself*) *are One*: And again, *ver.* 21. *That they may be One, as thou Father art in me, and I in thee.* So that our *Saviour* expresly asserts a *Likeness* of something *to this Union* on the one side; and this Author as expresly denies it on the other. In which (according to his blundering, undistinguishing way) he confounds [*Likeness*] and [*Sameness of kind*] as all One; as shall presently be further shewn.

In the next place, our *Saviour* (as plainly as Words can express a Thing) says, *That he and his Father are One, by a Mutual In-being, or In-existence in one another.* And this Man as expresly says, *That there is no* possible *way for them to be one but by Mutual-Consciousness.* But I on the contrary deny, That *Mutual-Consciousness* is *Mutual-Inexistence*, or *Mutual-Inexistence Mutual-Consciousness*, any more, than that *Being*, or *Existence* is properly *Consciousness*, or *Knowledge*; and therefore if *they cannot possibly be one, but by Mutual-Consciousness*, it is certain that they are not so by *Mutual-Inexistence*; which yet our Saviour, in Words properly and naturally signifying *Inexistence*, affirms that they are.

And the more intolerable is this Assertion in this Author, for that in *Pag.* 56. he affirms, that these Words of our Saviour *ought to be understood properly*; and if so, I hope they do not only exclude *Metaphors*, but all other *Tropes* and *Figures* also; for [*Proper*] is not, adequately opposed to *Metaphorical*, but to *Figurative*, whatsoever

ver the *Figure* be. And I do here affirm, That if our *Saviour's* Words be underſtood of *Mutual-Conſciouſneſs*, they do not ſignifie *Properly*, but *Figuratively*; and the *Figure* is a *Metonymy* of the *Subject* for the *Adjunct*; foraſmuch as in *God*, *Being*, or *Inexiſtence* are to be look'd upon as the *Subject*; and *Knowledge*, and the like Attributes as the *Adjuncts*. And therefore I do here tell this bold Man again, that for him to ſay, as he does, that the forementioned Words of our *Saviour* ought to be underſtood *properly*, and yet to interpret them to a ſence not *Proper*, but *Figurative* (which, by interpreting them of *Mutual-Conſciouſneſs*, he evidently does) is both an Abſurdity and a Preſumption, equally inſufferable. But in the

2d. Place I charge the forecited Paſſage of this Author with the ſame Abſurdity, for being as Contradictory to his own words, as it was to thoſe of our *Saviour*. For whereas he here ſays,

Firſt, *That this Oneneſs between the Father and the Son*, expreſſed in thoſe Words, *I am in the Father, and the Father in me, can be no other kind of Union, than an Union by* Mutual-Conſciouſneſs. And

Secondly, *That it is ſuch an one, that there is nothing in Nature like it.*

I deſire him to turn to *Page* 106. of his Book, where he tells us, *That the Fathers uſe ſeveral Examples, and allude to ſeveral ſorts of Union, thereby to form a Notion of the Unity of the Godhead in the Three Divine Perſons.* Let him, I ſay, read this, and tell me, Whether thoſe *Examples and Alluſions* could be of any uſe *to form a Notion of that Unity* to which they bore no *Reſemblance* at all? For I, for my part, ever thought, that there can be no Alluſion of one thing to another without ſome ſimilitude between them, and that a ſimilitude is always on both ſides; it being not poſſible for *Peter* to be like *John*, but *John* muſt be like *Peter* too. And if this Man does not yet bluſh at ſuch Contradictory Aſſertions, let him turn a little further to *Page* 126, 127. where he tells us particularly, that St. *Auſtin* explains this *Unity* by Examples of *Mutual-Conſciouſneſs*, and by ſeveral *Similitudes* (mark the words) of which the Unity of *Underſtanding, Memory*, and *Will* with the Soul of Man is alledged by him for *One*; and that a notable one too, for that *theſe Faculties* (as he there ſays) *are Mutually in one another*; and the Example of *Love* and *Knowledge* in the ſame Mind, is alledged by him as another ſuch a Simile, affirming them in like manner to *be Mutually in one another.* Now, I ſay, after all this, ought not the Reader to ſtand amazed, when he reads the Man firſt affirming that the *Unity* between the *Father* and the *Son Mutually exiſting* in one another by virtue of the *Mutual-Conſciouſneſs between them has nothing like it in Nature, nor has any Example, Metaphor, or Similitude, beſides it ſelf to allude to*; and yet afterwards producing ſeveral *Similitudes, Alluſions*, and *Metaphors* out of the *Fathers*, to explain both this *In-being*, and this *Mutual-Conſciouſneſs* by? *God* give him a better Memory; for as theſe things repreſent him, no Man living (would he but impart his skill) could be ſo fit to teach the *Art of Forgetfulneſs* as himſelf.

But after all, I muſt not omit to give the Reader notice of another of his Abſurdities, though of a lower rate, *viz.* That all along *Page* 57. he takes a *Pattern*, or *Example*, and a *Similitude*, or *Metaphor* for Terms equivalent; whereas a *Pattern*, or *Example* imports a perfect entire Reſemblance between it ſelf and the thing of which it is the *Pattern*, and indeed approaches next to a *Parallel Inſtance*; while, on the other ſide, an A-

gree-

greement in any one respect, or degree, is sufficient to found a *Metaphor*, or *Similitude* upon. And therefore tho it may easily be granted this Author, That there is no *Pattern*, or *Example* of such an *Union* as is between the *Father* and the *Son*; yet that does not infer, that there is nothing in Nature that bears any similitude to it; since this may very well be without the other, as that place in *John* 17. 11. and 21. has already proved.

And now I should here have finished my Remarks upon this particular Head, but that there is a certain Passage in order to his proving that there is nothing in Nature like *the Unity between the Father and the Son*, and it is this, *That in Substantial Unions, that which* comprehends, *is greater than that which is* comprehended: So that if Two Substances should be *United* by a *Mutual-Comprehension* of one another, the same would be both greater and lesser than the other, *viz.* greater as it *comprehended* it, and less, as it was *comprehended* by it, *P.* 57. Now this Proposition I will neither note as Paradoxical, nor absolutely affirm to be *false*. But so much I will affirm, *viz.* That it is nothing at all to his Purpose; and that he can never prove it to be *True*. For besides, that he still confounds an *Example*, or *Parallel Case* with a *Similitude*, I would have him take notice,

First, That this Maxime, *Omne continens est majus contento*, upon which he founds a majority of the thing *comprehending* to the Thing *comprehended*, is wholly drawn from, and founded upon the Observations made by the Mind of Man about *Corporeal Substances*, endued with Quantity and Dimensions; in which the *Substance Comprehending* is, and must be of a greater Dimension than the *Substance Comprehended*. But what is this to *Spiritual Substances*? Concerning which, I demand of this Author a solid Reason, Why Two such *Substances* may not be

 inti-

intimately United by a *Mutual-Permeation*, or *Penetration* of one another? For all that can hinder such a *Penetration*, or *Permeation* (as far as we know) is Quantity; which in *Spiritual Substances* has no place; and then, if such a *Mutual-Penetration* be admitted, these *Substances* will be *Mutually* in one another, and *United to one another*, not indeed by a *Comprehension* of one another, (of which there is no need, if such a thing could be) but by a *Mutual-Adequation*, or *exact Coequation* of one to the other; so that nothing of one *Substance* shall *exist*, or *reach beyond*, or without the other, but the whole of both by such a *Permeation*, *Mutually Exist* in each other. This, I say, I neither do, nor will affirm to be actually so, but I challenge this Author to prove that it *cannot be so*; and, till he can, it may become him to be less confident.

In the *next place*, I have one thing more to suggest to him about *Substantial Unions*, which he talks so much of, *viz*. That the Term is Ambiguous, and may signifie either,

First, The *Union* of Two or more *Substances* together, and so the *Father* and the *Son*, who are not *Two Substances*, but only *Two Persons* (as has been shewn in the foregoing Chapter) can never be *Substantially United*. Or,

Secondly, It may signifie the *Union* of Two, or more *Persons* in one and the same *Substance*; which is truly and properly the *Union* of the *Persons* of the *Blessed Trinity*.

And thus, though there is no Instance in *Nature* of *Persons* so *United*, yet by way of Allusion and Similitude, the *Union* of the three fore-mentioned Faculties of *Understanding*, *Memory* and *Will*, in *one and the same Soul*, (alledged by St. *Austin*) may pass for a small, or (as this Author himself calls it) *Page* 126. *Line* 28. *A faint*

faint Resemblance of the *Union* of the said *Three Divine Persons in the same Nature, or Substance*; which, according to his Excellent Talent of *Self-Contradiction*, he positively denies here in *Page* 57. and as positively affirms in that other now pointed at. In fine, this Assertion, *That the Father and the Son cannot possibly be One, or in One another* (which is here the same) *but by Mutual-Consciousness*, Page 57. Line 23, 24, 25. unavoidably infers, and implys, That they are not *One* by *Unity* of *Substance*, *Unity* of *Essence*, or *Unity* of *Nature*. For I am sure neither *Substance*, *Essence*, or *Nature*, are *Mutual-Consciousness*. And if the *Church* will endure a Man asserting this, I can but deplore its Condition.

PARADOX.

If we seek for any other Essence, or Substance in God, (says this Author) *but Infinite Wisdom, Power and Goodness, the Essence of God, though considered but as one Numerical Person, is as perfectly unintelligible to us, as one Numerical Essence, or Substance of Three Persons in the Blessed Trinity*, Page 69, 70.

Answer. This *Proposition* is false and Absurd, and to prove it so, I shall lay down these following Assertions.

First, That it is certainly much easier for Humane Reason to conceive one and the same *Divine Nature*, or *Deity*, as *Subsisting* in one *Single Person*, than in *Three distinct Persons*.

Secondly, That *Essence*, *Substance*, *Wisdom*, *Power* and *Goodness* are in the *Divine Nature* (which is a pure simple *Act*) all but one and the same Thing, or *Being*.

Thirdly, That, notwithstanding this, *Essence, or Substance, and Wisdom, Power and Goodness* are formally distinct from one another. That is to say, The *Conceptus Objectivus*, or proper *Essential Conception* of one does not imply.

imply, or involve in it the proper Conception of the other: Upon which Account one of them cannot properly be said to be the other.

Now these Three Things thus laid down, it is readily granted to this Man, *That Essence, or Substance, Wisdom, Power and Goodness are really one and the same Being*, and that therefore it is vain and foolish to seek for any *Essence, or Substance in God, which is not also Wisdom, Power and Goodness.* But this, by his favour, is not the point. For if he will nevertheless say, *That the Divine Nature expressed by one Infinite Essence, or Substance Subsisting in One Person, is as unintelligible, as the same Subsisting in Three distinct Persons*; Nay, that One and the same *Numerical Wisdom, Power and Goodness* considered, as *Subsisting* only in one *Person*, is not more Intelligible than the same, as *Subsisting* under Three; This is manifestly false, and contrary to common Experience, and without any further arguing the case, I appeal to the Reason of all Mankind, Whether it be not so?

PARADOX.

What is Intellectual Love (says this Author) *but the True Knowledge, or Estimation of Things? What is Justice and Goodness but an equal Distribution of, or a true and wise Proportion of Rewards and Punishments? What is perfect Power, but perfect Truth and Wisdom which can do whatsoever it knows?* Pag. 71, 72.

Answer. We have here a whole Knot, or Cluster of *Paradoxes*, but I shall take them asunder, and consider them severally: And because they run all in the way of *Interrogations*, I shall take them out of their *Interrogative Form*, and cast them into so many *Categorical Assertions.* The first of which is,

That Intellectual Love is nothing else but the true Knowledge and Estimation of Things.

This

This is false and Absurd. For *Love* is one Thing, and *Knowledge* another; each of them distinguished by *Essentially different Acts* and *Objects*, *Knowledge* importing no more than a bare Speculation, or Apprehension of the *Object*; whereas *Love* is properly an Adhesion to it: *Love Essentially* presupposes the *Knowledge* of the Thing *Loved*; but *Knowledge* cannot presuppose it self. *Knowledge* is the first *Act* of an *Intelligent Mind*, *Love* the second. And I would fain know, Whether this Man of *Paradox*, will affirm, That *God Loves* every Thing which he has *a true Knowledge and Estimation of?* But to give him one Argument for all, are not the Eternal Distinguishing Characters of *Two Persons* of the *Blessed Trinity* founded in the distinction of *Love* and *Knowledge* in *God*, the *Son* issuing from the *Father by way of Knowledge*, and the *Spirit* issuing from both *by way of Love?*

In the next place he affirms *Justice and Goodness to be the same Thing, and to consist both of them in a true and wise Proportion of Rewards and Punishments.*

But this also is false. These Two being as properly and formally distinguished by their *Acts* and *Objects*, as the Two former. And I do here tell this Author, That *God's Goodness* is the proper Qualification of his own Actions, without referring necessarily to any other besides; but that his Justice bears an *Essential Relation* to the Actions of others, *viz.* as *Rewardable*, or *Punishable*. And consequently *God* might have exerted innumerable *Acts* of his *Goodness*, though there had never been any *Object* for him to hav[e] exerted so much as one *Act* of his *Justice* upon. And to give him one Instance that may Convince any Man of sence of the vast difference of these two Attributes; [W]as that *Act of Creation*, by which *God* first Created the World, an *Act* of his Justice? Or did that *Act* consist in a *Wise proportion of Rewards*

wards and Punishments, before there was any *Act* of the Creature to be Rewarded, or Punished? But I am sure it was an *Act* of the *Divine Goodness*, whereby *God* communicated much of the Perfection of *Being* to someth ng without himself. Again, is Pardon of Sin an *Esse tial Act* of *God's Justice?* But I am sure it is an *Act* o his *Goodness*. Certainly this Man neither knows, nor cares what he says.

His Third Assertion is, *That perfect Power is nothing else, but perfect Truth and Wisdom.*

But this also is a gross *Paradox*, and as false, as that *Omnipotence* and *Omniscience* are not Two *distinct Attributes* of *God*. *God's Power* acts by and under the direction of *God's Wisdom*, and therefore neither is, nor can be *formally* the same with it. And besides this, all *Acts* of *Wisdom* and *Truth* proceed from *God* by a Necessity of *Nature*, but the *Acts* and Exercise of his *Power*, by a free determination of his *Will*. For in speaking of *God*, no Man says, That *God is Wise, Knowing, or True, or Acts according to these Perfections, because he will do so*; for he can neither be, nor *Act* otherwise; but we truly and properly say, That *God does this or that, because he will do it*; for if he had pleased, he might have chose, whether he would do it, or no. From all which, I conclude, That nothing could be more improperly and absurdly affirmed than, *That the Divine Power is nothing else but the Divine Truth and Wisdom.*

PARADOX.

In Men (says he) *it is only Knowledge that is Power; Humane Power, and Humane Knowledge, as that signifies a Knowledge how to do any Thing, are Commensurate; so that every Man can do what he knows how to do: Nay,* Knowledge, *is not only the Director of* Power, *but it is that* very Power *which we call* force, Page 72.

Answer.

Answ. This is so gross a *Paradox*, that, I think, it can need no other Confutation than to oppose the sense of all Mankind to it, nevertheless I shall offer this one Consideration towards the disproving the Identity of *Knowledge* and *Power*, *viz.* That a Man's Knowledge and Skill about the doing any Work of Art, may increase, as his power of Execution for the Actual doing the said Works may decrease, nay, wholly cease, and therefore they cannot be the same. For suppose a Carpenter disabled by Age, or Accident, that he cannot strike a stroke towards the building an House; does he therefore cease to know how to build it, while another shall build it wholly by the direction of his Skill and Knowledge? This Man may as well prove his Head and his Hands to be one and the same Thing, as *Knowledge* and *Power* to be so. But I shall go no further than this very Author, to confute this Author's Assertion, who has told us in *P.* 9. *l.* 3,4. *That we understand nothing of the Secrets and Mysteries of Nature; nor are concerned to understand them, any more than it is our Business to understand how to make either a Body, or a Spirit, which we have* no power *to do*, (mark that) *if we* did understand it, *and therefore it would be an useless piece of Knowledge.* Now I beseech the Reader to set these Two Assertions together, *viz.* that in *Page* 72. *That to know how to do a Thing is to be able to do it*, and that other in the *Page* 9. *viz. That though we understood how to make a Body, or a Spirit, yet we have no Power to do it.* I say let these Two Propositions be compared; and then I hope that for the future, *Knowledge how to do a thing*, and *Power to do it*, ought not, even according to this very Author, to pass for the same thing. In the mean time we see how one of his Assertions contains a gross Absurdity, and the other completes it with as gross a Contradiction.

PARADOX.

This Word Infinite (says he) *confounds our Notions of God*, p. 77.

Answer. This is false. The Thing indeed signified by the Word *Infinite*, exceeds and transcends our Notions, but the Word *Infinite* does not confound them. And I would have this Man take notice, that for an Object to surpass and be above our Thoughts, and to disorder and confound them, are very different Things. And moreover, that it is the height of Impudence and Ignorance too, to say, That *that Word confounds our Thoughts, Notions and Conceptions of God*; which all *Divines* and *Philosophers* in all Places and Ages have constantly expressed the *Nature* of *God* by: And which, after the Notion of his bare Existence, does, next in order, offer it self to the Mind of Man, in its Speculations of this Great Object.

PARADOX.

We know not (says he) *how far* Infinite *Wisdom and Goodness, and Power reaches; but then we certainly know, that they have their* Bounds, *and that the Divine Nature is the utmost* Bounds *of them*, p. 79.

To which I *Answer*, That for an *Infinite Wisdom* to have *Bounds*, and the *Bounds* of it to be the *Divine Nature* (which it self has no Bounds) is *in ipsis Terminis* an express, downright, and shameless Contradiction. See this further laid open in my 2d Chapter.

PARADOX.

This Creed (says he, speaking of the *Athanasian*) *does not speak of the Three Divine Persons as distinguished from one another*, P. 88. Line 21.

In reply to which, I am amazed to read an Assertion so manifestly false, and yet so positively uttered. For will this Author put out the Eyes of his Reader? He tells

tells us here that *Athanasius* (or whosoever else might be the Author of this Creed) *does not herein speak of the Three Divine Persons as distinguished from one another.* But I demand of him, does *Athanasius* here speak of them as of *Three Persons*, or no? If the first; then he does and must speak of them as *distinguished* from one another, for that without such a distinction they are not so much as *Three.* But if he does not speak of them *as of Three*, and as *of Three thus distinguished.* What then mean those Words of the Creed? *There is one Person of the Father, another of the Son, and another of the Holy Ghost?* Do these Words speak of these Persons *as distinguished*, or do they not? If they do; then what this Man has here said of the Creed, is shamelesly false; and if they do not express the said *Persons as distinct*, I defie all the Wit of Man to find out any Words that can.

PARADOX.

He tells us, *That the Title of the one Only true God cannot be so properly attributed to any one Person, but only to the Father*, p. 89.

Answer. This I have already shewn in *Chap.* 5. *p.* 137. to be both false and dangerous; as by direct consequence either making several sorts of *Gods*, or excluding both the *Son* and the *Holy Ghost* from the one true *Godhead.* At present I shall only say thus much, That [*the One only true God*] and [*the true God*] are Terms perfectly equivalent, and not only Commensurate but Identical in their signification; and withal, That this very Author himself affirms *Page* 186. *Line* the last, *That the Son must be included in the Character of the only True God*; which how he can be, without having this Character properly affirmed and predicated of him, and his suſtaining thereby the Denomination of the *only True God*, let this Confident, Self-contradicting Man declare if he can. In the mean time let me tell him further, That theſe Terms [*the True God*] and [*the only True God*] do both of them import an Attribute, or Denomination purely *Eſſential*, and by no means *Perſonal*, or *Oeconomical:* And moreover that every ſuch Attribute does and muſt agree to all the *Three Perſons* equally, and whatſoever equally agrees to them all, may with equal Propriety be affirmed of all and each of them, and conſequently that the Title of [*the One only True God*] may every whit as truly and properly be attributed to the *Son* and *Holy Ghoſt*, as to *the Father* himſelf. See more of this in my forementioned Chapter.

PARADOX.

I affirm (ſays he) *that the Glory and Majeſty and all the other perfections of the Three Divine Perſons are as diſtinct as their Perſons are.* And again, *Theſe perfections are as diſtinct as the Perſons, and yet as Numerically one and the ſame as the Godhead is*, p. 91.

Anſwer. The firſt part of theſe Aſſertions is utterly inconſiſtent with, and wholly overthrows the laſt. And it is indeed very horrid, as by inevitable conſequence inferring a Tritheiſme. For if the *Eſſential* Perfections of *God* (which in Truth are only the *Divine Eſſence* under ſeveral Conceptions and Denominations) are as *diſtinct as the Perſons*, whom the Church acknowledges to be *really diſtinct*, then it will and muſt follow, That in the *Trinity* there are *Three really diſtinct Eſſences, or Godheads*, as well as *Three really diſtinct Perſons*: And if they are thus diſtinct, it is impoſſible that the *Three Perſons* ſhould by vertue thereof, either be, or be truly ſaid to be, really one; ſo that this Author, we ſee, has herein

aſſerted

aſſerted a *Trinity* with a Witneſs; but as for any *Unity* in it, you may go look.

But I perceive he was driven to this falſe and abſurd Aſſertion by that Argument of his *Socinian* Adverſary urging him, That if the *Eſſential* Glory and Majeſty in *Father*, *Son* and *Holy Ghoſt* be but One, then it cannot be ſaid that their Glory is equal, their Majeſty co-eternal; foraſmuch as *Unity* is not capable of *Equality*; which muſt of neceſſity be between two or more. This, I ſay, no doubt drove him to this Inconvenience.

In Anſwer to which Objection, (though I owe not this Author ſo much Service) as I ſhall readily grant, That where there is an *Equality*, there muſt be alſo a *Plurality*, of ſome ſort or other, whatſoever it be: So I ſhall obſerve, That the *Divine Eſſence*, *Glory*, *or Majeſty*, (which I ſtill affirm to be but different Names of the ſame thing falling under divers Conceptions) and every other *Eſſential perfection* of the *Godhead*, may be conſidered two ways.

Firſt, Abſolutely and Abſtractedly in it ſelf, and as preſcinding from all *Perſonal Determinations*, in which ſence the *Divine Nature*, *Eſſence* (and every *Eſſential Attribute* included in it) is, and always muſt be taken, whenſoever, in Diſcourſe, it is ſpoken of, either as *compared with*, or *contra-diſtinguiſhed to* all, or any of the *Perſons*. And accordingly, in this ſence being *abſolutely One*, it is incapable of any *Relation of Equality*. Foraſmuch as *one Thing* conſidered but as *One*, cannot be ſaid to be equal to it ſelf. Or,

Secondly, This *Glory*, *Majeſty*, *or any other Eſſential perfection of the Godhead*, may be conſidered as ſuſtaining *Three ſeveral Modes of Subſiſtence in Three diſtinct Perſons*; which ſaid *Modes*, as they found a *Plurality in this Eſſential Glory*, *or Majeſty*, (though by no means *of*

it,

it) ſo this *Plurality* founds a Capacity of *Equality*; by virtue whereof, the ſame Glory according to its peculiar way of *Subſiſting* in the *Father*, may be ſaid to be equal to it ſelf as *Subſiſting* after another way in the *Son*, and after a third in the *Holy Ghoſt*; ſo that immediately and ſtrictly this *Equality* is between the Three ſeveral *Modes of Subſiſtence*, which this *Eſſential Glory*, or *Majeſty* ſuſtains, or (if you will) belongs to the ſaid *Glory*, for and by reaſon of them. And this is the true Anſwer to this *Socinian Objection*, which by a manifeſt fallacy proceeds *à dicto ſecundùm quid ad dictum ſimpliciter*, viz. That becauſe *Equality* cannot belong to the *Eſſential Glory*, or *Majeſty* of the *Godhead* conſidered *abſtractedly* from the *Divine Perſons*, therefore neither can it agree to the ſame *Glory*, or *Majeſty*, upon any other Account whatſoever, which is utterly falſe; foraſmuch as conſidered according to the *Three different ways* of its *Subſiſtence* in the *Three Perſons*, it may, as *Subſiſting* under any one of them be ſaid to be equal to it ſelf, as *Subſiſting* under the other Two.

PARADOX.

This Author repreſents Gregory Nyſſen *as firſt aſſerting a Specifick* Sameneſs, *or* Unity *of Nature, in the Divine Perſons (which alſo he makes all along to be ſignified by the* ὁμουσιότης) *and then aſſerting that this Specifick* Sameneſs, *or* Unity *of Nature, makes the ſaid Three Perſons* Numerically One, Page 118. the latter end.

Anſwer. This is too great an Abſurdity for ſo Learned a *Father* to be guilty of, and therefore ought to lie at this Author's own Door; for that a *Specifick Sameneſs*, or *Unity of Nature*, ſhould make any *Thing*, or *Perſon*, *Numerically One*, (any more than a *Generical Unity* can make Things

Things *Specifically One)* is beyond meaſure ſenceleſs and illogical.

PARADOX.

Though the Fathers (ſays he) aſſert the ſingularity of the Godhead, or the Numerical Unity of the Divine Eſſence; yet they do not aſſert ſuch a Numerical Unity, as where there is but one Perſon as well as one Eſſence, but ſuch a Numerical Unity as there is between Three, who are ὁμοούσιοι, of the very ſame Nature, but are not merely united by a ſpecifick Unity, but by an eſſential Union; and therefore are Three and One, Pag. 121. Line 15.

Anſwer. In theſe Words there are ſeveral Abſurdities, which he falſly charges upon the *Fathers*, but ought in all Reaſon to take to himſelf. As,

1. He ſuppoſes a *Specifick Unity*, and an *Eſſential Unity* to be *diſtinct Unities*: whereas every *Specifick Unity*, or *Union*, (call it, at preſent, which you will) is alſo an *Eſſential Unity*, or *Union*. For a *Specifick Unity* is one ſort of an *Eſſential Unity* (which in its whole compaſs contains the *Generical*, the *Specifical*, and the *Numerical*, and therefore thus to *contra-diſtinguiſh* a *Species* to its *Genus*, is fit for none but ſuch a *Logician* as this Author; it being all one, as if one ſhould ſay of *Peter*, That he is not only a Man, but alſo a Living Creature.

2. The ſecond Abſurdity is, That he owns a *Specifick Unity* of *Nature* in the *Divine Perſons* (which ſort of *Unity* I have abundantly proved in *Chap.* 7. the *Divine Nature* not to be capable of) for he ſays here of the *Divine Perſons*, *That they are not* meerly *United by a Specifick Unity*: which Words muſt imply, that however, ſo *United* they are.

3. He makes Two ſorts of *Numerical Unity*, contrary to all Rules of *Logick*, viz. *One*, where there are ſeveral

ral *Persons* of *One Nature*, as here in the ***Trinity***; and the other, where there is but *One Person*, as well as ***One Nature***. But let me here tell him, That the *Divine Nature* is every whit as *Numerically One* in the *Three Persons*, as if there were but one *Person* in the *Godhead*, and no more. And in this very Thing (as has been shewn) does the Mysteriousness of an *Unity in Trinity* consist. I say, The *Divine Nature* is as *Numerically One* in the *Three Persons*, as the *Humane Nature* was *Numerically One* in *Adam*, while there was no other Person in the World but himself; nay, much more so, since it is not *multiplicable*, as that was. And to affirm, That the *Numerical Unity* of the *Godhead* is not so perfect, or is not the very same, *Subsisting* in *Three distinct Persons*, as if we could imagine it to *Subsist* but in *One*, Subverts and Overthrows such *an Unity in Trinity*, as the *Church* in all *Ages* hitherto has maintained.

PARADOX.

Having told us, *That the Fathers universally acknowledged, the Operation of the whole Trinity* ad Extra *to be but One, and from thence concluded the Unity of the Divine Nature and Essence; for that every Nature has a Virtue and Energy of its own; (Nature being a Principle of Action,) and if the Energy and Operation be but One, there can be but One Nature.* He adds within four Lines after, *That this is certainly True, but gives no Account, how Three distinct Persons come to have but One Will, One Energy, Power and Operation; nor that any Account* (that he knows of) *can be given of it but by* Mutual-Consciousness, Page 124. Line 7, *&c.*

Answer. Were I not acquainted with this Man's way of Writing, I should be amazed to see him in so small a compass so flatly contradict himself. For will he, in the first place, assert, in the *Three Divine Persons* a *Nu-*

merical

merical Unity of Nature? And in the next, assert also, that this *Unity of Nature* is proved by *Unity of Energy* and *Operation?* And after this tell us, *That this gives no Account at all, how Three distinct Persons come to have but one Will and Energy, Power and Operation?* For does not *Unity of Nature* in these *Three distinct Persons* prove this? While the said *Unity of Nature* proves *Unity of Operation*, as the Cause proves its Effect, and *Unity of Operation* again proves *Unity of Nature*, as the effect proves its cause? This, any one of sence would think, is a fair, full, and sufficient Account how *Three distinct Persons, having all but One Nature, come thereby all to have but One Will, Energy and Operation.* And should any one else argue otherwise, I should think him *beside himself*; but this Author in this discourses *like himself*.

PARADOX.

Knowledge, Self-reflection, and Love are distinct Powers and Faculties in Men, and so distinct, that they can never be the same; Knowledge is not Self-Reflection, nor Love either Knowledge, or Self-Reflection; though they are inseparably United, they are distinct, Pag. 130. Line 11, 12, *&c.*

Answer. Here also is another knot of Absurdities. For,

First, *Knowledge, Self-Reflection*, and *Love* are not in Men *distinct Powers and Faculties* (as this unfledged Philosopher calls them) but only *distinct Acts*.

Secondly, Admitting that *Knowledge* were a *Faculty* (as it is not) yet I deny that *Knowledge* and *Self-Reflection* would make Two *distinct Faculties*, forasmuch as it is one and the same *Intellectual Faculty*, which both exerts an *Act* of *Knowledge*, and an *Act* of *Reflection* upon that *Act* of *Knowledge*, or upon it self as producing the said *Act*. For which Cause it is (as has been observed before) that Philosophers hold that the *Understanding* is *Facultas supra se Reflexiva*; all of them allowing both the *direct* and the *Reflex Acts* of *Knowledge* to issue from the same Faculty.

Thirdly, He says, That albeit the forementioned *Acts are distinct, yet they are inseparably United.* But this also is false; for (whether an *Act* of *Knowledge* may be without an *Act* of *Self-Reflexion,* as some, not without Reason, think it may) I am sure in Men (of whom alone we now speak) both an *Act* of *Knowledge* and of *Self-Reflexion* too may be without an *Act* of *Love* consequent thereupon: And if the former may be without the latter, then they are not *inseparably United,* as this Author here says they are.

PARADOX.

He says, *That Love is a distinct Act, and therefore in God must be a Person,* P. 133.

Answer. If this be a true and good consequence, then the Ground and Reason of it must be This, *That every distinct Act in God, is, and must be a distinct Person.* And if so, then every Decree in *God,* whether it be his Decree of *Election,* or of *Reprobation* (if there be such an one) or of creating the World, and sending *Christ* into it, and at last of destroying it, and the like, are each of them so many *Persons.* For every Divine Decree is an *Act* of *God,* and an *Immanent Act too,* as resting within him, and (as such) not passing forth to any Thing without Him; that Maxime of the *Schools* being most true, that *Decreta nihil ponunt in esse.* Nor is this all, but most of the *Divine Acts* are free also; so that there was nothing in the Nature of them to hinder, but that they equally *might,* or *might not* have been; which applyed to the *Divine Persons,* would make strange work in Divinity. In the mean time if this Author will maintain this Doctrine, *viz.* That *Acts* and *Persons,* are the same in *God,* (as, I think, he ought in all Reason to maintain the

immedi-

immediate conſequences of his own Aſſertion) I dare undertake that here he will *ſtand Alone* again; and that he is the only Divine who ever owned, or defended ſuch wretched Stuff.

PARADOX.

Theſe Three Powers of Underſtanding, Self-Reflexion, and Self-Love are One Mind, viz. *in Created Spirits*; of which alone he here ſpeaks, adding in the very next words, *What are meer Faculties and Powers in Created Spirits, are Perſons in the Godhead*, &c. Page 135. at the latter end.

Anſwer. This is a very groſs Abſurdity, and to make it appear ſo, I do here tell him, That the Three forementioned *Powers* are no more *One Mind*, than *Three Qualities* are *One Subſtance*; and that very Term [*Powers*] might have taught him as much; *Potentia* and *Impotentia* making one Species of *Quality*; under which all *Powers* and *Faculties* are placed. So that *his Three Powers of Underſtanding, Self-Reflexion*, and *Self-Love are One* only *Unitate Subjecti*, as being Subjected in One and the ſame Mind; but not *Unitate Eſſentiæ*, as *Eſſentially* differing both from one another, and from the Mind it ſelf too, in which they are. Certainly if this Man did not look upon himſelf as above all Rules of *Logick* and *Philoſophy*, he would never venture upon ſuch Abſurd Aſſertions.

PARADOX.

He tells us, *That the Son and Holy Ghoſt* Will *and* Act *with the Father; not the Father with the Son and the Holy Ghoſt*, Pag. 169. Line 13, 14, *&c.*

Anſwer. This is a direct Contradiction: For if the *Son* and *Holy Ghoſt* Will and Act with the *Father*, the *Father* muſt Will and Act with the *Son* and the *Holy Ghoſt*. And he who can find a diſtinct ſence in theſe Two *Propoſiti-*

 ons,

ons, and much more, affirm the first, and deny the latter, has a better Faculty at distinguishing than any Mortal Man, using his Sence and Reason, will pretend to. It being all one, as if I should say, *I saw* Thomas, William *and* John *together* ; *of whom* William *and* John *were in the Company of* Thomas. *but* Thomas *was not in the Company of* William *and* John. And I challenge any sensible thinking Man to make better sence of this Author's fore-mentioned Assertion if he can. But this must not go alone without a further cast of his Nature, by heightning it with another Contradiction too, which you shall find by comparing it with *Page* 188. *Line* 4. where he affirms, *That Father, Son, and Holy Ghost Act together*, having before expresly told us here, *That the Father does not Will and Act with the Son and Holy Ghost* ; which very Assertion also, (to shew him the further fatal Consequences of it) absolutely blows up and destroys his whole Hypothesis of *Mutual Consciousness*, by destroying that upon which he had built it. *For if the Father may and does Will and Act without the Son and Holy Ghost*, then farewel to the μία ἐνέργεια, and the μία κίνησις θελήματος, for they must never be alledged in this Cause more.

PARADOX.

Nothing can make God visible but a Personal Union to a Visible Nature, Page 234. Line 22, 23.

Answer. This is a most false Assertion, and directly contrary to Scripture. And to prove it so, I shall lay down these Four Conclusions.

First, That the *Godhead*, or *Divine Nature*, neither is nor can be visible to a Corporeal Eye, by an Immediate sight, or Intuition of the *Godhead* it self.

Secondly, That *God* is visible to such an Eye only by the special Signs, or Symbols of his Presence.

Thirdly,

Thirdly, That *God* is visible by a Body Personally United to him, only as the said Body is such a Sign, or Symbol of his peculiar Presence. And

Fourthly and Lastly, That a Body actually assumed by *God* for a Time, is during that Time as true, and visible a Symbol of his Presence, as a *Body*, or *Nature personally United* to him can be.

And thus it was, that *God* appeared visibly to the *Patriarchs* in Old Time, and particularly to *Abraham*, to *Gideon*, and to the Father and Mother of *Sampson*, who thereupon thought *that they should Die for having seen God Face to Face.* For generally all Interpreters hold the *Person* who thus appeared, to have been the *Second Person* of the *Blessed Trinity*, the *Eternal Son* of the *Father*; though sometimes called simply the *Angel*, and sometimes *the Angel of the Covenant*, from the Office he was then actually imployed in by his Father, as the Extraordinary Messenger and Reporter of his Mind to Holy Men upon some great Occasions.

This supposed, I desire this bold Author to tell me, Whether the *Second Person* of the *Trinity (God* equal with the *Father)* was *personally United* to the *Body*, which he then appeared in, or not? If not; then the forementioned Assertion, *That nothing can make God visible, but a Personal Union to a Visible Nature*, falls shamefully to the Ground, as utterly false. But if he was *Personally United to it*, then these *Paradoxes* must follow,

1. That he either laid down that *Assumed Body* afterwards, or he did not: if he did, then an *Hypostatical Union* with *God* may be dissolved; and not only so, but there may be also a Thousand *Personal Unions* one after another, (if *God* shall think fit to Assume a Body, and appear in it so often;) which would be contrary to the *Sence*

of

of all Divines, and to all Principles of sound Divinity, which own but one *Hypostatical Union* and no more. Or,

2. He still retains an *Union* to that *Assumed Body*, and then there is a double *Hypostatical Union*, viz. One to the *Visible Body* Assumed by him, in which he appeared of Old, and the other to that *Body* which he was Born with in the World. All which *Positions* are horrid and monstrous, but unavoidably consequent from the foregoing Assertion. But for the further illustration of the case I do here affirm to this Author, That *God* is as Visible in an *Assumed Body*, whether of Air, or Æther, or whatsoever other Materials it might be formed of, as in a Body of Flesh and Blood *Personally United* to him: I say, as *Visible*. For notwithstanding the great difference of these *Bodies*, and the difference of their *Union* and *Relation* to *God*, One being by a *Temporary Assumption*, and the other by a *Personal Incarnation*; yet no Corporeal Eye could discern this Difference, during the Appearance, but that one was, for the time, as Visible as the other; and therefore since both of them were truly Symbols of *God*'s peculiar Presence (the only way by which the *Divine Nature* becomes visible to a Mortal Eye) it demonstratively overthrows that positive, false Assertion of this Author, *That nothing can make God Visible, but a Personal Union to a Visible Nature.*

PARADOX.

All the Circumstances of our Saviour's Birth, and Life, and Death, were so punctually foretold by the Prophets, and so peremptorily decreed by God, that after he was come into the World, there was no place for his Choice *and* Election. *And he could not shew either his Love, or his Humility by* choosing *Poverty, Death,* &c. Page 242. Line 5.

Answer. This is False, Absurd, and Dangerous, and indeed next to Blasphemous; as overthrowing the whole

Oeconomy

Oeconomy of Man's Redemption by the Merits of *Christ*. For that which leaves no place for *Choice*, leaves no possibility for *Merit*. For all Merit is founded in *freedom of Action*, and that in *Choice*. And if *Christ*, after his *Incarnation*, had not this, he could not *Merit*. And whereas the Author says, *That Christ chose all this as the Second Person of the Trinity antecedently to his Incarnation*. I Answer, That this is indeed true, but reaches not the present Case. For what he did before he was Incarnate, was the *Act* of him purely *as God*; but a *Meritorious Action* must still be an *Humane Action*; which could not proceed from the *Second Person* before his Assumption of an *Humane Nature*. I readily grant and hold, That the Actions of *Christ's Humane Nature* received a peculiar Worth and Value from its *Union* with his *Divine Person*, yet still I affirm, that this Worth and Value was Subjected and Inherent in his *Humane Actions*, as such; and thereby qualified them with so high a degree of *Merit*. So that, whencesoever this *Merit* might flow, they were only his *Humane Actions*, *viz.* such as proceeded from him as a Man, that were properly and formally Meritorious.

And whereas this Author states the Reason of this his horrid Assertion upon the Predictions of the *Prophets*, and the *peremptory Decrees of God* concerning all that belonged to, or befell *Christ*, I do here tell him, That neither *Predictions* nor *Decrees*, though never so punctual and peremptory, do, or can infringe, or take away the freedom of Man's Choice, or Election about the Things so Decreed, or foretold; how difficult soever it may be for *Humane Reason* to reconcile them; and if this Man will affirm the contrary, he must either banish all *Choice* and *Freedom of Action*, or all certain *Predictions* and *peremptory Decrees* out of the World; let

him.

him choose which of these Two Rocks he will run himself against, for he will be assuredly split upon either. This vile Assertion really deserves the Censure of a *Convocation*, and it is pity, for the *Church's* sake, but in due time it should find it.

PARADOX.

Concerning *Person* and *Personality* he has these following Assertions, which I have here drawn together from several parts of his *Book*, viz. *The Mind is a Person*, Page 191. Line 21, 22. *A Soul without a Vital Union to a Body, is a Person*, Page 262. Line 17. *And the Soul is the Person, because it is the Superiour governing power, and Constitutes the Person*, Page 268. Line 28. *A Beast which has no Reasonable Soul, but only an Animal Life, is a Person*, &c. Page 262. Line 18, 19, 20. And again, *We may find the Reasonable and Animal Life Subsisting apart, and when they do so, they are Two*[*Persons*]*and but One* [*Person*] *when United*, Page the same, at the end of it. And lastly, *One Agent is One Person*, Page 268. Line 2.

Answer. In all these *Propositions*, so confidently laid down by this Man, there are almost as many Absurdities and Falsities as there are Words. I have already shewn this of some of them in *Chap.* 3. and therefore I shall be the briefer in my Remarks upon them here.

And first for that Assertion, *That the Mind is a Person*. To this I Answer, That the Mind may be taken Two ways.

First, Either for that *Intellectual Power*, or *Faculty*, by which the Soul understands and Reasons. Or,

Secondly, For the *Rational Soul* it self.

In the former sence, it is but an Accident, and particularly a Quality: In the second it is an *Essential* part of the Whole Man; and therefore upon neither of these

consequently Absurd to Assert any more. But the former is undoubtedly true. And to shew that it is so, we are to consider what Human Reason, and the Offices of it properly are; and so for the Humane Will, and the proper Acts and Functions of that. Now they are both of them *Intellectual Faculties*, and thereby distinguished from, and Superiour to all Acts of *Sensation*, whether External, or Internal, and all Acts of *Desire* and *Appetition*, proceeding from the Sensitive Appetite. And as they are superiour to them, so it is the proper Office of *Reason* to Arbitrate upon, Judge of, and Direct all the Apprehensions and Reports of the Senses, and upon such a Judgment passed upon them, to declare authoritatively, *What ought, or ought not to be done*; and in the like manner the *Will* is to Govern and Control all the *Inferiour Appetites, Desires*, and *Inclinations*, by an effectual disposal of them, to *what shall, or shall not be done.* And this is the Order and Oeconomy of all the *Rational* and *Sensitive Powers* and *Faculties* of the *Soul of Man*, and of the *Functions* and *Operations* respectively belonging to them. And now I desire any one to shew me, what use there is of a *second Reason*, and a *second Will*, and what are those particular, proper *Acts* proceeding from them, which are neither *Intellectual*, nor *Sensitive*. For if they are either of these, all such *Acts* have been fully accounted for, from the *Intellectual* and *Sensitive Principles* already mentioned, and therefore must needs be Superfluous. Again, I would know, whether these Two Reasons are *Subordinate*, so that one is subject to and governed by the other, or *Co-ordinate* and *Equal*, and neither of them Subject to, or Governed by the other? If they are *Subordinate*, the Inferiour is useless, since the *Acts* proceeding from both, being equally *Acts* of *Reason*, the Superiour can and may dictate all that the Inferiour can ſuggeſt immediately by it ſelf, and without the *Subordinate Operation* of the other; and what I have ſaid of an *Humane Reaſon*, will proportionably hold in an *Humane Will*: But if, on the other ſide, there are *Two Co-ordinate Reaſons*, and *Two Co-ordinate Wills*, neither of them ſubject to, or governed by the other, then, in the Direction and Diſpoſal of Mens Actions, they either ſuggeſt the very ſame Directions and Commands, or ſuch as are quite different, and ſometimes perhaps contrary. If the very ſame, then *One* of the *Reaſons* and *One* of the *Wills* are again ſuperfluous: For what need can there be of *Two* to ſuggeſt the very ſame things? But if theſe *Two Reaſons* ſuggeſt different, or contrary Directions, and theſe *Two Wills* exert *Two* different, or contrary *Influences* upon the Inferiour and Senſitive part, then the Soul muſt be diſtracted between both, and not able to proceed determinately to Action; but the *Two Reaſons* muſt diſpute the Matter, and the *Two Wills* muſt fight it out. And this will be the admirable Harmony and State of an *Humane Soul*.

If it be here Objected, That we ſometimes find mention in *Scripture* of a *Senſual*, or *Carnal Reaſon*, and of a *Senſual Will*: and that therefore *Two Reaſons*, and *Two Wills* muſt be admitted in each Man.

I Anſwer, That we Read in *Scripture* of the *Old Man* and the *New Man*, in *Perſons Regenerate*, and yet I cannot from hence infer, That *Two diſtinct Men* do, or can Subſiſt in *One Perſon*. And therefore as to that Objection of a *Carnal*, *Senſual Will and Reaſon*,

I Anſwer, That *Reaſon* is called *Senſual*, when it directs and preſcribes according to the Exorbitant Inclinations and Deſires of the *Senſitive Part*; and the *Will* is called ſo likewiſe, when it does not interpoſe its Sway and Authority, but ſuffers the *Senſitive Appetites* to take their

own

CHAP. X.

In which the Author's Grammatical, (*and such like*) *Mistakes, as they are found here, and there in his Writings, are set down, and remarked upon.*

COuld this Author have carried himself with any ordinary degree of Candor and Civility towards those, whom he wrote against, he had never had the least Trouble given him by me upon this Head of Discourse. But when I find him treating Learned Men with so much Disdain and Insolence, and much liker a rough, ill-bred *School-Master* domineering over his Boys, than a fair *Opponent* entring the Lists with an *Ingenuous Antagonist*, I must confess, I cannot think my self obliged to treat him upon such Terms, as I would an Adversary of a contrary Temper and Behaviour. One Man (and a very Learned one too) he flirts at, as if he could not distinguish between *Conjunctive* and *Disjunctive* Particles; Vindication of his Case of Allegiance, *pag.* 76. the Two last Lines. Another he *Scoffs*, or rather *Spits* at, as neither *understanding Greek nor Latine*. Vindic. Trin. *Pag.* 95. *Lin.* 25. and thereby, I suppose, would bear himself to the World as no small Critick in both. As for the *Socinians* (of which number this latter is) I do from my Heart Condemn their Opinions, as false, and destructive, not only of the *Christian*, but (in several

Instances) even of *Natural Theology* and *Religion* it self. Nevertheless I do not find, that these Men use to be reproached *for want of* Greek, *or* Latine, or for any Notable Defect of Parts, either Natural, or Acquired. *Faustus Socinus* was a Person undoubtedly of great Wit and Strength of Mind, and of Competent, though not very deep Learning; but his Uncle *Lælius Socinus* before him, and *Crellius* who lived some time after him, were Persons very well stocked with both; and so have been many more (indeed too many) besides these. And where the Case stands thus, I think, what the *Poet* said of *Probity* and *Integrity*, may very well be said of *Learning* also, viz. *That it is Commendable even in* an *Enemy*, how much soever we may blame him for the ill use of it. But this Author spares neither Friend nor Foe, but comes like a kind of Hurricano upon his Adversary, not vouchsafing him so much as one grain of Allowance, wheresoever he finds (or rather thinks he finds) him Tripping. And therefore, let him not, of all Men, complain that he is hardly dealt with, *if with the same measure, with which he has hitherto meted to others, it be measured to him again.*

Accordingly, I shall in this Chapter proceed to examine his *Grammatical, Vocabular* Mistakes. And that I may do this justly, and without the least shadow of unfair dealing, I will first set down the Table he gives us of the *Typographical Errata*, in the first Edition of his Book; that so we may distinguish, what ought to be laid at the *Printer*'s Door, and what at the *Author*'s.

The

CHAPTER X.

The Table of Errata *prefixed to the First Edition of the* Vindication of the Blessed Trinity, &c. *is as follows.*

PAge 50. Line 2. read περιχώρησις, P. 51. L. 15. for *Corinthus* read *Cerinthus*. P. 93. L. 26. for *ss* read *is*. P. 95. L. 32. for *his* read *Tres*. P. 96. L. 2. for *Persons* read *Personæ*, and L. 30. for *the* read *Three*. P. 105. Line 5. for *whence* read *when*. P. 155. Line 33. for *to* read *too*. Pag. 203. L. 15. for *we* read *He*. P. 214. L. 29. for *Convict* read *Convinc't*. P. 227. L. 10. for *World* read *Word*. P. 238. L. 18. dele *it*. P. 249. L. 18. read *Challenged*.

This is a true and exact Transcript of the Table of the *Errata* prefixed to that *Book*. (Whether the said Table be True, or no) concerning which, I cannot but observe, That most of these *Errata* are much more easily Corrigible by an Ordinary Reader (without any Admonition) than those that I shall mention, and remark upon. And I shall add further, That, had he but said [*That these and the like Errata the Reader is desired to Correct as he shall meet with them*] he should have heard of none of them from me; though I am pretty well satisfied, and so will any *Judicious Reader* be too, that as none of them in any probability are, so some of them (as they stand here placed in this Book) neither are, nor could be any one's but his own. But since he has laid in no such *Salvo*, and this stands as a full Account of the *Errata*; and not only so, but since in the Second Edition some Faults not mentioned in this Table, are Corrected, while others remain the same, or as bad, as in the First Edition, there is all the Reason in the World, that the Author ſhould be charged with that, from which he himſelf has thus diſcharged the *Printer*. And beſides, in the Second Edition of his Book, the Reader is deſired to take Notice, that there is no Table of *Errata* at all; by which we may juſtly conclude, That he reckoned it ſo *Correct*, as to need no further *Correction*. So that what I find there, I judge my ſelf, to have all the right that can be, to Account with him for.

A Letter to *Anonymus*, p. 1. Printed 1683.

And the rather, for that Ten Years ago he publickly declared in Print, *That he was reſolved in what he ſhould publiſh for the future, to Correct the Preſs himſelf*; though, on my Conſcience, it was one of the unfitteſt Employments (next to the *Writing of Vindications*) that he could take to; as, I doubt not, but this Chapter will pretty well ſhew.

Now the Words, which I intend to Remark upon, ſhall be of theſe Two ſorts.

Firſt, Such as may be conſidered ſingly in themſelves. And

Secondly, Such as muſt be conſidered in Conjunction with other Words, in Sentences and Forms of Speaking.

Of the firſt ſort the Reader may pleaſe to take notice of theſe that follow.

As in *Page* 16. *Line* 23. I find an extraordinary word called ἐκπορεοόμσεος: the meaning of which I would gladly know: For I can no more find it in any *Lexicon*, than I can in the Table of the *Errata*: And yet certainly it muſt be ſome excellent Word, as having ſtood its ground in both Editions of his Book. I confeſs I have been apt to think it ſtands for ἐκπορευόμενος; but why it ſhould do ſo, the Author (who, no doubt, is a *Grecian* in his Heart) may poſſibly give us a good Reaſon; but I, for my part, cannot.

Such

Such another Word we have cloathed indeed in *Greek* Characters, but, by no means, of *Greek* Extraction; and that is ἀκατωνόμιστον, *Pag.* 115. *Lin.* 11. I have read, I confeſs, of ἀκατονόμαστον, ſignifying *innominabile*, or *quod nominari non poteſt*; and I do not deny but that I find ἀκατωνόμαστον alſo; and that not only in the place here cited out of *Greg. Nyſſen*, but twice alſo in St. *Baſil's Hexaemeron* (from whence I quoted it ſo written, *Ch.* 7. *p.* 192.) But I very much queſtion, Whether the Word be ſo wrote in other and Ancienter Copies of thoſe *Father's* Works; and that for theſe Two Reaſons.

Firſt, Becauſe it muſt be derived from the *Preterperfect Tenſe* ὠνόμασται; and if ſo, then according to the Rule of *Grammar* in ſuch *Verbal Derivatives*, the Augment muſt be thrown away, and the Original Letter retained; as in ἔγερσις *ab* ἤγερσαι, ὁμαλισμὸς *ab* ὡμάλισμαι, and conſequently ὀνόμαστος *ab* ὠνόμασται. And that ὀνόμαστος with an *Omicron* is the Regular and proper Word, appears from thoſe Cognate Words ſo common amongſt the *Grammarians*, ὀνομαστικὴ & ὀνομαστικόν. Neverthleſs if ὠνόμαστος be admitted, it muſt be by the *Attick Dialect*; which very often (eſpecially in Compounds) puts an ω for an ο; as in ἀνώμαλος and ἀνώνυμος, and ſeveral other like Words.

But my Second *Reaſon*, why I think the Ancienter Editions of St. *Baſil* have it ἀκατονόμαστος with an *Omicron*, is, becauſe I find thoſe *Lexicographers* who write it ſo, quote this Word out of that very place of St. *Baſil's Hexaemeron*, where now it ſtands wrote ἀκατωνόμαστον; which ſurely proves that they found it not there ſo wrote then, when they quoted it from thence. But admitting that it may be ſo wrote, *viz.* with an ω as well as with an ο, yet what does, or can this make for our Author's new-coined ἀκατωνόμιστον? For till there can be be found such *Greek* Words as ὀνομίζω and ὀνομίζομαι to derive it from (which none ever yet met with, nor ever will) in vain shall we seek for ἀκατωνόμιςον any where but in this Author.

In the next place, to pass from *Greek* Words to *Latine*, or such at least as are *Latinized*, I would gladly know, who those *Anti-Nicene Fathers* were, who are mentioned by him, *Pag.* 24. *Lin.* 5. And whether they were *Arians*, or *Novatians*; who (as I take it) were the great Opposers of the *Nicene Council.* But that, I find, cannot be, since our Author tells us, *That the Persons, spoken of by him, were of the same Faith with the* Nicene Fathers. So that upon that Account, I should think, it ought to be the *Ante-Nicene Fathers.* And if so, I think the Author would do well to take notice, that there is a great difference between *Anti-Nicene* and *Ante-Nicene*, between such as lived *before* the *Council*, and such as were *against* it. And the more particular and exact notice ought he to take of it here, since (though the difference be only in an *Iota)* he yet knows what a Disturbance this little Letter made in the *Homoousian* and *Homoiousian* Controversie, even so great as to occasion the Convening of this Famous *Council.* Neverthelefs, that this word *Anti-Nicene* passed for good and current with this Author, is evident from hence, that it is (as well as some others) free of both Editions of this extraordinary Book.

Again in *Page* 105. *Line* 8. we are told of the *Favourites* of some Opinions. As to which, I had thought, that Men use to favour and countenance Opinions, and not to be countenanced and favoured by them. And yet the Word *Favourite* signifies *passively*, and so must be taken for one who *receives favour*, and not *actively* for one who *shews it.* And therefore if to represent any one

as

as the *Favourite of an Opinion* be not good ſence, I know no way, but by ſtriking it out, and putting *Favourer* in the room of it, to make it better.

In *Page* 106. *Line* 16. I read *Intenſion* uſed in the ſame ſence with *Intention*, or *Purpoſe*; and I muſt declare, that I never found it ſo uſed before.

And in *Page* 108. *Line* 31. I am told of the *Council* of *Lateran*; and I wondered a good while, what *Council* it ſhould be; for though I had heard of *ſeveral* Lateran *Councils*, yet I never heard of the *Council of the* Lateran, till I met with it here.

Likewiſe I find an Extraordinary Perſon in *Page* 43. *Line* 1. named *Lucifer Carolitanus*, and was thereupon in ſome thoughts with my ſelf, whether there might have been any place called in former times *Carolina*, or by ſome Name like it. But then out comes the Second Edition and alters it into *Caralitanus*; which (in my poor Opinion) looks very ſuſpiciouſly, as if ſome Body had a mind to Correct it, but knew not how. As for *Lucifer Calaritanus* ſo called from *Calaris*, now *Cagliari*, the Metropolis of *Sardinia*, I have heard much of him; but I will ſuppoſe our Author had ſome Body elſe in his Eye. And upon this occaſion, I cannot but take notice of ſome other *Writers* quoted by him, whom the World ſeems as much unacquainted with, as with this *Carolitanus*. As for inſtance St. *Hillary* in his *Apol. P.* 15. at the latter end. And *Albaſpinus* in his Defence of Dr. *Stillingfleet*, *Pag.* 165. *Lin.* 22. And *Nonnas* in his *Knowledge of Chriſt*, *Pag.* 218. Now St. *Hilary* indeed, a Famous Father of the Church, and Biſhop of *Poictiers*, and *Albaſpinæus* Archbiſhop of *Orleans*, Eminent for his Learned Works, and *Nonnus* who Wrote a Paraphraſe upon St. *John*'s Goſpel, in *Greek* Verſe, are every one of them known and celebrated by all. But as for St. *Hil-*

lary,

lary, Albaspinus and *Nonnas*, I never heard of them till this Author was pleased to bless the World with these New Names.

As for *Erronious* instead of *Erroneous*, and ἀγαιωσύνη instead of ἁγιωσύνη, they are small things, and ought to make no difference amongst Friends, though I have known many a poor *School-boy* forced to *Water his Plants* for a less Mistake.

But there is a Word of singular note, which I have met with at least six or seven times in this Book, and four times in one Page, *viz.* 227. and it is *Prosopopæa*, which also, as well as its Companions has given the Catalogue of *Errata* the slip, and so, weathered it out in Two Editions: But what to make of it, I cannot tell. There is indeed a certain Figure in *Rhetorick*, called *Prosopœia*, which I know well enough, but *Prosopopæa* I am wholly a Stranger to: And surely this Author could not mean the Figure προσωποποιΐα; forasmuch as the strict Literal signification of that is *fictio Personæ*. And I cannot imagine how this Author should mistake about this *Word* (of all others) having had so Excellent an Hand at the *Thing* signified by it; as having, I dare say, *made more Persons* than ever *God* thought fit to furnish the World with.

And to shew the Reader that our Author's store extends much further than one Book, I will present him with some more of the like Rarities out of some of his other Pieces.

As first in *Page* 65. of his Answer to the *Protestant Reconciler*, he makes mention of *Exorcisme*, *Chrysom*, *Unction*, *Dipping*, *Trine Immersion*, &c. as rejected by the *Church of England*. And here I was extremely at a loss to learn what *Chrysom* was; and after all my search, no *Lexicon* could inform me, till at last I hit upon a certain

tain little *Lexicon*, called, *The Bill of Mortality*, and there I found a Word very near it, as differing from it but by one Letter, which was *Chrisom*, signifying a Child that dies presently after it is Born: But then considering again, that the *Church of England* did not declare her self to reject such, I was as much at a loss as ever; till at length setting my Guessing Faculty on work, I concluded, that certainly it should be *Chrisme*, which is a *Greek* Word for *Unction*, as *Immersion* is a *Latine* one for *Dipping*. And this our Author should have taken notice of, for though he quotes it out of the *Reconciler*, yet since he neither rectifies it, nor reflects upon him for it, we may very reasonably suppose, that he took it for good Payment; and really thought, that it ought to be *Chrysom* as he found it. Otherwise he who had been so quick and sharp upon him at other turns, would, no doubt, have took him upon such an advantage, and well-favouredly exposed him for so foul a Blunder.

But to go on. In *Page* 209. *Line* 13. of the same Book, I find mention of the *Quadrigesimal Fast*. And this put me as much to a stand, as the other, to imagine what kind of *Fast* this should be. For the nearest and likest Word I could derive it from, was *Quadriga*, signifying a *Coach, Cart, or Waggon*. And accordingly as the *Jews* had their *Feast* of *Weeks*, and of *Tabernacles*, so I did not know, but the *Papists*, or some *Christians* like them, might have some *Fast*, called, *The Fast of Coaches, or Waggons*; and might possibly give it that Name from its being carried on with the Discipline of the *Whip* and the *Lash*, as *Coaches* and *Waggons* used to be. This Conjecture, I say, I made with my self. For I concluded, that this Author could not mean it of the *Lenten-Fast*; for that is called *Quadragesima*, or *Jejunium*

Quadragesimale, and issues from the Numeral *Quadraginta*, and so is quite another Thing from this *Quadrigesimal-Fast*; which I cannot find in all the *Rubrick* of our Church; though perhaps when those *Excellent Persons* spoken of, *Apology*, *P.* 5. *Lin.* 20. have finished their Intended *Alterations of our Rubrick*, we shall find it there too.

In the next place, let us pass to such of his Words as stand conjoyned with others in Sentences, or Forms of Speaking. And here let us first of all consider his absurd use of that form of Expression [*as I may so speak*] which he has at least Twenty times in this one Book: Now the proper use of these Words, is to bespeak excuse for that which they are joyned to, as for something that is *legendum cum veniâ*, and containing in it a kind of *Catachresis*, or at least some Inequality, some Defect or other in the Expression, with Reference to the Thing designed to be expressed by it. And this, I am sure, is all the true and proper Reason assignable for the use of these Words [*as I may so speak.*] But this Author applies and uses them, even when he pretends to give the properest and most Literal Account and Explication of Things, and such an one, as is not only better than all others, but even exclusive of them also, as the *only* True Account that can be given of them. As for instance, where he affirms *Self-Consciousness* to be the True and only *Formal Reason* of *Personality*, and *Mutual-Consciousness* to be the same of the *Unity* of the *Divine Nature* in the *Three Persons*, he ushers it in with those Words [*as I may so speak*] *Page* 56. *Line* 6, 7, 8, &c. which (according to what he holds about these Two Terms) is all one, as if I should say, *God* is an Infinite Eternal, Almighty Being *(as I may so speak)* and *God* is the Creator and Governor of the World *(as I may so speak)* and Man is a Rational Creature, having Two

Eyes,

Eyes, Two Arms, and Two Legs; *(as I may so speak)* all which is egregiously Absurd and Ridiculous. And the more so; for that this very Author reproaches one of his Adversaries (whether *Owen*, *Baxter*, *Lobb*, or the *Reconciler*, I cannot at present remember, but the Thing I perfectly do) for using the like Expression [*as I may so say*,] with great scoff and scorn, telling him thereupon, That *certainly no Man had ever more need of* [*so says*] *than he had*. Now for my own part, I think this *Author*'s [*so speaks*] are every whit as bad and contemptible as his Adversary's [*so says*] unless he can perswade the World, That a Man may *speak* an Absurd thing much more excusably than he can *say it*.

To this we may add some more such Absurd Expressions. As for instance, that in *P*. 55. *Lin*. 26. where he says, *That the Three Divine Persons are so United to each other, as every Man is to himself.* In which Words, besides the falseness of the Proposition; it being impossible for the *Three Divine Persons* to be so *United* to each other, as to be but *One Person*, which yet *every Man is*, we ought to note also the Absurdity of the Expression. For all *Union*, or *Unition*, is *Essentially* between two things at least; so that unless the *Man* be *One thing*, and *himself* another, He cannot be said *to be United to Himself*. He may, perhaps, be properly enough said to *be One with Himself*; but to say, *That he is United to himself*, is unpardonable Nonsence. Again, in *Page* 85. *Line* 8. He tells us, *That the Infinite Wisdom which is in the Father, Son, and Holy Ghost, is* [*Identically the same*] which is as much as to say, *That a Man is Wisely Wise*, *Honestly Honest*, *Learnedly Learned*, and the like: For though I know what it is to be *perfectly, or absolutely the same*, yet to affirm any Thing, or Person to be *Identically the same*, is an Idle, and a Nauseous Tautology. Likewise in

Page 182. *Line* 19. He tells us, *That God intercedes with no Body but himself.* Concerning which Form of Speaking, I must observe, That when the Term [*But*] is used as a Particle of *Exception*, it implys the Thing, or, Person excepted from others, to be of the *same kind*, or at least, *condition* with the rest, from which it was excepted. And therefore, unless *God* were a *Body*, it can with no Congruity of Speech be said, *That God intercedes with no Body but himself.* So that this also must pass for another Blunder. With the like Absurdity he tells us in *Page* 124. *Line* 15. *Where there are Two distinct and divided Operations, if any of them can act alone without the other, there must be Two divided Natures.* Now it is a Maxime in Philosophy, and that such an one, as, I think, ought to take place in *Grammar* too, That *Actionis non datur Actio.* And accordingly if the *Reason of Things* ought to be the *Rule of Words*, then to say, That *an Operation Acts, or Operates*, is extremely Senceless and Ridiculous.

But to proceed, he has a way of promiscuously applying such Words to *Things* as are properly applicable to *Persons* only, such as are [*who*] and [*whose.*] As for instance, he tells us of the Being of a Thing [*whose*] Nature we cannot conceive, *Page* 6. *Line* 11. And in the same Page, *Line* 23. *We may know* (says he) *that there are a great many things* [*whose*] *Nature and Properties we cannot conceive.* And in *Page* 7. *Line* 18. *It is so far from being a wonder to meet with any Thing* [*whose Nature*] *we do not understand*, &c. But is this Sence, or *Grammar?* Or does any Man say, *Reach me that* Book, [who *lies there*] *or that* Chair [who *stands there?*] No; certainly, none who understands what proper speaking is, would express himself so. And moreover (to shew that he can speak of *Persons* in a *Dialect* belonging only to *bare Things*, as well as he did of *bare* Things in words

proper

proper only to *Perſons)* he tells us of a *Son produced out of the Subſtance of* [its Parent] inſtead of *his Parent*, *Page* 257. *Line* 19. which is a way of ſpeaking every whit as improper and abſurd as the other. In the next place he has a cuſtom of joyning a Verb of the *Singular Number* with a Noun of the *Plural*, and ſo *vice verſâ*. As *there is Three Gods*, inſtead of, *there are Three Gods*, *Page* 2. *Line* 9. And *the Nature of moſt things* [are] *very dark and obſcure*, inſtead of [*is ſo*] *Page* 6. *Line* 20. which alſo is ſo Ungrammatical that it would not be endured in a *School-Boy*; it being as arrant a Solecism in *Engliſh*, as *Homines currit*, or *Socrates diſputant* would be in *Latine*. Likewiſe he often uſes the Particle [*then*] inſtead of [*than*] as, *The Scripture teaches more* [then] *Natural Reaſon does*. Pag. 148. Line 19. And *a more Glorious Authority* [then] *he exerciſes himſelf*, Page 173. Line 28. This, I ſay, is familiar with him, but withal exceedingly Abſurd, Improper, and not *Engliſh*. For [*then*] is a Note of Time, but [*than*] is a Note of Compariſon, importing a greater or leſſer degree of that Thing wherein the Compariſon is made; and is commonly joyned with the Words *ſooner*, or *rather*, but always with ſome word or other, denoting the *Comparative Degree* of a Thing. As, *ſuch* an one has more or leſs Strength, or Wiſdom [than] another. And I will Die *ſooner*, or *rather* [than] I will do ſuch a Thing, or the like. But no Man who Speaks, or Writes true *Engliſh*, will uſe theſe two words indifferently. But I muſt not omit that Notable Paſſage, *Page* 119. *Line* 25. where he tells us, That there is μήτε φύσεως μήτε ἐνεργείας τινα διαφορὰν ἐν τῇ Θεότητι. Theſe are the very words, and as they ſtand (though in conjunction with Two or Three *Engliſh* Words to complete the Sentence) do in my Opinion, carry much of the Air of a Solecism upon them;

ſo that according to the Conſtruction of them here, if it had been for my Life, inſtead of ſaying, *There is* τινὰ διαφορὰν, I would have ſaid, *There is* τὶς διαφορὰ, and ſo have joyned true *Greek* and *Engliſh* together.

And thus I have preſented the Reader with ſome of this Author's Ways and Forms of Expreſſion, which *Grammarians* call *Loquendi Genera*. From all which, according to the ſingular skill he has ſhewn in this ſort of Learning, it is to be hoped, that as he has already bleſt the World with a New Divinity and Philoſophy, ſo he will in due time oblige it with a new *Grammar* too.

And great need (as we ſhall preſently ſee) there ſeems to be of ſuch an one. In order to which, I ſhall mention but one more of this Author's Pieces. And that is a Book, Intituled, *A Defence of Dr.* Stillingfleet, *&c.*

In the beginning of which, there is a *Table of Errata* prefixed, that fills almoſt a whole Page; ſo that I verily thought, that it had ſo clearly carried off the whole Crop, as to leave no Gleanings behind. Nevertheleſs I ſhall preſent the Reader with this ſmall *Spicilegium* of what I gathered up after it; not mentioning any one Word that ſtands Corrected there.

In *Page* 53. therefore, and *Line* 10. He tells us of a Counterfeit *Epithite*; but what that is, I do not know. I have indeed often heard of an *Epithete* from the *Greek* ἐπίθετος and ἐπίθετον, ſignifying *quid appoſitum aut adjectum*, and imports properly, an Adjective joyned to a Subſtantive, and giving the Subſtantive a Denomination accordingly. But as for this Author's *Epithite*, it may, for ought appears, ſignifie ſomething to *ſtop Bottles*. For as for any other Signification (that I know of) it has none.

In

CHAPTER X.

In the next place, *Page 64, 65.* he quotes *Baxter* for an Expreſſion uſed by him, *viz. of ſuch People as talk through a Window on the West-end of* Moore-Fields; and calls it Mr. *Baxter*'s *Elegant Paraphraſes* for Madmen. But here (beſides the miſtake of *Paraphraſes* for *Paraphraſis*, which is only one Number put for another) our Learned Author muſt give me leave to tell him, That by this Paſſage, he ſeems not to underſtand what a *Paraphraſis* means. For a *Paraphraſis*, or *Paraphraſe* (to put it into *Engliſh* for his ſake) ſignifies properly a Tranſlation of ſome *Writing*, with Additions and Enlargements to Illuſtrate and Explain the ſence of them, and is therefore uſually called *Liberior Tranſlatio.* In which ſence we read of this or that *Paraphraſe upon the Pſalms*, and *Eraſmus*'s *Paraphraſe* upon the *New Teſtament*, and the like. So that unleſs the *Mad-men* here ſpoken of, were a certain *Book*, or *Writing*, and Mr. *Baxter*'s Words concerning them, an *Explicatory Tranſlation* of the ſaid *Writing*, this *Great-Good* Man could not properly call them a *Paraphraſe.* But what muſt we call them then? Why truly the forementioned Words might be properly enough called a *Periphraſis*, or *Circumlocution* (which, being ſo like the word *Paraphraſis*, might eaſily deceive a Man who cares not what he Writes) and when it is ſo taken, it is a certain Figure in Speech, whereby we expreſs a Thing by ſeveral Words, which otherwiſe might, and, for the moſt part, is expreſſed by one. As *Sophroniſci filius*, is a *Periphraſis* for *Socrates*, and *the Man who Conquered* Pompey the Great, is a *Periphraſis* for *Julius Cæſar*; and ſo to bring the matter home to Mr. *Baxter*'s Inſtance; that forementioned Expreſſion of, *Men who talk through the Windows at the Weſt-end of* Moore-Fields, is a proper *Periphraſis* for *Mad-men.* But as for a *Paraphraſe upon Madmen*, I leave it to this won-

derful

derful Person, to make a *Paraphrase* upon any Man, (whether Mad or Sober) if he can.

Likewise in *Page* 112. and the last Line, he tells us, out of *Calvin's* Epistles of a *Publica præcum formula.* Concerning which, though I must confess, that I do by no means aspire to be one of the Number of this Author's *Excellent Persons*, who were for *altering* our Liturgy, or Publick Form of Prayer. Yet, if it were expressed by *Publica præcum formula*, I should be one of the foremost who should desire that *Præcum* might be altered into *Precum*. In the mean time, why should any one who had read but a Page in *Calvin*, quote him for such a word as could not possibly drop from so Learned a Pen?

But it would be endless to descant particularly upon all this Author's *New-found Latine*, and Proprieties of Speech. And therefore to set them down briefly as they offer themselves. In *Page* 122. in the Quotation in the Margin, the Reader will find a most choice word, *viz. Conscionator*, not to be met with in any such puny *Author* as we commonly call *Classick*, but cited by him instead of *Concionator* out of the 57th Canon of our *Church*; which, I must tell him, is not an ordinary slip, but a foul *stumble*, attended with Two more in the same Quotation, *viz. Sique* for *Siqui*, and a lesser one, which is *Utrum*, for *Utrùm*; for that is no greater than the difference of a Noun from an Adverb, which, we know, is below a Person, Paramount to all rule, to take notice of. Though by his good leave the *Church of England* both Writes and Teaches better *Latine* to such as are disposed to learn it.

Again in *Page* 139. in the Quotation on the side, we have these Words cited out of the third *Book* of *Optatus Milevitanus. Recordamini quomodò à vobis jamdudum Matris Ecclesiæ membra distracta sunt, non enim [Unam-*

quamque

CHAP. XI.

In which is given some Account of this Author's *Temper and insolent way of Writing, as well in extolling himself, as in depressing and scorning his* Adversaries; *in both which he has not his Parallel.*

THough in all Contests and Controversies, how sharp soever on both sides, and just on one, there is still a duty, which every Man ows both to Decency and to Himself, always obligeing him to utter only such things, as may become him to speak, whatsoever his Adversary may deserve to hear; yet, as to the Adversary himself, it is, no doubt, a course justifiable beyond all exception, to take ones measures of Treating him, from the measures he has allowed himself of dealing with others. And, as I hope, for my own, and the Churches sake, to acquit my self as to the former part of the Rule, so let my Adversary take his lot as to the other. For I doubt not but to satisfie the World, (were it not superabundantly, from his own Writings, satisfied already) That he is a Person of such an insufferable Insolence both of Style and Temper, that all, that he has met with in the foregoing Chapters, has by no means paid off his Scores. In all his expressions concerning his Antagonists, he is infinitely ſcornful; and not only ſo, but very often alſo, extremely ſpiteful and malicious. For what but the height of ſpight could make him in his Vindication of his *Caſe of Allegiance* tax his Learned Adverſary, as an *Epicurean and an Atheiſtical Ridiculer of Providence*, only for maintaining, that the Paſſages and Events of Providence are not the Rule, which God will have us govern our Actions by; but the Precepts and Prohibitions of his Law? And what, but the ſame malice, could make him inſinuate that the ſame Author was inclined to *Popery and an Infallible Interpreter*, only for ſaying that one Text of Scripture was *obſcure* and *much controverted*? which yet St. *Peter* had ſaid of many *Paſſages of* St. *Paul's Epiſtles*, 1 *Pet.* 3.16. and yet without giving any wiſe man the leaſt occaſion from thence to think that he was then providing an Argument for the *Infallibility* of his ſuppoſed *Succeſſor*. And Laſtly, what but the bittereſt Rancour could make him charge his Adverſary, as if he had compared the ſwearing Allegiance to K. *W*. and Q. *M*. for the great and notorious Impiety of it, with the Villanies foretold by the Prophet of *Hazael*; only, becauſe he had told Him, that *as* Hazael *had changed his mind*; (notwithſtanding his confident Opinion of himſelf to the contrary;) *ſo had this Author too*? For who but one of equal Virulence and Ignorance would have ſtretched the compariſon, which reſpected only *the changing of Minds*, to a Compariſon as to the *merits of the Cauſe*, which it had no relation to at all? Indeed no more than that Reply of *Hazael*, *Is thy Servant a Dog*? was deſign'd to convince the Prophet, *That he had not four Leggs*, and not rather only to clear himſelf from ſuch a curriſh and belluine temper of mind, as thoſe Actions foretold of him muſt needs imply? And I ſuppoſe, when a certain Perſon ſpeaking of

Vind. Caſe, &c. p. 58. l. 26.

Vind. Caſe p. 48. and the two laſt lines.

Vind. of the Caſe, &c. p. 79. l. 10.

of the New Oath to a certain Bishop, said, *My Lord, I will be Crucified before I will take this Oath*, His meaning was not, that he thought the taking it more Painful and Tormenting than a *Crucifixion*, but that he had a greater unwillingness to take the one, than to undergo the other. And yet this was this Author's way of Treating a very Worthy Man, an old Acquaintance, and a fair Adversary. I am not at all concern'd to espouse or abett the Cause defended by that Learned Person. But this I do and ever shall averr, That there is a *Jus Belli*, in these Controversial, as well as in Military Conflicts, and consequently an obligation to Truth and Justice and common Ingenuity even in the exercise of the greatest Hostilities. But this Man's usage of his forementioned Adversary is not more Senseless and Illogical, than Disingenuous, Barbarous, and Unchristian. And so let the Reader take this as a Specimen of his impotent spleen and malice. After which, let us shew him in his next good Quality, his *Insolence*; and first in that Branch of it, which concerns his wonderful Opinion and Applause of Himself. B. K.

As to which, we shall first of all see him (as we have in some degree shewn him before) preferring himself before all the Fathers, as *much happier in giving an explication of the Trinity than they were*; and this, in such a fleering scoptical way, (scoptical I mean as to the *Fathers*, but highly *Commendatory* of himself) that it would even turn ones stomach to read his fulsom expressions. For he tells us, (and that with the most profound humility, no doubt) *p.* 101. *l.* 1. &c. *If that explication which I have given, be very consistent with, nay, be the true Interpretation of that account the Antients give of a Trinity in Unity, I hope it will not be thought*

thought an unpardonoble Novelty, if I have expressed the same thing in other Words, which give us a more clear and distinct apprehension of it, &c. And again *p.* 126. *l.* 2. *I hope this is no fault neither, to give an Intelligible explication of that, which all the Fathers taught, but were not equally happy in their explication of it.* No; for his comfort, no; to excell and outdo all the Fathers (if a man can do it) can be no fault at all. But before this be allow'd him, I do here require him to name and produce me but one (who acknowledges a Trinity) in the whole World, besides his own modest *self*, who ever preferr'd his explication of the Trinity for the *Happiness and Intelligibility of it*, before that given by the Fathers. I say, let him produce me so much as one affirming this, if he can. So that, in short, the Comparison here stands between the Fathers, and this Author: and we see the Preheminence given him above all the Fathers by the sole and single *Judgment of one Doctor*, and that Doctor is *Himself*: nay, and (which is more) to put the matter past all Comparison between him and them for the future, He tells us (as was also observed before in my 7th. Chapter) *That the Fathers neither knew how to speak their own Thoughts of the Trinity, nor indeed so much as to conceive of it aright, by reason of the* grossness of their Imaginations: *whereas, if they had* (as he adds) *but conceived of it, and expressed themselves about it, as he has done, all would have been plain, easie, and intelligible.* And as for Gregory *Nyssen*, (from whom he had Quoted more than from all the rest of the Fathers together) he gives him a cast of his Temper at last, *p.* 119. *l.* 5. and sends him away with this rap over the Pate, *That he could not tell what to make of him and his Reasonings; for that, in his judgment, he destroyed all Principles of Individuation.* And

in

in this manner we have him Pluming himself, clapping his Wings, and crowing over all the Fathers; for which and his quarrelsome domineering Nature together, most think, it is high time, that *his Comb were cut*.

In the next place, let us see what Elogies he bestows upon himself for his Archievements in the *Socinian* Controversie. Concerning which he tells the Men of that Persuasion, That after his Vindication of the Trinity *He believes they will talk more sparingly of Absurdities and Contradictions for the future*. p. 153. But, why I pray? Is it because this Author has got the *Monopoly* of them, and engrossed them all to himself? and that therefore the Laws will be very severe upon such as invade his Property? For, as for any other Reason, they have none, that I know of, to *talk more sparingly of Absurdities and Contradictions*, than they used to do, having so many more, out of his Writings, to talk of, than ever they had before. But he proceeds, and closes his Work with this Triumph over his Antagonist (and in him, I suppose, over all the rest of that Tribe) p. 272. *That he is pretty confident, that he will never be able to reason to any purpose in this cause again.* As for his *confidence*, none doubts of it; but as for his *Prediction*, if he proves no better a *Prophet* in what he here *foretells* of his Socinian Opponent, than in what he foretold of that Learned Person, who answered both his *Case of Allegiance*, and his *Vindication of it*. viz. *That if he would but well examine his Arguments before he answered them, he should expect to hear no more from him*: and if withall this Socinian be but able to handle him at such a Rate, as that close Reasoner has done, I dare undertake for him, that he shall go out of the World the most baffled Person, that ever lived in it. But why, *Vind. Case* p. *the last.*

for

for God's sake must the *Socinians* Reasoning Abilities (which his great Lord and Patron has given so high, so signal, and so peculiar an *Encomium* of) all of a suddain fail them, upon this Author's Publication of his book? what can the meaning of this be? Why the meaning of it is this. *Hic, vir, hic est*, &c. according to the words by which *Virgil* pointed out *Augustus Cæsar*. *This, This, is the Man*. This is that incomparable, mighty, and irrefragable Divine, who has wrote more convincingly and effectually against the *Socinians*, (if you will believe him) than all, that ever wrote against them before, put together. For notwithstanding all that has been wrote by those great Men, who from time to time have appear'd in this Controversie, the Controversie is still alive, and the *Socinians* continue writing and reasoning still: and even by this Author's confession (once at least) *to some Purpose*. For otherwise how could he say of his Socinian Adversary, *That he would never be able to reason to any purpose in this cause again*, if he had never reasoned so at all? But so far are the *Socinians* from being put *out of Countenance*, and much less *out of Heart*, by what this man has wrote against them, That I assure him, they look upon him as an Opponent according to their hearts desire; as having play'd a fairer Game into their hands than ever was dealt into them before: so that next to their wishing all the World their *Friends*, they wish they may always have such *Adversaries*. And therefore if they should resolve to *reason against him no more*, he will have great cause to thank either their Inadvertency for overlooking the great advantage given them, or their good Nature for not taking it. For the Book called by him *a Vindication of the Trinity*, is certainly like a kind of Pot or Vessel with handles quite round

See his four Sermons on the 1 John 14. p. 71. 72.

round it; turn it which way you will, you are sure to find something to take hold of it by.

And the truth is, upon a strict impartial comparing of things together, I cannot see any new Advantage that he has got over the *Socinians*, unless it be That he thinks his *Three Gods* will be too hard for their *One*. And perhaps it is upon Presumption of this, That he discharges that clap of Thunder at them in his Preface, where he tells us; *That having dipp'd his Pen in the Vindication of so glorious a Cause, by the grace of God he will never desert it, while he can hold Pen in hand.* In which words, methinks I see him ready Armed and Mounted (with his face towards the *West*) and brandishing his Sword aloft, all wreaking with *Socinian* blood, and with the very darts of his Eyes looking his poor *forgotten Friends* through and through. For in good earnest the Words sound very terribly to these Men; but most terribly of all to the Article it self: (which is like to suffer most by his *Vindication*): for thus to threaten that he will never leave off vexing it *as long as he can hold Pen in hand*, (which, I dare say, will be as long as he can tell Mony with it) This, I say again, sounds very dreadfully.

Nevertheless, as fierce and formidable as these words may represent him, he has yet, like a merciful Enemy, very great reserves of compassion. For otherwise how come so many *Socinian* Pieces wrote against him to lye so long unanswered? He has indeed lately wrote an *Apology for writing against the Socinians*; but where is the Apology for writing in such a prevaricating way against them at first, and for never writing against them since? For has he lost his glorious Polemick *Pen*? or has he lost the *use of his Hand*? or has he run himself *out of Breath*? If this last be his case (as by some *Asthmatick symptoms* one would think it is) he will

do

do well to call in his old Friend, and Defender, the *Footman*, to second him: especially since the contention, which now seems most likely to be, is, who shall *run* fastest from the Enemy, and keep furthest from Him.

William Giles sometimes of *Mark-lane.*

In the mean time I wonder that in the mannage of this disputation, he does not take the same course that other Learned Men in the like cases use to do. For he frequently taxes his Adversary with *Fallacies*; telling him that this is a *Fallacy* and that is a *Fallacy*: But why does he not express to his Reader, what the particular *Fallacy* is? there being no Sophism or Fallacy incident to Speech or Argumentation, but what falls under one of the Thirteen reckoned up by *Aristotle*. *Moreover*, while he is Animadverting upon the History of the *Unitarians*, he will, I believe, hardly get clear of a scurvy lapse in that History himself. For concerning the exposition given by the *Socinians* of that Text in the 3 *John* 13. where our Saviour tells the Jews, *That he came down from Heaven.* He writes thus: *Did* Socinus *find it so easie a Thing to reconcile this Text to his Darling Opinion, when he was forced to* Fast and Pray *for it, and to pretend* Revelation *because he wanted Reason to support it?* viz. *That Christ before he entred on his Prophetick Office, was taken into Heaven to be instructed in the Gospel, and then came down from Heaven again to publish it to the World.* p. 143. l. 19. *&c.* Now, the Person here spoken of, and intended by this Author, must needs have been *Faustus Socinus*, and I believe he will not pretend that he meant any other; which being supposed, This Remark of his will appear to have been a very great mistake. For neither was this the Text, about which this *Praying* and *Pretence of Revelation* was, (for *Fasting* is a word of this Author's putting

multo; and He who will digest the trouble of Reading this Authors Writings, will need no other Argument to prove it so. But as for those excellent Persons, whom he first slights, then *challenges*, and afterwards *flyes from*, by never replying upon them, I would have him know, that the World has already past it's judgment both upon them and him too: and therefore I would advise his *Haughtiness* for the future to forbear calling his Antagonists *Little Writers*, till by his Answers he has *made them so*.

A further discovery of his rude, undecent way of treating such as he writes against, is the Language he has bestow'd upon a certain Writer, a *Nonconformist* indeed, but yet a Man of Learning (as a much greater Man than this Author has found by experience) whom he calls a *Trifling Scribler, who understands little more than Quibbles and Jests*; Charging him withal with *Pertness* and *Folly* to complete his Character. *p.* 15. of his Preface to his Defence of Dr. *Stillingfleet*. And in the 12. *page* of the Book it self, and the five first lines, He represents him under the name of the *Inquirer*, as one, *who cannot understand plain and familiar sense*; *nor carry the Connexion of three or four Sentences together*. Very civil Language indeed, becoming a Scholar, a Divine, and a well-bred Man, to a Person who had not in the least provok'd Him. For my own part, I have no knowledge of the Man, but from his Writings; and upon the Stock of that knowledge have often wondred, that one so able to humble this Reviler, would take such gross Reproaches at his hands. Mr. Alsop.

But the Truth is, when I consider (as I noted first in my Preface) how patiently our whole Clergy has hitherto suffered him to call them *Fools* and *Hereticks*, by charging all those, as *such*, who concur not with him in holding the Three Divine Persons to be *Three*

distinct

distinct Infinite Minds or Spirits (which, I dare say, not one of them held at the time of his uttering this Lewd Reproach) I say, when I consider this, I have cause to surcease all wonder, that any Private Man should indure this insolent *Huff* to insult over him in such a manner. But I shall insist no further upon this master-piece of his scurrility, having in some measure accounted with him for it already. Only I shall add this, That as it is beyond example marvellous that any one single member of a Church should presume to load all the rest with such a charge, so it is yet a greater marvel that all should bear it.

It would be endless to set down all the dirty stuff that has flowed from his *Billingsgate* Pen. But to repeat and bring together so much as we have taken notice of, the Reader may be pleased to bear away in his memory such Expressions, and Appellations as these. viz. *Epicurean*, and *Ridiculer of Providence*, *Popishly inclined*, and *looking towards an Infallible Interpreter*, *Disaffected to, and a slanderer of the Government*, *Little Writers*, *Fools* and *Hereticks*, *errant Fopp*, *Trifling Scribler*, *shamefully Ignorant and Impudent*, *Fit to be sent to School again*, *One that understands little else but Jests and Quibbles*, *One that cannot understand plain and familiar sense*, *One that understands neither* Greek *nor* Latine, and the like. These are the choice Embellishments of his Style. But above all, that beloved word, *Nonsense*, is always ready at hand with him; and out it flies at all Persons and upon all Occasions. And hardly can he write three or four Pages together, but, right or wrong, he throws it in his Adversaries face. One would think that he was Born with the *Word* in his Mouth, and that it grew up with him from his Infancy, and that in his very Cradle he *Cryed Nonsense*, before he could *speak* it.

But

But to check this ungovern'd humour of his, in thus using this word at all Adventure; Let me tell him, that it is both a very rude, unmannerly *Word;* and most commonly, as applyed by him, a very *false Charge.* As for the rudeness of it, since he owns himself a *Son of the Church of* England, I think he would be much his own friend, if he would remember the Reprimand given him by his old *Acquaintance* and *Antagonist Doctor Owen*; who in his *Vindication*, &c. *p.* 72. having, upon occasion of some of his profane Scoffs, called him *Goodly Son of the Church of* England! immediately subjoyns, *That he intended it not as a Reflexion upon the Church it self*, but only *to remind this Man of his Relation to that Church. Which*, (he there says) *to his Knowledge, taught better Learning and better Manners.* In the next place, as for the falseness of the Charge in his usual application of this Word, I would have him know, That the Charge of *Nonsense* does not properly lye against every one who asserts a false Proposition, or is guilty of a mistake. For *Non sense* is not properly opposed to strict *Truth*, but to such plain and manifest *Truth* as is obvious to *Common sense.* For *Truth* oftentimes lyes deep, and abstruse, and requires a more than ordinary sagacity to reach and fetch it out; which that low Pitch of Reason, which we call *Common sense*, cannot always do. For in discourse a Man may be sometimes mistaken in laying his Foundation or Principle, and yet be very Clear and Rational in the Consequences he draws from it; and sometimes he may fail in drawing Consequences from a True and well-laid Principle; in both which cases, the whole discourse is certainly false and Inconsistent: Nevertheless (according to the common acception of the Word) this cannot be called *Nonsense.* It may indeed be called Error or Mistake; which is a weakness

ness cleaving too close to Human Nature, for any one of the same Nature to reproach another for it. But on the contrary, if every Thing, that is not strict Demonstration and certain *Truth*, must pass for *Nonsense*, I fear, it would overlay whole Volumes, and not only prevent the 2d 3d. and 4th. *Editions* of many Books, but shrewdly also endanger the *Sale* of the *First*: Especially if 2d. and 3d. by the unlucky escape of some scattering Copies, should chance all to appear in the space of Three or Four Dayes, As in the first Publication of a certain Book Entituled *The Case of Allegiance*, &c. it fell out. But great, no doubt, is the Art of Bestowing several Title-Pages, importing *divers Editions*, upon Books of one and the same Impression: and may serve to teach the World, what a fruitful Thing the Press is, when impregnated by the *Prolifick Genius* of some Writers; and that (when it is for the credit of any extraordinary Book and it's Author) it can bring forth *four*, *five*, or *six* Editions of it at the same time. Which certainly is a most Ingenious Contrivance; but whether it were the *Author*'s or the *Bookseller*'s, is a Question; though, some think, it uses to be done by a kind of *mutual-Consciousness* between both.

But to return to the Point in hand. According to the common use of the Word *Non sense*, He, who Discourses of Things obvious to the ordinary Apprehensions of Men, with gross and palpable contradictions of one thing to another, or with a plain, manifest Incoherence of one part of his Discourse with the other, that Man is properly and justly chargeable with *Nonsense*. And let those (in the Name of *Sense* and *Reason*) take it to themselves, who have most claim to it.

But because the best way of Illustrating Things is by

by example. I ſhall alſo take this courſe here. Thus for inſtance. For any one to own a Thing for a *great and ſacred Myſtery* (the very Notion and uſe of the word *Myſtery* importing ſomething *Hidden and Abſtruſe*) and at the ſame time to affirm it to be very *Plain*, *Eaſie* and *Intelligible*, is *Nonſenſe*. To ſay, That in Men *Knowledge* and *Power* are *Commenſurate*; nay That *Knowledge is Power*; ſo that whatſoever a *Man knows how to do*, he is by vertue thereof *alſo able to do it*, is contrary to the *Common Senſe* of all Mankind, and conſequently *Nonſenſe*. To ſay, *A Beaſt is a Perſon*, and yet to ſay withall, *That a Perſon and an Intelligent ſubſtance are Terms reciprocal*, is both *Nonſenſe*, and *Contradiction too*, with a Witneſs. To affirm, *That a ſpecifical Unity can make any Thing or Perſon Numerically One*, is *Nonſenſe*. To affirm, *That there are two diſtinct* Reaſons *and two diſtinct* Wills *in each Man, and thoſe as really diſtinct, as if the ſame Man had Two diſtinct Souls*, is *Nonſenſe*. And to affirm, *That the Body* (which is utterly void of any Intellectual Power, or Faculty) *is conſcious to all the Dictates and Commands of the Will*, is groſs and inexcuſable *Nonſenſe*. So that whereas this Author (according to his mannerly way) charges his Adverſary with *unintelligible Nonſenſe*. p. 227. l. 6. it muſt needs be granted, that he has much the advantage of him in this Particular; ſince all muſt acknowledge that his own *Non ſenſe* is very *Intelligible*.

And here I could eaſily direct him where he may be ſupplyed with ſeveral more ſuch Inſtances, as thoſe newly alledged; but that I think theſe may ſuffice for the Purpoſe they are produced for. In the mean time I would adviſe him for the future to uſe this rude Word more ſparingly, and cautiouſly; and to apply it only where the generally received way of ſpeaking applies it : And now and then alſo to caſt his eye upon his own Writings. Theſe things, I ſay, I would adviſe him to ; and to conſider withal, how unreaſonable and unjuſt it is, for him to beſtow about the *Word* ſo freely upon others, while he keeps the *Thing* to himſelf.

CHAP.

CHAPTER XII

CHAP. XII.

Containing a Brief Review, *and* Conclusion *of the whole* Work.

I AM at length come to a close of that Work, which I should much more gladly have been Prevented, than engag'd in, by being a *Reader*, rather than the *Author* of a Reply to this Man's strange, unjustifiable Innovations upon this great Article of our Religion. But it is now a considerable Time that the Book, here Animadverted upon, has walked about the World, without any Publick Controll; And though in private Discourse generally censur'd by all, yet, (as to the Point undertook by me) hitherto Answered by none ; which may well be Matter of *Melancholy Consideration* to all Hearty Lovers of our Church, and Ancient Christianity. Whereas, I dare say , had this Heterodox Piece been wrote and published in a Language understood by Foreigners, we should long since have had several Confutations of it sent us from abroad; and probably not without some severe Reflexions upon the *English* Church, and Clergy, for their silence in a Cause, which so loudly called for their Defence. To take off therefore this Reproach from our Church (in some degree at least) I have (while others, far more able to *Defend it*, chuse rather to sit still and *enjoy it*) ventur'd to set my weak Hand to the Vindication of a Principal Article of her Faith, against the rude Attacks of this bold Undertaker. In which, though I freely own, that all, that has been done by me in it, is extremely below the Dignity of the Subject, which I have employed my self in, yet I am well assured that I have fully and effectually answered this Man; and if it should prove otherwise, I must ascribe it to a peculiar Misfortune attending me; since none besides, has hitherto wrote against him, but has confuted him. In the Work I have here presented the Reader with, I have examined and gone over all that, I conceive, requires either Answer or Remark; and that according to the following Method and Order, which I shall here briefly set down.

I have, in the first place, laid my Foundation in the Explication and State of the Sense of the Word *Mystery*; which I shew, in General, signifies something *Concealed*, *Hidden*, or *Abstruse* in *Religious Matters*; and amongst Christian Writers not only that, but something also neither *Discoverable* nor *Comprehensible* by bare Reason: According to which, I shew, that this Author's frequent affirming, that his *Hypothesis* and Explication of the Trinity rendred the Notion thereof *very Plain, Easie*, and *Intelligible*, was utterly incompatible with the *Mysteriousness* of the same. I shew also upon what absurd Grounds he stated the Nature of a *Contradiction*; according to which, joyned with another of his Assertions, I shew, That no Man could be justly charged with *Contradiction*, though he discoursed never so incoherently and falsely upon any Subject whatsoever. From hence I proceeded to consider the *Ancient Terms* constantly received and used by *Councils*, *Fathers* and *Schoolmen*,

Schoolmen, in ſpeaking of the *God-head* and *Trinity*, which this Author in his Book had confidently and avowedly condemned, as *obſcuring* and *confounding* Men's Notions about theſe great Matters; and upon a diſtinct Explication of each of them, I ſhew the Propriety and ſingular uſefulneſs of them, both againſt all his exceptions, and above thoſe other Terms, which he would needs ſubſtitute in their Room: and under the ſame Head, I laid open the Contradiction of his *Vindication* and his late *Apology* to one another, as I had done before in my Diſcourſe about the Nature of a *Myſtery*. From hence I paſſed to his New Notions of *Self-Conſciouſneſs* and *Mutual Conſciouſneſs*; in the ſtrength of which two Terms he pretended to make a *Trinity in Unity* a *plain, eaſie, and intelligible Notion*; nay ſo very *plain, as to ſolve all Difficulties about it*; theſe being his very words. And as he pretended *Self Conſciouſneſs* to be the *formal conſtituent* Reaſon of *Perſonality* Univerſally, both in Beings Create and Uncreate. I firſt Demonſtrated the contrary in Created Beings; and that both from the general Reaſon of Things, and from Two manifeſt Inſtances; and withal examined and confuted ſeveral extremely abſurd Propoſitions, and Aſſertions advanced by him concerning *Perſonality*. From this I paſſed on, and proved that neither could this *Self-Conſciouſneſs* be the formal Reaſon of Perſonality in the Divine Perſons, ſhewing the impoſſibility thereof by ſeveral clear and unqueſtionable Arguments. And in the next place, with the ſame Evidence of Reaſon I proved, That *mutual Conſciouſneſs* could not be the ground or Reaſon of the Unity or Coaleſcence of the Three Divine Perſons in one and the ſame Divine Nature; and all this upon known, allowed Principles of Philoſophy,

phy,as well as Divinity. And so I Naturally went on to the examination of that monstrous Assertion of his,by which he holds and affirms the Three Divine Persons to be Three distict *Infinite Minds or Spirits* ; which I shew unavoidably and irrefragably inferr'd them to be *Three Gods* ; It being impossible for the God-head, which is essentially *One single infinite Mind or Spirit* , to be multiplyed into three distinct Infinite *Minds or Spirits,* without being multiplyed into as many *Gods.* This Opinion of his, I shew, was easie enough to be confuted; But for all that, I must here add further, that for the insufferable Scandal of it, it is much fitter to be *censured* by a *Convocation*, though even he himself should be *Prolocutor* of it. After this, since he had the Confidence to vouch his Hypothesis *for the constant Doctrine of the Fathers and the Schools*, I first proved it quite otherwise in the Point of *Self Consciousness*,and in his Assertion of Three *distinct infinite Minds* ; For the latter of which he quoted *Three* or *Four* Fathers, and *One* Sentence out of one *Schoolman*, viz. *P. Lombard* (which, one would think, was far from proveing it the *constant Doctrine* either of the *Fathers*, or, *the Schools)* and yet even these very Quotations, I shew were no more to his Purpose, than if he had alledged them to prove that Twice Three makes Twenty. And as for *Self Consciousness*, which is one of the Two main Branches, or members of his Hypothesis, he does not produce, nor so much as mention one *Father* or *Schoolman* in the behalf of it ; so exact is he in proving his *Doctrine* the very *same* with Theirs. And then, in the next place, for the proof of his *mutual Consciousness* from the *Fathers* and *Schoolmen*, I have distinctly considered his allegations for it, and forming them into Argu-

Arguments (such as the matter would afford) found them the saddest wofullest things to be called by that Name, that perhaps ever appeared in the World, since Argumentation was in use. And to complete his excellent and peculiar way of Arguing from the *Fathers* (for not so much as one *Schoolman* is cited in favour of *mutual Consciousness*) His whole business, I shew, was to reproach the *Fathers* as neither *able to conceive* rightly of the Trinity, nor yet *express* themselves Properly and Intelligibly about the same; and all this, because they neither conceived of it, nor expressed it, according to his Terms and Hypothesis, which yet he affirmed to be the *Constant Avowed Sentiments of those very Fathers*; though (God help them, poor Men) they were not so *happy*, as to know it. And this, I hope all the World will acknowledge, to be a most extraordinary way of proving a Thing from the Authority of the *Fathers*, by thus representing them as a Company of Dolts, who neither knew how *to think* or *speak*, as they should, upon the subject which they were professedly treating of. Upon which Head having finished my Answer as to the main Point I first engaged in, I proceeded to mark out, and Animadvert upon several of his *Paradoxical* Absurd Assertions, both in Divinity and Philosophy. And I did not only allege them for such, but also by the most commonly received and current Principles of both, effectually proved them such; and I referr it to any Man of clear and impartial Sense, upon a survey of the Particulars there distinctly examined and remarked upon, to pass as Judge between this Author and my self, whether the Proof falls at all short of the Charge. Next to which, because of his Insolent Reflexions upon some Learned Men, I took into consideration also his *vocabular* Sins, and manifold

Trans-

Transgressions of the *Laws* of Grammar and Philology: and whereas he had vilified his Adversary as *having neither Greek nor Latine*, I shew, that albeit the Charge had been never so true, yet that he was one of the unfittest Persons living to make it, for some certain Reasons fairly presented to him in that Chapter. And lastly to bring up the Rear of all, I thought it expedient to lay open the Temper of the Man, and his way of Writing; His Immoderate applauses of himself above all *before* him, or *about* him, together with his disdainful Treatment of all that come in his way, as if they were not worthy to *carry his Books after him.* Though (by what some of them have Wrote against him) it appears, that they have made too good use of their *own Books*, to be fit *to carry his.* In fine I have, in my Perusal of this Man's Writings, with the utmost exactness I was able, observed his way of speaking both of himself, and others; and upon the result of all do most seriously and sincerely affirm, That never did I (nor perhaps any one else) meet with so much confidence with so thin a Bottom to support it; and yet surely that Man ought to stand upon a very broad and firm Bottom indeed, who ventures to defie all the World.

And thus, to relieve the Readers memory, I have given him this brief draught or Scheme of the whole Work. In which, as it is this Author alone, whom I have undertook, so I think fit to declare, that if any one besides him, shall attempt an answer to this Discourse, I shall not in the least trouble or concern my self about him, whosoever he be; but if this Author himself shall be disposed to defend his New Notions and Hypothesis by a just and Scholastick Reply to what I have here offered against them, I will not fail

(God

(God affording me such a measure of Health and Strength as may enable me for Study) to attend his Motions upon this Subject, as soon, and as often as he pleases For I can hardly perswade my self that I have yet paid him all, that I owe him. Neverthelefs I must leave this Admonition with him, That I neither can, nor shall account such a Pamphlet, as his late *Apology*, a just and sufficient Answer to these *Animadversions*.

In the mean time, since the Reverend Dr. *J. W.* (spoken of in the precedeing Chapter) in his *Letters* about the *Trinity*, and *W. I.* another very Learned Person, in his 2*d. Letter* to the said Doctor, upon the same subject, have both of them been pleased to commend this Author *for several excellent Things in this Book*, I do with the greatest earnestness of Entreaty, as well as with the profoundest deference of Respect to their great Judgments beg of them, that they would by a kind of charitable Benefaction to such low, and mean Understandings as mine, vouchsafe to point out in Particular, what *those excellent Things* are, and in what Part of his Book they may be found ; and whether I have hit upon any of them in my *Three* immediately foregoing Chapters. For I have read the Book over and over; as (after I had took up Thoughts of Answering it) it concerned me, in all Reason, to do. And I do thereupon solemnly profess, that, according to the best of my poor Judgment, and that ordinary Measure of Learning which God has vouchsafed me, I can hardly find throughout the whole Work (unless perhaps, here and there a Passage or two against the *Socinians*) so much as one True, Through stroke either in *Divinity*, or *Philosophy*, or *Logick*, or even in *Grammar* ; and I confidently appeal to the ingenuous, and

An humble Address to the Learned Doctor. J. W. *and* W. I.

 unbyass'd

unbyass'd Reader, whether I have not in the foregoing *Animadversions* given very pregnant and particular Instances of this Author's gross Defects in every one of these. And therefore my poor Opinion and Advice is, That if these two Learned Men are resolved to persist in their Commendations of this Author (as there is nothing by which they can oblige him more) and withal to commend him upon sure, undenyable Grounds, they would hereafter wave all the forementioned Topicks of Commendation, and pitch upon his true excellency by commending him for his *Preferment*; for that certainly is very commendable.

And now, that I am taking my Leave of my Reader, (for this time at least) that I may not leave him with any just Distast or Grudg in his Mind against me, as if I had treated this Man too severely, I do assure him, that nothing has been here utter'd by Chance, or in the heat of any present Passion, but upon a due, calm, and sedate Consideration of what he had said *falsly* of others, as a Warrant for what was to be *truly* said of him. And I do further assure the Reader, that I would by no means have treated a Candid, Civil and well-bred Adversary, at the Rate, I have treated him, who has shewn no sign of any one of these Qualifications, either in his Writings or Behaviour. And therefore though to *accept Persons* be a Fault in the Sight of God and Man, yet certainly to *distinguish* them is none. I have used him, as I found him; and for what I found him, he may thank himself.

The Truth is, he has carryed on an offensive War with most that have Wrote; and there are very few, whom he has not, one way or other, struck at and Defied. So that the Matter being in effect brought to this

this Point, whether He ſhall be too hard for the World, or the World for Him, I hope it will not be long deciding. He has for a great while, and in a very audacious manner been Preying, and Privateering upon many a Worthy and good Name, and as far as he was able made prize of the Reputation of Men better than Himſelf: And therefore it is now high time for ſuch to think of repaying the good Turns done them, and for the injured World to retaliate upon the lawleſs *Aggreſſor*. For this is, and has been the *Cuſtom of Nations*; and all muſt grant it to be a moſt juſt, equal, and allowed courſe; and ſince it is ſo, 'tis to be hop'd, that this is not the laſt *Repriſal* that will be made upon him.

To the moſt Holy and Bleſſed Trinity, Three Glorious Perſons in one and the ſame Undivided God-head, be rendred and aſcribed all Honour and Praiſe, Thankſgiving and Adoration, now and for evermore. Amen.

THE END.

A TABLE of the Additions and Alterations made in the Second Edition of the Animadversions upon Dr. *Sherlock*'s Book of the *Trinity*.

PReface, Page 3. *over against* Line 22. *this Passage is added in the Margin*, [Dr. Owen *in his Vindication of Himself against this Author, gives him the Character of a* Scoffer, *and a* Censurer of other Mens Labours, Judgments, and Expressions. *Which* Witness *of his is* True; *and since it is so, Whether he, of whom it is True, deserves a* Rebuke, *or no, is left* to the World *to judge.* Owen's Vindic. against *Sh.* p. 129.]

Preface, p. 5. line 4. *This Passage in the first Edition, which shews,* That Tender Consciences are such Things as may some time or other put the Church not only to part with its Liturgy, Rites and Ceremonies, *but its very Faith also* for their sake, *is thus altered in the Second Edition*; [which shews, That there are some such Tender Consciences in the World, as (when opportunity serves) may put the *Church* not only to part with its *Liturgy, Rites* and *Ceremonies*, but its *very Creed* also for their sake.]

Preface, p. 12. l. 26. *after the words* paying the Scores of both, *this Discourse follows in the Second Edition.*

[*But now if either He himself, or any for him shall plead, That it was not fairly done to charge him with those* Blasphemies, *which he may (and perhaps does) pretend* to have been uttered by Him in the Perſon of his Adverſary, and as the genuine Conſequences of the Doctrine maintained by him.

To this I Anſwer. Firſt, That he, who pretends to ſpeak in the Perſon *of another, ought, according to all* Juſtice *and* Decorum, *to ſpeak only ſuch Things as that other, whom he* perſonates, *uſes to ſpeak, and conſonant to his known,* Avowed Sence. *But did his* Adverſary, *Dr.* Owen, *ever ſpeak ſo? Or uſe the Expreſſions here uttered by this Author? Whereas he declares himſelf concerning the ſaid Expreſſions thus, viz.* That he cannot mention them without begging Pardon for repeating ſuch horrid and deſperate Blaſphemies. Owen'*s Vindication againſt* Sherlock, *p.* 46. That they were fitter for a *Jew*, or a *Mahometan*, for *Servetus*, or *Socinus*, than a Son of this Church, *p.* 47. That he abhorred the Rehearſal of ſuch horrid Profaneneſs, *p.* 49. That they were odious Satanical Exprobrations of the Truth of Chriſt's Satisfaction, *ibid. And now can this Man pretend to ſpeak theſe Things in the Perſon of one who thus* Abhors, Abominates, *and* Deteſts *them? The Truth is, his whole Book is ſuch a lewd Miſrepreſentation both of the* Words *and* Sence *of his* Adverſary, *that if he has any* Bloud in his Body, *it muſt needs* fly in his Face, *and bid him* Bluſh *for ſuch* Unconſcionable Falſifications.

But Secondly, If he charges theſe Aſſertions as Conſequences of the Doctrine maintained by his Adverſary, *I muſt put him in mind of theſe two Things.*

1. *That to the juſt charging of any* Man *with the* Conſequences *of his* Doctrine, *or* Opinion, *the* Things *ſo charged, ought to be not only the* Real, *but alſo the* Plain, Direct, *and* Immediate Conſequences *of that* Opinion. *Foraſmuch as no Man ought in reaſon to be charged with the Remote far-fetched* Conſequences *of any* Propoſition *held by him*;

him; since he may in all Equity (if he disclaims them) be supposed ignorant of them, and that inculpably *too.*

2. *This* Author *is to know, That to the just charging of even any* Doctrine, *or* Opinion, *with such and such* Consequences, *though they follow never so* really *and* truly *from it, yet if they also lie any thing remote, and at some distance from the same, they ought first by* clear undeniable Arguments *to be proved to follow from thence, before they can justly and fairly be charged to do so.*

Which two Observations *thus premised; that I may lay the whole Matter before the* Reader *more particularly; he is to take Notice, That the* Doctrine, *which this* Author *loads with these* Blasphemous Consequences; *is,* That of the Necessity of a Satisfaction to be paid to God's Justice in order to the Pardon of Sin, and the Justification of Sinners. *And this I affirm to have been the* received Doctrine *of the* Church, *and the* General Opinion *of* Divines *in the Case*; *all asserting* the Necessity of such a Satisfaction; *though not All, I confess, upon the same* ground.

For First, *Some found this* Necessity *upon* the Necessary Egress of God's Vindictive Justice, *naturally acting and exerting it self where it meets with a* Proper Object.

But Secondly, *Others state this* Necessity *upon the* Decree *or* Purpose *of* God, *resolving to take this course for the* Pardon of Sin, *and no other. Which* Decree *and* Purpose, *though made freely, yet being actually passed and declared, it was not free for God to baulk the execution of it. His Veracity, Wisdom and Honour, as Supreme Governour of the World, not suffering him to let the Violation of his Laws pass without a due satisfaction made to his Justice. And this has been the Opinion of most Divines in this matter.*

Nevertheless, (whether upon either of these grounds, or some other) it is certain, that the Necessity of a Satisfaction was still held, and owned by the Church: *And yet upon supposal of* this Necessity *alone it is, (whatsoever ground it be stated upon) that this Author sets God forth in a most Profane manner*, as an Impotent Man venting his Rage and Passion without any sufficient Ground or Reason for it. *For, I am sure, no other Consideration can Answer, or come up to the* Impiety *of the forecited Expressions. And I freely appeal to the* Learned, *and* Unbyassed Reader, *Whether the said Passages can be placed to any other Account whatsoever.*

And if they cannot, I ask with what Conscience could this Man, of his own Head, invent such Hideous, Abominable Words, and then thrust them into his Adversary's *Mouth, whether he would, or no? Or charge them as the* necessary Consequences *of his* Doctrine, *without proving, or by any formed* Argument *so much as offering to prove them so? For surely he ought to have done this in the first place, and (since he knew that the* Learned Assertors *of this* Doctrine, *did and would deny these to be the Consequences of it to the very Death) he should by clear and solid* Ratiocination *have proved against them, (in spight of their Denial) that these were indeed the* True *and* Natural Consequences *of the said* Doctrine, *before he reproached them as such. But, it seems he was for doing* execution first, *and for* proceeding to Tryal afterwards; *though, as hasty as he was in the former, he has not yet done the latter, nor, I believe, ever will.*

Upon the whole Matter it is manifest, That it was not so much any thing Personal in Dr. Owen *(how bitter soever he was against him) as the* Doctrine *of* Christ's Satisfaction *asserted by the said* Doctor, *in common with the whole* Christian Church, *which this* Author *so vilely reflected upon; and discharged all those Blasphemous Scoffs at, in that Book of his; and consequently so far as he was the Author both of the Book and the Scoffs in it, he was as fit a Person to have joyned in the Address*

to

t the Morocco Ambassador, *as any Man in* England *besides*.

I do, I confess, charge this Author *with Asserting* Three Gods *(though He does not* in Terminis *express it) because of his Asserting* Three distinct Infinite Minds, *or* Spirits; *but then the Case here on my part is quite different from what it was on his. For in this, the Consequence of* Three Gods *from* Three distinct Infinite Spirits, *is* Direct, Manifest, *and* Immediate; *or rather, in Truth, is not so properly a* Consequence, *or* one Assertion *following from* another, *as* one *and* the very same *thing expressed in* other words, *which is the true account of this Matter: For the Words* [Infinite Mind, *or* Spirit] *are but a* Periphrasis *of the Thing signified by the Term* [God:] *And their perfect equivalence shall be fully demonstrated in my* Fifth Chapter.

From all which I conclude, That since there are (beyond all pretence of denial) several Horrid Blasphemous Expressions *in this* Author's *forementioned Book, which must and ought to be charged* somewhere; *and since his* Adversary *utterly disowns them all, both as to* Words *and* Sence; *and since the* Doctrine *it self, maintained by him, infers no such Thing, nor has this* Author *proved that it does so; but that the said Representations of it are peculiarly his own, and occur no where but in his Book (except possibly in the Writings of some of his old Friends the* Socinians, *and those such as the* Transilvanian Ministers) *it follows, that according to the strictest Laws of fair and just Quotation, all* the black Dirt *of those Impious and foul Passages which I have Cited from him, and charged upon him, ought to lie wholly at his Door, and let him (and his* Porter) *shovel it away thence as they are able.*

See a most Virulent and Blasphemous Book Wrote by these Men, and entituled, *Præmonitiones Christi & Apostolorum de abolendo vero Christo per Antichristum.*

As

As to what concerns the Licensing this Book, so severely and so justly reflected upon by Dr. Owen, *it did (it must be confessed) meet with a Person (as it were) framed for the very purpose*, &c.]

In the Book, *p*. 24. between *l*. 12. and 27. of the First Edition, this Addition and Alteration is made in the Second.

[*I must here remind him of* Two Things.

First, That he would be pleased to tell us how Men *can Write plainer and plainer of the Trinity* every Day after his New Notion of it has *solved all the Difficulties about it*, as in the forecited *p*. 85. *l*. 27. he positively tells us, *it does*. For (as I take it) where there *remains no Difficulty*, there must be the utmost degree of plainness; and withal, when Men are come to the utmost of any Thing, they can then go no further.

Secondly, I must remind him also, That the word *Plainer* in the *Comparative Degree*, does not couch under it the positive signification of *Plain*, &c. And much less *very plain and easie*: [Nay, so very plain as to have *all the difficulties of it solved*, as this Author has expresly affirmed]. So that if this be a *Scandalous Imputation*, it is easie to see to *whom the Scandal of it must belong*, &c.

P. 27. *l*. 25. after the word *Contradicted*, this Parenthesis is inserted in the Second Edition (*as nothing ought to be, which cannot be comprehended*.)

P. 74. *l*. 30. after the word *whatsoever*, three Lines from the bottom in the First Edition, this following Parenthesis is inserted in the Second. (For an *Hypostatick Union* and an *Hypostatick Composition*, *viz*. Such an one as makes a Compound Hypostasis, are quite different things: And this *Author* shall in due time be taught so much, if he has any thing to object against it.) Or, *&c.*

Page

Page 291. over against *Line* 12. of the First Edition, the following *Latine* Quotation is added in the Margin of the Second. *Qui personas in Deo modos tantúmmodo existendi, sive* τρόπους ὑπάρξεως *esse dicunt, ipsam Deitatem nequaquam excludunt, in qua conveniunt; Sed nihil aliud esse volunt, quàm Existendi modum, in quo differunt. Quare Pater non est modus tantùm existendi, sed Deus est, quemadmodum & cæteræ Personæ, verùm Deus est cum certo modo existendi, qui neque Filio convenit, neque Spiritui Sancto. Sic & Filius Deus est, non modus tantùm existendi, Sed Deus est cum certo modo Existendi, qualis neque Patri convenit, neque Spiritui Sancto. Ad eundem modum discriminis, & Spiritus Sanctus Deus est, non modus existendi tantùm; Sed deus est cum certo modo existendi, qualis nec Patri convenit neque Filio. Summa est, Personas in Deo non differre essentiâ, quia sunt unus Deus, sed Proprietate & modo Subsistendi. Twissus in Responsione ad Arminii Præfationem in extremâ Pag. Lin.* 20. *editionis Amstelodamensis apud Janssonium anno* 1632.

Page 342. after these words [*joyned true* Greek *and* English *together*] in the 4th *Line*, this following Discourse is to be inserted.

[But there is an extraordinary Passage in his Book of Judgment, *Chap.* 2. *Sect.* 1. *p.* 164. of the last Edition, (which should be the most correct) and I was doubting, whether I should charge it upon his Ignorance, or his Insolence; but both of them play their Parts very remarkably in it. For first he makes a most false, illiterate, and absurd Translation of a Verse, or rather part of a Verse in the New Testament, and then reproaches the received Translation as wrong, and very faulty, for rendring it otherwise. The place is in 2 *Pet. c.* 2. *v.* 4. εἰ γὰρ ὁ θεὸς ἀγγέλων οὐκ ἐφείσατο ἀλλὰ σειραῖς ζόφου ταρταρώσας παρέδωκεν εἰς κρίσιν τετηρημένους. In which he considers fiders only the words σειραῖς ζόφου ταρταρώσας, dividing them from the rest of the Sentence, *viz.* παρέδωκεν εἰς κρίσιν τετηρημένους, and by that means from the *Verb* in this *latter* part of it, which should govern the *Noun* in the *former*; thereby making σειραῖς to be governed not by παρέδωκεν (as it ought to be) but most falsely and Ungrammatically by ταρταρώσας, and so he renders σειραῖς ζόφου ταρταρώσας, *casting them*, viz. the Apostate Angels, *down into Chains of darkness*. And this interpretation he builds partly upon the pretended Reason of the Thing here discoursed of, and partly upon the signification of the word ταρταροῦν, but upon both of them very absurdly. From the Reason of the Thing he argues, that if ταρταρώσας should signifie the Apostate Angels *being cast down into Hell*, how could they be said upon Sentence passed upon them at the last Judgment, to be then cast into Hell, if they were there before? To which the Answer is very easie and obvious, That immediately upon their sin they were cast down into, and kept in those lower Regions called τάρταρος, or *Hell locally*, but not cast into *Hell-Torments*, till the last Judgment has passed upon them; so that with full accord both to Scripture and Reason we are to distinguish the *place of Hell*, where they now are, from the *Judicial penal Torments of Hell*, which they shall be adjudged to, and endure in that place hereafter; as we distinguish the Prison wherein Malefactors are kept, from the execution which they are there kept for; As indeed this Text with great significance alludes to both: So that his Argument from hence falls to nothing. His other Reason is from the signification of the word ταρταροῦν, which he affirms to signifie *only to cast down*. But on the contrary, I must here tell him first, That ταρταροῦν does not only import the Act of casting down, but (being derived

derived from τάρταρος) signifies also the Term *ad quem*, or the Place, into which this casting down is. And I refer him to all the *Greek* Lexicographers (not one of them excepted) whether they do not render ταρταρόω by *in Tartarum detrudo, dejicio*, or *præcipito*; and if so, how can σειραῖς possibly here agree with ταρταρώσας; for if τάρταρος be the Term *ad quem* of the Act, how can σειραῖς be so too; since one single Act can have but one Ultimate Term *ad quem?* And even this Man himself does not allow τάρταρος and σειραῖς to be one and the same thing. And besides this, I must tell him further, That if σειραῖς imported the *Term, Thing*, or *Place*, into which God cast down the Apostate Angels, it ought not to have been σειραῖς ταρταρώσας, but εἰς σειρὰς, forasmuch as the motion of casting down, importing a *Local descent* to something, the Dative Case cannot in true Grammar answer it.

And therefore the old *Latine* Version makes σειραῖς to import, not the *Term* to which, but the Instruments or means by which these Angels were thus brought down, rendring the Text thus, *Rudentibus Inferni detractos in Tartarum tradidit*, &c. which, as it is not strictly a *Translation*, but an arbitrary *Paraphrase*, so it is a very forced and unnatural one too; as importing not a *casting* but a *drawing down these Angels into Hell.* In which case, who must be the Person drawing them? For since God (to whom ταρταρώσας does and must here agree) ought to be considered by us as in the Highest Heaven, how can this drawing *down* be applied to him, which, in the Nature of it, supposes the Person *drawing* to be in that lower place, to which he is drawing others? For all *Traction* is a motion of the Agent forcibly bringing something to himself, but *Trusion* a motion by which he removes or forces something from himself.

It is clear therefore, that according to all the Rules of Grammatical Conſtruction, and proper ſpeaking, σειραῖς cannot be governed by ταρταρώσας· and that, therefore ſomething elſe muſt be ſought for to govern it, which can be nothing beſides παρέδωκεν. And then the whole Sentence will be properly and plainly tranſlated thus. Ταρταρώσας [God] *having caſt or thruſt them* [viz. *the Apoſtate Angels*] *down into Hell* [or the *Lower Regions*] παρέδωκεν σειραῖς ζόφου, *delivered*, or *put them into Chains of darkneſs*, τετηρημένους εἰς κρίσιν, *kept*, or *reſerved to* [or *for*] *Judgment*. And this is ſence and propriety of Speech, agreeable both to the Natural Signification, and the Grammatical Syntax of the Words. But the Tranſlation ſo imperiouſly and ignorantly given by this Man (in correction of that of the Church) is agreeable to neither. For it both divides one part of the Sentence from the other, from which it muſt not be divided, and then makes σειραῖς to be governed by ταρταρώσας, which cannot govern it, and quite cutts it off from παρέδωκεν, which alone can.

And now, ought it not to be matter of Amazement to all Men of Senſe and Sobriety, to ſee a Puny, who is not able to maſter three words of *Greek*, preſume to controul ſuch great Maſters of that Language, as the Tranſlators of the New Teſtament into *Engliſh* undoubtedly were? Nay, and thereby to reflect upon the Church her ſelf, which has received and owned this Tranſlation, and to whoſe Judgment and Authority (if he be ſo nearly related to her, as he pretends) he ows ſo great and *filial* a Deference? Let him rather inſtead of correcting the *Engliſh* Tranſlation (a Work which he was never born for) thank God, and the Tranſlators for it; there being few Men living more beholden to it than himſelf. And therefore leaving his forlorn Criticiſme

(as

(as new every whit as his Divinity) to shift for it self; I, for my part, like my *English* Bible, for his dislike of any part of it, better than before. For I can by no means see any force or consequence in this Argument, *viz.* That because this Author is much better at *quoting* a *Greek* Sentence than at *construing* it; therefore the *English* Translation of this Text in St. *Peter* is a *very bad Translation*: I say, I cannot admit, or yield to this Consequence.]

Page 347. of the First Edition after this Sentence [*In such a Case some are of Opinion, that where the words escape it, the Author himself ought to have it*] the following Discourse comes in *P.* 351. *Lin.*8. of the Second Edition beginning with these words.

[But because some perhaps will hardly be satisfied with so General a Charge without an Allegation of more Particulars, I shall here give the Reader a Catalogue of this Author's *Greek Errata* in the Second Edition of his Vindication of the Trinity (which should in Reason be thought the most correct) together with their Correction confronting them.

Greek Errata.	*Correction.*	
Νοεερὸν τὶ χρῆμα	Νοεερὸν τι χρῆμα	Pag. 102. Quotat.
εἶπεν	εἶπεν	
ἔν εἰμὶ	ἕν εἰμι	
ἐν ἐσμὲν--ἓν ἐσμὲν	ἕν ἐσμεν	
Punctum interrogationis post ἐσμεν pro Semicolo		
τελείαν	τέλειαν	
Ὁμούσιον ἐςὶν	Ὁμούσιόν ἐστιν	Pag. [illegible]
ἐπιδέχεταυ	ἐπιδέχεται	
ὀσιάς	οὐσίας	

	Greek Errata.	*Correction.*
	ἄνθρωπος ἐστὶν	ἄνθρωπός ἐστιν
	ἄνγέλου	ἀγγέλου
	ἦ--ῇ	ῇ
	ἀγγελος ἐστὶν	ἄγγελός ἐστιν
	Punctum interrogationis post ἐστιν pro Semicol.	
Pag. 107.	Θεὸς ἐστίν	Θεός ἐστιν
l. 14.	Ταυτ' οὐσιον	ταυτούσιον
Pag. 110. Quotat.	Συνεμμένους	Συνημμένους
	συνηθεία	συνήθεια
	ἐστὶ bis	ἐστὶ
	πρεῖς	τρεῖς
	ὑποστάσεις	ὑποστάσεις
	Θεοτήτα	Θεότητα
Pag. 113. Quotat.	Ἐστὶ	Ἔστι
	πολευθεῖας	πολυθεΐας
	παρητήσατο	παρῃτήσατο
	μὴ τὶς	μή τις
	νομισθείη	νομισθείη
2d Quot. ibid.	συγχώρει	συγχωρεῖ
	προμηθουμενη	προμηθουμένη
	διαφόρουε	διαφόρους
	οὐσία;	οὐσίας
	πληθοιτικῇ	πληθυντικῇ
Pag. 115. Quotat.	Ὑπο τινὸς	Ὑπό τινος
	ἀλλὰ τι	ἀλλά τι
Pag. 116. Quotat.	Καθ'.ἑαυτὸν	Καθ' ἑαυτὸν
	ἑκάστου	ἑκάστου
	ἐυέργεια	ἐνέργεια
	ὀνομαζονται	ὀνομάζονται
Pag. 119. Quotat.	Ἡθεία τὲ	Ἡ θεία τε
	ῇ	ῇ

ἀπαρ-

Greek Errata.	*Correction.*	
ἀπαῤῥίλλακτος	ἀπαράλλακτος	Pag. 119. l. 28.
διωςϱεὰν	διαφορὰν	Pag. 120. l. 26.
μίξιν τινα	μίξιν τινὰ	l. 27.
ἢ	ἤ	Pag. 121. l. 24, 25.
ἀπαῤῥέλλημτος	ἀπαράλλακτος	Pag. 122. l. 27.
ὁμουσιότης	ὁμουσιότης	ibid.
Αὕτη ὔν	Αὕτη οὖν	Pag. 12[illegible]. Quotat.
λόγω	λόγῳ	
ἐςὶ	ἐστὶ	
ὐδε	οὐδὲ	
ἀλλήλαις	ἀλλήλαις	
δόο	δυο	
ἀνάπαλιν	ἀνάπαλιν	
ἔν	ἕν	
διά τὲ	διά τε	
συναΐδιον	συναΐδιον	
τὴν τε	τήν τε	
συμπνοιαν	σύμπνοιαν	
εξυσίας	ἐξουσίας	
θυνάμεως	δυνάμεως	

Punctum interrogationis post ταυτότητα pro Semicol.

αλλήλαις	ἀλλήλαις	Pag. 125. Quotat.
ὁμουσιότης	ὁμουσιότης	Pag. 123. l. 19. Quotat.
ἔξωθέν τοῦ	ἔξωθεν τοῦ	
πατρος ἐστί	πατρός ἐστι	
ἀδιαρέτως	ἀδιαιρέτως	

ἁπλοῦν

	Greek Errata.	*Correction.*
Pag. 129. l. 27.	ἀπλῦν τὶ	ἁπλῦν τι
Pag. 165. l. 6.	ἀγαιωσύνης	ἁγιωσύνης
Pag. 200. l. 6.	ὁ Θεὸς μῦ ὁ Θεός μῦ	ὁ Θεός μυ, ὁ Θεός μυ.

Now all these *Errata*, one would think, make up a jolly *Company* to rendezvous together in the compass of less than half a dozen Pages of an *English* Book; a Company fit for our Author to march Triumphantly in the Head of.

Page 360. After [William Giles some time of *Mark-Lane*] in the First Edition in the Margin, is added in the Margin of the Second [*who Wrote (forsooth) in defence of our Author against the* Papists.]

Page 374. *Lines* 12, 13, 14. That Passage [*It is much fitter to be Censured by a Convocation, though even He Himself should be Prolocutor of it.*] is altered in *Page* 377. *Line* 9. thus------ [*Though even He Himself (since* John Goodwin *and* Hugh Peters *are gone off) should be Prolocutor of it.*]

And now, upon the issue of the whole Matter, I hope all Ingenuous, and Impartial Readers, all True Friends of our *English* Church and Old Divinity will allow, that I have treated an Insolent, Imposing Innovator, no otherwise than he has deserved; or rather indeed much short of it; and that None will Tax, or Censure me for what I have Wrote, but such as can think it reasonable for one Man to Trample upon, and Insult over his whole Profession, and to be Applauded, or at least endured in such a Presumption.

For

For my own part, I can by no means judge ſo; and as I abhor ſuch Pride in others; ſo, I hope, I ſhall never be guilty of the leaſt degree of it my ſelf. I thank God, I account not the meaneſt of my own Profeſſion my Inferiour; and if I ſhould be tempted to think any one *Below* me, it ſhould be only ſuch an one as thinks himſelf *Above* all the World beſides.

FINIS.